Against Capital Punishment

Against Capital Punishment

The Anti-Death Penalty Movement in America, 1972–1994

Herbert H. Haines

OXFORD UNIVERSITY PRESS
New York   Oxford

Oxford University Press

Oxford   New York
Athens   Auckland   Bangkok   Bogotá   Buenos Aires   Calcutta
Cape Town   Chennai   Dar es Salaam   Delhi   Florence   Hong Kong   Istanbul
Karachi   Kuala Lumpur   Madrid   Melbourne   Mexico City   Mumbai
Nairobi   Paris   São Paulo   Singapore   Taipei   Tokyo   Toronto   Warsaw

and associated companies in
Berlin   Ibadan

Copyright © 1996 by Oxford University Press, Inc.

First published in 1996 by Oxford University Press, Inc.,
198 Madison Avenue, New York, New York 10016

First issued as an Oxford University Press paperback, 1999.

Library of Congress Cataloging-in-Publication Data
Haines, Herbert H.
Against capital punishment: the anti-death penalty movement in
America, 1972–1994 / Herbert H. Haines.
p. cm.   Includes bibliographical references and index.
ISBN 0-19-508838-7; 0-19-513249-1   (pbk)
1. Capital punishment—United States.   I. Title.
HV8699.U5H35   1996
364.6'6'097309047—dc20   95-20114

1 3 5 7 9 8 6 4 2

Printed in the United States of America
on acid-free paper

for Cynthia

Preface

One of the most satisfying times in a scholarly career is when a research project comes along that melds several of one's academic interests. This book represents such a convergence. Since my undergraduate years, I have focused much of my attention on various deviance, crime, and social control topics. I have written rather little along these lines, but I have taught courses in these fields to students at three academic institutions. And since my first year of graduate study, I have also been fascinated by social constructionist theories of social problems; i.e., theories about how people organize, devise shared understandings of putative social conditions that they find undesirable, and attempt to change them. The third of my primary interests is social movement analysis, and it is in this area that most of my research has been done. For a person with this array of concerns, what could be more appropriate than a book about a social movement that seeks to do away with one of the most controversial practices in twentieth-century criminal justice?

This project, like most of the research I have undertaken, was born in the classroom. I first began thinking seriously about the death penalty in 1987 while I was designing a course on the sociology of violence. Both in academic and popular discourse, talk about "violence" is too often restricted to *deviant* applications of physical force. This obscures the fact that lethal and nonlethal aggression are woven into public affairs and that institutionalized forms of violence are worthy of critical examination in their own right. To compensate for the usual myopia that characterizes this subject, I added units on warfare, police violence, and capital punishment to the more standard topics of street crime, spouse abuse, and the like. As I explored the voluminous literature on the death penalty over the next couple of years, I noticed that aside from Michael Meltsner's book on the NAACP Legal Defense Fund's litigation in the 1960s and early 1970s (1973), works that focused on "antigallows" reformers of earlier eras and a smattering of articles in mostly historical journals, anti-death penalty *activism* had been ignored. As surely as nature hates a vacuum, a researcher is loath to walk away from a topic that has been so underexplored.

This book is the culmination of over four years of research. Supported by a small travel grant from the National Endowment for the Humanities in 1991, I began to explore American anti-death penalty activism through the Sara B. Ehrmann Collection at Northeastern University, Boston, which contains the papers of the Massachusetts Council for the Abolition of the Death Penalty and the American League to Abolish Capital Punishment. Both organizations were formed in the aftermath of the executions of Nicola Sacco and Bartolomeo Vanzetti, radical Italian immigrants convicted—erroneously, in the view of many—of a double robbery-murder in 1920. The ALACP kept the abolitionist flame alive through much of this century and provided more recent activists with a tradition on which to build. I then traced the more recent phases of the struggle over capital punishment through large and small newspapers, using major newspaper indexes and the "Newsbank" database at Cornell University's Olin Library. I was a participant-observer in several movement conferences and meetings across the United States between 1990 and 1994. Grants from the National Science Foundation (#SES-9109494) and the Research Foundation of the State University of New York made it possible for me to work full time during 1992 collecting data on anti-death penalty activism of the 1970s, 1980s, and 1990s. During 1992 and early 1993, I combed through the records of major movement organizations and the private papers of individual activists, collecting more than 5,000 pages of documents for analysis, and I interviewed nearly 50 leading figures in the movement. Those who spoke with me do not comprise a representative sample of death penalty opponents, nor do their views reflect the "other side" of the death penalty debate. But neither a representative cross section nor a "balanced" sample is necessary given the objectives of this book. Capital *litigation* is a massive topic in itself and one that, unlike the *"political"* branch of the struggle, has received a good deal of scholarly attention. Thus, many of the attorneys who have left their mark on the capital punishment system in America have not been interviewed for this book. The people I chose to contact make up a large portion of the leadership of the anti-death penalty *social movement,* the abolitionist core who set the strategic course of the battle against capital punishment over the past two decades.

I owe a debt of gratitude to many individuals for assisting me in this investigation. Henry Schwarzschild, William Bowers, and John Galliher provided encouragement in the formative stages of the project. William Bowers, Frank Hearn, Richard Kendrick, Craig Little, Louis Masur, and Joane Nagel provided helpful criticism on various phases of the project or read portions of the manuscript. Several people were generous enough to give me access to their private papers or to the files of the organizations they serve: Hugo Adam Bedau (Tufts University, the National Coalition to Abolish the Death Penalty, and formerly president of the American League to Abolish Capital Punishment); Pat Clark (Death Penalty Focus of California); Leigh Dingerson (National Coalition to Abolish the Death Penalty); Jonathan Gradess (New York State Defenders Association); Joe Ingle (formerly of the Southern Coalition on Jails and Prisons); Damaris Walsh McGuire (New Yorkers Against the

Death Penalty); Ali Miller (Amnesty International USA); Michael Nelson (Dunstable, Mass.); Eric Prokosch (Amnesty International); Henry Schwarz-schild (formerly of the American Civil LIberties Union Capital Punishment Project); Paula Sites (Indiana Public Defender Council); Barbara Sproul (Hunter College, City University of New York); Donna Schneweiss (Amnesty International USA and Kansas Coalition Against the Death Penalty); and Margaret Vandiver (University of Memphis).

There are three people who deserve special acknowledgement. Two of these are Hugo Bedau and Constance Putnam, whose hospitality and personal assistance went beyond what any researcher might reasonably expect. If ever there was a gold mine of information about an American social movement, it lies in the study of their Concord, Massachusetts, home, and I was allowed to dig in that mine, alone and undisturbed, for three days. I am also especially indebted to Rick Halperin of Southern Methodist University and Amnesty International USA. Without the remarkable network he has set up to collect and disseminate news accounts concerning the death penalty and human rights issues, it would have been quite impossible for me to keep abreast of recent events.

I also thank Jeanne Holiday of the Mudd Library, Princeton University, for her assistance with the ACLU Archives, and my student research assis-tants—Adrienne Chickering, Tobi Clarke, Michelle Pless, Stephanie Smith-son, and Kathy Zucker—who made substantial contributions in library work, transcribing recorded interviews, and coding.

Three people at Oxford University Press have worked directly with me on this book, and I am most grateful for their contributions. David Roll was the first to express enthusiasm for the project, and he advised me in the early stages of my writing. When David left Oxford, Gioia Stevens assumed his responsibilities. She might have viewed my book as a "stepchild," passed into her care by another, but she never did so. Lisa Stallings not only dealt gently with some of my bad habits as a writer, but spotted inadvertent inaccuracies that might have gone unnoticed by a less conscientious editor.

Above all, I have benefited from the overwhelming cooperation of the people whose work this book is about, the activists who have devoted them-selves to opposing capital punishment in the United States. Only one of the dozens of people I approached for interviews refused me. The rest invited me into their homes and offices, answered all my questions, and offered unsolic-ited insights about their movement. Many volunteered to track down docu-ments for me or to open their files for my use. I am deeply indebted to all these people. I may not tell their stories quite the way they themselves would, but I have done my best to get those stories right. Any errors of fact or chronology are my responsibility alone.

Finally, I thank my wife and children for their patience and understanding, particularly during the period when I was away from home so often and again during the final weeks of writing.

Cortland, New York   H.H.H.
July, 1995

Contents

Against Capital Punishment

Introduction: Death Penalty Abolitionism in America

Capital punishment[1] is in decline as the twentieth century nears its end. Once a virtually universal practice, only about 100 of the world's 180 or so nations still take the lives of those who commit serious violations of their laws (Amnesty International USA 1989a:259–262; Hood 1989:7–33). Executions have become especially rare among industrialized democracies. A few retain capital statutes dealing with extraordinary crimes such as treason, but only Japan, parts of the former Soviet Union, and the United States still carry out death sentences for "ordinary" crimes of violence.

But for at least the time being, the United States stands in stark contrast to the international trend. Capital punishment is flourishing here. After going without executions from 1967 through 1976, 38 states and the federal government have passed revised capital-sentencing statutes that meet the stiffer constitutional requirements the Supreme Court laid down between 1976 and 1983. By the time these words appear in print, at least two more states — Iowa and Wisconsin — may well have brought back the death penalty. Since 1983, the Court has removed a number of procedural impediments on the states, and the rate of electrocutions, gassings, and lethal injections has grown as a result. Thirty-eight persons were put to death in 1993, more than in any year since John F. Kennedy sat in the Oval Office. The number fell to 31 in 1994, but all indications point to a rising tide of harsh justice through the remainder of the decade. Nearly 3,000 convicts now await their dates with the executioner (see Table 1).

The phoenixlike resurgence of America's death penalty has been accompanied, and perhaps facilitated, by a corresponding wave of public enthusiasm. Surveys reveal a consistent pattern of support for capital punishment, in which around 75 to 80 percent of the persons polled agree that murderers should be executed.[2] These results indicate a dramatic reversal of opinion since the mid-1960s when, for a brief period, capital punishment advocates found themselves in the minority (Zimring and Hawkins 1986:39). The sustained enthusi-

TABLE 1.   Convicts Under Sentence of
Death, 1980–1994

Year	Number	Year	Number
1980	618	1988	2,182
1981	924	1989	2,250
1982	1,137	1990	2,412
1983	1,289	1991	2,465
1984	1,464	1992	2,575
1985	1,642	1993	2,848*
1986	1,838	1994	2,948**
1987	1,982		

*As of April 20, 1994.
**As of October 20, 1994.
Source: NAACP Legal Defense Fund; U.S. Justice
Department, Bureau of Justice Statistics.

asm of Americans exceeds anything seen in most other Western countries. For example, Virginia activist Marie Deans described the difference in atmosphere she encounters when traveling in Europe:

> It's wonderful to go over there, because they treat you with such warmth, you know. Here, we get hate mail, nasty phone calls in the middle of the night, people calling you names and writing nasty letters to the editor about you, and stuff like that. And you go over there, and it's like culture shock! . . . This has not happened to me once, this has happened to me *many* times in England and Ireland and Scotland. I'll get in a taxicab and they hear this southern accent and they want to know where I'm from. And I can tell them I'm *from* South Carolina but I live in Virginia. And they'll say "That's one of those state's that's killing people all the time!" They *talk* about this stuff! *Taxi drivers* wanting to know what's *wrong* with us![3]

Of course, not all Europeans agree with those Deans has encountered. Many citizens of the United Kingdom, France, and elsewhere would prefer that executions resume in their lands. But these attitudes rarely lead to serious reintroduction drives. In the United States, by contrast, elected officials scramble to capitalize on pro-death penalty sentiment.

Why is this country bucking what appears to be a world-historical trend away from capital punishment? There are probably several reasons. The most important may be America's special curse — levels of violent crime so high as to be unique in the industrialized world. We are at much greater risk of being robbed, raped, assaulted — and especially murdered — than citizens of countries such as Germany, Great Britain, Canada, and Japan. Americans have grown increasingly angry and fearful about the situation in their streets, and the death penalty has become a symbol of that mood, a red button waiting to be pressed by politicians and journalists alike.

But another piece of the answer lies with the weakness thus far of the anti-death penalty movement (ADPM) in this country. Such a movement exists. Its members call themselves "abolitionists," as did nineteenth-century opponents of slavery. Some of them are lawyers who specialize in capital defense and who struggle to overturn the convictions of death-sentenced inmates in appellate courts. Others are policy advocates who lobby state legislators, plead with governors to grant clemency, and attack capital punishment in countless public debates, call-in talk shows, and op-ed columns from coast to coast. Still others are Christians who work with death-sentenced prisoners and their families out of a sense of religious duty. Some abolitionists are single-minded in their dedication to contesting what they see as state-sanctioned murder, whereas others see the death penalty as one human rights violation among many that must be addressed.

The diversity of the movement often leads to philosophical and strategic disputes, but so far it has managed to avoid the factional splintering that has plagued other crusades in America. Nevertheless, the anti-death penalty movement has been unable to stem the resurgence of executions. There have been too few members, too little money, and too little broad appeal in the messages the movement has tried to deliver. Clearly, a strong anti-death penalty movement would not be enough to bring capital punishment to a quick end. But it is a necessary precondition. For we in the United States have exhibited a great capacity for self-deception on matters of crime and justice. Only a reasonably large, vigorous, and well-provisioned army of activists could turn the country around on this issue, and that army has not yet emerged.

Based on information gleaned from the statements of media commentators and politicians, one might quickly conclude that popular support for the death penalty is irreversible. This is not necessarily the case. The death penalty remains a highly controversial subject, and executions raise issues that, in a nation founded on principles like equal justice, individual rights, and due process, regularly capture widespread attention. In one recent three-year period, for example, three capital cases received sustained front-page coverage from coast to coast:

• On April 21, 1992, Robert Alton Harris died in California's gas chamber. Harris's case had been the focus of enormous attention because he was the first convict to be executed in that bellwether state since the early 1960s — thus putting to rest the image of capital punishment as primarily a southern phenomenon — and because he was said to suffer from the effects of fetal alcohol syndrome. A serious attempt to have the execution televised was blocked by the courts. And months later, death penalty opponents battled with the state over whether a videotape of his death, alleged to be graphic proof of the cruelty of death in the gas chamber, should be made public.

- On January 5, 1993, child killer Westley Allan Dodd was executed in Walla Walla, Washington. His death received widespread media coverage because it employed a method that hadn't been used in the United States in 28 years: hanging. The fact that Dodd had *chosen* hanging over the option of lethal injection added to the macabre celebrity of the case.

- On January 4, 1995, Jesse DeWayne Jacobs died from a lethal injection in Texas. Jacobs, who the state had first accused of murder, was later seemingly absolved of killing the former wife of his sister's boyfriend. The case was notorious because prosecutors changed their account of the crime after Jacobs had been convicted. During his trial, they alleged that he had shot the victim after his sister, Bobbi Hogan, had persuaded him to try to scare the woman into giving up custody of her children. In Ms. Hogan's subsequent manslaughter trial, the same prosecutors alleged that she, not Mr. Jacobs, had fired the fatal shot. Accomplices in capital murders are subject to the death penalty under Texas law, but even staunch advocates of capital punishment were disturbed by the inconsistency in the state's story. This was the latest in a series of Texas cases involving the execution or near execution of men for crimes they may not have committed.

In spite of the widespread approval that capital punishment enjoys, the details of cases like those of Harris, Dodd, and Jacobs stir deep feelings of ambivalence, even among persons who are philosophically committed to the death penalty.

Furthermore, the very momentum of capital punishment seems to contain the seeds of future crises and debates whose outlines are only gradually becoming apparent. For example, the steady rise in the population of the nation's death rows virtually guarantees that one of two things will occur. The first possibility is that further curtailment by the courts of the legal grounds for appeals will produce an unprecedented bloodbath, with hundreds of executions a year taking place in American prisons. The other is a continuation of the status quo, a slow and uncertain form of justice that almost everyone — retentionist and abolitionist alike — sees as unsatisfactory. Moreover, the sheer cost of capital prosecutions, which has been estimated to range from 1.8 million to $15 million per case (New York State Defenders Association 1982; Magagnini 1988), is forcing state and county governments to make exceedingly difficult choices: should they cut expenditures for schools, police protection, and human services in order to pay the bill for a handful of death penalty cases? The sheer expense involved is coming to be seen as an intractable problem that may soon bring capital punishment in the United States to a critical juncture.

Against Capital Punishment traces the evolution of anti-death penalty activism, with emphasis on the period since 1972. The book draws on current social movement theory in order to account for both the movement's successes in preventing the use of capital punishment on a truly massive scale (certainly a distinct possibility in a nation with nearly 20,000 homicides a year) and for its inability to pull this country along in the same current that is carrying the remainder of the democratic West.

Historical Cycles of American Abolitionism

The death penalty has been in almost continual use in this country since the early Colonial period. The first person to lose his life at the hands of an executioner in what was to become the United States was Captain George Kendall, who was put to death in 1608 (Espy and Smykla 1987). Since that time, some 14,000 men, women, and even children have been put to death. This figure excludes thousands of lynching victims (Bedau 1982:3). Their crimes included not only murder, but also rape, theft, witchcraft, counterfeiting, and a wide variety of other transgressions.

Through most of the nation's history, the proposition that authorities had the legal and moral right to take the lives of those who committed serious crimes was taken for granted by the bulk of the citizenry. Nevertheless, organized opposition to capital punishment is not a recent development. On the contrary, abolitionism has existed in one form or another since the eighteenth century. Prior to the American Revolution, anti-death penalty sentiment was primarily confined to such groups as the Quakers and to occasional essayists who criticized it as a violation of scriptural dictates, an ineffective deterrent, or a disproportionately severe punishment for crimes other than murder (Masur 1989:4). But such reformers were up against formidable obstacles. The public was accustomed to executions, which took place in public. Since incarceration was not yet a common means of punishing serious offenders, a society without a death penalty was difficult to imagine.

After the Revolution, the debate over capital punishment became more visible. Abolitionism was almost indistinguishable from the prison reform movement at this stage. Thus, some of the vocal critics of executions were associated with such groups as the Philadelphia Society for Alleviating the Miseries of Public Prisons, and some were among the most important intellectual and political leaders of the time—Benjamin Rush, Benjamin Franklin, and Thomas Jefferson.[4] They drew their rhetorical ammunition from European reformers like Cesare Beccaria, whose *Essay on Crime and Punishments* was published in the United States in the 1770s and was frequently cited by prison reformers and abolitionists (Post 1944:38). Beccaria claimed that the certainty of punishment, not its severity, was the key to deterring crime, and that capital punishment was less helpful in preventing murder than life imprisonment at hard labor. The writings of English prison reformer John Howard were also used by American reformers in their speeches and pamphlets.

Although Beccaria provided a convenient source of debating material, his work was not the only source of abolitionist sentiment during the post-Revolution years, nor even the primary one. America was fertile ground for anti-capital punishment reform for reasons of political ideology. There was a growing distaste in many quarters for unfettered state power (Friedman 1993: 63). The rule of law, and the impulse to *reform* wrongdoers rather than to dispose of them, seemed to symbolize the difference between the monarchy that the patriots were casting aside and the enlightened republic they sought to build. It was a "republican, religious language unlike anything in Beccaria" that framed the issue for Americans after Independence had been secured (Masur 1989:54). Similarly, the spread of a liberal theology undermined biblical justifications for capital punishment. Mercy, rather than divine retribution, came to be seen by many religious Americans as the true spirit of the scriptures.

Although antigallows sentiment was present during the Colonial period and received a significant boost from the Revolution, it did not take the form of a coordinated social movement. The history of *organized* abolitionism has been cyclical, achieving its highest levels of visibility and influence during four protest phases. The first of these peaked during the 1830s and 1840s. The second occurred just prior to the turn of the twentieth century and persisted until the outbreak of World War I. The third cycle came in the mid-1950s and 1960s. The fourth began in the late 1970s and is still under way.

The First Abolitionist Era

By the 1830s, anti-death penalty agitation had grown stronger and more radical in its demands: whereas relatively few had called for *complete* abolition of the death penalty during the eighteenth century, many more did so by the early 1830s. Prominent Americans lobbied for abolition bills in several state legislatures during this period (Mackey 1976: xviii, xix; Mackey 1982:113–122; Davis 1957:32). By the end of the 1850s, antigallows agitation had secured de jure abolition of capital punishment in Michigan, Rhode Island, and Wisconsin. Additionally, Maine passed a law that required its governor to issue a specific order for an execution to take place, and specified that such an order could be handed down no sooner than a year after the trial's completion. The so-called "Maine Law," which was later copied by other states, had the effect of abolishing executions de facto. Some of these victories were soon reversed. But short-lived as the successes of this era were, they were also quite unprecedented.

The greater receptivity of the nation to calls for the elimination of the death penalty in the 1830s and 1840s can be understood in terms of several trends that were under way during that time. The first was a general climate of reform in the handling of people on society's margins. The Jacksonian era witnessed not only serious consideration of proposals to abandon the gallows, but also calls for radical change in the treatment of the poor, the orphaned, the mentally ill, and the criminal (Rothman 1971). Another contributing factor was a growing faith not just in the *desirability* of reforming deviants of all stripes, but in the *capacity* of enlightened individuals to do so successfully (Mackey 1976:xx). Likewise, the middle-class preference for "internal restraints and private punishments" continued to evolve (Masur 1989:5). All these currents lent strength to anti-death penalty forces in the 1830s and 1840s.

While some anti-death penalty activists sought the total abolition of hangings—successfully in some cases—the primary legacy of the first abolitionist era turned out to be the elimination of *public* hangings. Public executions in America had always been justified on "educational" grounds; the spectacle of a wrongdoer meeting his maker on the village green or courthouse lawn was intended to terrify potential criminals and make them think twice about committing capital crimes. But public hangings troubled many Americans of the early nineteenth century. It was feared that they might provoke sympathy for the condemned, threaten public order, and brutalize the entire community. Many abolitionists thought, naively, that ending the spectacle of public executions would undermine the most fundamental justification for capital punishment itself (Masur 1989:95–113).

"Private" hangings — hangings conducted within prisons before a small, select audience of witnesses — were adopted by Rhode Island, Pennsylvania, New York, Massachusetts, and New Jersey during the 1830s, and 15 states had restricted executions to prisons or prison yards by 1849. A few abolitionists worried that moving executions behind prison walls would merely conceal their horror and ugliness, and thus delay the final resolution of the issue. They were probably correct. Making the process private may have undermined the retentionists' deterrence argument somewhat, because a hanging that few saw with their own eyes would be less terrifying to potential lawbreakers than one conducted under the gaze of the whole community. The arrival of a system of execution behind closed doors, however, also prevented abolitionists from capitalizing on growing public distaste of the gruesome details of these events.

The anti-death penalty movement began to lose its momentum during late 1840s, due largely to the distracting effects of the Mexican War and to growing North-South tensions over slavery. The decline reveals what may have been a key weakness of antigallows groups before the Civil War: they were made up of "generalized reformers" who were occupied not only with seeking to eliminate capital punishment but also with prison reform, antislavery agitation, and other controversial issues of the time. Their interests and energies were spread rather thin, and external events siphoned off much of the momentum and resources that had fueled their efforts against hanging. Abolitionist activity virtually ceased by the mid-1850s and remained dormant during the post-war period. The few truly active reformers of this period struggled, with some success, for the elimination of laws that made execution mandatory on conviction for murder (Filler 1952:132–133). Some reformers assumed that this would lead rapidly to total abolition. But like the demise of public executions, the introduction of judicial discretion in capital cases seems to have robbed abolitionists of one of their most potent arguments; namely, that mandatory capital punishment led juries to acquit the guilty in order to avoid being a part of official killings.

The Second Abolitionist Era

The ADPM entered a second era of vigor and influence during the last few years of the nineteenth century. This revival rode the waves of Populist and Progressive reform and benefited from the growing appeal of both "scientific" corrections and a socially conscious form of Christianity (Mackey 1976:xxxii). The movement was also affected by New York's introduction of a new technology of execution, the electric chair, in 1890 (Barry 1979:61). Critics claimed that electrocution amounted to a form of torture, a modern equivalent of burning at the stake, and they launched a new round of assaults on capital punishment.

Anti-death penalty activism during this period was based primarily at the state and local level. Among the more important of the state groups was the Anti-Death Penalty League in Massachusetts formed in 1897. There was little national coordination through most of this period, although the Chicago-based Anti-Capital Punishment Society of America and the Committee on Capital Punishment of the National Committee on Prisons became active during the second decade of the twentieth century. Organized opposition to abolition came not so much from religious leaders, as it had in the nineteenth century, but from judges, prosecutors, and the police. The basic claim of the retentionists was that the deterrent effect of the death penalty was unique among punishments, and that abolition would subject the nation to an unprecedented onslaught of violent crime (Dressner and Altschuler 1975). Some also argued that the elimination of *legal* executions would simply invite an increase in lynching, and that crime-prone immigrant and black populations could only be held in check by the terror of the hangman's noose (Galliher, Ray, and Cook 1993; Mackey 1976:xxxv).

The movement enjoyed even more success during this second cycle than it had during the earlier one. Ten states banned executions outright during this period: Colorado (1897), Kansas (1907), Minnesota (1911), Washington (1913), Oregon (1914), North Dakota (1915), South Dakota (1915), Tennessee (1915), Arizona (1916), and Missouri (1917) (Bowers 1984:9; Galliher, Ray, and Cook 1993; Zimring and Hawkins 1986:29). Abolition bills came close to enactment in several other states, passing one legislative house but failing in the other. History repeated itself, though: most of the legislative victories were reversed, as had been those of the first reform era. This time, the abolitionist spirit fell victim to the generally violent and nativist atmosphere surrounding World War I (Schwed 1983:17–18; Mackey 1976:xxii–xxiv; Filler 1952:134) and the later economic reversals (Galliher, Ray, and Cook 1993).

The American League to Abolish Capital Punishment

Although the second cycle of anti-death penalty agitation ended with the outbreak of World War I, a new organization emerged during the 1920s that kept the flame alive through the succeeding four decades: the American League to Abolish Capital Punishment. The ALACP was founded in 1925, the midpoint of a bleak decade for death penalty opponents. It was first based in New York City, later moved its headquarters to California, and finally settled in Brookline, Massachusetts. The League's primary goals through most of its 47-year lifespan were to assist and coordinate campaigns for state abolition bills and to educate the public concerning the moral and practical problems with the death penalty. In both of these missions, the ALACP relied heavily on well-known people who served at various times on its executive committee: prison wardens Lewis Lawes (Sing-Sing), Thomas Mott Osborne (Auburn), and Miriam Van Waters (Massachusetts Reformatory for Women); attorney Clarence Darrow; psychiatrist Karl Menninger; and academics Thorsten Sellin, Donal MacNamara, and Hugo Bedau. These individuals gave speeches and wrote articles and pamphlets that the ALACP distributed throughout the nation. Several also served as presidents of the League. During the 1920s, the ALACP managed to support campaigns for legislative abolition of capital punishment in at least 11 states, providing testimony and mailing tens of thousands of pieces of literature a year. The results of the legislative attacks on capital punishment throughout the 1920s, 1930s, and 1940s, were discouraging: inevitably, abolition bills either died in committee, were defeated by one or the other state legislative body, or were vetoed by governors. In addition to its lobbying during the 1920s, the League also established a research committee to carry out some of the first systematic empirical investigations on such questions as deterrence and racial discrimination in capital sentencing (ALACP 1929).

The viability of the league varied greatly over time. In its early years, it benefited from the furor surrounding the Sacco-Vanzetti and Leopold-Loeb cases, and its membership and fund-raising success boomed. But the Great Depression and World War II were devastating for most social movement organizations, and the ALACP was no exception. It barely survived the 1940s. A modest revival occurred in the 1950s when Sara B. Ehrmann took over as executive director. Through Mrs. Ehrmann, who had directed the Massachusetts affiliate for years and had become involved with the death penalty when her husband served as assistant defense counsel for Sacco and Vanzetti, the ALACP provided a crucial link to the reemerging abolitionism of the 1950s and 1960s.

The Third Abolitionist Era

The third major cycle of death penalty abolitionism began in earnest during the 1960s, and by the time it ended, the master strategy for ridding the nation of capital punishment had shifted from the legislative arena to the courts. In turn, that strategic shift set the stage for the most recent chapter in the attack on capital punishment that is the main subject of this book.

The legal battle against capital punishment will be discussed more fully in chapter 1, but a brief overview of the movement in the 1950s and 1960s is in order here. By the time the third cycle of abolitionism began, the average yearly rate of executions had already been declining for decades, for reasons that are not altogether clear (see Table 2). Public opinion still supported capital punishment, but judges and juries nevertheless had been sending fewer and fewer convicted criminals to death row since the late 1930s. The average number of executions per year fell to 128 during the 1940s, a decline of 50 per year over the previous half-decade. The early 1950s brought an average of

TABLE 2.   Number of Executions by Year in
the United States, 1930–1970

Year	Executions	Year	Executions
1930	155	1951	105
1931	153	1952	83
1932	140	1953	62
1933	160	1954	81
1934	168	1955	76
1935	199	1956	65
1936	195	1957	65
1937	147	1958	49
1938	190	1959	49
1939	160	1960	56
1940	124	1961	42
1941	123	1962	47
1942	147	1963	21
1943	131	1964	15
1944	120	1965	7
1945	117	1966	1
1946	131	1967	2
1947	153	1968	0
1948	119	1969	0
1949	119	1970	0
1950	82		

*Source: National Prisoner Statistics Report: Capital Pun-
ishment 1984*, p. 12. Washington, D.C.: Bureau of Justice
Statistics.

only 83 hangings, gassings, and electrocutions per year (Zimring and Hawkins
1986:30). Philip Mackey (1976:xlii) speculates that the lingering shock of the
Holocaust may have been partly responsible for this. A growing awareness of
the trend toward abolition in Europe may also have played a role (Bedau 1982:
23). In any case, the decline in capital punishment was most noticeable in
northern and western states, and less so in the South.

With capital punishment already in spontaneous decline in America, several new state-level abolitionist organizations appeared in the late 1950s and
the 1960s. Many of these, such as the California-based Citizens Against Legalized Murder, the Ohio Committee to Abolish Capital Punishment, and the
New Jersey Council to Abolish Capital Punishment, were at least loosely
affiliated with the ALACP. Others were independent, including California's
People Against Capital Punishment, the New York Committee to Abolish
Capital Punishment, the Oregon Council to Abolish the Death Penalty, and

the National Committee to Abolish the Federal Death Penalty (Mackey 1976: xlvi–xlvii).

The reemergence of organized anti-death penalty activity in the United States was stimulated in part by the report of Great Britain's Royal Commission on Capital Punishment (1953; Christoph 1962:76–95), which concluded that the application of the death penalty in Great Britain had already been limited to so few crimes and so few criminals that further restrictions were unrealistic. Therefore, the commission reasoned, "the real issue is now whether capital punishment should be retained or abolished" (Royal Commission 1953:212). This came as close to a call for abolition as the commission's charge allowed.[5] Eleven years later, Great Britain hanged its last convict, and Parliament formally struck down the death penalty in 1969.

The Royal Commission had a dual impact in the United States. Its report provided American abolitionists with fresh documentation for their arguments, and its very existence suggested that the question of abolition was one that a modern, civilized nation ought to take seriously. An American law professor, Herbert Wechsler, who had served as an adviser to the Royal Commission, also served on the American Law Institute (ALI) committee that was working on a Model Penal Code for use by state legislatures. The committee voted 18 to 2 to recommend abolition of the death penalty by the states, but the ALI convention eventually declined to adopt that recommendation (Meltsner 1973:21–23).

In addition to developments abroad, American abolitionism profited from the notorious Barbara Graham and Caryl Chessman cases in California. Graham was put to death in the gas chamber in 1955 despite her claims of innocence, and her case became the basis of a best-selling book and a popular Hollywood motion picture. Chessman had killed no one, but was condemned to die for kidnapping with bodily harm in the course of a series of sexual assaults. This violated California's "Little Lindbergh Law" and carried the penalty of death. Something of a publicity hound, Chessman not only insisted on representing himself at trial, but published three popular books during his 11 years on San Quentin's death row. The case generated widespread sympathy; many believed Chessman was innocent, and even some of those who thought him guilty were nevertheless troubled by irregularities in his trial. His supporters included Eleanor Roosevelt, Aldous Huxley, Ray Bradbury, Marlon Brando, and Albert Schweitzer. When Chessman was finally put to death in 1960, angry mobs attacked U.S. embassies in several countries (Brown 1989; Schwed 1983:73–91).

Anti-death penalty forces managed to pass abolition bills in Alaska, Hawaii, and Delaware during the late 1950s. During the 1960s, Oregon and Iowa abolished the death penalty outright, whereas West Virginia, Vermont, New York, and New Mexico elected to retain it only for extraordinary offenses (Bowers 1984:9). But abolitionists faced frustrating difficulties lobbying for the repeal of death statutes, pursuing clemency for individual convicts, and struggling to change the generally hostile climate of opinion. Beginning in 1963, civil rights attorneys associated with the NAACP Legal Defense and

Educational Fund (LDF) began a series of courtroom attacks on racial disparities in southern death sentences for rape. In 1965, the strategy was broadened
to a multi-issue assault on the constitutionality of capital punishment in general, that is, for white as well as black offenders and in murder as well as rape
cases. LDF lawyers, later joined by attorneys from the American Civil Liberties Union, hoped to bring about a moratorium on executions while this campaign was in progress (Bedau 1977; Zimring and Hawkins 1986:33–38):

> The politics of abolition boiled down to this: for each year the United States
> went without executions, the more hollow would ring claims that the Ameri-
> can people could not do without them; the longer death-row inmates waited,
> the greater their numbers, the more difficult it would be for the courts to
> permit the first execution. A successful moratorium strategy would create a
> death-row logjam. (Meltsner 1973:107)

The switch to a primarily legalistic strategy was successful, at least in the
short run. No convict was put to death in the United States between 1967 and
1977. The key victory, however, came in the Supreme Court's 1972 ruling in
Furman v. Georgia, which effectively struck down all the nation's death penalty laws on the basis of the arbitrary and discriminatory manner in which
capital punishment was administered. The decision came on a narrow five-to-
four vote, with each justice in the majority submitting a separate opinion.
Furman represented a remarkably fragile victory. Death penalty opponents
who had been tempted to celebrate the final demise of executions in this nation
soon realized that their goal had not been achieved once and for all. The
justices' opinions left open the possibility that states might yet devise death
penalty statutes that were constitutionally permissible, and a new round in the
struggle would begin. That is precisely what occurred.

The Fourth Abolitionist Era

The reaction to the Supreme Court's *Furman* ruling was immediate and tumultuous. Self-styled "law and order" advocates decried the decision as an open
invitation to anarchy. A flurry of legislative activity ensued, and within two
years 28 states had adopted new death penalty statutes. These revised laws
attempted to remedy the constitutional defects identified in the LDF cases,
either by making the death penalty mandatory for certain types of crimes – an
approach that was later struck down by the Court – or by introducing sentencing standards to make the process less arbitrary (Williams 1978:71). In a set of
three 1976 decisions,[6] the Supreme Court upheld the more rationalized sentencing procedure, thereby reopening the door to the death chamber in America.
The first execution of the post-*Furman* era came when Gary Gilmore died in
front of a Utah firing squad on January 17, 1977.

Since the return of capital punishment in the United States, the anti-death
penalty movement has revived. It no longer consists of lawyers and litigation
strategies alone. Rather, it has come to consist of scores of organizations with
widely varying degrees of involvement in the struggle. A recent publication

lists 34 national level organizations,[7] 20 national religious organizations with official policy statements against the death penalty, and 147 regional, state, and local groups that are involved in some manner with the ADPM (National Coalition to Abolish the Death Penalty 1990). Those organizations that are truly active on the issue, rather than only nominally abolitionist, engage in a variety of activities. Some secure the services of lawyers to handle the appeals of individual death row convicts or otherwise minister to their needs. A few lobby state legislatures to prevent the reinstatement or expansion of the death penalty. Others coordinate informational programs to change public opinion on what they characterize as state-sanctioned murder. Some organize occasional demonstrations, including "vigils" outside prisons where convicts are scheduled to be put to death. On the national and regional levels, the most influential ADPM organizations are Amnesty International USA, the American Civil Liberties Union, the NAACP Legal Defense and Educational Fund, and the National Coalition to Abolish the Death Penalty. Many of the state and local groups are affiliated with one of these national organizations.

The anti-death penalty movement is not a *mass* movement on the order of the civil rights, feminist, or pro-choice/right-to-life movements. In some respects, it resembles the "professional social movements" first discussed by McCarthy and Zald (1973): its major activists are neither death-sentenced inmates nor former convicts, but rather moral entrepreneurs who speak for those under direct threat of execution; the resources that fuel their efforts are derived from sources other than the direct beneficiaries of those efforts; and a large portion of the membership of the movement is "paper" membership — that is, it represents either members of multi-issue groups that have affiliated with an anti-death penalty coalition or of members of multi-issue groups that deal with the death penalty as one project among many. On the other hand, a chronic shortage of funding forces the movement to rely mostly on highly dedicated, unpaid volunteers. There would *be* no organized outcry against capital punishment if it were not for these true believers. Thus, the ADPM is a far cry from such fully professionalized movement organizations as Common Cause.

Additionally, the tactics of the ADPM differ radically from current mass movements. Anti-death penalty demonstrations have become relatively rare in recent years. There is at present no "radical flank" (Haines 1988) that employs disruptive or violent tactics to harass the criminal justice system. There *is* a great deal of lobbying, letter writing on behalf of death-sentenced inmates or favored legislation, and "public education" on the flaws of capital punishment. Theoretical "purists" might suggest that the ADPM is not a social movement at all, but rather an *interest group*[8] — albeit an interest group that is morally motivated and active around a distinctively social issue rather than some narrow group interest. It is unwise, however, to make too sharp a distinction between collective action vehicles that rely primarily on unconventional tactics and those that operate within the system. Protest movements that are excluded from the polity and interest groups that are parts of it are not two qualitatively different phenomena, but rather two ranges on the spectrum of collective action. Moreover, politicized collectivities have a way of shifting between conventional and unconventional tactics over time, and often gain and lose membership in the polity (Tilly 1978). It would be foolish to see the ADPM as an inappropriate subject for social movement analysis simply because its *current* tactical repertoire emphasizes routine politics.

Death Penalty Abolitionism and Modern Social Movements

This book has two objectives. First, it seeks to describe the struggle against the death penalty in America since the early 1970s — to tell the stories of the organizations that have been at the front lines of the battle, the activists who have made those organizations run, the strategic choices they have made, and the victories and defeats they have experienced. These are dramatic stories, even heroic at times — stories that intersect important fault lines in the American sociocultural bedrock. They have gone almost untold thus far, at least as far as the historical and social scientific literature is concerned. But this will be a sociological work as well as a historical one; it will seek to *explain* the movement as well as describe it. In attempting to understand the course that the abolitionist challenge has taken and the decidedly mixed results it has achieved, this study will borrow conceptual tools from contemporary social movement scholarship. Thus, before returning to the anti-death penalty movement itself, a brief survey of recent developments in social movement analysis and their relation to this investigation is in order.

Social movement theory is now in a fertile period on both sides of the Atlantic. Resource mobilization (RM) theory, which dominated the field in America during the 1970s and part of the 1980s, is being challenged by newer interpretive approaches that emphasize ideational aspects of collective action and the social construction of public issues. A fruitful dialogue has also been initiated with proponents of the "new social movements" approach (Cohen 1985; Klandermans 1986; Melucci 1980, 1981, 1989; Pizzorno 1978; Touraine 1985) that developed primarily in Europe. Resource mobilization theory was itself a theoretical challenger, part of a "second generation" of social movement theories, only two decades ago.

The "first generation" theories that resource mobilization supplanted comprised the "classical model" of social movements (McAdam 1982). These theories differed from one another in many ways, but they shared two important characteristics. The first was a microsociological focus. Writers in the collective behavior school stressed the emergence of norms out of ongoing processes of social interaction and their role in the appearance of mass movements (Turner and Killian 1957; Smelser 1962), whereas others emphasized alienation (Kornhauser 1959) or relative deprivation (Feieraband, Feieraband, and Nesvold 1969; Gurr 1970). Regardless of the specific explanation of protest and insurgency, early theories directed attention to the social-psychological level — to the individual characteristics or motivations of movement participants that set them apart from nonparticipants. The other common characteristic of first generation theories was the tendency to view movements and their participants as deviations from the "normal." Eric Hoffer (1951), for example, believed that movements drew their converts from among socially marginal and psychologically flawed persons, and that such persons frequently shifted between seemingly contradictory causes. Similarly, Lewis Feuer (1969) portrayed American student protest during the Vietnam era as the outcome of unresolved conflicts in early life. Not only did these portrayals turn out to be empirically inaccurate, but they revealed a deep antipathy toward social movements that masqueraded as objective scientific inquiry. Other observers of modern collective action did not share the reductionism of Hoffer and Feuer, but nevertheless interpreted movements as "outbursts" of irrational mass behavior that were symptomatic of various sorts of system malfunctioning (Kornhauser 1959; also see Gusfield 1962).

A second generation of social movement theory emerged in the 1970s and the early 1980s, with the development of the resource mobilization perspective (McCarthy and Zald 1973, 1977; Oberschall 1973) and the closely related, sometimes overlapping, political process model (McAdam 1982; Tilly 1978). These theories differed in important ways from the older approaches. Whereas first generation theories had focused on the explanation of individual participation in collective action and on the largely social-psychological factors that were thought to motivate it, the second generation theories shifted attention to the dynamics of formal movement organizations (Buechler 1993; Ferree and Miller 1985) and to the political environment in which they operate. Resource mobilization theory spawned studies of movement fund-raising, strategy, organizational structure, coalition building, interorganizational competition, and movement-countermovement interaction (for example, Barkan 1986; Cable 1984; Freeman 1973; Gamson 1975; Haines 1984; Jenkins and Eckert 1986; Jenkins and Perrow 1977; Staggenborg 1988, 1989, 1991; Zald and Useem 1987). Meanwhile, political process scholars examined the existing organizational structures out of which movements grow, shifts in the receptivity of political systems over time, and the manner in which these affected mobilization (for example, Gale 1986; McAdam 1982; Morris 1984; Shorter and Tilly 1974; Snow and Marshall 1984; Tarrow 1989; Zald and McCarthy 1987).

The newer theories of social movements also differed radically from classical theories in respect to the "normality" of collective action. Whereas first generation theorists had tended to marginalize social movements and to view participation as an irrational and expressive type of conduct, those working within the emerging tradition saw protest as the product of rational assessment of costs and benefits, as a normal extension of conventional political behavior (McCarthy and Zald 1977; Tilly 1978; Zald 1992). Whereas classical theories saw fluctuations in collective grievances as essential preconditions for the emergence of insurgency (even if they did not necessarily take those grievances seriously), RM theorists recognized that the existence of discontent does not guarantee collective *action*. They proceeded from the working assumption that dissatisfaction is either constant within society (Jenkins and Perrow 1977;

Tilly 1978) or relatively easy to orchestrate if adequate resources are available (McCarthy and Zald 1973, 1977). In either case, grievances were "bracketed" as unproblematic.

Resource mobilization and political process theories have enhanced our understanding of collective action in Western societies enormously. They have helped to counteract some of the biases of the older paradigm, and they have shed light on features of social movements that are now seen as crucially important by scholars across the theoretical spectrum (Zald 1992). But dissatisfaction, particularly with resource mobilization theory, began to build during the 1980s. Critics accused RM of paying excessive attention to formal movement organizations while ignoring nonbureaucratic groupings and diffuse communities of participants (Buechler 1993; Killian 1981; Turner and Killian 1987; Zald 1992), overestimating the importance of elites and other exogenous supporters while underestimating that of aggrieved groups themselves (McAdam 1982; Morris 1984) or ignoring the manipulative impact of such support (Haines 1984, 1988; Jenkins and Eckert 1986; McAdam 1982), and employing an unrealistic economic model of movement participation (Ferree 1992; Fireman and Gamson 1979; Friedman and McAdam 1992; Rosenthal and Schwartz 1989). Based on these critiques, a third generation of social movement theory is emerging. This new line of analysis does not take the form of a single theoretical tradition, at least not yet. Moreover it does not seek to replace the resource mobilization and political process models, but to round out the picture of collective action that they have drawn.

The major thrust of the third generation of social movement theory is to "bring meaning back in"; that is, to reverse the neglect of ideology, problem definition, and claims making that followed from resource mobilization's obsession with structure (Klandermans 1984). Much of the "new social movement" literature, for example, has emphasized the role of collective identity (Melucci 1989; Stoecker 1995; Taylor and Whittier 1992; also see Friedman and McAdam 1992) — in essence, a sense of "we-ness," common interest, and efficacy — in sustaining activism in feminist, environmental, peace, and similar movements. A particularly important segment of third generation research has pertained to the social construction and framing of issues by activists (Best 1989; Gamson and Modigliani 1989; Klandermans 1992; Snow, et al. 1986; Snow and Benford 1988, 1992).

The concept of "frames" is based on the work of Erving Goffman (1974), who was concerned with interpretive structures by which people organize experience in everyday life. Snow, Rochford, Worden, and Benford (1986) have applied this notion to the study of collective action, defining a movement frame as an interpretive scheme that defines some aspect of the environment, such as gender discrimination, the irradiation of food, or the execution of convicted murderers, as intolerable and as remediable through some prescribed set of actions. A key objective of framing activity is to create a consensus as to the need for change (see Klandermans 1988; Klandermans and Tarrow 1988) and a willingness to contribute to the effort (Snow and Benford 1988:199–204).

In order for a social movement to mobilize effectively, it is important that it package itself in a manner that appeals to potential supporters. It must resonate with beliefs that are held by those it hopes to win over—it must "push the right buttons," as it were. David Snow and his colleagues have suggested that the packaging of causes, which they call "frame alignment," takes four primary forms:

- *Frame bridging* occurs when the movement's frame and that of a group of potential supporters are sufficiently congruent that the activists can win their support by merely pointing out the consistency.
- *Frame amplification* involves the clarification and strengthening of a movement frame by linking it to values or beliefs held by the public.
- *Frame extension* occurs when a movement stretches its diagnosis and prescription regarding a social problem, linking it to a popular set of beliefs in order to appeal to potential adherents.
- *Frame transformation* is an action movement actors employ when they try to bring about a change of outlook among potential supporters to win them over to the movement's point of view as to the causes and cure of the problematic social condition. In other words, frame transformation requires the cultivation of new values that support what the movement is trying to accomplish. This is a very difficult task, and according to Snow et al. (1986), it generally takes too much time to be of practical use.

The potential mobilizing value of a particular movement frame depends on three sets of constraints (Snow and Benford 1988). *Infrastructural* constraints include the salience of the frame's values and symbols to the target audience, the breadth of those ideational elements, and their interrelatedness. *Phenomenological* constraints include the degrees to which the frame is believable to intended target audiences (its "empirical credibility") and harmonizes with the audiences' experiences (its "experiential commensurability") and with existing cultural constructions of events (its "narrative fidelity"). Finally, the mobilizing potential of a frame is affected by the movement's timing; that is, the point within historical cycles of protest at which it appears.

In all forms of alignment except frame transformation, movement leaders try to relate their goals to the *existing* values of the public. "They are thus in a certain sense both consumers of existing cultural meanings and producers of new meanings, which are inevitably framed in terms of organizers' reading of the public's existing values and predispositions" (Tarrow 1992:189).

Analytical Framework

Resources and the Struggle Against Executions

This investigation of anti-death penalty activism draws its research foci from second and third generation theories. For one thing, it pays close attention to the *resource base of the movement*: How much money and how many members have been available for the fight against capital punishment, and what other forms of resources have been available? Did increases in the availability of such resources *precede* escalations in the amount and intensity of anti-death penalty protest (lobbying, litigation, and demonstrating) by abolitionists during the post-*Furman v. Georgia* era as resource mobilization theory predicts? Or was the relationship between funding, membership, and activity levels more complex? What have been the sources of funding for ADP organizations, and have funding sources constrained the way in which capital punishment has been contested over the past two decades? We will see that the ADPM as a whole has suffered from chronic underfunding throughout the period from 1972 to the present, and that it has had a relatively weak organizational base at the local and state levels. These deficits have made it difficult to mount a challenge that might have a reasonable chance of bringing executions to an end in the United States, but have not been so limiting as to prevent abolitionists from slowing their advance. Contrary to a core RM argument, however, the intensity of abolitionist activity over the past 20 years seems not to be a direct function of available resources; anti-death penalty work has varied in more direct relation to changing opportunities in the legal and political arenas than to changes in available resources.

Organizational Infrastructure of the Abolition Movement

The investigation also examines the *organizational infrastructure* of abolitionism during its most recent phase. Studies of the civil rights movement (McAdam 1982; Morris 1984) showed that black churches, colleges, and other institutions were extremely important in spreading the struggle for racial justice. They provided mobilization sites, concentrations of potential supporters and participants, leadership, and channels of communication (see McAdam 1982: 125–142), all somewhat protected from external constraints by opponents. Similarly, much will be said in this book about the infrastructure from which the ADPM grew and the manner in which that infrastructure conditioned the movement's ideology and tactical repertoire. Several of the primary movement organizations emerged as special projects within established organizations that were dedicated to other goals. This was true of Amnesty International (a human rights group headquartered in the United Kingdom), the NAACP Legal Defense and Educational Fund, Inc. (a civil rights law firm emphasizing issues affecting African Americans), and the American Civil Liberties Union (which specializes in the preservation of constitutional freedoms). In each of these cases, anti-death penalty tactical decisions have been shaped in part by the orientation of the parent organization. Another major group, the National Coalition to Abolish the Death Penalty, was built on the foundation of a coalition that had originally been formed to seek amnesty for Vietnam War draft resistors. Religious groups were especially well represented within this predecessor coalition. While NCADP has evolved considerably since its early days, its "roots" have exerted a considerable impact on the manner in which it has worked against capital punishment. The organizational infrastructure on which the contemporary anti-death penalty movement was built has constrained the way in which activists have framed the issue.

Political Opportunity and the Death Penalty

Another focus of this study is the impact of *political climate and opportunity structure* on anti-death penalty activity, which draws from political process models. As was noted earlier, organized opposition to capital punishment in America has followed a cyclical pattern and ADP forces achieved most of their successes during distinct eras. Between those eras, the ADPM declined into relative obscurity and isolation. Such alternation between activity and abeyance is common among social movements (Taylor 1989), and the political process model suggests one possible reason: the overall vulnerability of political institutions to challenges varies over time. Relatively "open" periods may come about in a wake of economic or electoral crises (Piven and Cloward 1977; Tarrow 1988a, 1988b; Nagel 1990) or perhaps as a result of the "inspirational" effect of successful challenges in other arenas (Tarrow 1988b:435), for example, the civil rights movement during the 1960s. On the other hand, more particularized events, such as the sudden and unexpected rise of a sympathetic politician to high office or a favorable judicial decision, may present opportunities for mobilizing around particular issues (see McAdam 1982:40). In short, political process theorists expect "cycles of protest" and "cycles of reform" (Tarrow 1988a) to occur when a favorable "structure of political opportunities" (Eisinger 1973; McAdam 1982:40–43) exists.

In one respect, the recent history of the ADPM supports the predictions of political process models. The third peak in anti-death penalty activism occurred in the midst of the 1960s, a period characterized by diverse forms of collective action and generally liberal outlooks within the federal government's executive and judicial branches. In fact, the effort that produced the short-lived judicial ban on capital punishment (1972–1976) was a direct outgrowth, both organizationally and ideologically, of the 1960s civil rights revolution. The last two decades, on the other hand, have seen the decline of many of the 1960s social movements and a sharply conservative turn in the national political climate. The ADPM has been forced to assume a more defensive stance during this period, concentrating most of its efforts on stemming the trends toward death penalty reinstatement and increased numbers of executions. The rightward trajectory of the Supreme Court is particularly important in connection to the specific issue of capital punishment; it became clear early in the first Reagan administration that the federal courts could no longer be counted on to limit the application of the death penalty in any significant way. As we will soon see, however, the constriction of previously available opportunities to contest the penalty did *not* lead to the demobilization of abolitionists. On the contrary, the movement expanded, albeit in new directions.

Issue Construction and Frame Alignment

A final theoretical focus, and a key to the fate of the anti-death penalty movement in the United States thus far, concerns the manner in which the issue of capital punishment has been defined by its opponents. The chapters that follow discuss a wide array of alleged defects in the policy of executing convicted criminals, ranging from what abolitionists see as the inherent evil of state-sanctioned killing to racial discrimination in death sentencing to its economic costs. Based on the work of the new social constructionists, the alignment of anti-death penalty claims and strategies with public beliefs about violent crime will be discussed in detail, particularly in chapter 6. Indeed, the central argument of the book is that frame alignment difficulties — including the tendencies to utilize *frame transformation* rather than *frame extension* strategies and to de-emphasize the types of issues that have the most widespread appeal — are the primary reasons for the slow growth of the ADPM and for it shortage of both resources and grassroots organizational strength.

Although the main concern of this book is the *fourth* cycle of American abolitionism that began in the late 1970s, the narrative cannot begin at that point. Rather, it must begin with the rise of *lawyers* to leadership during the 1960s and with their decision to get the Supreme Court to declare that the official policy of killing killers is in violation of the Constitution of the United States. It was this dramatic strategic shift, and the unprecedented judicial reaction it brought, that set the stage for the resurgence of the anti-death penalty movement in the 1980s and 1990s. Thus, it is to the constitutional strategy that we turn next.

1

The Fall and Rise of Capital Punishment: 1965–1976

Leslie Horton, awaiting execution for rape in Florida, was enjoying a visit with his family the morning of June 29, 1972, when a guard stepped in and asked "Can you stand some more good news today?" The Supreme Court, the guard informed him, had just abolished the death penalty. Earlier that morning, Chief Justice Warren Burger had announced the Court's decision in the case of *Furman v. Georgia* (408 U.S. 238, 1972), which by the narrowest of margins declared all existing capital statutes in the United States to be in violation of the Eighth and Fourteenth Amendments to the Constitution.

Eighty of the other 86 death-sentenced prisoners at the Florida State Prison Farm got the good news from the radio as they returned from watching a Clint Eastwood movie. Death row erupted in "hollering, hooting, and the exuberant rattling of cell doors." Some shouted "Right on, Mr. Justices." Some mockingly cursed President Nixon, who had campaigned on a punitive "law and order" platform. And at least one wept with joy (Waldron 1972).

Elsewhere, the response was less enthusiastic. President Nixon reiterated his belief that capital punishment is a superior deterrent to violent crime, and told reporters that he hoped the ruling would not extend to federal death sentences for kidnapping and hijacking (Robbins 1972). Jere Beasley, the lieutenant governor of Alabama, fumed that "a majority of this nation's highest court has lost contact with the real world." His counterpart in Georgia, Lester Maddox, called the decision "a license for anarchy, rape, murder" (quoted by Meltsner 1973:290). Police chiefs were nearly unanimous in their condemnation of the Court's action. Gallup polls were soon reporting a sharp realignment of popular opinion in favor of capital punishment (Zimring and Hawkins 1986:39–40).

The Road to *Furman*: 1965–1972

A decade earlier, anyone suggesting that the nation's highest court would ever render a judgment like *Furman* would not have been taken seriously. Debates over capital punishment had raged for two centuries in America, but they had taken place almost exclusively in *political* forums — in state legislatures and governors' offices. Although the New York Committee to Abolish Capital Punishment had systematically used the courts to try to block executions in the 1950s (Neier 1982:196), no one on either side of the controversy had seriously claimed that executions per se were fundamentally inconsistent with any part of the U.S. Constitution. After all, they were common at the time the document was written, and continued unabated in the decades thereafter. How, then, could the Founders possibly have seen capital punishment as a form of "cruel and unusual punishment?"

That this basic question was not entertained does not mean, however, that the death penalty had never come before the federal courts. Prior to the late 1960s, two types of capital cases were heard. First, there were appeals by condemned prisoners based on alleged violations of constitutional rights before or during their trials. Among the most important of these is the case of the Scottsboro Boys, who were convicted of raping two white women and sentenced to die in Alabama. In 1932, the Supreme Court (*Powell v. Alabama,* 287 U.S. 45) ordered a retrial on the grounds that the defendants had been inadequately served by their court-appointed lawyers.[1] A 1936 ruling (*Brown v. Mississippi,* 297 U.S. 278, 80 L. Ed. 682) reversed the conviction and death sentence of a black defendant whose confession had been extracted under torture by deputy sheriffs. Appeals such as these were rather infrequent until the expansion of federal habeas corpus during the early 1960s opened up new possibilities for convicts struggling to save their own lives (Hoffmann 1989: 176–177).

The second type of challenge heard by the federal courts involved claims that particular *mechanical aspects* of executions constituted cruel and unusual punishment. In the cases of *Wilkerson v. Utah* (99 U.S. 130, 1878) and *In re Kemmler* (136 U.S. 436, 1890), the Supreme Court denied the claims that death by shooting and electrocution, respectively, violated the Eighth Amendment. A method of execution could be viewed as unconstitutionally cruel only if it involved an *unnecessary* degree of pain, was *intended* to produce extreme suffering, or was inherently barbarous — for example, burning at the stake or breaking on the wheel. In perhaps the most bizarre capital case to come before the Court, *Louisiana ex rel. Francis v. Resweber* (329 U.S. 459, 1947), the justices refused to halt the *second* electrocution of a teenaged prisoner who had survived a botched first try. The Court concluded that the necessity of repeating the execution resulted from an honest mistake, not any conscious plan to torture the unfortunate convict. A year after the first attempt, the boy was strapped into the chair a second time and killed.[2]

The notion that *all* forms of execution are violations of the fundamental rights guaranteed to all Americans, regardless of the method employed or the particulars of the legal procedures leading to the death chamber, was unheard of until the 1960s. During that tumultuous decade, it came to be the cornerstone of a major assault by a band of lawyers who were, for a brief time, the advance guard of the abolition struggle.[3]

The Rise of the Litigators

The new strategy of attacking capital punishment through the *courts* was designed and directed by lawyers associated with two organizations: The NAACP Legal Defense and Educational Fund, Inc. (LDF) and the American Civil Liberties Union (ACLU).

The LDF was founded in 1939 as a civil rights law firm. It was closely associated with the National Association for the Advancement of Colored People, but was kept separate from the NAACP so that it could receive tax-deductible contributions—which the parent organization, due to its involvement in lobbying, could not. LDF lawyers like Thurgood Marshall used carefully crafted test cases to broaden opportunities for African Americans, especially in education. Its most glorious victory came in *Brown v. Board of Education* (347 U.S. 83, 1954), the case that swept away the legal basis for racially segregated public schools. After the school desegregation cases, LDF attorneys tackled a broad range of other issues, including equal employment, housing, voting rights, and the legal defense of civil rights protesters in the trenches of the South. In these areas, as well as in its later assault on the death penalty in America, the Legal Defense Fund made use of a large network of cooperating attorneys around the country—lawyers who were not on the LDF payroll but whose work it helped to coordinate (Meltsner 1973:5-10).

The ACLU came together in 1920, founded by a group that included Clarence Darrow and Felix Frankfurter—the latter a future Supreme Court justice like Thurgood Marshall. Its mission was always considerably broader than that of the Legal Defense Fund, in the sense that it directed its efforts at preserving the liberties guaranteed to Americans in their Bill of Rights rather than orienting itself toward any specific constituency (Walker 1990:46). The ACLU also differed from the LDF in that its activities were primarily defensive in character; that is, it sought to prevent encroachments on constitutional rights rather than actively seeking their expansion (Meltsner 1973:4). In addition to litigation, the ACLU has engaged in lobbying, policy advocacy, and public education throughout its history.

Until 1965, the ACLU did not have an official position on capital punishment. There was considerable disagreement among its members over the issue, which the organization did not consider to be a civil liberties matter and thus not an appropriate area to address (Epstein and Kobylka 1992:45–46; Schwed 1983:113). Even though there were no unambiguous grounds for including execution within the ACLU mandate, the ACLU board—after considerable internal debate and prodding from its branches in California, New York, and Florida—adopted an abolitionist policy (Dorsen 1968:269-278; Neier 1982: 196-197).

The Legal Defense Fund, on the other hand, had been defending blacks in capital rape cases since 1950.[4] According to Jack Greenberg, who headed the LDF during the peak of its attack on the death penalty, LDF lawyers had "frequently debated the possibility of attacking the constitutionality of the death penalty on racial grounds" (Muller 1985:164). But during the years of the Kennedy administration, two things happened to encourage such a concerted assault.

The first of these precipitating events was a pair of important law review articles in 1961 suggesting that the death penalty might be vulnerable to attack by litigators. In one of these articles, antitrust attorney Gerald Gottlieb (1961) made the novel suggestion that although the Framers of the Constitution clearly accepted capital punishment, executions might nevertheless be considered inconsistent with *contemporary standards of decency,* and therefore in violation of the Eighth Amendment prohibition of "cruel and unusual punishments." The same year, Walter E. Oberer (1961) pointed to what he viewed as a possible *procedural* flaw in capital sentencing. He charged that the practice of excluding potential jurors with moral scruples against the death penalty, called "death qualification," was likely to produce juries that were inclined toward guilty verdicts. That is, "[i]n order to give the state a jury willing to bring in a death sentence, the law had stacked the deck against the defendant's claim that he was not guilty" (Meltsner 1973:24).

The second and even more important development came in the form of an unexpected signal from Supreme Court Justice Arthur Goldberg that the Court might be receptive to constitutional arguments such as those suggested by Gottlieb and Oberer. The message came when the Court was deciding whether to hear the appeal of a death-sentenced rapist (*Rudolph v. Alabama,* 375 U.S. 809, 1963). A majority of six voted against granting certiorari, but Goldberg—with Justices Brennan and Douglas concurring—filed a dissenting opinion that maintained that three questions deserved the Court's full consideration. The first of these was whether, in view of the worldwide trend against the death penalty as a punishment for rape, such an application is a violation of the "evolving standards of decency" that go along with the moral evolution of society.[5] Second, Goldberg said the Court should determine whether death is a disproportionate penalty for any crime in which no life is taken. Third, he said that it should ask whether lesser punishments can serve the same legal purposes as execution—thus making death for rape "unnecessary cruelty."

Justice Goldberg's reservations about capital punishment were not the results of a sudden revelation. In a 1973 speech, he stated that his doubts had been growing since his days as a lawyer, well before his appointment to the Supreme Court (Barry 1979:68n). During his first full term on the Supreme Court, Goldberg assigned his new clerk, Alan Dershowitz, the research possible Eighth Amendment arguments against the death penalty. Dershowitz maintains that Goldberg understood full well that the Court was unlikely to overturn the penalty at that time, but was nevertheless "convinced that we should start the ball rolling on this issue" and get "lawyers and judges to start thinking about raising constitutional challenges to capital punishment" (1982: 307). Prior to his landmark dissent, Goldberg had circulated a memorandum to the justices expressing the view that the death penalty was barbaric and that, while the others may not agree, they should at least consider the Eighth and Fourteenth Amendment issues involved. According to Dershowitz, it was Justices Warren and Black, the "liberals" on the Court, who were most upset.

Chief Justice Warren worried that abolishing or limiting the death penalty would undermine the Court's public credibility on more important issues like desegregation. It was at Warren's request that Goldberg agreed not to publish the memorandum, but rather to express his views in the form of the dissenting opinion in *Rudolph* so as "to alert the criminal defense bar to the fact that at least three justices had some doubts about the constitutionality of capital punishment in some contexts" (Dershowitz 1982:307–309; also see Urofsky 1987:189). "Of course," Dershowitz recently said, "I sent copies of the dissenting opinion to every lawyer in America who I knew . . . " (Gray and Stanley 1989:331). The Goldberg dissent was, then, an intentional signal.

Legal Defense Fund lawyers heard Goldberg's call to action loud and clear. But because the Supreme Court was still being widely attacked for exceeding its proper role and making unpopular decisions, particularly in the racial arena, they reasoned that the Court was not likely to strike down capital punishment on Eighth Amendment grounds in one judicial stroke. Thus, the LDF chose to attack the death penalty *indirectly*. They began working on a strategy that would attack the *process* by which convicted criminals were sentenced to die. There were two parts to this strategy. One involved a concerted assault on racial discrimination in death sentencing and the other pertained to selected trial procedures in capital cases.

Racial Discrimination in Southern Rape Cases

The racial angle was a natural outgrowth of the LDF's primary mission. It was common knowledge to any attorney working in the South that death sentences there were not meted out in a color-blind fashion. Rather, black defendants were much more likely to be condemned when their victims were white, and especially when the charge was rape. LDF attorneys had, in fact, already raised this issue — unsuccessfully — in a 1950 Virginia appeal (*Hampton v. Commonwealth,* 190 Va. 531, 58 S.E.2d 288), and had planned to do so again a decade later (*Hamilton v. Alabama,* 270 Ala. 184, 116 So. 2d 906, 1960), until the defendant's sentence was reduced to life imprisonment. Justice Goldberg's failure to include racist sentencing as one of the issues casting a constitutional shadow on the death penalty was a major disappointment to the LDF (Muller 1985:166). The issues that he did mention, however, suggested that discriminatory sentencing might nevertheless get a favorable hearing if it were adequately documented.

As a first step in supporting the discrimination claim, director-counsel Jack Greenberg appointed Frank Heffron in 1964 to make a preliminary study of racial patterns in rape sentencing in southern states. The young attorney's research revealed that bias did indeed appear to exist and that a case could be made that widespread violations of the equal protection clause of the Fourteenth Amendment were occurring. But for such a claim to stand a reasonable chance in the courts, a much larger data collection effort would be required (Meltsner 1973:34–35, 75–78).

Attempts to induce foundation heads to underwrite empirical research on rape sentencing were unsuccessful, and Greenberg was forced to use money from the general fund to support it (Meltsner 1973:35). He and Anthony Amsterdam, who was to become the guiding force behind the litigation campaign, hired students from the Law Students Civil Rights Research Council to travel throughout the South during the summer of 1965, collecting data on rape cases from court records. Marvin Wolfgang, head of criminology and a colleague of Amsterdam's at the University of Pennsylvania, oversaw the data analysis. During 1965 and 1966, the preliminary data were introduced as evidence in a number of rape trials, in order that sentencing might be delayed until the analysis was compete (Meltsner 1973:86–90). In the end, few were surprised at the findings: even after an array of aggravating and mitigating factors are held constant, black men who raped white women were significantly more likely than white rapists to be sent to the death chamber.

Procedural Issues in Capital Sentencing

Besides discriminatory sentencing, the Legal Defense Fund also based its challenge to capital punishment on three common features of capital trials at the time: (1) the exclusion of "scrupled jurors"; (2) the simultaneous determination of guilt and sentence in a single trial; and (3) the lack of precise standards to guide juries in deciding whether to condemn a defendant to death (Barry 1979:67–70).

The standard practice at the time was to excuse from a panel any prospective juror who had conscientious objections to capital punishment. From the prosecution's standpoint, this made perfect sense. A death sentence required a unanimous vote, so the presence of even one juror who would not be a party to such a sentence precluded the desired outcome. The LDF's challenge to this process rested on the argument that had first been raised by Oberer in 1961 — that "death qualified" juries were not only unrepresentative of the community and inclined toward death sentences, but that they were also more prone to finding defendants guilty in the first place. Consequently, juries purged of those with misgivings about capital punishment deprived defendants of their right to a fair trial.

Another procedural element of capital sentencing to which LDF attorneys took exception was the practice of deciding the issues of guilt and sentence in the course of the same trial. This procedure was used in all but five death penalty states, and it put capital defendants in a precarious position. Rules of evidence generally limited their ability to introduce information about their character or background unless it was directly relevant to the question of guilt and innocence. But this is precisely the type of evidence that juries need to hear in order to decide between execution or imprisonment. If the accused chose to testify on his own behalf to get such information before the jury, he might well assist in his own conviction, because biographical facts that might encourage leniency in sentencing might also destroy any chance of acquittal. Moreover, the prosecution would then be free to bring up the defendant's past criminal record during cross-examination (Friedman 1993:309–310; Meltsner 1973:68–69).

The Legal Defense Fund's third procedural argument pertained to the absence of sentencing standards in capital cases. Most states abandoned the practice of making execution mandatory on conviction for a capital offense during the nineteenth and early twentieth centuries. This was done to avoid a phenomenon called "jury nullification," the acquittal of guilty defendants by jurors who were unwilling to send them to the gallows. But in granting juries the discretion to choose between life and death, lawmakers had made the decision essentially arbitrary. Without guidelines as to when a death sentence was legally appropriate, jurors were free to make their determination based on anything they wished, including personal prejudices, and were not required to explain themselves. To some extent, the same could be true of other criminal trials as well. In *capital* prosecutions, however, it was usually the jury rather than the judge that was given the responsibility of passing sentence. More fundamentally, the LDF attorneys maintained that *"death is different,"* that extraordinary safeguards must be in place when a human life, rather than a temporary loss of liberty, hangs in the balance. If we must retain capital punishment in America, they argued, capital trial juries must at least be supplied with relatively precise standards to use when passing sentence (Meltsner 1973:69–70; Schwed 1983:117).

It is critical to note that LDF's procedural claims were as relevant to the cases of murderers as to those as rapists, and as relevant to the defense of white defendants as to blacks. The campaign against the death penalty began to take on a momentum of its own, such that by late 1966, its architects had made a conscious decision to try to stop *all* executions. They were almost compelled to do so by the legal arguments they had forged.

> Once the Fund had taken on the fates of southern black rapists . . . , it was only logical to argue for these procedural safeguards wherever such argument would fend off executions. The very nature of these legal arguments called out for their broadened application, even if the courts chose to ignore or reject the racial claims in granting the right to the procedural safeguards. Similarly, once the Fund formulated a viable argument which attacked the imposition of death on Eighth Amendment grounds and which seemed to interest courts sufficiently for them to grant stays of execution while they considered that argument, there was no ethical way of denying it to any convict facing execution. (Muller 1985:168–169)

The capital punishment campaign had carried the LDF beyond its original civil rights mission for the first time in its history. The costs were considerable. Not only were the LDF's cooperating attorneys now going to defend whites as well as African Americans, but "even . . . whites culled from the most racist segment of society" (Muller 1985:159). In addition, the campaign was going to require a massive expenditure of resources while directly benefiting, if successful, only about 600 individuals. The LDF would not be able to pick and choose its test cases and build judicial receptivity for progressively tougher issues, as it had in its litigation against segregated schools and restrictive covenants. And it was going to find itself defending one of the most unattractive and despised collection of clients imaginable, a far cry from well-dressed, nonviolent, churchgoing blacks from Alabama. A public opinion backlash loomed as a distinct possibility (Muller 1985:170–184).

The Moratorium Strategy

It was clear even at the time that bringing the machinery of capital punishment to a permanent halt would require more than courtroom victories. It would require victories at the level of state government as well—more frequent exercise of gubernatorial clemency for condemned inmates and, hopefully, even the repeal of capital punishment statutes by a state legislature or two. To set the stage for this dimension of the abolition struggle, the LDF and ACLU devised what they called the "moratorium strategy." Its main goal was to create a logjam of death-sentenced prisoners whom the states would be able to confine on death row but not put to death. Eventually, the states would be forced either to abolish capital punishment or to initiate a massive wave of executions. It was hoped that state legislatures and governors would not have the stomach for the latter.[6] Additionally, the moratorium strategy was intended to demonstrate that abolition would not open a floodgate of violent crime and, contrary to the centuries-old retentionist claim, that the Republic could survive without capital punishment.

But being lawyers, the moratorium strategy's planners saw the ultimate benefit of such a strategy as coming through the courts. Attorney and law professor Anthony Amsterdam put it this way:

> . . . we felt if we could . . . stop executions for a while, then when we got up to the state or federal Supreme Court it would be harder for justices to turn down our appeals based on the Constitution and start the executions up again. Once we stopped the executions, the courts would then have to face the awful reality that a decision in favor of capital punishment would start the bloodbath again. (Amsterdam, quoted by Wolfe 1973:244–245)[7]

Implementing such a multifaceted campaign was a complex and expensive task, and one that fell most heavily on the shoulders of the Legal Defense Fund. The ACLU's broad civil liberties agenda kept its lawyers busy. Thus, by mutual agreement, it deferred to the LDF on legal issues and participated in the courtroom struggles mostly as amicus curiae. The ACLU concentrated on lobbying and community education (Schwed 1983:113–114).

Funding represented a problem, because the LDF budget was too restricted to pay for the levels of activity that the moratorium strategy required. The resources for the project were found when the Ford Foundation gave a $1 million grant to the LDF to form a National Office for the Rights of the Indigent in 1967. It is fairly certain that Ford officials did not initially see this project as having much to do with capital punishment, but Greenberg reasoned that this was precisely the arena in which the class bias of the criminal justice system was most extreme. For this reason, the money was used to pay for death penalty work. The LDF was already handling the appeals of more than 50 death-sentenced inmates, and the moratorium strategy would require it "to intervene directly in hundreds of cases in over thirty of the forty-two jurisdictions whose law still provided for the death penalty" (Meltsner 1973: 108).

A recent graduate of Harvard Law School, Jack Himmelstein, was hired as the coordinator of the campaign. Himmelstein set about organizing a national network to serve as its vehicle. The network consisted of cooperating attorneys, interested academics, leaders of existing abolitionist groups, journalistic allies, and sympathetic corrections officials. Their responsibilities were to share information, provide ammunition for the lawyers' arguments, and, most importantly, to keep the New York headquarters informed of any impending execution dates in their areas so that petitions for stays could be filed in time (Wolfe 1973:144–146; Meltsner 1973:112–113).

The cooperating attorneys around the country who were allied with the LDF were usually unfamiliar with the organization's carefully devised strategy and were not experts on defending death-sentenced clients. The task of handling death row appeals was daunting. To assist them in preventing any executions from occurring in the United States, Himmelstein distributed "last-aid kits"—a bound packet of habeas corpus petitions, applications for stays of execution, legal briefs laying out an array of constitutional issues, and other materials. With a kit in hand, even inexperienced lawyers could go to court and make sophisticated claims for a stay of execution (Meltsner 1973:112).

Whereas Himmelstein was the formal coordinator of the strategy, law professor Anthony Amsterdam was its guiding genius. Amsterdam's career as a student, civil rights litigator, and anti-death penalty legal technician is legendary. He is regarded with awe, even by his legal adversaries. Stories have circulated for years about the way he repeatedly astounded judges with his detailed knowledge of case law and with the creativity of his written and oral arguments. Amsterdam graduated from the University of Pennsylvania Law School at the top of his class in 1960, simultaneously earning a master's degree in art history at Bryn Mawr. He gave serious consideration to becoming an art historian rather than a lawyer, but settled on law after winning a prestigious position as Supreme Court Justice Felix Frankfurther's clerk. Amsterdam, who was to gain fame as a specialist in criminal defense, next became a U.S. district attorney for the District of Columbia, and thus gained a year's experience on the prosecutorial side of the law.

At the age of 26, Amsterdam joined the faculty at the University of Pennsylvania. He later moved to Stanford and then to New York University. He first became associated with the Legal Defense Fund in 1963, when he began handling civil rights cases. By 1965, he was devoting more than half of his time to the LDF. His leadership in the nationwide struggle against the death penalty—devising strategy and advising the lawyers for hundreds of individual inmates—was provided while he was fulfilling the usual responsibilities of a law professor (Meltsner 1973:80–81; Wolfe 1973:230–232).

One of Anthony Amsterdam's early accomplishments in the ADP struggle came in a class action lawsuit on behalf of all prisoners under sentence of death in Florida. Governor Claude Kirk, Jr., came into office in 1966 promising to enforce the death penalty and to clear out the backlog of 50 death row residents in his state—many of whom were without legal counsel. To prevent this, two Miami attorneys loosely affiliated with the ACLU and LDF departed from the case-by-case approach that dominated death row law at the time and brought suit against the state of Florida on behalf of *all* its condemned prisoners. This was an unprecedented use of the writ of habeas corpus, one that borrowed a technique commonly seen in commercial law. Amsterdam became involved, and a federal judge surprised almost everyone by responding with a temporary stay for all the state's death-sentenced inmates. The LDF immediately filed for a similar mass stay in California, where another pro-death penalty governor—Ronald Reagan—had assumed office. In both states, the attorneys attacked the arbitrary manner in which death sentences are handed down, the provision of appointed counsel for only one appeal, and the exclusion of scrupled jurors, and charged that capital punishment is cruel and unusual punishment (Meltsner 1973:126–143; Wolfe 1973:233–246).

Although subsequent court decisions in Florida and California were not wholly favorable to the LDF and ACLU, executions in those states were successfully stopped. In fact, the moratorium was working nationwide. Only one execution occurred in 1966. The next year, two men were put to death—Aaron Mitchell in California and Luis Jose Monge in Colorado. No one knew it at the time, but the next American execution was a decade away. Meanwhile, the death row logjam that was the goal of the moratorium strategy was building. Between 1966 and 1967, the number of inmates awaiting execution rose from 351 to 415.

Jackson *and* Witherspoon

During 1968, decisions in two important cases added significantly to the Legal Defense Fund's drive for a moratorium on capital punishment in America. The cases were *United States v. Jackson* (390 U.S. 570) and *Witherspoon v. Illinois* (391 U.S. 510).

The issue in *Jackson* was a feature of a kidnapping statute, the "Lindbergh Law," which made defendants vulnerable to a death penalty only if their case went before a jury. Defendants charged under the law were thus coerced into pleading guilty to avoid risking execution. A U.S. district court overturned the law on these grounds. On appeal, the Supreme Court ruled that the law itself was constitutional, but that portions of it violated defendants' Fifth Amendment right against self-incrimination and their Sixth Amendment right to a trial by jury.

At issue in *Witherspoon* was the exclusion from capital case juries of persons with moral doubts regarding capital punishment. Witherspoon's attorneys introduced data from Hans Zeisel's research that indicated that "death qualified" juries were indeed conviction-prone, as knowledgeable observers had long suspected. The LDF and the ACLU supported that claim in amicus curiae briefs (Meltsner 1973:121–122; Wolfe 1973:257–258). When Witherspoon's appeal reached the Supreme Court, it was ruled that the trial court's guilty verdict could stand, but that only the most absolute form of opposition to the death penalty warranted exclusion from a jury. That is, courts would only be allowed to excuse those potential jurors who stated that they would never vote for a death sentence under any circumstances. To purge persons with more conditional objections deprived defendants of due process of law. Although the justices sidestepped the key issue, the *Witherspoon* ruling nevertheless seemed to represent a considerable victory for abolitionists, because it finally allowed persons with at least some reservations about capital punishment to sit on capital case juries.[8] Taken together with *Jackson,* it also lent credibility to the procedural side of the LDF's campaign and allowed litigators to keep condemned men alive while further developing the judicial assault on the death penalty (Barry 1979:73–75). For the moment, it seemed that a steady momentum toward judicial abolition was building.

Boykin *and* Maxwell

Two other cases of the late 1960s, however, suggested that the momentum toward abolition was fragile. One of these was *Boykin v. Alabama* (395 U.S. 238, 1969). Edward Boykin had pleaded guilty to five counts of robbery for crimes committed during the spring of 1966. The proceeds from these crimes had ranged from $140 to $373 and only one shot had been fired—a warning shot that had ricocheted and slightly injured one person. Although the crimes were relatively minor in terms of the violence involved, Alabama was a state in which robbery could still bring the death penalty. In spite of his guilty plea, the jury returned a death sentence for each of the five counts.

The obvious disproportionality of Boykin's sentence led the Legal Defense Fund to use it as a test case, and they hoped that the Supreme Court's willingness to hear the appeal meant that the Court might consider the Eighth Amendment ramifications of capital punishment. In what has been called perhaps the most ingenious legal brief ever presented to the U.S. Supreme Court, Anthony Amsterdam (a) invoked the concept of evolving standards of decency to support the claim that continuing to execute robbers when nearly all of the states have ceased to do so is clearly cruel and unusual;[9] (b) pointed to the lack of sentencing standards for Alabama capital juries; and (c) reminded the justices that Boykin had pleaded guilty without knowing he might still receive a death sentence.

When the Court's decision was announced on June 2, 1969, abolitionists were disappointed that it was based on the narrowest of the legal issues raised in the appeal. Boykin was granted a new trial because he had been allowed to plead guilty without understanding the jeopardy in which he was putting himself. But the members of the Court passed over Amsterdam's fundamental Eighth Amendment claim concerning execution for the crime of robbery. This confirmed the LDF's fears that the "cruel and unusual punishment" argument was unlikely to be a serious weapon against the death penalty, and that the matter would ultimately be settled on Fourteenth Amendment grounds (Schwed 1983:123–124).

It was unclear to Amsterdam and his colleagues why the Supreme Court was continuing to decide capital appeals on narrow grounds and avoiding the central constitutional issues. Doing so merely put off the inevitable, cluttered its docket, and permitted the pileup on the nation's death rows to continue. The most likely explanation was that the Court was waiting for a case that, unlike Boykin's robbery conviction, would have implications for a large group of death-sentenced inmates (Wolfe 1973:283–284). *Maxwell v. Bishop* (398 U.S. 262, 1970) seemed to fill that bill.

The LDF's involvement in *Maxwell,* which involved a black man sentenced to die in Arkansas for the rape of a white woman, had begun in 1966. It was one of the cases in which the LDF had originally sought to raise the sentencing discrimination argument based on the Wolfgang-LDF sentencing data. The Eighth Circuit Court of Appeals had at first refused to review the case, but was ordered to do so in 1967 by Supreme Court Justice Byron White. The case was argued before the Eighth Circuit in 1968 by Alabama lawyer E. Graham Gibbons with support from LDF (Wolfe 1973:276). Writing for the Eighth Circuit, Harry Blackmun — soon to occupy a seat on the Supreme Court himself — acknowledged that Wolfgang's data demonstrated a historical pattern of biased sentencing, but still rejected the claim on the grounds that these data did not pertain specifically to the jury that had convicted and sentenced Maxwell himself (398 F.2d 138, 8th Cir., 1968).

On appeal to the Supreme Court, the LDF again raised the discrimination issue, but added arguments against standardlessness and the single-verdict procedure. Certiorari was granted on the latter two. Amsterdam, assessing the makeup of the Court, thought there was a five-to-four majority in his favor. While the *Maxwell* case was pending, however, Justice Abraham Fortas was forced to resign in the midst of a conflict-of-interest scandal. Amsterdam had been counting on Fortas to be part of the five-vote majority. In addition, Chief Justice Earl Warren announced his retirement. These developments put the resolution of *Maxwell* on indefinite hold while the two outgoing justices were replaced. Warren was replaced by Warren Burger as chief justice. But President Nixon ran into trouble when he tried to fill the other vacancy. Two consecutive nominees, Clement Haynesworth and G. Harrold Carswell, were rejected. Eventually the seat was given to Harry Blackmun, who had recently written for the Eighth Circuit in turning back Maxwell's appeal. Due to his prior involvement in the case, Blackmun was disqualified from ruling on it again, leaving a four-to-four deadlock. Despite all its efforts, the LDF was forced to abandon *Maxwell* as the crucial test case on the constitutionality of the death penalty.[10] When the Court did finally rule on the case in 1970, it again sidestepped the central constitutional arguments and gave Maxwell a new trial on *Witherspoon* grounds. But in a footnote, the Court agreed to hear two more cases that raised the same issues — *McGautha v. California* and *Crampton v. Ohio.*

1970–1972: The Culmination of the Constitutional Attack

The LDF/ACLU siege of capital punishment in the United States had, by 1970, brought more than its share of ups, downs, and unexpected twists in the road. Its final two years were no exception.

Unlike earlier LDF cases that reached the Supreme Court, *McGautha* and *Crampton* both involved the crime of murder. But the issues that the lawyers pursued were not new ones. They were, in fact, the issues that *Maxwell* had failed to resolve. Both defendants had been sentenced to die by juries that had been given no clear instructions as to how they should determine the men's fates. And while McGautha's trial was bifurcated, with separate guilt and sentencing phases, Crampton's death sentence had come at the end of a single-verdict trial. Amsterdam and his colleagues had been attacking both of these procedures for years as inconsistent with the due process clause of the Fourteenth Amendment, but neither matter had been settled. Both cases were in the hands of private attorneys, but the LDF filed amicus curiae briefs. There was an air of desperation among the abolitionist attorneys. If these cases were lost—which seemed to be the most likely outcome—the de facto moratorium on executions in the United States would probably end and the floodgates into U.S. death chambers would open.

The Supreme Court announced its decisions in both cases on May 3, 1971, and the news was not good. Neither the absence of sentencing guidelines nor single-verdict trial procedures were deemed unconstitutional. The vote was six to three. Justice Harlan, the author of the majority opinion, wrote that it would be unwise and probably futile to try to determine a priori the factors that would warrant a death sentence. Furthermore, he reasoned, any attempt to do so would probably backfire in defendants' faces by, in effect, restricting the jury's ability to act mercifully. On the single-verdict issue, Harlan acknowledged that separate guilt and penalty phases are preferable to single-verdict trials. But, he wrote, the Constitution does not guarantee that the *best* procedures must be followed in criminal prosecutions, only that grossly unjust ones must be avoided. It does not protect defendants from having to make risky tactical choices at trial, such as whether to increase their risk of execution by remaining silent on the issue of guilt and innocence.

The *McGautha* and *Crampton* rulings represented major defeats for the abolitionists. They demolished two of the central procedural arguments on which the LDF had pinned its hopes for six years (Barry 1979:75). The third issue, scrupled jurors, had met with partial success in *Witherspoon,* but had not been as damaging to capital punishment as had been hoped. The LDF's use of the issue of racism in death sentencing, even though limited to rape cases, had thus far been sidestepped by the justices. This left them no choice but to take up the Eighth Amendment claim directly, a claim that had always seemed to be a long shot, and all the more so since the *Boykin* ruling a year earlier. If the Court refused to hear such an argument, or if it proved unsuccessful, the three-and-a-half-year-old moratorium on executions in the United States would be over, and the lawyers would be back to the business of struggling to save the lives of individual clients (Meltsner 1973:231). If the odds against a frontal attack on executions as cruel and unusual punishments seemed high before, they seemed even more so in the face of an odd concurring opinion in *McGautha*, authored by Justice Hugo Black. Black made it a point to state that, since executions were common when the Constitution was written, the cruel and unusual punishment clause was irrelevant to the question of the death penalty. He added that if capital punishment is to be abolished, this should be done by elected legislators and not appointed judges. Amsterdam and the other lawyers had to ask themselves why Black would have gone out of his way to offer these comments when the case at hand involved no Eighth Amendment claims. Was it a thinly veiled signal that the LDF's only remaining constitutional issue would be dead on arrival (Barry 1979:77)?

The LDF braced for the worst. In anticipation of a bloodbath, an emergency conference was held in mid-May at Columbia Law School. The lawyers who attended the meeting "carried off several pounds of legal memoranda, prepared under Himmelstein's supervision, to be used if the Court refused to extend the moratorium" (Meltsner 1973:246). In addition to standard lawyerly fare, the Columbia conference also included discussions of the need to focus some of abolitionism's energy once again on the *political* front (*New York Times* 1971). The central conclusion to be drawn from the *McGautha* and *Crampton* decisions, Amsterdam told the conferees, was that the Supreme Court could not be expected to take favorable action on the death penalty any time soon. Therefore, it was necessary to begin trying to convince the public of the need for abolition and to support legislative efforts at the state and national level. This, in turn, required the creation of a "functional network" of anti-death penalty organizations to do public education and lobbying work on a large scale. Hugo Bedau, president of the American League to Abolish Capital Punishment, set out to organize such a network.[11] But events of the summer of 1971 put these plans on hold.

Contrary to abolitionists' fears, executions did not resume in the wake of the *McGautha* and *Crampton* rulings. Justice Black's curious opinion notwithstanding, the fundamental question of whether the death penalty constituted cruel and unusual punishment cried out to be settled once and for all.

Several things happened at the dawn of the 1970s that made it more and more important for the Court to settle the issue. First, the Fourth Circuit Court of Appeals ruled in late 1970 that death sentences for rape were cruel and unusual if the crimes neither took nor endangered human lives (*Ralph v. Warden*, 438 F. 2d 786, 4th Cir. 1970), and the attorneys general of Maryland, North Carolina, South Carolina, and Virginia soon filed an appeal. Then Winthrop Rockefeller, the lame-duck governor of Arkansas who abhorred executions, commuted the sentences of all the state's death row prisoners before leaving office. In a similar action, Pennsylvania's attorney general, Fred Speaker, unilaterally ordered the removal of the electric chair from the state's death chamber, calling it unconstitutional and obscene. The incoming governor, Milton Shapp, believed that Speaker had overstepped his authority, but nevertheless promised that executions would not be resumed during his term in office (Meltsner 1973:229–238). By 1971, nine states had abolished the death penalty, four more had no one on death row, and anti-death penalty bills had reached the floor of state legislatures in California and Massachusetts, as well as the U.S. House of Representatives (Wolfe 1973:363–371). These were precisely the types of actions the moratorium strategy had been designed to bring about. Combined with the unprecedented population explosion on America's death rows, which had reached 694 by the end of 1971, they put added pressure on the Supreme Court to issue a definitive ruling. So did escalating public concern over "law and order." Less than two months after the *McGautha* and *Crampton* decisions were announced, the Supreme Court agreed to hear a package of four appeals and to issue a conclusive decision. Two of the cases, *Aikens v. California* (406 U.S. 813, 1971)[12] and *Furman v. Georgia* (408 U.S. 238, 1972), involved convicted murderers. The other two, *Branch v. Texas* (408 U.S. 238, 1972) and *Jackson v. Georgia* (408 U.S. 238, 1972), were rape cases. All four defendants were black and all the victims were white.

By the time the cases came before the Court, two more Nixon appointees were on the bench. William H. Rehnquist and Lewis F. Powell, Jr., the newcomers, were both conservatives and strict constructionists, that is, adherents to the philosophy that the role of the judiciary is to interpret the Constitution narrowly and not to make policy. Amsterdam and the LDF team could count on only three justices—William Brennan, William O. Douglas, and Thurgood Marshall—to support their position. Warren Burger and Harry Blackmun were clearly hostile, and Rehnquist probably was as well. Thus Powell, Potter Stewart, and Byron White were the swing votes, and the LDF needed two of them to win (Meltsner 1973:279).

Oral arguments were set for January 17, 1972. Anthony Amsterdam was slated to present the abolitionist case in *Aikens* and *Furman*. Jack Greenberg would argue *Jackson,* and *Branch* would be handled by Dallas attorney Melvin Carson Bruder. In the weeks leading up to the momentous date, the LDF team had refined its Eighth Amendment claim based on suggestions Amsterdam had solicited from a wide array of allies. The core of the team's arguments that day was that the death penalty, *as administered in the second half of the twentieth century,* was inconsistent with evolving standards of decency. Modern sensibilities had resulted in far less frequent application of the penalty. Concern had increased over the possibility of tragic errors in death sentencing, as had demands that rigorous standards of due process be set up in capital cases. As a result, swift justice had given way to long and complex trials, to automatic appeals, and, thus, to extended delays between trial and execution. This succeeded in turning the experiences of death-sentenced inmates into a form of extended psychological torture. All this would be true even if the legal mechanisms of capital punishment worked evenhandedly. But, the attorneys pointed out, they didn't. The death penalty operated in a unjustifiably selective manner; which murderers and rapists got put to death was determined neither by how heinous was their crime nor by any other specific characteristic. It was determined by the whims of particular juries, and sometimes by the race or

unattractiveness of particular defendants. Numerous amicus curiae briefs —
prepared by several professional associations (corrections, psychiatry, defense
lawyers), religious groups, nine governors, and civil rights organizations —
supported the LDF's position in the cases (Meltsner 1973:255–257).

June 29, 1972: Death Takes a Holiday

Abolitionists had no reason to feel optimistic as they awaited the outcome of
the 1972 cases. Most of their issues had been shot down or sidestepped since
the anti-capital punishment campaign began seven years earlier, and they now
faced the additional obstacle of a block of Nixon appointees who tended
toward a unified hard line on matters of criminal law (Meltsner 1973:287).
Amsterdam and his team had given it their best shot, but nearly all the signals
the Supreme Court justices had given off pointed to an impending defeat,
albeit a narrow one.

Nearly everyone was shocked, then, when Chief Justice Warren Burger
announced on the morning of June 29 that the death penalties of Furman,
Jackson, and Branch — and all other death-sentenced inmates in America —
were overturned. The vote was five to four; Brennan, Douglas, Marshall,
Stewart, and White made up the majority, while Blackmun, Burger, Powell,
and Rehnquist dissented. The news struck the Legal Defense Fund's New York
headquarters like an earthquake:

> Within minutes the story began to appear on every major wire-service ticker.
> Calls jammed the LDF switchboard. Lawyers and secretaries produced tran-
> sistor radios. General disbelief. Numbness. Tears in people's eyes. Slowly
> smiles replaced gaping jaws; laughter and embraces filled the halls. "This
> place looks like we just landed a man on the moon," [staffer Douglas] Lyons
> shouted into a phone. (Meltsner 1973:290)

That evening, while a rock band they called "The Eighth Amendment"
played in the library of their headquarters on Columbus Circle, LDF staffers
celebrated into the wee hours (Greenburg 1994:451). But the elation of June
29 soon gave way to a realistic assessment of what had happened. The death
penalty as Americans had known it was relegated to history, that much was
clear. But it was not at all certain that the nation had seen its last execution.
Even the five justices in the majority were divided as to *why* existing death
statutes could not remain in effect. Brennan and Marshall felt that capital
punishment could not be considered constitutional in any form. Brennan concluded that execution is uniquely degrading to human dignity and cannot be
shown to serve any legitimate purpose better than incarceration. Both agreed
that executions had become so infrequent and so constrained by legal safeguards as to betray their rejection by society, and Marshall felt certain that the
rejection would be even more complete were the public more knowledgeable
of the actual facts of capital punishment.

The remaining majority justices did not agree that death as a legal punishment was *inherently* unconstitutional. Justice Douglas explicitly rejected the

portion of the LDF's case that rested on evolving standards of decency. In fact, he viewed it as dangerous; making one portion of the Bill of Rights historically relative threatened to open the door to reinterpretation of the other nine Amendments (Woodward and Armstrong 1979:208). For him, the problem was that death-sentencing procedures were so discretionary that discrimination against minorities and the poor became inevitable. The pivotal votes of Justice Stewart and White also hinged on untrammeled discretion, but in slightly different ways. Stewart wrote that the death sentences of Furman, Jackson, and Branch

> are cruel and unusual in the same way that being struck by lightning is cruel and unusual. For, of all the people convicted of rapes and murders in 1967 and 1968, many just as reprehensible as these, the petitioners are among a capriciously selected random handful upon whom the sentence of death has in fact been imposed. . . . Racial discrimination has not been proved, and I put it to one side. I simply conclude that the Eighth and Fourteenth Amendments cannot tolerate the infliction of a sentence of death under legal systems that permit this unique penalty to be so wantonly and so freakishly imposed. (408 U.S. 309)

For Justice White, the problem with the rare and arbitrary application of capital punishment in contemporary American society was that it negated any legitimate function the penalty might otherwise serve. In particular, it could not be an effective deterrent. Unless capital punishment could be administered in a way that made it effective in controlling crime or doing justice, it could not be allowed to exist.

Because only two of the justices had ruled that executions by their very nature violate the Constitution, it was clear that some sort of "improved" death penalty could rise again in the aftermath of *Furman*. But it was unclear what alterations in current practice would be required. Because arbitrariness was the basic defect for three members of the Court, there remained the possibility that a *mandatory* death penalty for certain kinds of crimes might pass muster. Death statutes that included clear sentencing guidelines might also stand a chance, though the *McGautha* decision made that seem less likely. Still, comments made by the justices who had dissented in *Furman* revealed doubts even about these avenues (Schwed 1983:141–142). The situation was anything but clear, but a major victory had been achieved by abolitionist litigators. Chief Justice Burger practically invited state legislators to enact revised capital sentencing statutes, but he believed privately that "[t]here will never be another execution in this country" (Woodward and Armstrong 1979: 219). Jack Greenberg stated that capital punishment in the United States was finished (*New York Times* June 30, 1972), but Amsterdam was a bit more cautious in his optimism:

> Even if some kind of mandatory legislation were passed, by the time this could happen and a new round of appeals go through the courts, nine or ten years would have elapsed without any execution in this country. It's almost

inconceivable that executions could be resumed under those circumstances. (quoted in Wolfe 1973:411)

In fact, the nation would go 9 years, 7 months, and 15 days between executions.[13] But contrary to Amsterdam's hopes, capital punishment *would* resume in America.

Political Opportunities, Prior Organization, and Resources Before Furman

Before proceeding to the continuation of America's struggle over the death penalty during the mid-1970s, a summary of the theoretically significant features of the years leading up to the Supreme Court's landmark 1972 decision is in order. As noted in the introduction, this study of anti-death penalty activism is organized around issues raised by second- and third-generation social movement theories. In summing up the trajectory of this activism during the phase that produced the moratorium on executions and ultimately the *Furman* decision, the first questions to be addressed concern the opportunities for contesting capital punishment policies, the links between movement structures in adjacent time periods, and the availability and utilization of collective action resources.

The phase of abolitionist history that we have been examining was unique in that *political* strategies, aimed at legislative abolition at the state level, were relegated to the margins. For the first time, *lawyers* became the shock troops of the anti-death penalty movement. This transformation occurred, first, because political abolitionism had produced generally poor results.[14] Reformers had succeeded in ridding a number of states of capital punishment over the years, but generally only for a short while. Legislative victories are by nature fragile — laws that are made during one legislative session can be unmade during the next. Executions usually returned after a relatively few years, often on the heels of a spectacular crime or a wave of ideological fervor.

The second and more important reason for the rise of the lawyers was the sea change in the federal judiciary that took place during the 1950s and the 1960s. During Earl Warren's tenure as chief justice from 1953 to 1969, the Supreme Court handed down a series of revolutionary decisions in the areas of civil rights and criminal law. The civil rights decisions[15] helped to thrust issues of racial discrimination into the forefront of the national consciousness. The criminal law decisions multiplied protections for persons accused of crimes, including their rights to the assistance of lawyers (*Gideon v. Wainwright,* 372 U.S. 335, 1963; *Escobedo v. Illinois,* 378 U.S. 478, 1964), to avoid self-incrimination (*Malloy v. Hogan,* 378 U.S. 1, 1964; *Albertson v. Subversive Activities Control Board,* 382 U.S. 70, 1965) and double jeopardy (*Benton v. Maryland,* 395 U.S. 784, 1969), to confront and cross-examine witnesses (*Pointer v. Texas,* 390 U.S. 400, 1965), to be promptly informed of their rights on arrest (*Miranda v. Arizona,* 384 U.S. 436, 1966), and to protection from the use of illegally obtained evidence by prosecutors (*Mapp v. Ohio,* 367 U.S. 643, 1961; *Katz v. United States,* 389 U.S. 347, 1967).

Thus, a Supreme Court that was receptive to litigation based on broadened notions of civil rights and due process represented a window of opportunity for abolitionists, a chance to escape from the legislative treadmill of repeal and reinstatement on which they had been trapped since the dawn of the nation's history. The possibility that the death penalty might be unconstitutional meant that it might be banished *irrevocably,* sidestepping the fickle sentiments of the public and elected lawmakers. If capital punishment were to be banished by judicial fiat, the abolitionist litigators reasoned, the nation would get used to living without it.

Improved governmental responsiveness to civil rights demands did not occur in a vacuum, of course. To a large extent, it was the fruit of years of struggle and sacrifice by the civil rights movement. For if the 1950s were, for advocates of social change, a frozen sea, the civil rights movement tore through it like a huge icebreaking vessel. In its wake it left relatively open waters through which other ships could sail: movements for peace, environmental protection, women's and gay rights—and for the abolition of capital punishment. The civil rights movement paved the way by mobilizing members who would later venture into those other movements, by loosening up the political center and making it more receptive to demands for change of various kinds, and by raising issues that could be applied to other causes.

To characterize the Warren Court/civil rights era as a "window of opportunity" is to emphasize that the opening was temporary. It may have seemed to LDF and ACLU people in 1965 that the new era of liberal constitutional interpretation was inevitable and permanent, that the window would never close. But midway through the Nixon years, it became clear that this was not so. The "law and order" politics that emerged in the late 1960s made the wholesale elimination of executions in America less likely, and by the time *Furman* was argued, a farsighted few among the lawyer-activists were already talking about a revival of the political/community action flank as an *adjunct* to their efforts in court. But virtually everyone, attorneys and laypersons alike, understood that the lawyers were still in charge.

So the shift in the "structure of opportunities," toward which the political process model directs our attention, produced a corresponding shift in the strategic character of the movement. What can be said of the *organizational infrastructure* of anti-death penalty work, one of the key concepts of resource mobilization theories? Was the pre-*Furman* assault on the constitutionality of capital punishment independent of what had gone before, or was it an extension of existing organizations and structures, as resource mobilization theory predicts? In large measure, the lawyer-dominated third phase of American abolitionism was organizationally independent of earlier anti-death penalty efforts. This is not surprising, because there was only a scant abolitionist infrastructure to draw on in the 1960s. On the national level, only the American League to Abolish Capital Punishment still survived, and it was more a symbol than a viable organization. State groups had formed in the 1950s, but they hardly comprised a mass movement.

Abolitionists whose involvement went back to the 1950s or earlier, like Sara Ehrmann and Donal MacNamara, were important to the emerging legal challengers as sources of inspiration and information. They were indispensable in keeping the abolitionist flame alive during the "doldrums" of the mid-twentieth century (Haines 1993). But they were part of a very small and rather loosely knit community of abolitionists, not a preexisting network that could ease mass mobilization. Hugo Bedau and Doug Lyons, whose involvement dated back only to the late 1950s, served vitally important roles to the LDF and the ACLU. Bedau summarized the core arguments of the movement in "The Case Against The Death Penalty," a pamphlet distributed by the ACLU,[16] and worked closely with the LDF in its efforts. He had also been centrally involved in a successful 1963 anti-death penalty referendum campaign in Oregon (Bedau 1980), as well as in earlier abolitionist efforts in New Jersey (Bedau 1967). Lyons, who had become almost fanatically involved with the abolitionist cause during the Chessman controversy when he was all of 11 years old, and who later founded a group called Citizens Against Legalized Murder (CALM),[17] published a nationally distributed newsletter that kept sympathizers informed of impending executions and other developments across the country. He built the best library of death penalty-related books and articles then available, and worked on the staffs of both the LDF and the ACLU after he graduated from the University of California at Berkeley.

Unlike the litigators, both Lyons and Bedau had close contacts with Sara Ehrmann and others of the earlier generation of abolitionists.[18] And technically, they were both the directors of abolitionist organizations (CALM and what was left of the American League to Abolish Capital Punishment). But the services they rendered to the campaign against capital punishment in the 1960s were performed as individuals, not as representatives of preexisting social movement groups. The existing organizations out of which the constitutional campaign of the 1960s and 1970s emerged were the LDF and the ACLU themselves. These were not segments of an *abolitionist* movement at all, both having come to the issue quite late. And given that it was the LDF that was the true leader of that battle, it is most accurate to say that the third wave of abolitionism was rooted more in the *civil rights movement* than in prior anti-death penalty struggles. As a consequence, the constitutional attack was based more on issues and strategies that had emerged out of the struggles for African American rights and the defense of the Bill of Rights than on earlier abolitionist claims and tactics.

The mobilization of *resources* for the fight against capital punishment has always been difficult, and the 1960s phase of the fight was no exception. Contrary to one version of resource mobilization theory, the LDF/ACLU campaign did not originate because of a sudden increase in available resources. On the contrary, resources were extremely tight, and the decision to move into this area was made with rather little consideration of the funding implications (Muller 1985:180–181).

The difficulties of raising money for abolitionist litigation had to do with the constituency of the movement as much as with the issue itself. Often unpopular movements can manage to attract financial support and motivate participation by concentrating their efforts on the aggrieved population for whom they speak. The civil rights struggle did this during its early days, using black churches and colleges as mobilization sites (McAdam 1982; Morris 1984) and relying on large numbers of small contributions (Haines 1988:101-104). Even relatively poor constituents, collectively, can often provide funds and materials for substantial levels of collective action. But the most direct beneficiaries of anti-death penalty work, death-sentenced inmates, are utterly incapable of providing monetary or other material resources for work on their behalf or of participating in any active way. When faced with a powerless constituency, movements normally turn to "conscience constituents" — people who do not stand to benefit directly from collective action but who are motivated to provide support by a sense of moral obligation. Both the farm workers' movement (Jenkins and Perrow 1977) and certain of the civil rights organizations, particularly during the later stages of the movement (Haines 1988), did this. But here too, the struggle against the death penalty has always been severely disadvantaged. It is difficult, to say the least, to raise money to help those who make up perhaps the most despised group in America (Muller 1985) and who, additionally, are physically segregated and made visible only through generally unfavorable media images.

As we shall see, these difficulties in acquiring adequate resources to fight capital punishment continued to plague the movement throughout the years since *Furman*. During the phase we have been examining, when the battle was being waged primarily in the federal courts, abolitionists did manage, however, to make do with quite limited sources of funds. The Legal Defense Fund's major expense during this period was empirical research on various aspects of death sentencing. To facilitate such research, the organization diverted money from its general fund (money that had been contributed not for the abolitionist cause but to underwrite the LDF's larger civil rights mission), utilized a foundation grant that was intended more generally for indigent defense (Meltsner 1973:109; Barry 1979:71), and relied heavily on the cheap labor of law students and on volunteers (Meltsner 1973:86). The LDF was also able to accomplish a great deal through its heavy reliance on "cooperating attorneys," who it directed but did not have to pay. Thus the major organization in the pre-*Furman* phase of the movement — LDF — was a "professional social movement organization" (McCarthy and Zald 1973) that could draw on the moral dedication and flexible schedules of a nationwide network of attorneys to do much of its work. Consequently, the shortage of resources was a limitation, but not a crippling one.

Framing the Death Penalty Debate

Because the abolitionism of the 1960s differed from that of earlier eras in terms of its central strategy (litigation rather than political action) and the organizational bases of its key decision makers (civil rights/civil liberties movements rather than traditional abolitionism or prison reform), it stands to reason that the death penalty issue would also be *framed* in new ways. Such was indeed the case. Traditional abolitionist arguments—for example, the failure of execution as a deterrent, the inhumanity of executions, the danger of fatal miscarriages of justice—did not disappear from the debate. Rather, they were recast as *constitutional* issues whose historical origins lay in the civil rights and civil liberties movements. The wrongfulness of executing human beings for their crimes was no longer to be cast as merely *morally* objectionable, but as violations of specific provisions of the Eighth and Fourteenth Amendments: capital punishment wasn't just *wrong,* it was contrary to "evolving standards of decency" and thus *cruel and unusual*; it wasn't merely *discriminatory,* it was inconsistent with equal protection under the law and with standards of due process to which every citizen is entitled. Thus the framing of the issue took on a technical character, and the success of abolitionist claims making depended less on its alignment with the ethical sensibilities of the citizenry than with its formal legal validity.

On that June morning in 1972, the shift of anti-death penalty efforts from lobbying and persuasion to litigation seemed an unqualified success to most observers. After all, the goal that had eluded traditional abolitionists for two centuries had been achieved in about seven years of concentrated work by a handful of bright and dedicated lawyers. The death penalty had vanished, perhaps permanently, from every state and territory of the United States. The lives of more than 600 inmates then awaiting execution, and untold numbers of future offenders, had been saved.

But it would soon be clear that the organizational and strategic transformation of the anti-death penalty movement carried a price tag. Through most of the moratorium period, the majority of citizens and their elected officials had remained rather passive about the issue. They supported the death penalty in principle, but they did not clamor for it. But the decision to bypass public opinion set off a backlash. It focused media attention and elevated capital punishment to the status of a major policy issue (Epstein and Kobylka 1992: 83). Not only did a rising proportion of the nation's citizens express support for capital punishment and anger at the way in which the decision had been taken out of their elected representatives' hands, but those representatives began to claim a mandate to reinstate it. Conceivably, then, the constitutional attack may have helped to bring the trend away from capital punishment to a premature end. The Supreme Court might have held its ground and struck down the new statutes as they had the old. But the justices were stung by the widespread disapproval of the *Furman* ruling, and reversed themselves only four years later.

As the depth of the nation's reaction to the *Furman* decision became apparent, capital punishment opponents were ill prepared to withstand it. They were caught off-guard, much like those who had successfully opposed legal prohibition of abortion were surprised by the rapid mobilization of right-to-life forces after *Roe v. Wade.* The rise of litigators to a dominant position in the movement had exacted yet another cost: it had contributed to the withering away of whatever was left of citizen-based, political abolitionism. It had been difficult enough to hold that kind of abolitionist organization together in any case, but the success of the litigators had made it seem that there was nothing left for them to do. The lawyers were in charge and seemed to have things well in hand.[19] But the coming years would be rougher than the abolitionists imagined.

The Struggle Against Restoration: 1972–1976

In 1966, public opinion polls had revealed that only 47 percent of the American public supported capital punishment, marking the first time in history that a majority of the nation sided with the abolitionist cause. But there had been little time for the LDF and its allies to celebrate. Eleven months later, those same polls revealed that 13 percent of respondents had changed their minds — probably in response to growing concern about crime and urban disorder. The proportion opposed to the death penalty fluctuated around 45 percent between 1969 and 1972. In the aftermath of the *Furman* ruling though, the public took an increasingly hard line. On November 8, 1972, two-thirds of California voters endorsed a referendum that amended the state constitution so as to revive capital punishment.[20] By March 1973, national polls indicated that 63 percent favored a return of executions, and the figure reached two-thirds a year later (Zimring and Hawkins 1986:39). Abolition, it seemed, had arrived in the midst of rising support for capital punishment. In fact, by meshing with popular resentment of the federal government imposing its will on the states, abolition had itself *contributed* to the public's growing enthusiasm for the execution of violent criminals.

That the death penalty could be banished over the objections of a large segment of the public is actually not surprising. Franklin Zimring and Gordon Hawkins point out that support for execution stood at 70 percent in Great Britain when Parliament declared an experimental moratorium in 1965 and increased by six percent over the next year (1986:40). The gradual elimination of the death penalty in Canada, beginning with the systematic commutation of all death sentences and ending with final abolition by Parliament in 1976, and the defeat of a 1987 bill that would have begun the process of restoring capital punishment in that country, were both accomplished despite continued opposition by a majority of the electorate (Comack 1990; Fattah 1983; Jayewardene 1972). Similar patterns have been noted in New Zealand, which staged its last hanging in 1957 (Newbold 1990).

The post-*Furman* backlash was swift in the legislative arena as well. The gears of restoration began turning within weeks of the decision. Governor Reubin Askew of Florida signed a new death penalty bill on December 8, 1972, making his state the first to officially restore capital punishment (*New York Times* December 9, 1972). By May of the next year, 12 more states had revived the sanction (*New York Times* May 10, 1973), and 31 had done so by the spring of 1975 (*New York Times* April 21, 1975).

In their attempt to put the nation's executioners back into business, legislators faced something of a dilemma. As noted earlier, it was not entirely clear what type of death penalty, if any, the Supreme Court would be willing to let stand. The situation at the time is aptly summarized by Hugo Bedau:

> To be sure, it was clear that all then-current (nonmandatory) capital statutes, at least for such crimes as murder and rape, were no longer enforceable. At fault principally was their maladministration, which permitted "freakish" and "arbitrary" (as well as racially discriminatory) factors to play a decisive role in sentencing. But precisely why this freakish pattern of death sentencing was in violation of the eighth amendment, rather than merely an offense to extraconstitutional moral sensibilities, remained unclear, especially since virtually the same freakish pattern had been held not unconstitutional a year earlier in *McGautha v. California*. . . . (1987:166)

Two primary forms of capital laws emerged from the confusion. In some states, lawmakers reasoned that all arbitrariness could be removed from capital sentencing if death were made *mandatory* for certain crimes, specified in advance. The mandatory death penalty was truly an anachronism. It had begun its disappearance from American criminal procedure in the early nineteenth century and had virtually vanished by the time the courts had started to look into the constitutionality of capital punishment.[21] Nevertheless, 16 states responded to *Furman v. Georgia* by enacting mandatory death penalty laws. These states were Delaware, Idaho, Indiana, Kentucky, Louisiana, Mississippi, Nevada, New Hampshire, New Mexico, New York, North Carolina, Oklahoma, Rhode Island, South Carolina, Tennessee, and Wyoming (Barry 1979:90n). The most common crimes for which death was legally required under those statutes were the murder of a police officer, multiple murder, a killing by a person already serving a life sentence, and murder-for-hire.

The other strategy for devising a legally acceptable death penalty involved a device the Court, in *McGautha,* had refused to require: the formalization of sentencing guidelines by means of specified aggravating circumstances. Five states — Georgia, Illinois, Montana, Texas, and Utah — allowed death sentences only when such circumstances were found. They included many of the same factors written into mandatory schemes: the killing of a law-enforcement officer, the commission of murder in the course of another felony, multiple murder, and murder by a prisoner. Arkansas, Colorado, Florida, and Nebraska went further, specifying *mitigating* circumstances that sentencers were required to weigh against aggravating factors such as mental impairment, youth, and extreme emotional disturbance at the time the crime was committed. Four other states — California, Connecticut, Ohio, and Pennsylvania — passed legislation requiring a death sentence in cases where aggravating circumstances were present but no mitigating circumstances were found. These laws amounted to "quasimandatory" death penalties (Barry 1979:87–90).

Thus, the situation after 1972 was uncertain. The executioner had made his triumphant return, at least on paper, and several different types of capital-sentencing schemes awaited the Supreme Court's scrutiny. Abolitionists were aware that another landmark decision was forthcoming, but that it was unlikely to come before 1976. In the meantime, there was much to be done.

Anti-Death Penalty Activity After the Furman Decision

During the roughly four years that elapsed from the day the Supreme Court struck down existing death penalties in America and its decision in *Gregg v. Georgia* (428 U.S. 123, 1976), which allowed for the introduction of more rationalized capital sentencing schemes, abolitionists continued to pin their hopes on the judiciary. Some were confident that litigators would be able to handle the reinstitution challenge.[22] Others were more aware that their recent success might be suddenly reversed, but felt that they had at least bought some time. The longer it took for the Court to rule on the constitutionality of mandatory sentencing and guided discretion statutes, the better prepared the attorneys would be to press their case and, they hoped, the harder it would be for the justices to be a party to the reintroduction of a sanction for which many of them shared a personal distaste. During the years immediately following *Furman,* anti-death penalty forces attempted to marshall empirical ammunition for the upcoming courtroom battles, took the first steps toward rebuilding a *political* wing for their movement, and, of course, continued to litigate.

Research. Following the Supreme Court's *Furman* ruling, Anthony Amsterdam, Jack Himmelstein, and Hugo Bedau discussed whether the decision was likely to spell the true end of the death penalty in the United States. They agreed that it might, but only if abolitionists acted quickly to fend off the inevitable legislative reaction. Doing so would require both rapid implementation of the Court's ruling and developing an arsenal of solid social science evidence on pivotal issues.[23] Thus, one of the first concrete steps in preparing for continuing litigation was the organization of a systematic empirical research initiative. Amsterdam and his allies did not expect the results of scientific investigations to sway judges' decisions, for the legal issues before them could not be settled once and for all by empirical data alone. Rather, the litigators saw social science as providing solid foundations on which judges could justify their rulings (Caswell 1974:53). Consequently, it was important to identify those issues that would loom large in future courtroom battles and to persuade sociologists, psychologists, and other researchers to apply their expertise to those issues in a useful manner.

After an initial meeting between LDF attorneys and more than two dozen academics at Columbia University in October 1972,[24] the primary responsibility for directing the research initiative fell on the shoulders of Bedau. Bedau, a professor of philosophy at Tufts University, had fought capital punishment since 1957 and had been involved in one capacity or another with each of the abolitionist organizations operating at the national level. In addition to his 15 years of advocacy, he had edited the best-known book on the subject (Bedau

1964) and established the wide contacts in academia that would help in attracting researchers to death penalty work.

The biggest obstacle facing the research effort was a lack of funding. With the sole exception of Marvin Wolfgang's LDF-financed investigation of rape sentencing, no study of capital punishment in the United States had ever received monetary support.[25] In early 1973, Bedau secured a $32,000 grant from the Russell Sage Foundation to coordinate the development of a research agenda, and over the next six months, he and sociologist Elliot Currie met with over 100 invited academics at research centers across the nation.[26] Attempts during 1973 and 1974 to secure additional funding for a five-year, $150,000 capital punishment research project were unsuccessful (Bedau 1977: 96).

Nevertheless, 25 research ideas were developed. Only two of these were funded and under way by mid-1974, but other studies were initiated after the Sage project folded. Foremost among the studies conducted within four years of the *Furman* case were investigations of the factors underlying public opinion on the death penalty (Ellsworth and Ross 1976; Gelles and Straus 1975; Sarat and Vidmar 1976; Vidmar and Ellsworth 1974), further work on discrimination in capital sentencing (Reidel 1976; Wolfgang and Reidel 1976; Zimring, Eigen, and O'Malley 1976), the functioning of mandatory capital-sentencing schemes (Bedau 1976), and deterrence (Bailey 1975, 1976; Bowers and Pierce 1975; Passell 1975).

Mobilization. In the years leading up to the *Furman* victory, the LDF lawyers found themselves more and more in driver's seat of the abolitionist movement. The battle against capital punishment was now in the litigators' hands, and it would be they who would win or lose it. Everyone else, including ACLU people in the New York headquarters and in the state civil liberties unions around the country, deferred to them.[27] Legal campaigns like this one are delicate. They require careful planning and coordination. Cases must be taken up in proper sequence to erode adverse precedents gradually. Although the anti-death penalty campaign showed "little of the sort of architectural planning" that had characterized earlier LDF litigation on housing and school desegregation (Muller 1985:174–175), it was nevertheless helpful for the other abolitionists, the nonlawyers, to stay out of the LDF attorneys' way. Any actions that might adversely effect the climate in which federal judges decided key legal issues were best avoided. Thus, even the ACLU was staying more on the sidelines by 1972.[28]

But in spite of the consensus that the future of capital punishment would ultimately be decided by the "nine old men" behind the bench in Washington, Amsterdam, Himmelstein, and Greenberg understood that their resistance to restoration would ultimately need to be backed up by some degree of lobbying and public education.[29] These elements had been missing from the movement for years, and the LDF itself possessed neither the expertise nor the resources to provide them. The American League to Abolish Capital Punishment was moribund, having experienced a dramatic decline in financial support. That left the ACLU as the only organization capable of directing the nonlitigational aspects of the struggle.

On December 14, 1972, Jack Himmelstein met with ACLU executive director Aryeh Neier and several of his staff to discuss possible roles for the ACLU in fighting new capital legislation. He explained that the LDF would need the assistance of ACLU attorneys in some states to finalize the vacation of death sentences, but that the most pressing need was for the ACLU to "take over entirely whatever work could meaningfully be done on the legislative front." Neier agreed that the lobbying effort could be handled by his organization, though not at a level that was adequate to the challenge—that is, with a full-time lobbyist in each state.[30] An informal and rudimentary ACLU "Capital Punishment Project" emerged from this discussion, embodied in the person of Doug Lyons. Lyons had by this time moved from Berkeley to New York and was working as a volunteer at the ACLU headquarters. His responsibilities with the new project included coordinating public education efforts, monitoring the status of capital punishment bills in the various states, serving as liaison with state ACLU chapters and other abolitionist organizations, and handling the collection and distribution of general information about the issue.[31] Lyons left to begin law school in the fall of 1973. His replacement was Sheila Levine, who led the project until September, 1975. When she, too, resigned to become an attorney, freelance journalist Deborah Leavy became the third director of the Capital Punishment Project until 1978 (serving as co-director with Henry Schwarzschild after 1976). Whereas Lyons and Levine had served as unpaid volunteers, Leavy was at least on the payroll as a part-time employee. The ACLU's commitment to the principle of abolition was not in question, but the organizational status of these capital punishment specialists illustrates how low the project ranked among its institutional priorities before 1976. This may well have been due to Neier's judgment that the abolitionist momentum in the political and public opinion arenas had been reversed and that litigation remained the most effective way to prevent the execution of convicted criminals (Neier 1982:207). After 1976, as we shall see in chapter 2, major defeats in the courts led the ACLU to "put the Project on a more substantial and regular footing" (Schwarzschild 1979a).

On the state level, some ACLU affiliates were rather actively involved in trying to prevent the executioner's return. ACLU of Northern California, for instance, provided funds and staff for the "No on Proposition 17" campaign in California (American Civil Liberties Union of Northern California 1972). In 1975 and early 1976, several state affiliates were also active in the trenches. They mounted a statewide letter-writing campaign and telephone chain in Kansas, sponsored public hearings on a restoration bill in New Jersey, joined with other groups to sponsor a series of community meetings on the death penalty in Vermont, and lobbied against restoration and death penalty expansion efforts in California.[32] But capital punishment work was considered a low priority in most state ACLU branches. Levine lamented that "[b]ecause the death penalty project is not as current as 'Privacy' or as dramatic as 'Rights of Children,' the smaller overworked affiliates are forced to make decisions and many of our project's activities have lost-out." Many members felt "that this is one project that can slide until the issue is before the Supreme Court again."[33]

Levine tried hard to increase the anti-death penalty activity of ACLU affiliates, but she also attempted to expand the organizational network of the movement during her brief tenure, and these efforts were intensified by her successor.[34] At the very least, a larger coalition of organizations willing to go on record in opposition to capital punishment would provide an added measure of legitimacy. Expanding would also provide a larger army of people to lobby and track capital cases around the country. In spite of Levine's efforts and those of others, however, the size of the anti-death penalty movement between 1972 and 1976 remained extremely small, and the intensity of its work remained very low.

Continuing LDF Litigation. The lawyers who had assumed the leadership of the struggle against capital punishment during the 1960s had no chance to rest on their laurels following their surprising victory in 1972. First, in order for *Furman* to take effect, the highest court in each state had to take action to implement it. So the Legal Defense Fund's first task was to seek "a clear, broad, firm implementation of *Furman* in every capital punishment state and the vacation of the death sentences of everyone on death row. . . ."[35] Then the LDF filed challenges to the new death penalty statutes nearly as fast as the state could enact them. The justices had, in a sense, boxed themselves in: *Furman* had declared arbitrary application of death sentences to be unacceptable after *McGautha* had pushed the most likely remedy, sentencing guidelines, out of bounds. Anthony Amsterdam and his colleagues hoped that the Supreme Court would go further than it had in *Furman v. Georgia* and strike down the death penalty once and for all. But that outcome seemed extremely unlikely in the short term.[36] Thus, the more immediate objective of continuing LDF litigation was to extend the five-year-old moratorium. If that could be done, the prospect of a torrent of executions would make it difficult to reopen the death chamber.

The first case the Supreme Court agreed to hear, *Fowler v. North Carolina* (285 N.C. 90, 1974; 428 U.S. 904, 1976), involved one of the 29 death row convicts being represented by LDF attorneys. Under the revised North Carolina capital statute, Jesse T. Fowler had received a mandatory death sentence for killing an acquaintance during a dice game. Thus, the case promised to be a showdown on the most common variety of post-*Furman* death-sentencing law. Oral argument was heard on April 21, 1975. A rather ominous and unexpected development from the LDF's standpoint was the filing of an amicus curiae brief by Solicitor General Robert Bork in support of the North Carolina death penalty. Bork attacked the characterization of capital punishment as cruel and unusual, and citing a recent study by economist Isaac Ehrlich, he maintained that frequent expressions of doubt about the deterrent effect of executions were unfounded. Bork's involvement in the *Fowler* case threw the considerable weight of the solicitor general's office behind the LDF's opponents, and amounted to the assertion of a federal interest in capital punishment (Epstein and Kobylka 1992:97–98).

Fowler did not resolve the matter, however, because the illness of Justice William O. Douglas and his subsequent retirement prevented the Court, now split four to four on the death penalty, from reaching a decision. Instead of rehearing oral arguments before a fully reconstituted Court, the justices agreed to rule on a package of five other cases in October, after Douglas's successor had been confirmed. Two of those cases, *Woodson v. North Carolina* (428 U.S. 280, 1976) and *Roberts v. Louisiana* (428 U.S. 325, 1976) pertained to mandatory death penalty statutes. *Gregg v. Georgia* (428 U.S. 123, 1976), *Proffitt v. Florida* (428 U.S. 242, 1976), and *Jurek v. Texas* (428 U.S. 262, 1976), on the other hand, involved challenges to guided discretion statutes. According to Rupert Barry (1979:103), the cases were unusual in two respects. Each of the defendants had been convicted of "felony murder," that is, of killing in the course of committing another serious crime. Such offenses constituted less than a third of all homicides at the time. And whereas most homicide victims were black, then as now, the victim in each of these cases was white. These five cases were selected because they were relatively straightforward and presented no "side issues" (Woodward and Armstrong 1979:431). The differences among them concerned details of the sentencing schemes that had delivered the men to death row.

In *Woodson* and *Roberts,* the LDF team claimed that "mandatory" death sentencing, as used in North Carolina and Louisiana, failed to resolve the problems that the justices had found objectionable in 1972 — the arbitrariness and capriciousness in the determination of who is to live and who is to die. Rather, it merely shifted discretion from juries to other players in the judicial process: the prosecutors who determined the initial charge, the judges who accepted or rejected plea bargains in potentially capital cases, the higher courts which either heard or refused to hear appeals of those cases, and the governors who could grant or withhold clemency in the convict's final weeks or days. As in the past, the attorneys also restated their bedrock conviction that capital punishment entailed cruel and excessive punishment regardless of the legal niceties that preceded it.

The arguments in the three other cases were similar. The briefs filed by attorneys representing Gregg, Proffitt, and Jurek maintained that the bifurcated trials and aggravation/mitigation schemes that had been put in place in the states of Georgia, Florida, and Texas failed to produce evenhanded justice. Like mandatory sentencing, "guided discretion" laws had only a minimal impact on one of several decision points, and aggravating factors were defined too vaguely to make sentencing truly rational. More fundamentally, procedural fine-tuning failed to change the fact that state-sanctioned killing violated evolving standards of decency in contemporary society. Executions could not be reconciled with the spirit of the Eighth Amendment.

Opposing the abolitionist attorneys were state attorneys from the states whose laws were being challenged. Together, they claimed that: where discretion existed, it was justifiable, not arbitrary; capital punishment serves a legitimate purpose in criminal justice; capital punishment cannot be seen as "unusual" or unconstitutionally cruel; and racial discrimination is not a significant factor in the selection of criminals for execution (Epstein and Kobylka 1992: 104–105). Solicitor General Robert Bork again submitted a lengthy amicus brief, as he had in the *Fowler* case, maintaining that death was not qualitatively different from other punishments under the Constitution. And he again introduced the deterrence findings of Isaac Ehrlich in order to discredit the 1972 argument that the death penalty served no useful purpose.[37]

On March 30 and 31, oral arguments in the *Gregg* package of cases were heard. They did not go well for the abolitionists. Some of the justices seemed hostile, and according to witnesses, Anthony Amsterdam's presentation came across as self-righteous and disrespectful at times. Justice Stewart, who had sided with the majority in *Furman,* sparred with Amsterdam over the question of whether discretion in death cases was any less acceptable than in any other criminal case, and other justices were equally aggressive. The questions they directed to the state attorneys were less sharp than those directed to Amsterdam and his colleagues. Robert Bork made his appearance during the second day of oral argument, when the *Woodson* and *Gregg* cases were heard. Clearly, he was speaking to a friendly audience, and he handled himself well. If the inclinations of the Court were not already obvious to everyone in the room, they became so when Justice Powell invited Bork to expand on his views of the deterrence issue, and then gave him five additional minutes at the podium in which to do so (Epstein and Kobylka 1992:107–109).

Abolitionists had to endure months of waiting before the decision was announced, and they braced for bad news. Deborah Leavy and Henry Schwarzschild, who had joined her on the ACLU Capital Punishment Project, used the time to plan a "Governors' Commission Against Execution," to be composed of present and past governors willing to urge fellow state executives to exercise their clemency powers and stop executions in their states.[38] They also scheduled an emergency meeting for the week the Supreme Court was to announce its decision "to discuss organizational strategies" in case the ruling in *Gregg* allowed some or all of the capital-sentencing laws to stand.[39]

Gregg and *Woodson*

John Paul Stevens replaced William O. Douglas on the Supreme Court before the 1976 death penalty cases were heard, and abolitionists assumed that the fate of capital punishment rested largely in his hands. Because Stevens had never issued a ruling on the issue, no one could predict which way he would go.[40] But when the Supreme Court announced its decision in *Gregg v. Georgia* and its companion cases on July 2, 1976, Stevens's vote wasn't as critical as both sides had expected it to be. By a seven-to-two margin, the fundamental assertion that capital punishment is inherently cruel and unusual under the U.S. Constitution was laid to rest. The justices permitted the death-sentencing schemes of Georgia, Florida, and Texas to stand, concluding that three elements were sufficient to safeguard against arbitrary sentencing: (1) guided discretion, that is, sentencing guidelines that detail specific elements of crimes that make state-imposed death an appropriate sentence; (2) special consideration of mitigating circumstances; and (3) the requirement of automatic review by state appeals courts.

The swing votes were cast by Justices John Paul Stevens, Potter Stewart, and Lewis Powell. It was obvious, they agreed, that the Framers of the Constitution had accepted the death penalty as legitimate. They dispensed with the "evolving standards" claim by pointing out that elected representatives in at least 35 states had already reinstated the penalty in the wake of *Furman*. Could they all be acting against the wishes of their constituents? And how could the U.S. Supreme Court justify substituting its moral judgment for that of the people?[41] Thurgood Marshall and William Brennan dissented, seeing nothing in the revised statutes to change their 1972 assessments of capital punishment.

The same day that the Court upheld guided discretion schemes, it narrowly struck down North Carolina's and Louisiana's mandatory death penalties. In their rulings on *Woodson* and *Roberts,* the majority reasoned that rigid sentencing structures that failed to take account of the particular circumstances of crimes and the criminals responsible for them were inconsistent with *Furman v. Georgia*. To require execution for *all* persons convicted of certain crimes certainly eliminates unbridled discretion, but at too high a cost. The Court wanted the life or death decision to be bounded and rationalized, but was not willing to sacrifice individualized sentencing totally (White 1987:6). The margin in *Woodson* and *Roberts* was five to four. Justices Burger, Rehnquist, White, and Blackmun, dissenting, would have allowed the mandatory sentencing schemes to stand.

In granting its approval to sentencing standards, the Court had been forced to find a way around its own *McGautha* ruling, issued only five years earlier (Epstein and Kobylka 1992:81). Early in May 1976, Justices Stewart, Powell, and Stevens struggled for a theory with which to declare guided discretion schemes constitutional without explicitly overruling the 1971 decision. To do so would be to admit that the Court had used faulty reasoning in *McGautha* (Woodward and Armstrong 1979:436–37). In the end, the task of reconciling the *Gregg* and *McGautha* decisions was assigned to Justice Stewart. His solution was to stress that the Court was not now making sentencing standards and bifurcated trials an absolute requirement in states that wished to retain capital punishment; it was merely declaring this approach to be constitutionally permissible. Both White and Stevens thought this approach appeared contrived, but with time running out before the end of the 1976 session, they concluded that it was the best they could do. Whether out of discomfort over the strained reasoning or not, it was reported that Justice Stevens's hands shook and his voice cracked as he read the *Gregg* decision to the packed Supreme Court chamber on July 2 (Woodward and Armstrong 1979:436–439).

In retrospect, it is reasonable to wonder why the Supreme Court didn't simply abolish the death penalty and be done with the legal mess it had created. Impending executions and the appearance of inconsistencies in the Court's rulings on the issue had certainly caused enough personal agony for several of the justices to make such a final resolution attractive. And outright abolition would seem to have been the next logical step following the *McGautha* and *Furman* rulings, as Lewis Powell initially predicted when the 1976 cases were first deliberated. But it is too easy to assume that Supreme Court justices behave like philosopher-kings, gravitating inexorably toward the conclusions that logic and precedent dictate. In fact, they are far from immune to the impact of both presidential and public pressure (Caldeira 1991; Epstein and Kobylka 1992:21–32; Marshall 1989). So why did the Supreme Court pull back from abolition? Why did it change course on the death penalty in 1976? The transition from a liberal Warren Court to a conservative Nixon/Burger Court was not the whole answer, because the shift was from five to four against capital punishment to seven to two for it. The most likely explanation for the Court's change of direction lies in public opinion. Both Stewart and White, who had been in the majority in *Furman v. Georgia,* but who switched sides four years later, cited the post-*Furman* public and legislative reaction in their opinions. Both made reference to California's constitutional referendum, to a Massachusetts referendum in support of the death penalty, and to the opinion poll trends (Zimring and Hawkins 1986:66–67). Thus, *Gregg v. Georgia* can be seen in large part as a surrender to vox populi. Normally, such a surrender would be an abdication of judicial responsibility. Judges are supposed to interpret the law and the Constitution, whether or not it leads them toward decisions that the citizens find acceptable. However, the Legal Defense Fund's strategy of applying an "evolving standards" argument effectively invited the justices to take the backlash into consideration. If the people wanted the death penalty back, standards must not have evolved so much as abolitionists had claimed.

With *Gregg,* the door to America's death chambers opened wide. The long-awaited "bloodbath" was now a real possibility. As it turned out, through, executions would remain infrequent events for several years to come. From 1976 through 1983, the Supreme Court continued to grant certiorari to a large number of appeals by condemned inmates. In hearing those appeals, the Court attempted to refine the legal machinery that would lead a small proportion of convicted murderers to their demise. As this process was played out, abolitionists struggled to reassert themselves in the arenas of legislative action and public education.

One hundred and ninety-nine days after the ruling in *Gregg v. Georgia* was announced, Gary Mark Gilmore was strapped into a chair in the Utah State Prison at Point of the Mountain and shot through the heart, ending America's historic moratorium on executions.

2

The Return of the Executioner: 1976–1982

Assessing the meaning of the Supreme Court's ruling in *Gregg v. Georgia* 10 days after it was announced, an ACLU document did not mince words:

> . . . the overwhelmingly important first fact is that *The Supreme Court has now rejected the major constitutional arguments against the death penalty which have stopped executions in the United States during the past ten years.* . . . [The constitutional] attack has failed, and the resumption of executions — possibly in numbers unknown since the 1940's — is imminent.[1]

Death penalty opponents had good reason to be concerned. Almost 500 post-*Furman* death-sentenced inmates now resided in the prisons of 35 states, and there was no reason to expect those states to drag their feet in putting them to death now that they had permission to do so.[2] But the long-dreaded (or eagerly awaited, depending on one's point of view) "bloodbath" wasn't truly imminent after all. The Supreme Court would spend the next several years fine-tuning the death-sentencing process it had allowed to reemerge. The nation would not see executions in significant numbers until the mid-1980s.

Refining the Death Penalty Process

Between 1976 and 1982, the U.S. Supreme Court continued the "torturous effort to contain capital punishment within the rule of law" that had begun with *Furman* (Weisberg 1983:305). It did so by agreeing to hear a long series of appeals to individual post-*Furman* death sentences. In bringing these appeals before the Court, the defense bar sought not only to overturn as many death sentences as possible, but also to achieve the long-term objective of proving to the courts that it was administratively and intellectually impossible to make the death penalty operate in a constitutional manner (Weisberg 1983: 322). Many of the Court's rulings during this period adhered to the principle that "death is different" from other punishments and thus required enhanced due process protections. Consequently, the cumulative effect of the decisions was to constrain the manner in which death sentences could be applied.

For example, one important set of rulings concerned the specificity and range of aggravating and mitigating evidence that is admissible in the penalty phase of a capital trial. In 1977, the court struck down a Louisiana law that required the death penalty for the murder of a police officer (*Roberts v. Louisiana*, 431 U.S. 633) because it made no provision for the consideration of possible mitigating factors. In an important 1978 case, the Court prohibited statutory limitations on the sorts of mitigating factors that defense attorneys could present to juries (*Lockett v. Ohio*, 438 U.S. 586, 1978; *Eddings v. Oklahoma*, 455 U.S. 104, 1982). That is, whereas aggravating circumstances had to be enumerated in advance by the law itself, the same limitation did not apply to evidence that might lead to a more merciful sentence. Defense counsel were thus given an advantage over the prosecution—the freedom to introduce any aspect of a defendant's character or record, or anything about the crime, that might prevent a sentence of death (White 1991:13).[3] In another 1978 ruling (*Presnell v. Georgia*, 439 U.S. 637), the Court reversed a state court's decision to uphold a death sentence based on an aggravating circumstance on which the trial jury itself had not relied.

Other Supreme Court rulings during the post-*Gregg* years further expanded due process rights in death sentencing. Defendants were guaranteed protection against death sentences for crimes in which no life was taken, such as forcible rape (*Coker v. Georgia*, 433 U.S. 584, 1977; *Enmund v. Florida*, 458 U.S. 782, 1982). Courts were prohibited from basing death sentences on vaguely defined aggravating circumstances (*Godfrey v. Georgia*, 446 U.S. 420, 1980) and from excluding potential jurors who merely acknowledged that they would be "affected" by the fact that execution was a possible outcome (*Adams v. Texas*, 448 U.S. 38, 1980). The justices barred the imposition of a death sentence on retrial when the original proceeding had resulted in a life sentence (*Bullington v. Missouri*, 451 U.S. 38, 1981), as well as the introduction, during the penalty trial, of damaging psychiatric testimony derived from pretrial examinations in which defendants had not been warned that their statements might be used against them (*Estelle v. Smith*, 451 U.S. 454, 1981). The overall thrust of the justices' decisions through 1982, then, was that capital punishment was constitutionally permissible only under elevated standards of due process. The states could put its worst criminals to death, but not without negotiating a procedural "obstacle course" (Berger 1982) unique to capital cases.

The apparent advantage granted to capital defendants did not end even with their conviction and sentencing. They were also given access to a uniquely long and elaborate appellate process, a process that saved many of their lives and delayed the end of many others. The process varies slightly from state to state, but the typical outlines during the period before 1983 are as follows: death sentences were automatically appealed to the highest state court, regardless of the wishes of the condemned prisoners. Appeals in this first round were limited to the trial record and any procedural errors it might reveal. If the state's highest court affirmed the conviction, the prisoner could appeal to the U.S. Supreme Court to review the case. The Supreme Court, however, agreed to hear only two or three percent of such appeals — usually those that presented legal issues of widespread importance.

If the request for review was denied, a second cycle of appeals, called state postconviction proceedings, was available. The claim would first be filed in the lower court, often the same court in which the trial took place, then in the higher state courts, and, finally, in the U.S. Supreme Court once again. In this round, appeals were not limited to the trial record. For instance, an inmate might claim that his defense attorney had represented him in an incompetent manner, or that newly discovered evidence suggests he is innocent and should be heard in court.

If, after two rounds of appeals, the convict was still under sentence of death, he or she could file for federal habeas corpus review. At this stage, only alleged violations of rights guaranteed by the U.S. Constitution could be considered. Federal habeas proceedings would begin in a U.S. district court and, if denied there, proceed through the U.S. Circuit Court of Appeals and, finally, to the U.S. Supreme Court. Once all these avenues of relief were exhausted, there remained the possibility of "successor" *habeas* petitions based on new issues. It is important to understand that only direct appeals in state courts were truly *guaranteed* to death-sentenced inmates; they could ask to have further appeals heard in court, but there were no assurances of success. Moreover, inmates were not necessarily guaranteed the right to a lawyer beyond the first appeal. This varied by state, and many death row inmates had to draft their appeals themselves. Thus, the reality of the appellate process was often quite different from what the public perceived it to be. Nevertheless, only those convicted of capital murder had access *on paper* to such an elaborate series of appellate proceedings. The result was a tremendous amount of delay in carrying out death sentences. For those offenders who ultimately had their sentences carried out, "justice" was usually not done for many years.

"Let's Do It": Gary Gilmore and the Return of Executions in America

For a while after the *Gregg* ruling, it was uncertain which state would be the first to put a convicted murderer to death. Texas, Georgia, and Florida seemed likely candidates, but the "winner" in this macabre race turned out to be Utah. Gary Mark Gilmore was convicted there on October 7, 1976, of two killings earlier in the year, and scheduled to face a firing squad on November 15. The ACLU, through its Utah affiliate, immediately began legal proceedings to block the execution, and succeeded in obtaining a stay a week before it was scheduled to happen. Gilmore, though, had decided that he preferred "to die like a man" rather than spend his life behind bars, and he persuaded the Utah Supreme Court to lift the stay.[4]

At year's end, Gilmore was still alive. Those wishing to prevent his death, including not only the ACLU but Gilmore's mother as well, had managed to secure two more stays of execution—one from the governor and one from the U.S. Supreme Court—over his vigorous objection. Abolitionists were in the extremely awkward position of acting against the expressed wishes of a death row inmate and clearly adding to his psychological distress by doing so. So great was Gilmore's distress, in fact, that he made an unsuccessful suicide attempt on November 16. His refusal to appeal his sentence "forced the ACLU to explain, and explain again, that [their] quarrel was not with Gilmore but with the state of Utah, that the right at issue was not the 'right to die' but the right of the state to kill one of its citizens" (Leavy 1977).

The last of Gary Gilmore's scheduled execution dates was set for January 17, 1977. The day before, however, ACLU lawyers were pleading with a U.S. district court judge to issue yet another restraining order on the grounds that the Utah Supreme Court had not formally upheld the constitutionality of the state's death penalty law. The judge did so at 1:05 A.M. on January 17, setting off a chaotic struggle during Gilmore's last hours. Attorneys for the state of Utah immediately rushed off to Denver in a Utah National Guard aircraft in hopes of getting the Tenth Circuit Court of Appeals to overturn the stay. They were accompanied by a Utah ACLU attorney who would argue that the circuit judges lacked the authority to issue such a ruling (Cooper 1977). Prison officials continued their preparations for an early morning execution. So did Gilmore, who, learning of the judge's order in the middle of a surprisingly cheerful final visit with family members, became so enraged that he required sedation.

At 7:37 A.M., a specially convened panel of the Tenth Circuit Court ruled that the execution could proceed. A desperate call from a pay telephone was made to Alvin Bronstein, another ACLU lawyer who was waiting in the U.S. Supreme Court with a final stay application in his hand. Justice Byron White reportedly denied the application at 7:45 (Utah time), as Gilmore was being taken to the prison warehouse that would serve as the site of his execution. A few minutes later, Justice Thurgood Marshall also turned it down (Cooper 1977).

Without waiting to find out whether the U.S. Supreme Court would act on the ACLU's final application for a stay, Utah authorities proceeded with the execution of Gary Gilmore. He was strapped into an old chair that faced a curtain of black sheets. Behind the curtain were five anonymous riflemen. When asked by the warden if he had any last words, the prisoner paused, then said "Let's do it!" A hood was placed over Gilmore's head, and he was shot in the chest at 8:07 A.M. One rifle fired a blank. Bullets from the other four weapons all pierced his heart, and he was pronounced dead two minutes later (Nordheimer 1977).

As if the nation needed time to catch its breath after the Utah drama, no one else was put to death in 1977 or 1978. It was actually not that at all, but simply the still sluggish and deliberate functioning of the nation's legal machinery that accounted for the delay. Through 1983, executions remained rare events in the Unites States (see Table 2.1).

TABLE 2.1.   U.S. Executions, 1976–1982

Date	Name	State	Method of Execution
1/17/77	Gary Gilmore	Utah	Firing squad
5/25/79	John Spenkelink	Florida	Electrocution
10/22/79	Jesse Bishop	Nevada	Lethal gas
3/9/81	Steven Judy	Indiana	Electrocution
8/10/82	Frank Coppola	Virginia	Electrocution
12/7/82	Charlie Brooks	Texas	Lethal injection

Only two of the six inmates to die during the 1976–1982 period, John Spenkelink and Charlie Brooks, put up a legal fight. The rest were "consensual" executions, that is, convicts who refused to cooperate with the appeals to which they were entitled. Thurgood Marshall and William Brennan called them "state-administered suicides" (Turner 1979). It is impossible to say with any certainty that these inmates were "selected" in order to undercut abolitionist efforts or residual public misgivings over the resumption of capital punishment. But the eagerness of these men to die and to confront through the media those who wanted to keep them alive undoubtedly served those ends very well. So did the fact that five of the six convicts were white. This did much to ease the return of a practice so frequently accused of racism over the years (Neier 1982:210–211).

The Slow Reawakening of Abolitionism

So far as public visibility was concerned, the first evidence of resistance to capital punishment's comeback came in the streets. On Christmas Eve 1976, in anticipation that the state would soon be executing its first convict, small groups of protesters staged vigils in Alabama, Georgia, Florida, Kentucky, Mississippi, North Carolina, South Carolina, Tennessee, and Texas. These actions took place outside prisons, statehouses, and governors' mansions, and they were loosely organized by a two-year-old organization called the Southern Coalition on Jails and Prisons (*New York Times* 1976b; Wicker 1976). The coalition had been formed by Southern Prison Ministries, a Christian service group. Its purpose was to work on a variety of prison reform issues, and it turned its attention to the death penalty in 1976.[5] A second round of events, mostly prayer vigils, was staged across the nation on the weekend after Gilmore's death. Over the Easter weekend of 1977, the coalition organized a "Witness Against Executions," in which between 1,000 and 3,000 abolitionists from across the nation gathered in Atlanta. They carried a mock electric chair and wooden cross from the Martin Luther King, Jr. Community Center to the state capitol, where they prayed and heard speakers like former U.S. Attorney General Ramsey Clark and Rev. Ralph Abernathy decry the nation's return to killing convicted murders (Wicker 1977; McNulty 1977a). Smaller supporting demonstrations were held in Philadelphia and other cities (Smith 1977). The selection of Easter as the time for these demonstrations was intentional, as Rev. Murphy Davis of the coalition explained to journalists:

> "Jesus was the victim of a state execution, and for a lot of us, the execution and his Resurrection mean we don't have to pay the price with human life. The giving and taking of lives belongs to God." (Murray 1977)

Public demonstrations by abolitionists, albeit mostly smaller ones, continued throughout the late 1970s. Several protests were staged by an ad hoc group called People Against Executions, or PAX. PAX was formed at the initiative of Tony Dunbar, who served as the coordinator of the Southern Coalition on Jails and Prisons from 1974 to 1976, and later as the southern regional coordinator for Amnesty International. Its purpose was to do something that other ADP organizations were unwilling to do: employ dramatic direct action tactics.[6] As the 1979 execution of John Spenkelink approached in Florida, several PAX activists, along with Spenkelink's mother Lois, chained themselves to the fence around Governor Bob Graham's home and briefly occupied his office in hopes of being arrested. Graham refused to have the protesters arrested, but their action achieved a good deal of publicity anyway. The same year, PAX organized an event in Washington, D.C., called "Florida Day." Mock executions were held near the Supreme Court building, and 25 of the nearly 200 participants were arrested when the "bodies" were dumped on the building's steps (Kroll 1988). PAX protesters attempted to disrupt Governor Graham's speech renominating President Jimmy Carter at the 1980 Democratic National convention. During the speech, Lois Spenkelink stood in front of demonstrators in black robes and hoods who hoisted a large banner reading "Governor Graham killed my son" (*Miami Herald* 1980). The group also held a sit-in at the Georgia governor's office, demonstrated against the execution of Robert Sullivan in 1983 (Ingle 1990:58–62, 145–146), and performed abolitionist street theater in San Francisco (*San Francisco Examiner* 1983; *Los Angeles Times* 1979). In addition to the PAX protests, small bands of protesters continued to hold vigils at the site of all executions until the mid-1980s. They were often outnumbered by boisterous pro-death penalty demonstrators on hand to celebrate the imminent demise of a convicted murderer. For years, though, abolitionists refused to let a convict be put to death without their being there to bear witness. After the mid-1980's, activists shifted attention from witnessing to finding attorneys to handle the appeals of the growing list of inmates facing execution dates.

Other opponents of capital punishment concentrated on providing legal assistance to inmates facing execution. As of 1976, the corps of attorneys who had been working on capital cases found itself overwhelmed by the sheer number of inmates who would soon be having execution dates set. To help deal with the problem, the ACLU recruited volunteer lawyers to represent individual condemned prisoners, as well as laypersons to assist them in the preparation of those cases.[7] The Legal Defense Fund continued to steer most of the litigation efforts and training of volunteer lawyers.

In addition, the Southern Poverty Law Center sponsored the formation of "Team Defense," a group of attorneys based in Atlanta. Team Defense was headed by Millard Farmer, a white Georgian from a wealthy family who had become passionate in his opposition to the death penalty after spending the earlier portion of his career in a "straight, uptight law practice" (Gray and Stanley 1989:107). Farmer and his colleagues defended only indigent clients, and tried to bring specialized expertise in capital law, as well as aggressive courtroom tactics — resources normally available only to clients with money — to the penalty phase of their trials. They challenged the composition of jury pools, sought to prolong trials in order to force jurors to become better acquainted with defendants, and introduced large numbers of motions so as to establish grounds for subsequent appeals. Farmer once had six judges disqualified in a single case (McNulty 1977b; *New York Times* 1976a; Oney 1979).

The National Coalition

The idea of forming a multiorganizational "network" to broaden the attack on capital punishment had been bandied about within the ACLU as early as 1971, when Hugo Bedau and Aryeh Neier discussed the matter.[8] Within days of the *Gregg* ruling, concrete steps were taken to make the concept a reality. The result of these efforts was the formation of the National Coalition Against the Death Penalty (NCADP, later to be renamed the National Coalition *to Abolish* the Death Penalty).

Before the Court handed down its ruling, a meeting was called by Deborah Leavy and Henry Schwarzschild, who had joined Leavy as codirector of the ACLU's Capital Punishment Project, to discuss organizational strategies against legislative reenactment. At that July 8 meeting, a smaller group was selected as a working party to structure the coalition. It included representatives of the ACLU, the LDF, the Southern Poverty Law Center, and the United Methodist Church.[9]

Henry Schwarzschild emerged as the major architect of the national coalition. Schwarzchild had fled Nazi Germany with his parents in 1939 and settled in New York City. After participating in the southern civil rights movement, he joined the ACLU in 1971 and took charge of the organization's effort to achieve an amnesty for Vietnam draft resisters who wished to return home. As part of that effort, Schwarzschild had established an interorganizational structure called the National Coalition for Universal and Unconditional Amnesty to help pressure President Gerald Ford to pardon those who had left the United States to avoid military conscription. Its affiliates included a wide range of religious, human rights, peace, and civil rights groups. Newly elected President Jimmy Carter granted a general amnesty when he took office in 1976, and the coalition was dissolved. Schwarzschild's availability for reassignment during the summer of *Gregg,* along with his intellectual abilities and prior experience with coalition building, made him a natural choice for the ACLU Capital Punishment Project and for the job of organizing the NCADP. He built the death penalty coalition out of many of the same organizations that had been recruited into the earlier draft-amnesty coalition.[10]

NCADP was intended to fill much the same role as the defunct American League to Abolish Capital Punishment: to serve as a national voice of the abolitionist community — at least those who were not litigators — and to stimulate and coordinate anti-death penalty activities on the part of its affiliates. The coalition took a very long time to achieve organizational viability. For the first five years of its existence, the NCADP was virtually a one-person affair, operating from Henry Schwarzschild's desk at the ACLU headquarters in New York. The coalition did not acquire its first "office" until 1983, when the American Friends Service Committee provided a desk at its Philadelphia headquarters. The NCADP had virtually no money in those years; major contributions for 1981 totaled only $9,200.[11] Its organizational affiliates numbered around 50 from 1977 to 1979,[12] and there were 40 state coalitions in place in 1979 (Schwarzschild 1979). Most of these state coalitions, however, existed mostly on paper, with no office, no paid staff, and minimal funding.

Owing to the organizational weakness of the NCADP and its lack of resources before 1983, the concrete activities it engaged in were relatively limited. The coalition pressured governors to veto death penalty bills,[13] cosponsored the 1977 Witness Against Death demonstration in Atlanta, encouraged the clergy to mobilize grassroots religious opposition to the death penalty, and attempted to establish itself as a clearinghouse for information on the issue. It was not until the mid-1980s that NCADP had the funds and the staff to assume a higher profile.

As weak as the NCADP was during its early years, it nevertheless lent important measures of credibility and legitimacy to the abolitionist cause. The stance of the ACLU itself was well known among legislators and other public officials, so the pronouncements of Neier, Leavy, or Schwarzschild in the media or before a congressional subcommittee were somewhat predictable. The existence of the National Coalition Against the Death Penalty carried the force of its affiliates' reputations — for example, the U.S. Catholic Conference, the United Methodist and United Presbyterian churches, the National Urban League, the National Council on Crime and Delinquency, and the American Orthopsychiatric Association.

The NCADP gave the appearance of a broader range of active opposition to capital punishment than, in fact, may have existed at the time. Moreover, the coalition provided a focal point for the rudimentary national network of abolitionist organizations operating on both the national and state levels. That meant, for example, that key participants in the ADP programs of the LDF, ACLU, Amnesty International, and a host of other affiliated groups served on its board of directors and met regularly with each other. When NCADP began sponsoring yearly conferences in 1981, this function was enhanced. The result was a degree of coordination that would have been missing without the coalition structure.

Amnesty International

The year after the NCADP was formed, another major actor entered the fray: Amnesty International. AI is a global human rights organization founded in 1961, initially to work for the release of persons imprisoned around the world for the nonviolent expression of their political beliefs ("prisoners of conscience"). As the years went by, AI expanded its work into other areas: fair trials for political prisoners, an end to "inhuman and degrading punishments" such as torture, and most recently, work against extrajudicial executions and "disappearances" (Amnesty International USA 1991). The strength of the organization has been a product of its large worldwide membership, its reputation for impartiality, and the grounding of its work on the Universal Declaration of Human Rights and other international standards.

At first, the death penalty was an issue for AI only insofar as it was used against prisoners of conscience, but the organization's dedication to the abolitionist cause gradually broadened. In 1971, AI requested the United Nations and the Council of Europe to "make all possible efforts" to eliminate capital punishment globally and asked its own national branches in retentionist countries to work for abolition. Three years later, AI pledged itself to oppose "by all appropriate means the imposition and infliction of death penalties and torture or other cruel, inhuman or degrading treatment or punishment of prisoners or other detained or restricted persons whether or not they have used or advocated violence."[14]

The major step toward committing AI to the abolitionist cause came in 1977, when its international visibility had reached a peak as a result of having been awarded a Nobel Peace Prize. Capitalizing on its newfound celebrity, AI convened an international conference on the death penalty in Stockholm, Sweden. More than 200 delegates from 50 nations took part, including Hugo Bedau, Henry Schwarzschild, Deborah Leavy, and Ramsey Clark from the United States. At the conclusion of the meeting, the conferees issued "The Declaration of Stockholm," which condemned the death penalty as "the ultimate cruel, inhuman and degrading punishment," as a violation to the right to life that is inherently vulnerable to political abuse and that serves no legitimate purpose. The declaration formalized AI's "total and unconditional opposition to the death penalty, its condemnation of all executions, in whatever form, committed or condoned by governments, and its commitment to work for the universal abolition of the death penalty."[15]

Within the board of directors of the United States section, anti-death penalty sentiment had already been building in the months before the conference in Sweden. When an Alabama convict named John Evans was scheduled to be electrocuted, the ACLU and the Southern Coalition on Jails and Prisons requested that AIUSA send representatives to a protest at the prison. According to Larry Cox, who would later become the first national death penalty coordinator for AIUSA, nobody wanted to go. People preferred to work on issues that were less controversial than capital punishment, and this "wasn't an issue anybody felt strongly about." Nevertheless, Cox reluctantly agreed to represent Amnesty at the demonstration. Although Evans's execution was stayed, the event was a turning point for Cox and for AIUSA. He returned to New York with a newfound passion, lobbied in support of a greater AIUSA presence on the issue, and even participated in PAX-sponsored civil disobedience in Florida in 1979.[16]

Now that AI was a component of the movement, it was able to add an international dimension to what was otherwise strictly a domestic issue. Although AI is headquartered in the United Kingdom, it is organized into national "sections" around the globe, the largest of which is now in the United States. These sections, in turn, consist of local community "groups" of anywhere from a handful of activists to more than 100.[17] From its inception, the organization's primary tactics in the human rights field entailed careful investigations of alleged human rights abuses, rapid distribution of accurate information about individual cases to its local groups around the world, and the orchestration of massive letter-writing campaigns among its multinational membership. No less important, AI has commanded the attention of the news media, especially in America and Europe. These methods have allowed the group to tear away the veil of secrecy surrounding torture, "disappearances," and improper arrests and detention. Once it became involved in combatting state-sanctioned killing, AI was able to bring to bear a sort of pressure that had rarely been used against any criminal justice practice in America: mass appeals from citizens of other nations calling for mercy for death-sentenced inmates. The most successful such case to date may have been the campaign to save the life of Paula Cooper, condemned to die in Indiana for a murder she participated in at the age of 15. Over a million Italians signed a petition on her behalf, and similar efforts in West Germany and Belgium produced thousands of letters to Indiana state officials (Schmetzer and Kamin 1987). Even Pope John Paul II called for mercy for Paula Cooper, and her sentence was eventually commuted. She will become eligible for parole at the age of 45.

AI's entrance into the movement also introduced an entirely novel abolitionist frame: *the incompatibility of capital punishment with international human rights standards.*[18] Executions under judicial authority were clearly unlike many of the other targets of Amnesty pressure in that several human rights agreements addressed the use of executions but did not unambiguously prohibit them. *The Universal Declaration of Human Rights,* which is the bedrock of AI's work, states that all human beings are endowed with a right to life and with a right to be protected from cruel, inhuman, or degrading treatment. Article 6 of *The International Covenant on Civil and Political Rights,* which the United Nations General Assembly adopted in 1966, established a number of safeguards and restrictions on the use of the death penalty among member nations. The Human Rights Committee set up by that document interpreted Article 6 as suggesting "strongly . . . that abolition is desirable." General Assembly *Resolution 2857,* first adopted in 1971 and formally reaffirmed in 1977, stated that " . . . in order fully to guarantee the right to life, as provided for in article three of the Universal Declaration of Human

Rights, the main objective to be pursued is that of progressively restricting the number of offenses for which capital punishment may be imposed, with a view to the desirability of abolishing this punishment in all countries." In 1984, the *United Nations Economic and Social Council Safeguards Guaranteeing Protection of the Rights of Those Facing the Death Penalty* were adopted by the General Assembly. The "ECOSOC safeguards" prohibit the execution of juveniles and endorse the right to appeal and to seek commutation of death sentences. In 1989 the General Assembly went further by adopting the Second Optional Protocol to the International Covenant on Civil and Political Rights Aiming at the Abolition of the Death Penalty, which binds signatory nations to abolishing capital punishment. Regional treaties in Europe and the Americas do the same.

Even before 1977, AI worked to strengthen human rights standards and thus increase its leverage on the issue of capital punishment. But the absence of explicit and binding prohibitions of the death penalty in international law did not prevent AI from criticizing it in those terms. And although American abolitionists outside of AI have not made frequent reference to specific human rights doctrines, they have followed AI's lead in pointing out that the United States is virtually alone among Western democracies in continuing this practice. The United States is in company with the likes of the People's Republic of China, Iran, Iraq, and several former Soviet republics — not particularly "good company" from the perspective of most American citizens.

At its outset, AI's involvement in the American abolitionist movement was rocky. The internal contention began with the recommendations of a death penalty committee appointed in 1978 by AIUSA's board of directors to plan how the U.S. section would implement the Stockholm Declaration. A majority on that committee agreed in principle that massive publicity and letter writing, from the New York headquarters down to the local group level, ought to be employed in connection with each and every impending execution. This set off a debate that soon became quite acrimonious. Some board members, particularly attorney Arthur Michaelson, were concerned over the scope of the proposed death penalty program, its "potentially divisive nature," and the effect it would have on AIUSA's work on its more traditional concerns.[19] It was not that Michaelson favored the death penalty or that he saw it as outside of AI's mandate; indeed, he had participated in the preparation of an amicus brief that AIUSA submitted to the Supreme Court when the *Gregg* and *Woodson* cases were under consideration. Rather, it was a matter of the priority that death penalty work would receive and the impact of that work on the organization. Going beyond AIUSA's longstanding opposition *in principle* to anti-death penalty *activism,* the critics believed, would change the organization for the worse. The proposed death penalty program would inevitably focus the activities of the U.S. section on the United States itself rather than on other countries, and thus would threaten to squeeze out AIUSA's traditional mission of aiding prisoners of conscience.[20] Additionally, it would threaten to tarnish AI's moral halo, precisely when the organization was on the verge of becoming well established in this country. According to Michaelson, "steamrolling tactics" by abolitionist hard-liners on the Death Penalty Committee were propelling Amnesty International USA in this direction.[21]

For those who were advocating a full-scale assault on the death penalty, the issue was one of remaining true to AI's principles. Barbara Sproul, a Hunter College professor who chaired the Death Penalty Committee through much of this period, maintains that capital punishment was difficult for some members of AIUSA because it is harder to "romanticize" than other human rights issues. It was easy to imagine prisoners of conscience "as being, in essence, Tom Jeffersons"—as morally pure and heroic figures, abused by evil tyrants. It was easy to work on behalf of persons so imagined, and one received a certain prestige for doing so. Death row prisoners convicted of criminal violence, on the other hand, represented the hard cases that many Amnesty activists preferred to ignore:

> . . . the source of the problem was that those who presumed that prisoners of conscience weren't political, and . . . who wanted to romanticize them and always presume that they were sort of saintlike characters, now were faced with the prospect of getting involved in a *political* act on their own. There's nothing "political" about working for democracy in the Soviet Union or Brazil. All of a sudden we're now going to be asked to work for *unpopular* characters, which they never presumed a prisoner of conscience to be—although in those countries prisoners of conscience were *enormously* unpopular! And now we're going to be asked to work for people who aren't prisoners of conscience, [but] murderers, who were extremely unsavory characters, and who one's neighbors thought ought to be executed![22]

By mid-September 1978, AIUSA's board passed unanimously a resolution to "proportion" death penalty work so as to remain primarily devoted to prisoners of conscience. This resolution at first seemed to satisfy Michaelson and other critics. But he soon began complaining that the resolution was being ignored and that abolition work was receiving more than its share of emphasis. He claimed, for example, that material sent out from New York to local group leaders in 1979 "just reeks with unmeasured failure to give any heed to the resolution which had been unanimously passed by the Board. . . ."[23]

Death penalty work was not universally welcomed at the local group level either. By November 1978, 50 local AIUSA groups had responded to a request that they appoint a "death penalty coordinator" and that the designated person begin educating him or herself in preparation for future actions. Local death penalty coordinators were then to assume responsibility for involving their group in a major worldwide campaign planned by the London headquarters for 1979. By June 1980 there were 100 local groups with death penalty coordinators, which exceeded the expectations of the committee. That number had risen to around 150 a year later. Several of these groups, though, worked primarily against the death penalty in nations to which they had been assigned: the Soviet Union, Iraq, Trinidad/Tobago, Nigeria, or Japan.[24] Moreover, a representative of AIUSA at a Vienna, Austria, AI conference said that only about one-third of the groups with death penalty contacts could truly be called "active" on the issue. One person often did all the work and felt isolated from the rest of the members.[25]

Larry Cox continued to encounter a lack of enthusiasm for death penalty work when he met with local groups around the country, and even felt the need as late as 1984 to make a speech at the annual general meeting in which he reminded the membership of the rationale for AIUSA's opposition to capital punishment. In that speech, Cox argued that the struggle against the death penalty was inseparable from the struggle against torture and political killings by governments.

> It's apparent that many Americans, even some members of Amnesty International, are genuinely horrified at the thought that in places like Chile or South Korea prisoners are taken, strapped down, and electric shock is applied to their bodies until they are in excruciating pain, but find it acceptable, or at least less alarming, that in a place like Florida prisoners are taken, strapped down, and electric shock is applied to their bodies until they are dead. Many Americans, it is clear, are shocked and horrified that drugs are used in a place like the Soviet Union, not to cure people but to cause pain to prisoners, but find it acceptable, in fact find it humane, that in a place called Texas drugs are used not to cure people, . . . but to poison prisoners to death.
> . . . [T]he very meaning of human rights is that they are inalienable. Human rights are not awards given by governments for good behavior, and they cannot be taken away from people for bad behavior.[26]

As time passed, it became apparent that taking up the fight against executions did not measurably damage AI's standing in the United States. More than a decade after he first resisted abolition work, Arthur Michaelson acknowledged that the death penalty issue did not distort AIUSA's overall mission as he initially feared it would.[27] He has also reached the conclusion that there were very few defections among the membership or at the board level, a view shared by other past and present death penalty staff at AIUSA. One very public resignation that did occur involved conservative columnist William F. Buckley, who left AIUSA's board of directors over what he characterized as the "stupidity" of the Stockholm Declaration and the "inevitable sectarianization of the amnesty movement" that it entailed (Buckley 1977).[28] Buckley's presence among AIUSA's directors had been useful as a means of broadening the organization's appeal across the political spectrum, but few were sorry to see him leave because it was charged that he had used AI data in a selective and ideological manner in his newspaper columns and television series *Firing Line*.[29]

Nor did local activists leave AIUSA in significant numbers. Unlike some Amnesty sections, notably that of Sweden, AIUSA did not *require* its members to participate actively in the full range of mandate issues. Thus, those who had joined the organization primarily to help prisoners of conscience, political prisoners, or victims of torture were free to retain that emphasis. The only restriction was that they were not to stand in the way of their group's ADP work or to express support, *as a member of Amnesty International,* for capital punishment. Because anti-death penalty work was not made mandatory or dealt with heavy-handedly, there was little resistance at the local level to AIUSA's abolitionist stance.[30]

In addition to dissent among AIUSA's membership, there was another potential roadblock to its working against the death penalty *in the United States* during the late 1980s: Amnesty International's organizational rules. Since 1968, AI members were prohibited from working directly on behalf of *individual* victims of human rights abuses within their own countries. Lobbying their own government for ratification of international rights treaties or abolition of capital punishment was not banned, just the sort of work on individual cases that had always been AI's specialty.[31] There were two reasons for these guidelines. First, the "own country" rule helped to protect members from reprisals, because they would never be called on to criticize their own government. Such protection might seem unnecessary for activists in the United States, Great Britain, or Sweden, but it could be vital to their counterparts in a number of African, Asian, or eastern European nations. The rule was also intended to enhance AI's credibility as an impartial advocate of fundamental human rights. Whether or not a particular individual qualifies as a "prisoner of conscience" or a "political detainee" is often a matter of judgment. So may be the validity of an alleged torture victim's story, so the investigation of such matters and the determination of whether they merit AI's intervention has always been left to staff researchers at the International Secretariat in the United Kingdom.

The "own country" rule was frequently debated within AI, but it became crucial in connection with capital punishment work. If strictly enforced, the rule would prohibit the U.S. section from addressing the death penalty in America and would force AIUSA to rely solely on appeals from abroad. Leaders of the U.S. section decided that they could neither speak credibly on the issue nor ask the American membership to work against the death penalty worldwide if the executions at home were to be placed off limits.[32] Consequently, in 1980, AIUSA asked the London headquarters to relax the rule so members could work on this issue. Ali Miller, who headed AIUSA's Death Penalty Program beginning in 1990, explained that the American section had always reasoned that death sentences and impending executions were not matters of interpretation like many other human rights abuses. When charges of torture, for example, are raised by opposition groups and denied by political regimes, AI often faces a difficult task in determining the facts. But death penalty cases in the United States are entirely different. Neither the nature of the charges nor the date of scheduled execution require any subjective evaluation whatsoever. Miller and her colleagues at AIUSA headquarters argued that the concern for objectivity that is the basis of the "own country" rule is moot with respect to the death penalty in the United States.[33]

The International Secretariat denied AIUSA's request for an across-the-board exemption, but allowed the U.S. section to request permission to make appeals on behalf of individual death-sentenced inmates as their cases came up. For the next two or three years, London gave its authorization routinely.[34] This arrangement worked relatively well until the mid-1980s, when the pace of executions in the United States picked up and negotiations between the New York and London offices were renewed. Although the U.S. section was granted more and more autonomy for its abolitionist efforts at home, the tension within AI's global structure has yet to be fully resolved.[35]

Another Amnesty International policy that might have impeded its participation in the ADPM concerned restrictions on entering into coalitions or joint actions with other organizations. As with work within activists' own countries, the concern here was image and credibility. If a national section or local AI group were to cooperate in some way with an organization that was ideological in character, opponents would be able to capitalize on the incident, and AI's carefully groomed image of nonpartisanship would be tarnished. Thus, AI's policy is to prohibit any level of the organization, including local groups, from joining coalitions, cosponsoring events with other groups, or participating in any other joint action without official approval.

Had AIUSA been forced to stand completely aloof from existing anti-death penalty organizations in the United States, its effectiveness would have been quite limited. But London allowed the American section to join the NCADP very early on—in 1978. The rationale for this was that the coalition was a single-issue organization with no political or ideological agenda. AIUSA's participation, however, must be renewed yearly by the International Secretariat. Any effort to broaden the coalition's goals beyond merely the abolition of capital punishment could result in AIUSA's withdrawal.[36]

Out of the Courtroom: 1976–1982

By the late 1970s, the major national players in the anti-death penalty struggle were in place, if not fully mobilized and organizationally robust. The LDF continued its role as the legal arm of the movement, but it was now joined by three other groups with varied roles to play. The Southern Coalition on Jails and Prisons and the ad hoc PAX created visible, dramatic actions in the "streets" when the state took a life. The ACLU's Capital Punishment Project, which from 1977 to 1990 was embodied mainly in the person of Henry Schwarzschild, was the movement's public education/policy advocacy arm. Schwarzschild kept track of reinstatement bills as they moved through state legislatures, testified in committee hearings, distributed literature, participated in debates, and carried the abolitionist banner before radio and television audiences (Schwarzschild 1979:5–8). He made as many as 150 speeches a year.[37] In 1977, the ACLU released a set of draft amendments to be introduced "by legislators and others who wish to insure strict due process where capital punishment legislation is inevitable." A carefully worded preface reiterated that the organization's opposition to capital punishment was absolute and that it did not endorse any form of fine-tuning of the penalty of death, but if such a penalty must exist, it might as well be as fair and nondiscriminatory as possible. Included were amendments designed to ensure the appointment of qualified defense lawyers for indigent defendants, the selection of unbiased juries, and fair appellate procedures.[38]

The National Coalition to Abolish the Death Penalty occupied another slot on the nonlitigational side of the movement, although the NCADP was, by Schwarzschild's admission, far too much a "weak reed" to contribute more than broad organizational endorsement until well into the 1980s. The NCADP campaigned for gubernatorial vetoes of death penalty legislation in the aftermath of *Gregg,* and focused much of its meager resources on mobilizing the religious community behind abolition. In 1982, the coalition was the primary sponsor of an "Interfaith Week Against the Death Penalty," during which supporters distributed press releases, circulated petitions signed by local religious leaders, and held interfaith services based on the theme of abolition.[39] With only $8,600 in funding that year,[40] however, the NCADP was incapable of mounting any large-scale challenges.

Amnesty International brought to the movement a global membership pool, significant organizational and monetary resources, and a global human rights frame that sought to take the death penalty debate beyond the cramped vocabulary of criminal justice. During the six years after the return of capital punishment to America, its efforts were more visible than those of any other organization. In 1979, AI staged a major news conference at the United Nations headquarters in New York to explain its position and release a 206-page report on capital punishment around the world. The report summarized what AI saw as the major problems with the death penalty: it is irreversible and error-prone, a poor deterrent, inhumane, and a violation of the spirit of numerous human rights standards that many retentionist nations had signed. The report also included a detailed review of the use of executions in the nations of the world.

Then, as always, AI's assault on capital punishment was global in scope; the United States was just one of a large number of nations that persisted in executing its own citizens, and thus only one of a large number of targets.[41] In bringing pressure to bear on the United States, AI did not rely primarily on its American activists. The International Secretariat sent "missions" to Florida, California, Ohio, Georgia, and Washington, D.C., in 1979 to discuss the matter with state and federal officials (Amnesty International 1987:7–8). In 1980, the West German section launched a four-month campaign in which its members wrote letters of protest to American governors. In a large-scale campaign during 1982, each of 13 death penalty states was "adopted" by various foreign AI sections, whose members monitored developments there and flooded political leaders, churches, and newspapers with letters. The London headquarters also issued "Urgent Action" requests for each impending execution in the United States.[42] Urgent Actions are used by AI when its researchers determine that an individual is in immediate danger of torture, "disappearance," or execution. A network of tens of thousands of volunteers in 60 nations are rapidly notified and asked to send politely worded airmail letters, telexes, or telegrams to relevant officials on the person's behalf. In U.S. death penalty cases, those appeals were generally requests for clemency.

In addition, members were asked always to include a reminder that Amnesty International totally opposed all uses of the death penalty, regardless of the charge, and considered executions to be violations of the right to life and the right not to be subjected to cruel, inhuman, or degrading treatment as guaranteed in the Universal Declaration of Human Rights.

The other major effort by AI to contest capital punishment in the United States during the first part of the reinstatement era was its call for the appointment of a presidential commission on the death penalty, similar to the British Royal Commission and a Canadian parliamentary committee, both of which issued reports during the 1950s. It was hoped that such a commission would look into fundamental human rights issues, the possibility that violations of U.S. Constitutional guarantees were continuing after *Gregg*, the impact of capital punishment on crime and the legal system, and possible criminal justice alternatives.[43] According to Tony Dunbar, who at the time was AIUSA's southern states coordinator, such a commission would be instrumental in stimulating national discussion of the issue in a forum other than the courts and in spawning "an objective body of information" to guide the ensuing debate.[44] President Carter did not respond to a formal request in April 1980 that he appoint such a commission, and the idea was dropped when Carter was defeated by Ronald Reagan in November. It was feared that any capital punishment commission appointed under the Reagan administration would be stacked with death penalty supporters and would conclude that its use should be expanded.[45]

Summary

When the death penalty became constitutionally permissible again in 1976, lawmakers in many states responded to what they perceived to be the desires of the electorate by passing new capital-sentencing laws. Judges in those states began sentencing people to die, and America's death rows began to refill. Although capital punishment had returned with a vengeance, executions were slow in starting.

The reason only six convicted murderers were executed through 1982 was the Supreme Court justices' intention to reinvent capital punishment. The Court rendered decisions in a series of cases that established death as a unique criminal penalty and subjected it to a number of special limitations. To put a human being to death for his misdeed, the agents of the State would have to jump through procedural hoops more challenging than those they would confront in any other type of case. Defendants in capital cases were the beneficiaries of an enhanced version of due process, enjoying advantages unknown to other accused criminals. These included a dual trial with separate guilt and penalty phases, wider latitude to present favorable evidence than the prosecution was entitled to, and access to an unusually complex appeals process.

Obviously, the decision by the Court to allow capital punishment to return was a defeat for the lawyer-dominated abolitionist movement. But on the other hand, the Court in its post-*Gregg* decisions *did* respond favorably to various abolitionist claims. Consequently, there was still hope that the litigators would be able to limit the penalty's application and possibly set the stage for an eventual "Furman II"—a final decision abolishing the death penalty once again on constitutional grounds. Some persons within the movement saw the importance of revitalizing "political" abolitionism; that is, efforts to turn public opinion against capital punishment, to prevent its reinstatement by state lawmakers, and perhaps even to get a legislature or two to abolish it. But because public opinion was so lopsided and the legal arena seemed still to hold possibilities, this branch of the movement was slow in getting started. Both the ACLU Capital Punishment Project and the National Coalition to Abolish the Death Penalty raised their voices against executions, but both were organizationally weak throughout this period. The Southern Coalition on Jails and Prisons and PAX were important sources of visibility thanks to their use of direct action tactics. The decision of Amnesty International to fight the death penalty was a watershed event for the movement, but AI's struggle was years in the making, owing to the need to resolve sticky issues in its internal guidelines and the necessity of convincing its own members that the execution of murderers was really a human rights issue. A great deal of AIUSA's work in the post-*Gregg* years was spent doing so.

Political abolitionism in the late 1970s and early 1980s, then, was weak and ill formed. Thanks to the hesitant resumption of executions, it could afford to be. However, everything started changing in 1983.

3

The Reemergence of Political Abolitionism

Although it was not clear at the time, 1983 was a turning point in the national struggle over capital punishment in the United States. The justices of the U.S. Supreme Court retreated from their involvement in the procedural details of capital sentencing. As a result, many of the available grounds for lifesaving appeals began to evaporate and the pace of executions started to climb gradually from year to year. These were bad omens for a movement that had for almost 20 years leaned heavily on the skills of lawyers to combat the state-sanctioned extermination of convicted killers. But the legal setbacks of the period from 1983 to the present did not diminish the intensity of the abolitionist movement. Rather, they stimulated a change in its strategic direction. Litigators are still involved, to be sure. But now they struggle to save individual lives rather than mount coordinated challenges to the institution of capital punishment itself, as they did in the 1960s and 1970s. The broader attack has shifted from the courts to the arenas of legislative politics and public persuasion. Activists have emphasized new issues, including the danger of fatal miscarriages of justice, the fiscal and system costs of the death penalty for the criminal justice system, and the unique ethical dilemmas of juvenile and mentally retarded offenders. The shift has been fraught with difficulties — few abolitionists expect the nation to stage its final execution any time soon — but it has not been totally without signs of success. Cracks in public support for the death penalty have been exposed but not fully exploited. A backlog of death-sentenced inmates is building, one which dwarfs that of the 1960s moratorium years, and the willingness of Americans to endorse really large numbers of executions every year is still very much in doubt.

In the first part of this chapter, we will explore the Supreme Court's change of heart about the special legal status of the death penalty and the impact of that change on the fates of the men and the handful of women on death row. The chapter will then consider the adjustments that major ADP organizations made to the changed environment they were up against, including the development of new "incremental" approaches to undermining support for capital punishment, the switch from "reactive" to "proactive" tactics, and the effort to mobilize new constituencies—especially the religious community, ethnic minorities, and the families of murder victims.

"Deregulating Death": 1983–1994

In the first seven years after the *Gregg* ruling, the Supreme Court ruled in favor of 14 out of the 15 death-sentenced inmates whose appeals were fully argued before it. As we have seen, it tacitly endorsed the theory that the taking of a human life by the State in punishment for a crime is the most awesome of all legal decisions and that it must therefore be done only after unusually stringent due process requirements have been fully met. But suddenly, in late 1982, the Court reversed itself. In a series of decisions that continued through that decade and into the next, the Court "essentially announced that it was going out of the business of telling the states how to administer the death penalty phase of capital murder trials" (Weisberg 1983:305).

One of the cases that signaled the Court's reversal was *Barefoot v. Estelle* (103 S. Ct. 3383, 1983). The defendant in *Barefoot* had been sentenced to die in large part because of psychiatric testimony that he would be likely to commit further violent offenses in the future if he were not killed. But as even the American Psychiatric Association acknowledged, such testimony is notoriously unreliable. The accurate prediction of future individual conduct is presently beyond the capacity of behavioral science, and such testimony is no more trustworthy than the flip of a coin. Nevertheless, the Supreme Court saw nothing unconstitutional in allowing juries to base their life or death decisions on it. Perhaps more important, the *Barefoot* ruling held that federal circuit courts are not required to grant stays of execution or to give a full hearing to a death-sentenced inmate's claim that his habeas corpus right had been improperly denied. The circuit court could, that is, summarily decide against the appeal without a full consideration of its merits. This ruling introduced a paradoxical twist to the "death is different" doctrine. Because in a death penalty case the state cannot apply the prescribed punishment—that is, kill the inmate—until the appeal is completed, it is important to do away with any procedure that draws out the process unnecessarily. The result of this and later rulings on federal habeas corpus was that, henceforth, death-sentenced inmates were *not* entitled to a safeguard that would be available, for example, to a convict serving a 25-year prison term (see Denno 1992:440–441; 448–449). Another 1983 case, *California v. Ramos* (463 U.S. 992), upheld that state's requirement that capital juries be advised that a sentence of life without opportunity for parole could be commuted by a future governor—that life without parole, the only alternative to a death sentence in the penalty phase of California capital trials, did not necessarily make permanent incarceration a certainty. Ramos's lawyers had tried to argue that this instruction was misleading and prejudicial.

Also in 1983, the Supreme Court backtracked on its previous insistence that aggravating circumstances be statutorily specified in unambiguous terms. In *Wainwright v. Goode* (464 U.S. 78, 1983), the justices found no objection to a penalty trial in which the sentencer had relied on an aggravating circumstance, future dangerousness, that was not found in the state statute. In *Zant v. Stephens* (462 U.S. 862, 1983), they refused to overturn a death sentence based, in part, on an aggravating circumstance that was later invalidated as unconstitutionally vague by the Georgia Supreme Court. Finally, the decision in *Barclay v. Florida* (464 U.S. 874, 1983) affirmed a death sentence in which the trial judge had overruled the jury's recommendation (as he was allowed to do in that state) and sentenced the defendant to die based on aggravating circumstances that had no clear basis in either the facts of the case or in Florida's rather detailed capital-sentencing law.

After 1983, the death penalty rulings of the U.S. Supreme Court were a lopsided string of defeats for the defense bar. Appellate courts were freed from the responsibility, implied in the *Gregg* ruling, of insuring that death sentences were being handed down consistently in all similar cases (*Pulley v. Harris,* 465 U.S. 37, 1984). The prosecutor's latitude to challenge prospective jurors for moral scruples about capital punishment was broadened, (*Wainwright v. Witt,* 469 U.S. 412, 1985; *Lockhart v. McCree,* 476 U.S. 162, 1986), as was the freedom of trial courts to impose death sentences on accomplices who neither killed nor intended to kill during the crime (*Cabana v. Bullock,* 474 U.S. 376, 1986; *Tison v. Arizona,* 481 U.S. 137, 1987). Claims of ineffective trial counsel were made more difficult to raise on appeal (*Strickland v. Washington,* 467 U.S. 1267, 1984). After first prohibiting "Victim Impact Statements," in which the emotional consequences of the crime on the victim's family are introduced as evidence during the penalty phase of capital murder trials, due to the risk that they would contribute to arbitrary and capricious sentencing decisions (*Booth v. Maryland,* 482 U.S. 496, 1987), the Court reversed itself and allowed their use (*Payne v. Tennessee,* 501 U.S. 802, 1991). Florida's system of allowing trial judges to impose the death penalty against the recommendations of the jury was upheld (*Spaziano v. Florida,* 468 U.S. 447, 1984). The imposition of death sentences on convicted murderers who are mentally retarded (*Penry v. Lynaugh,* 492 U.S. 302, 1989) or as young as 16 (*Stanford v. Kentucky,* 492 U.S. 361, 1989) were both ruled to be constitutional. Laws *requiring* juries to impose the death sentence if they find at least one aggravating circumstance and no mitigating circumstances, despite their seemingly mandatory nature, were upheld (*Blystone v. Pennsylvania,* 494 U.S. 299, 1990). So were denials of all further appellate review of a case based on the failure to file a state-court appeal on time (*Coleman v. Thompson,* 111 S. Ct. 2546, 1991)[1] or to present crucial facts properly in a state-court appeal (*Keeny v. Tomayo-Reyes,* 116 L. Ed. 2d 652, 1992). The justices virtually prohibited the raising of new issues in second petitions for federal habeas corpus (*McCleskey v. Zant,* 111 S. Ct. 1454, 1991). In a decision that shocked even many death penalty supporters, the Court ruled that the Constitution did not guarantee the right to a full hearing of new evidence of a condemned inmate's innocence that had not been available at the time of the original trial (*Herrera v. Collins,* 498 U.S. 925, 1993). Federal habeas corpus, which has led to the identification of constitutional errors in over 40 percent of the cases reviewed, has been cut back severely and appears likely to be further curtailed in coming years.[2]

McCleskey v. Kemp

The hostility of the federal courts to anti-death penalty litigation after 1982 was crystal clear. But one Supreme Court decision, more than all the others, signaled the futility of continuing to place hope for abolishing the death penalty on the constitutional strategy that had once been so successful. That case was *McCleskey v. Kemp* (481 U.S. 279, 1987).

The *McCleskey* case was handled by the Legal Defense Fund and represented the last gasp for a line of attack that it had used since first taking on the death penalty in the 1960s: racial disparities in capital sentencing. Virtually everyone on the anti-death penalty side of the issue was convinced that such disparities had not abated under post-*Furman* sentencing schemes, particularly those that pertained to the race of murder *victims*; the murder of white people seemed to be taken more seriously by prosecuting attorneys than the murder of nonwhites. An earlier attempt to raise the race-of-victim issue in the Fifth Circuit Court had failed due to methodological shortcomings of the statistical evidence presented in support of the claim. That evidence had controlled for only one aggravating factor, leaving open the possibility that the disparities were caused not by racial bias but by other legally and morally relevant features of the crimes. The court implied in its ruling that more adequate data might support a successful challenge, so the LDF enlisted David Baldus and a team of his colleagues from the University of Iowa to undertake a methodologically sophisticated study of death sentencing in Georgia. The study was funded by the Edna McConnell Clark Foundation.

The opportunity to introduce the findings of this study arose in an appeal by Warren McCleskey, a black man convicted of killing a white policeman in Fulton County, Georgia. One of his claims was that his death sentence had been imposed on the basis of his and his victim's respective races. The findings of the Baldus study were introduced by the LDF to show that the state of Georgia had applied its post-*Furman* death-sentencing statute in a way that purposefully discriminated against persons convicted of killing white people, especially if the killer was black, thus violating the Eighth Amendment of the Constitution (Baldus, Woodworth, and Pulaski 1990:309–311). In raising this issue, the LDF had come full circle; it wanted to show that one of the defects in the older system of capital punishment that had led to the Court's majority to condemn it as arbitrary and capricious in 1972 was still operating full force in that same state.

The data presented in the *McCleskey v. Kemp* arguments were impressive. They demonstrated that out of the 2,484 murders that took place in Georgia between 1973 and 1979, two-thirds involved African American killers and

African American victims. But convicted murderers who killed whites were far more likely to receive death sentences than those who killed blacks. Even after controlling for 39 aggravating and mitigating factors,[3] statistically significant race-of-victim disparities remained. Only four percent of black murder convicts received death sentences as compared to seven percent of whites. But the killers of white victims were far more likely to receive a death sentence as the killers of blacks. *Black* killers whose victims were white were particularly vulnerable, as Table 3.1 demonstrates.

Table 3.1 shows clearly that the taking of white people's lives was treated much more seriously by Georgia trial courts than the taking of black people's lives, even after legitimate aggravating and mitigating factors are taken into account. This was true in spite of the fact that blacks were victimized far out of proportion to their numbers. And in white victim cases, black defendants were in especially deep trouble. The principle source of the racial disparities, according to Baldus's work, were the decisions by prosecutors whether or not to seek death sentences and whether or not to allow defendants indicted for murder to plead guilty to the lesser charge of voluntary manslaughter. In both decisions, killers of African Americans received a break (Baldus, Woodworth, and Pulaski 1990:327–328).

McCleskey's claims and the statistical evidence they were based on were rejected by Federal District Court Judge Owen Forrester, who ruled that the data lacked validity and that, even if they had been more trustworthy, the constitutional question before him could not be answered through multiple regression or any other purely quantitative means. The LDF appealed the ruling to the Eleventh Circuit Court of Appeals, where it lost by a nine-to-three vote. Unlike Forrester, the Court of Appeals granted the validity of the Baldus study, but the majority said the data failed to show a sufficient level of disparity between white and black victims to prove that there was an *intent* to discriminate. The decisive blow to the discrimination claim, and to the hope that the lawyers might yet rid the nation of capital punishment once and for all, came in the Supreme Court on April 22, 1987, by a five-to-four vote.[4] The majority accepted the findings of the Baldus study, but ruled that statistical evidence was irrelevant to a broad challenge to capital punishment. Although

TABLE 3.1. Killer-Victim Racial Combinations and Death Sentences in Georgia, 1973–1979

Race of Killer/Victim	Number with Death Sentence	Percentage
Black/white	50 of 233	22
White/white	58 of 748	8
Black/black	18 of 1,443	1
White/black	2 of 60	3

Source: Adapted from Baldus, Woodworth, and Pulaski 1990: 315.

such methods might be sufficient to settle other Fourteenth Amendment claims, such as jury discrimination or equal employment opportunity, they did not apply to death sentencing because juries are expected to make decisions on the basis of "innumerable factors that vary according to the characteristics of the individual defendant and the facts of the particular capital offense."[5] Other kinds of discrimination claims are different in that there are fewer relevant variables to be taken into consideration.[6]

Moreover, Justice Powell's lead opinion in *McCleskey v. Kemp* stated that because perfect uniformity is impossible in criminal justice, accepting McCleskey's claim about racial disparities would open up the entire justice system, not just capital punishment, to similar challenges. Perhaps most important, Powell also wrote for the majority that the data the LDF had presented in support of the claim proved nothing about the presence of racial bias *in Warren McCleskey's particular case,* that is, among the prosecutors who chose to put him on trial for his life or the jurors who decided he should be executed. It might have turned out differently. In a 1994 biography, Justice Powell revealed that since leaving the Court he has become convinced that capital punishment is unworkable. If he had it to do over, Powell said, he would vote against the death penalty in any case that came before him, including *McCleskey v. Kemp* (see Coyle 1994; *New York Times* June 11, 1994). Had Powell reached this conclusion before 1987, the subsequent course of capital punishment in America might have been radically different.

The *McCleskey* decision represented the defeat of the last broad-based legal attack on capital punishment in the abolitionists' arsenal. It was now apparent to almost everyone that if capital punishment was to be eliminated in the United States any time in the near future, the end would not come as a result of litigation. Only a radical change in the ideological makeup of the Supreme Court could change that bleak prognosis, and no such change in the Court's center of gravity was likely for many years to come. In a sense, opponents were back where they had started in the middle of the 1960s. Lawyers would have to return to the task of saving individual lives, not pursuing a test-case strategy. The death penalty would have to be seen as a political issue again.

Thus, whereas the *McCleskey* ruling was seen by all abolitionists as a disaster, though not a completely unexpected one, it was also taken by some activists as a sign that a change of course for their movement was long overdue. Attorney David Bruck, for one, saw *McCleskey* as an opportunity in disguise:

> *McCleskey* can't be seen as a defeat in its own right. Rather, it's a ratification of the defeat that the abolition movement has been suffering in the United States ever since 1972. But I suspect that *McCleskey* will also prove to be the rebirth of abolition. [It] is the end, for now, of our enervating reliance on the courts to stop the death penalty for us. After *McCleskey,* the fight returns to where it was during the years when abolition was gaining ground rather than receding. This is where the struggle belonged all along: In our legislatures, our churches, and our labor, professional and community organizations. [This] is

how abolition came about in other Western democracies. In France, in Britain, in Canada, in Australia, there came a moment when the future of the death penalty rested on a vote in the legislature. If the vote was in favor of executions, prisoners would be executed. There was no backstop, no court poised to intervene and assume responsibility for the question of life and death. In each country, when the crucial vote came, the public still favored retention of the death penalty. But in each country, the legislators took responsibility, used their own judgement, and voted for abolition. They did so because the responsibility was theirs, and because they could not evade the knowledge that in this last third of the twentieth century, the killing of prisoners in peacetime is a practice which has simply run its course. (Bruck 1987)

In referring to lack of popular endorsement for abolition in other nations, Bruck did not mean to imply that American activists could ignore public sentiment. He meant only that the Supreme Court's abdication of oversight made it impossible for elected representatives to pass the buck any longer. In another article, he wrote that ADP activists

. . . don't need to convince *everyone.* 70–80% majorities are needed before executions actually take place: a divided population (i.e., 60% for, 40% against) won't carry out executions, because the death penalty loses its political potency when the division is that sharp. So our objective is just to chip away at the current 'critical mass' of support: if 15% or 20% changes back to opposing the death penalty, we might well [see] a return to the moratorium conditions that prevailed in the 1970s. (Bruck 1986:1)

During the month after the decision, the NCADP began to focus its efforts on state-by-state organizing and on discussions of new strategies for "community and legislative action." AIUSA and the NCADP began using the *McCleskey* case as a means of generating more opposition to capital punishment among minority organizations.[7] The ACLU took the lead in lobbying Congress for a federal "Racial Justice Act," which would prohibit racial bias in death sentencing and restore the ability of inmates to challenge their sentences based on "accepted statistical methods" like those in the Baldus investigation.[8]

Organizational Growth After 1983

When the courts began slamming doors in the faces of ADP litigators during the 1980s, it spelled the end of a major period of opportunity that the abolitionist movement had enjoyed and relied on since the days of Earl Warren. But the closing off of chances to challenge the death penalty in court did not destroy the abolitionist movement, as a simplistic political opportunity model might suggest it would. Rather, the period after 1983 was one of slow but steady organizational *expansion* and strategic *redirection* for the ADPM. AIUSA funding of its death penalty program more than doubled during the mid-1980s, from $31,475 in fiscal year 1982–1983 to about $70,000 in fiscal year 1987–1988,[9] and AIUSA was devoting approximately 18 percent of its Action Unit budget to the death penalty by 1989. Cutbacks have taken place in all areas of AIUSA's budget in the 1990s, but by nearly all accounts, neither fund-raising woes nor the poor climate for abolition produced a decline in the emphasis on death penalty work within the organization.[10] The NCADP underwent an even greater budgetary expansion, as can be seen in Table 3.2.

The upward trend in NCADP revenues reflects a process of organizational revitalization that became most apparent with the hiring of an energetic new director, Leigh Dingerson, in 1987, as well as greater sophistication in fund-raising among the staff. Clearly, funding levels such as those within the coalition and AIUSA are not adequate to the goal of eliminating capital punishment, as will be discussed later. Nevertheless, the increases were significant given the generally poor outlook for curbing executions in the United States. In 1983, the coalition was finally able to open its first office in a tiny donated space at the Philadelphia headquarters of the American Friends Service Committee. According to the NCADP's director at the time, that first office was barely large enough to hold a pair of desks.[11] In 1987, the coalition moved to a more spacious office in Washington, D.C., accommodating a staff that grew to four full-time, paid people and several volunteers and interns. Direct-mail fund-raising was initiated, 501 (c)(3) tax status was approved to attract tax-deductible contributions, and proposals for foundation grants were submitted.[12] The majority of NCADP's income is obtained from individual donors, including both major contributors and people who give in the $25 to $50 range. Organizational affiliates are asked to contribute according to a sliding scale. Small groups with low budgets of their own pay annual coalition dues of $50, whereas affiliates with incomes over $500,000 contribute $2,500.[13] In 1981, the NCADP's bimonthly newsletter *Lifelines* began publication and the first national conference was held in Washington. Regional conferences were begun four years later. Thus, although the NCADP is still small in terms of its staff and budget, it is far more active than in the early years, when it was little more than a paper organization.

AIUSA's involvement in capital punishment in the United States also expanded during the mid-1980s. As we have seen, it had begun informally under

TABLE 3.2. National Coalition to
Abolish the Death Penalty, Annual
Revenues, 1981–1991

Year	Revenues	Year	Revenues
1981	$ 9,200	1987	$ 46,691
1982	unavailable	1988	73,556
1983	unavailable	1989	137,038
1984	26,608	1990	211,511
1985	35,662	1991	221,487
1986	46,778		

Source: Miscellaneous NCADP financial reports.

the coordination of a "death penalty committee." But in 1984, death penalty work achieved the status of a formal and permanent AIUSA program with its own full-time coordinator, Charles Fulwood. Under Fulwood and his successors, Magdaleno Rose-Avila and Ali Miller, AIUSA became much more attentive to the development of strategies appropriate to the situation in the United States. There evolved a greater measure of autonomy from the International Secretariat in London, and coordination with the rest of the anti-death penalty movement improved. Meanwhile, the level of involvement by local and student groups continued to increase. In 1988, a worldwide "Human Rights Now" tour of Amnesty-sponsored rock concerts contributed to a massive increase in the number of young people participating in the organization's work. This influx of new members benefited the Death Penalty Program. And finally, the 1983–1994 years brought two worldwide, year-long campaigns against the death penalty. One of these focused exclusively on the United States, and the other included the United States among several target countries.

The intensity of the ACLU's work on capital punishment is more difficult to gauge than that of the rest of the national movement. At the national level, the Capital Punishment Project was a one-man operation, for all practical purposes, after 1976. Its director, Henry Schwarzschild, lacked even a secretary to handle routine correspondence throughout most of his tenure. Controversy erupted as early as 1979 over the project's place within the ACLU, prompting its leadership to appoint a committee to consult abolitionists inside and outside the ACLU "about the best contribution the ACLU could make . . . , given its limited resources."[14] The committee sought to determine whether the focus of ACLU's efforts should continue to be on the original core charge of public advocacy, on community organizing,[15] or on litigation. Schwarzschild took the position that, given extremely limited resources, the project should stick to its policy advocacy/public education role. Much of his opposition came from the southern states, where there was strong sentiment to move in the direction of mobilizing poor people and African Americans against the punishment that so selectively targeted them (Schwarzschild 1979: 13–14). The committee concluded that the most important changes required were for the Capital Punishment Project to be given more funding and a higher priority[16] within ACLU and for much more emphasis to be placed on developing a network of state-level groups to fight the battle from the bottom up.[17]

Not much had changed by 1983, save that the NCADP was beginning to exist independently of Henry Schwarzschild and, thus, was taking over some of the burden he had previously shouldered alone. The Capital Punishment Project remained the smallest of the ACLU's various projects in terms of both staff and budget.[18] Given both the apparent lack of progress in holding back the tide in either the courts or the legislatures and the termination of an outside grant that provided much of its support, its continuation was never assured. This is not to say that the ACLU ever contemplated renouncing its stated opposition to executions or asking its affiliates around the country to cease work on the issue. The question was whether a discrete unit, however small and underfunded, should continue to exist at the national level. Henry Schwarzschild's status within his organizational home base was far lower than in the abolitionist movement as a whole, where he was always among a small group of recognized leaders. But he often referred to the temptation to leave the ACLU because of its lack of commitment to his work. "I have persisted in this work," he wrote in 1983, "not because I needed the job, but because under such unfavorable conditions (without a secretary for the past five years, without associates, without legal back-up staff, without administrative help) I know that the contribution we make in this field has been extraordinarily valuable, indeed essential."[19]

Schwarzschild continued as director of the ACLU Capital Punishment Project until he retired at the end of 1990, but remained very active in the NCADP thereafter. There were concerns in other organizations that Schwarzschild's departure would lead the ACLU to withdraw from the abolitionist movement,[20] but it did not. He was replaced as director of the Capital Punishment Project by Diane Rust-Tierney, who was formerly a legislative counsel based in Washington, D.C. The Capital Punishment Project has since operated out of the Washington office, across the street from the Supreme Court building. Under Rust-Tierney, the Capital Punishment Project continues its traditional responsibility for public education and policy advocacy, and was the leader in organizing opposition to the expansion of the federal death penalty.

In sum, the anti-death penalty movement has become better organized at the national level since the focus of abolitionism shifted away from the courts. The ACLU has not made a strong commitment to its Capital Punishment Project, but AIUSA and the NCADP have become better organized, staffed, and funded. Nevertheless, robust *national* organizations are not enough to prevail in battles that are fought largely at the *state* level, and this is where the anti-death penalty movement has been weak. Among the NCADP's affiliates are a large number of state coalitions. But only a handful of these—in particular, coalitions in California, Massachusetts, New York, and Illinois—have substantial resources. Death Penalty Focus of California, itself a coalition, had a budget of over $141,750 in 1992, up from about $70,000 in 1990. New Yorkers Against the Death Penalty managed to raise over $100,000 in grants by the same year,[21] and an anti-death penalty political action committee was established there. Local AI groups work on death penalty issues, as we have seen, but rarely is such work high in their agenda. Several ACLU affiliates are very active, particularly that of Northern California. However, their involvement is usually weighted more toward death row appeals and less toward lobbying and public education. Indeed, the movement's "grassroots deficit" is one of its major impediments, as we will see in chapter 6.

Once bolstered by more solid organizational bases and freed from their subservient role as "second-stringers" to their litigator colleagues, anti-death penalty activists began during the 1980s to devise new strategies. The following sections of this chapter will examine elements of these emerging movement strategies—elements that do not lend themselves to straightforward chronological presentation. The first of these concerns changes in the way in which ADP activists criticized the death penalty, in hopes of appealing more effectively to popular views. Another was the attempt to replace the movement's *reactive* approach with a more aggressive and *proactive* one. Finally, abolitionists recognized the necessity of trying to reach out to new constituencies, especially religious groups and people of color, and to bring them into the struggle against the electric chair, the gas chamber, and the injection needle as instruments of crime control.

Reframing the Death Penalty

During the legalistic era of the 1960s and 1970s, the ADPM often behaved as though the attitudes of the American people did not matter very much. What mattered was the Constitution and its interpretation by federal judges. If the judges could be convinced that capital punishment violated the Eighth and Fourteenth Amendments, executions would be consigned to the history books, and the fight would be over for good. But with the gradual realization that victory would not be achieved that way after all, abolitionists began to turn their attention back to identifying the soft spots in public approval of the death penalty.

Death and Taxes: Mobilizing Around Cost in Kansas

The most novel of these newer arguments was *cost*. Supporters of capital punishment are often heard to say that one of its many advantages is its cheapness. Even if it is true that the threat of being put to death is no more effective in deterring homicide than the prospect of a life sentence, the argument goes, executions are surely far less costly than the thousands of dollars per year that it takes to maintain a convict in the penitentiary. Clearly, the maintenance of prisoners *is* expensive. Prison construction costs in the early 1980s were estimated at $70,000 per bed (Allen and Latessa 1983), and the annual operating expenditures for state correctional facilities in 1990 averaged $15,777 per prisoner (U.S. Department of Justice, Bureau of Justice Statistics 1992b:18). The per capita expenditures on state and local justice systems that year stood at $261.02 (U.S. Department of Justice, Bureau of Justice Statistics 1992c:7). Why should law-abiding citizens have to see their taxes go to feed, clothe, and house those who have taken innocent human lives?

At one time, the financial advantage of executing criminals was self-evident. But with the advent of enhanced due process requirements in capital cases—bifurcated trials, relatively specific statutory criteria for death sentences, and protracted appeals—it soon became apparent that capital punishment was no longer a bargain. A study by the New York State Defenders Association (New York State Defenders Association 1982) was among the first to show why this is so. It estimated the costs to counties and the state of capital trials and direct appeals (that is, the first step in the appellate process) should

TABLE 3.3. Estimated Costs of Death Penalty in
New York State

Trial, Guilt and Penalty Phases	
Defense Costs	
Attorneys	$212,700
Investigators	80,000
Experts	60,000
	$352,700
Prosecution costs	$ 845,400
Court costs	300,000
Total trial cost	$1,498,100
Direct Appeal to the Court of Appeals	
Defense	$ 80,000
Prosecution	80,000
Total cost, direct appeal	$160,000
U.S. Supreme Court Review	
Defense	$ 85,000
Prosecution	85,000
Total	$170,000
Total Cost for Trial, Direct Appeal, and Supreme Court Review	
To state	$ 817,700
To county	1,010,400
	$1,828,100

Source: New York State Defenders Association 1982.

the bill then before the New York state legislature be enacted. The results of the study (see Table 3.3) revealed that whereas the execution itself might be inexpensive, the costs of delivering an inmate to the execution chamber would not.

Not only did the NYSDA estimates conclude that the costs of capital prosecutions would be far higher than expected should the state reenact it, they also found the cost of a death penalty *trial alone*—nearly $1.5 million—would exceed the cost of sentencing the same defendant to prison for the rest of his or her life—$602,000 (New York State Defenders Association 1982: 23).[22]

The explanation for the high cost of prosecuting capital cases was found in the unique features of post-*Gregg* capital trials:

- Because a life is at stake, guilty pleas are unlikely. Such pleas frequently save authorities the expense of a trial in cases where less is at stake.
- The proposed New York law made costly promises concerning the quality

of the defense counsel that would be provided to indigent people charged with capital offenses.

• Capital trials are usually lengthy, owing to the higher number of pretrial motions and the importance for both sides of careful jury selection.

• Both prosecutors and defense counsel, if they take their jobs seriously, run up unusually high bills for the services of investigators. This is true not only in the guilt phase of the trial, but especially in their preparation of aggravating and mitigating evidence for the penalty phase.

• Both sides bring in more expert testimony in capital trials. Forensic scientists, psychiatrists, and polygraph experts often ask for fees of hundreds of dollars per day.

• The maintenance of segregated death rows with special security requirements adds to the cost.

• Appeals are more common in capital than in noncapital cases. Surprisingly enough, the cost of appeals appears to account for far less of the total bill than the trial itself, but this portion is hardly negligible.

The NYSDA estimate of $1.8 million per capital case was criticized by the sponsors of the New York death penalty bill for, among other things, exaggerating the likely cost of defense counsel. The authors denied this, insisting that their estimates were reasonable in terms of the proposed statute before the State senate and assembly in Albany. It is now recognized that studies in other states have yielded more realistic estimates, but they are nevertheless generally consistent with the New York investigation.[23] Although specific costs vary from state to state, the features of capital prosecutions that are primarily responsible for making them so expensive are the same everywhere. In every state studied so far, it appears that the legal bills for capital punishment render it more expensive than even the most severe alternative—life imprisonment without parole. Moreover, the NYSDA estimates were conservative in one crucial sense: they covered only one round of appeals. Had the reinstatement bill passed in the early 1980s,[24] New York might, in fact, have incurred further expenses as inmates pursued extended challenges to their sentences.

As a result of the New York cost estimates and studies in other states, ADP activists began to suspect that the costliness of the death penalty might be turned against it.[25] The first practical test of this tactic came not in New York, but rather in Kansas in 1986. Like other states, Kansas's death penalty had been voided by the Supreme Court in 1972. But unlike most states, Kansas did not reinstate capital punishment in the aftermath of *Furman v. Georgia.* Death penalty bills were passed by the legislature in 1979, 1980, 1981, and 1985. Each year, though, they were vetoed by Governor John Carlin, a Democrat who opposed capital punishment but had pledged during his campaign that he would not stand in the way of the desires of his constituents. However, he had changed his mind when the time came to sign the 1979 bill into law, and he stuck to his guns for the remainder of his tenure. When Governor Carlin left office in 1987, his replacement was an outspoken death penalty supporter, Republican Mike Hayden. Hayden made the reinstatement of capital punishment a central selling point in his campaign. He invited Kansas lawmakers to have a death penalty bill on his desk as soon as possible in the 1987 term so that he could make its signing one of his first official acts as governor.

With the arrival of the new governor, abolitionists faced a crisis. Kansas was something of a symbol for the movement. As a generally conservative midwestern state with an "Old West" image and a dominant Republican Party, it might have been expected to reactivate its gallows as soon as the Supreme Court had opened the door. But thanks to a small but dedicated band of activists and a governor who had been willing to gamble his political career on a matter of moral principle, the state was still death penalty-free. During previous fights over the issue, opposition to reinstatement had been based on familiar themes. Testimony against an ill-fated 1986 bill, for example, characterized capital punishment as morally wrong, of no deterrent value, and unfair to minorities (*Topeka Capital-Journal* 1986). But with the state in the midst of a fiscal crisis that had brought $60 million in across-the-board state budget reductions and significant cuts in human services and health care, the leaders of the Kansas Coalition Against the Death Penalty met with other activists at the NCADP's November 1986 conference in New Orleans and were persuaded to build their case largely on the question of whether Kansans were willing to foot the bill (Woolf 1987).

Jonathan Gradess, of the New York State Defenders Association and the NCADP, had been developing the fiscal angle since the 1982 study was undertaken. He was encouraged by the media interest that the issue had generated, and had made a presentation about it at the New Orleans NCADP conference. Gradess was then brought to Topeka by Kansas abolitionists, where he met with lawmakers and helped organize the antirestoration campaign.[26] The Board of Indigent's Defense Services for the state released estimates in December 1986 that the creation of a new office to try the 70 to 80 capital cases that might be expected each year would cost about $1.4 million (Wood and Pepper 1987). David Gottlieb, a professor from the University of Kansas School of Law, testified that total costs to local and state government could exceed $15 million, including nearly $7.5 million for new death row facilities (Myers 1987). An estimate by the Legislative Research Department was even higher, projecting annual expenses of $10.9 million for capital defense costs alone (Hanna 1987), plus an additional $1.3 to $3 million more for postconviction costs (Gottlieb 1989:461). Forty-year "life" sentences would cost an estimated $323,500.

When the bill had passed in the state house and reached the state senate, supporters of reinstatement took two tacks. First, some agreed with the governor that "the issue of capital punishment should not be debated or considered on the basis of cost" (Blankenship and Boyette 1987). But while stating that they would refuse to debate the matter on economic grounds, they also presented competing cost estimates based on the assumption that Kansas would face very few capital trials and that a new death row would be unnecessary, at least in the near term (Hanna 1987; Leech 1987).

In a surprising outcome, the Kansas senate defeated the death penalty reinstatement bill when it finally came to a vote in early April. This was the first defeat of a capital punishment bill by the Kansas legislature since 1907. The 22–18 outcome came about because six lawmakers who had been expected to support the measure unexpectedly changed their votes. It is difficult to say how decisive the cost argument was in this outcome. One of those who switched positions cited it as the major factor in his change of heart (Jones 1987). Others cited moral qualms about the death penalty and the fear that an innocent person might someday be executed. In all likelihood, the outcome of the vote rested on a complex mix of factors. Unlike in past sessions, Kansas legislators knew that any bill they passed in 1987 would, in fact, become law. This put the responsibility squarely on them, and some seem to have flinched. The abolitionists' introduction of the issues of capital punishment's cost and its potential damage to the criminal justice system specifically and the state budget generally probably had an impact when the issue came to the floor. The argument changed the terms of the discussion, allowed the ADP forces to take the initiative, and gave some lawmakers—those who had misgivings about the death penalty but were afraid to go public with those misgivings for fear of incurring the wrath of their constituents and the governor—a new and more acceptable language with which to justify their vote.[27] In any case, the 1987 defeat of capital punishment in Kansas kept the issue from being seriously considered in that state for two years. It was beaten back again in 1989, and in 1990 Governor Hayden reluctantly signed a 40-year mandatory minimum sentence for first-degree murderers that was, in essence, a substitute for a death penalty. Finally, in 1994, Governor Joan Finney allowed the death penalty to return to her state after a 22-year absence.[28]

Nevertheless, the issue of cost has remained an important feature of abolitionist frame alignment since the mid-1980s, especially in Idaho, Iowa, Wyoming, and Wisconsin. Alaska rejected the death penalty on the basis of the costs of creating a death row,[29] and cost was also a major factor in Minnesota when Governor Carlsen opposed its reinstatement in 1991.[30]

Miscarriages of Justice

Although the surprising costliness of putting convicted murderers to death was first introduced into the debate during the 1980s, concern over the possibility of miscarriages of justice has a much older pedigree. It was expressed at least as early as the 1820s by reformer Edward Livingston, and throughout the nineteenth and twentieth centuries by such critics as Charles C. Burleigh, Horace Greeley, William Howells, and Sing-Sing warden Lewis Lawes (Mackey 1976), as well as by the American League to Abolish Capital Punishment.[31]

The possibility that an innocent person might be tried, convicted, and executed for a crime that he or she did not commit seems much more remote during the post-*Gregg* era, thanks to the special procedural requirements the courts and legislatures put into effect. However, events in the late 1980s revived the issue. In 1987, Hugo Bedau and Michael Radelet published a law review article that made a strong case that the danger of fatal miscarriages was real. The authors used a variety of published and unpublished sources to locate information on "potentially capital cases" in the United States during the twentieth century. These were cases in which defendants were liable to be sentenced to death.[32] Defendants in these cases were coded as innocent if there were: (a) later decisions by authorities that indicated an error had occurred, such as an executive pardon or judicial reversal, or (b) some unofficial action indicating error, such as a reliable confession by another person or the weight of the evidence as judged by others who subsequently studied the case. The former accounted for 80 percent of cases Bedau and Radelet identified, whereas the latter accounted for the remaining 20 percent.

In their article, Bedau and Radelet identified 350 persons who they believed had been wrongfully convicted of potentially capital offenses between 1900 and 1985. Of these, 139 were sentenced to die. Of the 23 death sentences that were actually carried out, only one of the executions occurred after 1976.[33] In a subsequent book on the topic of miscarriages, Radelet, Bedau, and Constance Putnam (1992) extended their analysis through 1991 and concluded that an additional 66 erroneous convictions occurred between 1985 and 1991. But there were no additional executions of persons the authors believed to be innocent. According to the U.S. House Judiciary Committee's Subcommittee on Civil and Constitutional rights, a total of at least 45 death sentences were found to be in error between 1976 and 1993 (see Table 3.4).

Several of the recent cases involved well-publicized close calls, in which convicts were discovered to be innocent and released from death row after nearly being executed. The most media attention went to the case of Randall Dale Adams, who spent 12 years in a Texas prison and came within three days of lethal injection before his conviction was overturned in 1989. The appellate judges who finally released him ruled that Dallas prosecutors had used perjured testimony and had knowingly suppressed evidence in order to obtain a conviction against Adams for the slaying of a police officer in 1976 (*Dallas Morning News* 1989; Malcolm 1989). Adams's case became especially well known because it was the subject of a film, The *Thin Blue Line,* produced by Errol Morris. Also released from prison in 1989 was James Richardson, a Florida man convicted in 1968 of poisoning his seven children. Richardson's life was saved by the *Furman* decision in 1972, but he remained in prison for 18 more years before it was determined that his children's babysitter most likely committed the killings. As in the Adams case an appeals court ruled that the official who had prosecuted Richardson had withheld crucial evidence at the trial (Minor 1989).

Another notorious near miscarriage involved a black school custodian, Clarence Brandley, who was erroneously convicted of the rape and murder of a 16-year-old white girl. Forensic evidence suggesting that the crime was committed by a white man was "misplaced" and never mentioned to the jury. Other evidence pointing to a different suspect was ignored by the police who investigated the crime. One of those police officers, while interviewing Brandley and one of his coworkers soon after the crime, is alleged to have told Brandley, "One of you two is gonna hang for this. Since you're the nigger, you're elected" (Davies 1991:23). Brandley spent almost nine years on death

TABLE 3.4. Erroneously Sentenced Inmates Released from Death Row, 1976–1993

Year of Release	Name	State	Year of Conviction
1976	Thomas Gladish	New Mexico	1974
	Richard Greer	New Mexico	1974
	Ronald Kleine	New Mexico	1974
	Clarence Smith	New Mexico	1974
1977	Delbert Tibbs	Florida	1974
1978	Earl Charles	Georgia	1975
	Jonathan Treadway	Arizona	1975
1979	Gary Beeman	Ohio	1976
1980	Jerry Banks	Georgia	1975
	Larry Hicks	Indiana	1978
1981	Charles Giddens	Oklahoma	1978
	Michael Linder	South Carolina	1979
	Johnny Ross	Louisiana	1975
1982	Anibal Jarramillo	Florida	1981
	Lawyer Johnson	Massachusetts	1971
1986	Anthony Brown	Florida	1983
	Neil Ferber	Pennsylvania	1982
1987	Shabaka Waglini	Florida	1974
	Perry Cobb	Illinois	1979
	Darby Williams	Illinois	1979
	Henry Drake*	Georgia	1977
	John Knapp	Arizona	1974
	Vernon McManus	Texas	1977
	Anthony Peek	Florida	1978
	Juan Ramos	Florida	1983
	Robert Wallace	Georgia	1980
1988	Jerry Bigelow	California	1980
	Willie Brown	Florida	1983
	Larry Troy	Florida	1983
	William Jent	Florida	1980
	Earnest Miller	Florida	1980
1989	Randall Adams	Texas	1977
	Jesse Brown**	South Carolina	1983
	Robert Cox	Florida	1988
	Timothy Hennis	North Carolina	1986
	James Richardson	Florida	1968
1990	Clarence Brandley	Texas	1980
	Patrick Croy	California	1979
	John Skelton	Texas	1982
1991	Gary Nelson	Georgia	1980
	Bradley Scott	Florida	1988
1993	Kirk Bloodsworth	Maryland	1984

(*continued*)

TABLE 3.4.   Erroneously Sentenced Inmates Released from
Death Row, 1976–1993 (continued)

Year of Release	Name	State	Year of Conviction
1993	Federico Macias	Texas	1984
	Walter McMillan	Alabama	1988
	Gregory Wilhoit	Oklahoma	1987

*Drake was retried and sentenced to life in prison. But the parole board became
convinced of his innocence and freed him based on testimony by his alleged
accomplice and the medical examiner.
**Brown was acquitted of murder on retrial, but convicted of related robbery
charges.
Source: U.S. House of Representatives Subcommittee on Civil and Constitutional Rights, 1993.

row before letter-writing campaigns, street demonstrations, and the provision
of free legal counsel led to his release in 1990 (MacCormack 1990).

Naturally, abolitionists have sought to capitalize on the issue of erroneous
death sentences. They have tried to draw the nation's attention to the issue
through press releases, reports, and speeches, and they have rallied around
particular convicts as exemplars of what is wrong with the death penalty as a
whole. There are, of course, many condemned inmates who claim to be innocent. Most of these attract few, if any, supporters outside the prison. But
others, like Clarence Brandley, have eventually been transformed into causes
celebres. More recently, Texas inmate Gary Graham became a focal point for
activists in that state and across the nation. Graham, who is black, was sentenced to die for the killing of a 53-year-old white man, Bobby Grant Lambert,
during a 1981 robbery. Graham admitted to having committed a string of ten
robberies during the same time period, but vehemently denied the murder
charge. According to his supporters, there is an abundance of evidence that
Graham was not the murderer. They maintain that he was convicted solely on
the basis of a single, highly suspect witness, even though numerous other
witnesses have either been unable to identify Graham or maintain that he was
not the man they saw at the crime scene. There was no other physical or
circumstantial evidence to tie him to the crime. Like many falsely convicted
individuals, Graham was represented at his trial by a court-appointed attorney
who displayed little enthusiasm or competence. He was also hindered by a
Texas rule that new evidence of innocence must be introduced within 30 days
of the trial's conclusion. Neither the existence of other witnesses who would
testify that Graham was the wrong man, nor affidavits from relatives that he
was with them at the time of the crime, nor police ballistics tests that ruled out
his gun as the murder weapon became known until after the time limit had
passed. Texas authorities refused to hold a hearing on the new evidence.

By 1993, a "Gary Graham Justice Coalition" and a "Gary Graham Legal
Defense Committee" had been organized to publicize the details of his case
nationwide. Petitions were circulated through AI and NCACP channels. Civil

rights leaders such as the NAACP executive director, Benjamin Chavis, and celebrities, such as actors Danny Glover, Edward Asner, Mike Farrell, Harry Belafonte, and Martin Sheen and film director Spike Lee, spoke on his behalf and appealed for a new trial. Thanks to those efforts and to the legal work of the Texas Resource Center, one of several federally funded agencies around the country that now handles the appeals of some death-sentenced inmates, Graham's execution was twice stayed. Eventually, the Texas Court of Criminal Appeals ruled in April 1994 that "truly persuasive claims of innocence" based on newly discovered evidence may be presented in state habeas proceedings. Consequently, Graham received an opportunity to prove his innocence. The ruling amended the state's time limit on new evidence, but only where inmates could meet what one dissenting judge called "an impossibly high standard of proof" of their innocence (*Capital Report* 1994).[34]

Although "near misses" have been widely publicized by abolitionist organizations and have attracted considerable press attention, the impact of the innocence issue on the death penalty debate is limited in two ways. Because most of the cases of erroneous death sentences in the twentieth century occurred before the Court-imposed reforms in capital sentencing, the problem of mistaken executions is often dismissed as having been solved. And because there are relatively few instances in which clearly innocent persons have been not only convicted *but actually put to death,* death penalty supporters can characterize such episodes as indications of how *well* the nation's procedural safeguards worked, not how poorly. After all, the vast majority of the system's "mistakes" had been caught and corrected. From a narrowly legalistic perspective, this point is probably well taken. From a more humanistic point of view, however, it neglects the fact that not only is the wrongly convicted person deprived of a number of years of freedom, but he or she is put through the excruciating experience of death row confinement. That is, prisoners who have narrowly escaped execution for crimes they did not commit have already suffered what is probably the worst part of the death penalty: months or years of psychological torment, often confined to a cramped death row cell for as many as 23 out of every 24 hours, with little to take their minds off their impending fate. The unique psychological experience of living under sentence of death has been commented on by a number of scholars and psychiatrists (see Bluestone and McGahee 1962; Johnson 1990a; Streib 1987:155–64; West 1975). Arguably, then, a wrongfully convicted death row prisoner who is fortunate enough to escape execution has escaped only the final part—and in some ways, the easiest—of the process. If this interpretation is correct, the system has *not* worked, and a tragic error has *not* been avoided.

If incontrovertible *proof* of a fatal miscarriage were found *soon after an execution occurred,* it might well provide an enormous boost to the anti-death penalty movement. This is unlikely to happen, however, because there is little inclination—and few resources—to pursue the matter after an inmate is dead. Thus, as in the cases of Roger Coleman and Leonel Herrera, the matter is buried with the convict. Nevertheless, the shadow of doubt concerning the infallibility of the judicial system seems to temper the enthusiasm of many people for capital punishment and continues to attract a good deal of media coverage (Haines 1992). For these reasons, the "innocence issue" will continue to be stressed by abolitionists.

The "Incremental Strategy": Probing for the Soft Spots in Public Opinion

In directing attention to the high cost of capital punishment and the risk that innocent people might fall victim to society's impulse to fight violence with violence, abolitionists were engaging in *frame extension*. That is, they were seeking to broaden their message "so as to encompass interests or points of view incidental to [their] primary objectives but of considerable salience to potential adherents" (Snow, et al. 1986:472–473). But even before these two issues were raised in a systematic way, activists had begun to probe for other "soft spots" in public attitudes toward capital punishment. Given that litigation had become a dead end and that large majorities of Americans expressed their support for capital punishment, were there doubts that might be exploited? This question was the foundation of what came to be called the "incremental strategy," that is, the strategy of chipping away at the popularity of the death penalty piece by piece.

One of the architects of the incremental approach was Charles Fulwood. In 1984, Fulwood was hired by Amnesty International USA as director of its death penalty program. His background was in civil rights. He had been with the Student Nonviolent Coordinating Committee in the 1960s, the Voter Education Project in Atlanta, and the Maynard Jackson and Andrew Young campaigns. As an "outsider," his perspective on how to do human rights work was somewhat distinctive. It was based in the realities of the South, where most of the executions were occurring. Fulwood believed the approach that AI had been using, responding to each announcement of an execution date with letters requesting clemency, was getting nowhere:

> [I]t was a ritual that made people feel good and made them feel like they
> were having a constructive impact, but what they were doing was pissing off
> governors and parole boards *and,* above all, the attorneys that were representing some of these clients. Because [those attorneys] were telling us "This is
> doing no good, and it's actually inflaming the situation, *and it's irrelevant!*"
> You know, it has absolutely no impact whatsoever. . . .[35]

Fulwood and his colleagues at AIUSA decided to mobilize the Urgent Action mechanism only when a death row convict had a *serious* execution date rather than merely a preliminary and technical one, and only when *all* appellate issues had been exhausted. In place of case-by-case responses, Fulwood decided to shift to a more aggressive and politically sophisticated strategy. He wrote a lengthy planning paper soon after assuming his duties at the New York headquarters.[36] Passed by the board of directors, it stressed the importance of moving away from crisis work on individual cases and toward attacking the *institution* of American capital punishment. It argued for trying to change

American opinion indirectly by identifying and exploiting people's doubts about the death penalty and by targeting specific population groups — especially young people, minorities, and due to the spread of the lethal injection method, health professionals. It recommended that AIUSA be prepared to offer specific legislative solutions, short of the ultimate goal of total abolition, to the death penalty's flaws.

A first step in the new strategy was to be a public opinion poll, designed to go beyond the superficial question "Do you support or oppose executing convicted murderers" that was typical in opinion surveys and that produced such discouraging results time after time. Amnesty's survey would distinguish between the "hard core" and "soft core" retentionists, and identify the subissues around which the latter might be persuaded to change their minds. In 1986, AIUSA commissioned such a public opinion poll in Florida. Unlike previous polls, this one explored the more subtle aspects of respondents' attitudes. How solid was their support for or disagreement with capital punishment? What characteristics of the death penalty were they least comfortable about? Would they still prefer the execution of murderers if certain alternative punishments were available? Fulwood and Scharlette Holdman, a Florida abolitionist, worked with Cambridge Survey Research to design questions that would yield answers to such questions, and the survey was conducted in February, April, and June 1986.

Many American abolitionists were unenthusiastic about the decision to probe public opinion on the issue of capital punishment. The figures produced by the Gallup surveys were discouraging enough. But according to Magdaleno Rose-Avila, who was deeply involved in AIUSA's death penalty work during this period and who succeeded Fulwood as director, many ADP activists feared that a detailed poll might reveal that things were even worse than they thought, that there was no hope.[37] The AIUSA poll did in fact reveal that the support for capital punishment in Florida was overwhelming, so much so that the prospects for its abolition in the short term were remote. Eighty-four percent of those surveyed responded that they either "strongly favored" or "somewhat favored" the death penalty.

Although disappointing, the result did not come as a surprise. What *was* surprising was the finding that death penalty support in Florida, though widespread, was far less solid than commonly supposed. Three-fourths of the respondents believed death sentences were applied arbitrarily, and nearly half saw capital punishment as racially discriminatory, biased against the poor, and no more than a short-term solution to more fundamental problems of the criminal justice system. Less than half of them favored the execution of convicted persons under the age of 18 (35 percent), persons guilty of unpremeditated murders of family members or friends (34 percent), persons with histories of mental illness (28 percent), or the mentally retarded (12 percent). The poll found that many Floridians seemed to favor capital punishment only because no better alternative was available. Expressed support dropped precipitously when respondents were asked to choose between execution, life without parole, and life without parole combined with restitution to the victim's family

(Amnesty International USA 1986). This was interpreted to mean that many citizens did not so much *demand* the death penalty. Rather, they found it *acceptable* in a system that seemed unable to come up with anything better.

On the one hand, the new understanding of public opinion on the death penalty suggested that abolitionists might attack it by endorsing the types of alternatives people favored—life imprisonment without any possibility of parole, for instance. But this was touchy, to say the least. Many, and probably most, anti-death penalty activists are nearly as opposed to warehousing offenders in prison without any hope of freedom as they are to killing them.[38] Consequently, nothing remotely resembling an endorsement of life without parole was possible for the movement.

But the polls also suggested to Fulwood and others in the movement the wisdom of pursuing *wedge issues* like the execution of juvenile and mentally retarded offenders. Neither of these issues were new to the ADPM—both had been addressed as side issues by the American League to Abolish Capital Punishment decades earlier—but concentration on the goal of *abolition* had subordinated both in the ALACP's efforts. For Fulwood,

> the notion was that if we had a sustained campaign over a long period of time—say 10 to 15 years—using this . . . approach, that we would now begin to sort of close the net for those people who would be eligible for a death sentence. The idea was to focus on *doubt*, rather than feeling like you had to convince somebody to be against the death penalty *all the time*—although we always said, you know, that we [in Amnesty International] are *fundamentally opposed* to this as a matter of policy, because this is a human rights violation, etc. etc. etc. And that was sort of the context we set for it. We said "Look, Amnesty takes the position that the death penalty is a human rights violation. Period." Then we went *on* to say, you know, "Look at these issues: juveniles, mentally retarded, violation of international law. . . . "[39]

At first, even to shift from capital punishment itself to subissues like these was controversial within the abolitionist movement. It had the appearance of a retreat from the more fundamental moral issues that were at stake. For some, the incremental strategy seemed to imply that the death penalty could be "reformed"—that a death statute that exempted juveniles and the mentally ill or retarded, or a death penalty that was administered fairly across racial and social class categories, would somehow be an "acceptable" one. This, the *purists* felt, must never be implied.[40] Thus, abolitionists were rather slow to board the incrementalist train, and Fulwood ran into resistance in the AI hierarchy itself. After the 1984 strategy paper was approved by the AIUSA board, Fulwood was summoned to London to consult with the International Secretariat (IS). He recalls feeling as if he were being "taken to the woodshed." For two days, he debated various aspects of the plan at Amnesty's headquarters before leaving for a death penalty conference in Stockholm, Sweden, where the discussions continued. The British were concerned that the Americans were exceeding their authority in making such a major policy change without consulting the IS. And both the IS and the Swedish section, which was known within AI for the hard line it took on human rights principles, were concerned that incrementalism violated the principle of absolute opposition to the death penalty in any form.[41]

In the end, the international hierarchy was flexible. In 1988, the International Executive Committee formally adopted a statement that work by national sections toward "measures short of total abolition" were consistent with AI policy so long as they always made it clear that Amnesty International was absolutely opposed to the death penalty in any form and for any reason.[42] Compromises were made by AIUSA, but the incremental strategy survived:

> . . . I think there emerged a certain appreciation for what I was doing. You have to balance this with political reality. You just can't bury your head in the sand and say "*This* is our mandate and *these* are our principals and *these* are our operating procedures," etc. etc. You've got to at least look out the window. Even if you don't go outside, you've got to at least look out the window. You just can't let your whole world be defined by operating in a vacuum. I think that they [the International Secretariat in the United Kingdom], again, appreciated that.[43]

Once the London headquarters' lukewarm blessing was obtained, AIUSA began stressing the subsidiary issues that had been identified as hopeful ones. It threw its weight behind efforts on the state level to exempt from eligibility for execution those with subnormal intelligence and those who committed murders when under the age of 18. In 1991, these were the foci of a special AIUSA campaign. In seeking "MR bills," AIUSA worked closely with the Association for Retarded Citizens and other lobbying groups. In fact, it preferred for those groups to take the lead in state-level lobbying so as to avoid the appearance that MR bills were abolitionist Trojan horses[44] — which, in a certain sense, they were. And AIUSA's unsuccessful effort to stop the 1992 execution of Johnny Garrett,[45] a Texas inmate convicted for a killing he committed at the age of 17, was intended, in part, to focus public and media attention on juvenile offenders on death row.

Resistance to incremental approaches gradually subsided in the rest of the anti-death penalty movement as well. At the NCADP conference of November 1987, for instance, it was agreed that "total abolition is not presently achievable in most parts of the U.S., but that efforts limiting the application of the death sentence are worthwhile." For the first time, there were conference workshops on the juvenile offender and mental retardation issues,[46] and beginning in 1988 the coalition included both of these statutory exemptions in its legislative goals. The next year, director Leigh Dingerson asserted that the continued stream of negative court decisions "give abolitionists marching orders for future work on juveniles and mental retardation" and revealed that the NCADP would soon begin working with other national, state, and local organizations on a coordinated series of legislative campaigns against the executions of inmates in these categories.[47]

In addition to juvenile and mental retardation exemptions, the NCADP and ACLU also concentrated on working for the passage of what eventually became known as the Racial Justice Act. The RJA, as noted earlier, would have had the effect of nullifying the *McCleskey* decision by allowing inmates to challenge their death sentences with statistical evidence of biased sentencing patterns in their states. Even this incremental measure disturbed some people, because it aimed at "improving" capital punishment by removing one of its most disturbing features, racial discrimination.[48]

Incrementalism provided the ADPM with something it badly needed: a more realistic legislative agenda that abolitionists and their allies could pursue. Juvenile offenders and mentally retarded convicts were issues that the movement might win on, and it needed victories badly. According to Fulwood, death penalty activists found themselves

> . . . actually passing legislation in the states, and picking up more support and picking up people who otherwise would never have been involved in this . . . that was the way that we got civil rights organizations involved. Because there was something *specific* for them to do! You know, rather than just having some state senator who's sympathetic introducing a bill to abolish the death penalty but can't get two additional votes for it! We were able to get sponsors for legislation that would *restrict* the death penalty, and then use it as an educational tool to wear down the opposition, to create so much doubt and ambivalence about it so that there would not be the political will to continue.

This is not to say that the incremental battles were easy. Thirteen states and the federal system have set 18 as the age threshold for death sentencing.[49] Despite widespread public support for the exemption of juvenile offenders, however, no state has taken action to raise its existing statutory age limit. "MR bills" have fared somewhat better. In 1991, a year in which activists devoted a great deal of effort to achieving statutory provisions prohibiting the execution of mentally retarded convicts,[50] such bills failed to pass in 15 of the 16 states where they were introduced. But eight states had enacted them by June 1993 (*Capital Report* 1993). The list grew to ten by mid-1995. Legislation to reduce racial inequities in death sentencing has been a long shot for the movement, but one that has the added advantage of helping stimulate greater black and Latino involvement.

Becoming Proactive

Most of the anti-death penalty movement's tactics through the mid-1980s were *reactions* to events over which the movement had little or no control; an impending execution date, the introduction of a reinstatement bill or a death penalty expansion bill (adding new classes of capital crimes, like drive-by shootings, for example), or efforts to streamline federal habeas corpus. Since the mid-1980s, leaders of ADPM organizations have repeatedly stressed the necessity of getting off the treadmill and moving in the direction of a more "proactive" approach.

One aspect of this, as we have seen, was Amnesty International's de-emphasis of its traditional "urgent action" letter-writing approach in American death penalty cases. On a much smaller scale, the NCADP made use of a similar approach through the "National Execution Alert Network." The incremental strategy did not entail a rejection of appeals for clemency, but simply a broadening of the abolitionists' repertoire so as to seize the initiative. Letter-writing campaigns, particularly when those letters come from outside the state in which the execution is taking place, seemed to be having little direct effect.[51] Several of the activists interviewed for this book, some of whom are based in AI, expressed this pessimistic view. For instance, Ali Miller, who directed AIUSA's Death Penalty Program from 1990 to 1993:

> . . . we're trying to get away from letter writing and this focus on last-minute clemency efforts. Because it's both frustrating and often futile. Although it's worthy and important to mark every execution, and letter-writing and press toward an execution date can be an important part of a clemency process, it can only be a *part,* and it has to hook into an existing clemency process which basically has to be run on the ground by the folks in that state. Generally [it's] the lawyers and critical folks in the state who can make it happen. Otherwise, at best all we're doing is making the governor or the clemency board a tad uncomfortable. At worst, it's falling on deaf ears. . . . Nobody should fool themselves that letters alone stop executions.[52]

Rick Halperin, a Texas activist and former AIUSA chairperson, saw the resistance of decision makers to outside pressure as particularly fierce in his state, which leads the nation in executions:

> It sounds callous to say, but I'm telling you in all seriousness, people in this state [Texas], legislators in this state, the attorney general, any elected official or the pardon and parole board, the governors . . . they don't give a damn what anybody thinks. We've seen it under male governors, female governors, Democrats, Republicans. They absolutely just don't care. That's not to say that people shouldn't write letters and fax because they need to and they have to, but it's just very, very, very difficult to do this work in this state.[53]

One substitute for seeking clemency in individual cases was the expansion of media work; that is, making a greater effort to achieve favorable press attention to the abolitionist cause. This expansion went hand in hand with frame alignment efforts discussed earlier. Regardless of how well issues like cost-effectiveness and the risk of error resonate with the attitudes of the people, they cannot affect the climate of public opinion unless they are made known through the electronic and print media of the nation. This has sometimes been difficult in the past. Media concentration on stories about violent crime, especially on television, is sensational and gripping. It usually encourages emotional identification with the victim and the victim's family as well as the demonization of the perpetrator, and thus tends to drive up the demand for harsher criminal justice policies. Whereas crime stories are simple and direct, many of the criticisms of severe punishments like the death penalty are complex and counterintuitive. For example, opinion surveys that revealed unexpected amounts of ambivalence and discomfort with capital punishment often went virtually unnoticed. Despite prodding, some newspapers were reluctant to report them,[54] and when they *were* reported, it was often done in a somewhat misleading manner. Consider the following newspaper headlines, each of which appeared in 1992:

"Texans Give Thumbs up to Executions" (Fair 1992)

"Death Penalty Support Still Strong in State" (Skelton 1992)

"Californians Back Death Penalty, Poll Says" (Chiang 1992)

Each of these headlines appeared above a newspaper story about surveys that revealed a widespread preference for *alternatives* to the death penalty, were such alternatives available. The high levels of *abstract* support for capital punishment were to be expected, the preference for alternatives was not. Yet it was the former that jumped out at readers. To increase favorable press coverage of the anti-death penalty movement's claims, abolitionist groups have tried to develop media contacts and become more skilled in dealing with the press. AI has been relatively successful in this regard, owing to its prominence and credibility. The reports it issues on a wide range of human rights issues *do* generate headlines, even when the issue is capital punishment in America rather than torture in the Sudan.

Outside of AI, the most straightforward effort to get better press coverage of the issues raised by the ADPM was the establishment of the Death Penalty Information Center (DPIC) in 1990. The center was the brainchild of Fenton Communications, a public relations firm with links to the movement. Initial funding was provided by the MacArthur Justice Project, part of the J. Roderick MacArthur Foundation.[55] The NCADP's director hoped that such a national media center would "change the momentum of the death penalty debate through a proactive press campaign against it."[56] Officials of the MacArthur Foundation apparently intended DPIC to be an objective source of information on the death penalty for the media to use in its coverage of the issue, not a part of the abolitionist movement per se. DPIC's staff would produce reports on particular issues that seemed likely to influence the public's views, such as racially biased sentencing, the risk of miscarriages of justice, and the widespread perception that murderers who do not get death sentences are back on the street in a very short time. The center would oversee the distribution of those reports to media outlets and be ready to provide further information to the press and to appear on radio and television talk shows.

The idea of a separate Death Penalty Information Center was not greeted enthusiastically by everyone within the upper ranks of the movement. Some NCADP board members worried that DPIC would be too heavily influenced by the litigators on its board and thus focus too much on *legal* issues rather than the ones likely to mean something to the public. Others did not understand why the NCADP itself should not receive the funding for coordinated media work, since it was already well positioned for such a role. To still others, these concerns amounted to no more than a "turf battle"; what difference did it make who got the money, as long as the job got done?[57] From the outset, the relationship between DPIC and the movement was somewhat ambiguous.

Although the center was supposed to be neutral and independent of abolitionist organizations, it was also supposed to provide assistance to those organizations concerning their press relations.[58] Its office was even located within the NCADP office suite in Washington until 1992, although its operations and budget were separate.

The Death Penalty Information Center was officially launched in June 1990. Its first director was Michael Kroll, a journalist, long-time abolitionist, and veteran of the direct action group PAX. Kroll was supported by an administrative assistant and by Fenton Communications. The DPIC's annual budget was approximately $200,000, a substantial sum in comparison to abolitionist organizations. Over the next two years, the center's major activities were the following:

- distribution of a general press packet on the death penalty to media across the country;
- a series of press briefings by Kroll and attorneys Steven Bright and Bryan Stevenson with reporters from *The New York Times, The Wall Street Journal, The Washington Post,* and major television networks;
- a press "campaign" on racism in death sentencing in the Chattahoochee Judicial District of Georgia;
- press releases on unfairness in the imposition of the death penalty in Philadelphia and prosecutorial misconduct in capital cases;
- appearances by Kroll, Bright, and Stevenson on a number of television and radio programs; and
- workshops on effective press work at the NCADP national conferences of 1990 and 1991.[59]

Kroll resigned as director of DPIC in June 1992, in order to return to his native California. The MacArthur Justice Center board was unhappy that only one major report—the Chattahoochee report—had been released in the first 18 months of DPIC's existence, that DPIC had been unable to achieve as much major television coverage as had been hoped, and that the press was continuing to highlight individual "villains" rather than systematic problems with the death penalty. They were also unhappy that DPIC had so far failed to capitalize on a list of former prosecutors, corrections professionals, and sympathetic relatives of murder victims that it had enlisted as "new voices" against the death penalty. A funding cutoff was threatened. The NCADP was displeased as well, feeling that DPIC had, in fact, focused more on legal issues than on matters that were likely to interest the public at large, and had not coordinated its activities with NCADP affiliates at the state and local levels.[60] Kroll's duties were assumed by Richard Dieter, a lawyer and justice reform activist, in 1992. At the same time, DPIC moved out of the NCADP suite to office space in Fenton Communications. MacArthur Justice Center funding has continued, and with Dieter as its director, DPIC has issued reports on the cost of capital punishment (Dieter 1992), cost-effective alternatives to the execution of convicted murderers (Dieter 1993), miscarriages of justice (U.S. House of Representatives Subcommittee on Civil and Constitutional Rights 1993), and the chaotic state of capital prosecution in Texas (Dieter 1994).

Another proactive strategy by anti-death penalty activists in recent years involved trying to take the issue back from politicians who had learned to use it for their own purposes. By the end of the 1980s, many U.S. politicians began to sense that the crime issue generally, and capital punishment specifically, represented the electoral mother lode. Being perceived as "soft on crime" was suicidal, and representing one's opponent as being insufficiently serious about dealing with lawbreakers was an excellent campaign tack. The first question put to Democratic presidential candidate Michael Dukakis during a 1988 televised debate with George Bush asked him how he would feel about the death penalty if his wife Kitty were brutally raped and murdered. His answer made him sound detached and overly intellectual on the issue. Bush battered Dukakis on the crime issue for the remainder of the campaign. The most infamous expression was the "Willie Horton" television commercial. The commercial highlighted acts of violence committed by a black convict who had been free under a Massachusetts prison furlough program while Dukakis was governor. The fact that the program had been in existence well before he took office was lost in the clamor, and opportunistic candidates across the nation took notice.

Political manipulation of capital punishment increased in the 1990 midterm elections. Candidates across the nation, and particularly in Florida, Texas, California, and Michigan gubernatorial races, used television commercials that bragged of their concrete efforts while governor or state attorney general to have convicted murderers executed. One such spot showed Texas candidate Mark White walking past portraits of inmates he had helped to execute while serving a previous term as governor. Andrew Young, the former civil rights activist and Atlanta mayor, reversed his longstanding opposition to capital punishment while pursuing the Democratic nomination for governor of Georgia (Oreskes 1990). Abolitionists were encouraged that many of the candidates who most fiercely pushed their stand on the issue went down to defeat. This undermined what was becoming a central piece of conventional campaign wisdom: that the death penalty was a "hot button" issue on which many voters would decide how to cast their vote.[61] Still, abolitionists hoped to avoid a replay of the 1990 feeding frenzy as the 1992 elections approached. Leigh Dingerson initiated an NCADP campaign, dubbed "STOP IT!," to take the death penalty out of the elections.[62] It encouraged activists at the state and local levels to confront pro-death penalty candidates at campaign appearances and to try to "expose" the cynical manner in which they were using the death penalty as a political ploy. The idea was to show that most candidates *knew* that executions failed to bring any noticeable improvement in public safety and wasted scarce resources, but were not honest or courageous enough to say so publicly. And the STOP IT! campaign placed particular emphasis on exposing the exploitation of subtle racism by candidates relying heavily on the issue, much as the Willie Horton ad had done four years earlier. The NCADP sought to show that "crime," in election-year rhetoric, was little more than a code word for "race." In sum, Dingerson's idea was to take the death penalty out of the elections by showing that it was being used by dishonest candidates to insult the intelligence of the electorate. This was a delicate task, because the tax-exempt NCADP could not endorse particular office seekers.[63]

NCADP's campaign experienced some small victories during the summer and fall. It was most successful in low-profile contests for state legislatures, district attorneys, and state attorneys general.[64] One higher profile success came in the race for U.S. senator from Illinois, when the Illinois Coalition persuaded candidate Carol Moseley Braun to reassert her *absolute* opposition to capital punishment after she had begun to waver under pressure. But in most elections of national importance, STOP IT! did not have a great impact. The death penalty did not become as much of a key issue in the 1992 elections as expected because, in many races, both candidates endorsed it.[65] Democratic presidential candidate Bill Clinton, in particular, did not fall into the trap that had crippled the Dukakis campaign. He made a point of advancing a "tough" anticrime image, albeit one that placed more emphasis on crime *prevention*. And he returned to Arkansas, where he was governor, to sign death warrants during the campaign. This was hardly the manner in which the ADPM had hoped to see the death penalty vanish as an election-year issue. In other elections, capital punishment did not play a major role simply because pro-death penalty candidates chose not to try to capitalize on their opponents' anti-death penalty positions. But in 1994, capital punishment reemerged as a campaign issue. Governor Mario Cuomo, whose veto had prevented reinstatement for over a decade in New York, was defeated—in part for his allegedly soft position on crime. The death penalty also figured prominently in gubernatorial and legislative races in California, Iowa, Missouri, and Nebraska (Kotok and Gertzen 1995). In many of these races, it was not satisfactory merely to support capital punishment; several candidates were battered by their opponents merely for not showing enough enthusiasm about the matter.

The last and most recent expression of the ADPM's turn toward proactivity entails efforts to persuade prosecuting attorneys *not* to seek death sentences in cases where they might be inclined or pressured to do so. Given the combination of statutory aggravating factors and significant extralegal details present, some crimes have all the earmarks of death penalty cases. They include killings of white victims by black assailants, multiple-assailant cases where one defendant might be coerced by the threat of capital punishment to testify against another, and highly publicized murders in which the defendant is without the financial means to mount a serious defense.[66] Some of these same crimes may also include important mitigating circumstances like mental retardation or a history of physical abuse against the accused.

The classic strategy in such cases is a legal one: the prosecutors seek the death penalty and the defense attorney attempts, with greater or lesser degrees of enthusiasm and skill, to avoid a death sentence. At the time the research for this book was in progress several ADPM groups, including AIUSA and Death Penalty Focus of California, were discussing the feasibility of approaching prosecutors in advance to try to discourage them from asking for the death penalty.[67] When the surviving family members of the victims are opposed to the death penalty, they might prevail on the survivors to express their preference that the killers not be sentenced to die. In counties with budgetary problems, abolitionists have stressed how avoiding a long and expensive trial could save a great deal of money for better uses.[68] Preemptive strikes can also focus on the age of defendants or seek to involve their home communities in forestalling capital charges. In one such case, anti-death penalty activists in Oklahoma took up the case of Jesus Manuel Corrales, a 16-year-old male charged with the murder of a white teenager. After the Oklahoma County district attorney announced his intention to seek the death penalty in order to set an example for local gang members, a coalition called "Save Our Children" was formed. It included the NAACP, Amnesty International, the ACLU, and various child advocacy and Latino community groups.[69] Corrales eventually pleaded guilty to first-degree murder and was sentenced to life imprisonment without parole. Days after entering the plea he changed it to not guilty, claiming that he had been forced into the earlier plea bargain by his attorney.[70] As this is written, an appeal is still pending.

Attacking the death penalty on the "front end" is a long shot because of the public's angry and fearful mood about crime. The pressure to seek the maximum penalty can be intense, and a choice not to do so is sometimes taken as a sign that one crime is not seen by the authorities as being as "bad" as others. This is often a very touchy matter given the racial and class issues that may be involved. Moreover, approaching prosecutors about individual cases is not an attack on the death penalty itself. It is merely an attempt to reduce the body count. As we shall see in chapter 4, the choice between case-by-case lifesaving and broad attacks on capital punishment as a criminal justice *policy* is a contentious one within the movement.

The Struggle to Diversify

John McCarthy and Mayer Zald (1973) set off something of a theoretical firestorm when they pointed out that collective action has often flourished in recent decades without much mass participation, especially that of the direct beneficiaries of movements' efforts. It can rely instead on relatively small numbers of "professional" reformers who eschew large-scale actions like public demonstrations in favor of lobbying, litigation, and publicity. The bills for such activities, McCarthy and Zald contended, are often paid not by the aggrieved parties for whom the movement speaks, but rather in large part by "conscience constituents"; that is, people driven by normative motivations rather than self-interest.

The suggestion that such "professional social movements" in fact represented the new wave of collective action in industrial societies was soon questioned by other movement analysts, as noted in the introduction. These critics countered that indigenous organization and resources are more important than resource mobilization theorists were suggesting (McAdam 1982; Morris 1984)

—that the aggrieved population itself usually plays a crucial role. Although it is undoubtedly true that social reform has become a rather specialized "profession," most social movements clearly have built on a pool of people who benefit directly from their activities. Most active feminists, for example, as well as those who merely write checks to the National Organization for Women or other feminist organizations, are women themselves. Most rank-and-file civil rights activists are African Americans or other ethnic minorities. The vast majority of committed gay rights advocates are gay men and lesbians. But the direct beneficiaries of the anti-death penalty movement are convicted murderers, and for a variety of reasons, they are rarely able to take a direct role in a collective movement against the institution that seeks to kill them. [71]

Not only does the ADPM lack a natural constituency that would participate out of self-interest, but it has tended to recruit from a vary narrow band of American society throughout its history. Its ranks have been filled mostly by middle-class white people with professional backgrounds and liberal politics. The same is often true today, especially in some state-level abolitionist groups. For example, William Bowers, a death penalty researcher who has also been involved in anti-death penalty activism in Massachusetts, laments the failure of abolition forces in that state to recruit from a wider range of groups:

> But this is really an interesting notion, I mean a fascinating thing here—youth and minorities and people of color being in or out of this movement. I look at the Massachusetts situation, [where the state abolitionist organization is dominated by] middle-class, sometimes religiously oriented, you know, Unitarian-Universalist-type, Friends-type people of this state—we're utterly lacking in getting minorities and disadvantaged people behind this thing! [And] we're not getting young people. Oh God, you go to those meetings and there's nobody at the meetings you haven't seen there for three years. There's nobody, *nobody* you haven't seen before. And they're all *real old people!* [72]

As ADP organizations have become more stable since the mid-1980s, their leaders have also become more concerned about the homogeneity of their membership and have made conscious attempts to enlarge and broaden the movement. No one is turned away, to be sure, but the most concerted efforts have been directed toward increasing the participation of church people, victims' families, students, and—most importantly—people of color.

Mobilizing the Religious Community

The teachings of Jewish and Christian scriptures on capital punishment are ambiguous. The Old Testament makes what seems to be approving reference to punishing as many as 33 offenses by death. They range from murder to chronic disobedience of one's parents' commands. Even animals that fatally injure a human are subject to execution (Exod. 21:28–29). But two other passages seem to prohibit or discourage punishing by death:

Thou shalt not kill. (Exod. 20:13)

Say unto them, "As I live," saith the Lord God, "I have no pleasure in the death of the wicked, but that the wicked turn from his way and live. Turn ye, turn ye from your evil ways; for why will ye die, O house of Israel." (Ezek. 33:11)

There are few direct references to capital punishment in the New Testament. But unlike the Old Testament's harsh treatment of sin and punishment, it stresses forgiveness and mercy. Throughout the centuries, Americans seeking biblical support for execution have cited the Old Testament, and abolitionists have cited the New Testament. Jewish scholars, who might be expected to support the death penalty for scriptural reasons, generally have stressed how Jewish law *in practice* placed so many procedural limitations on capital punishment as to virtually abolish it (Kazis 1967; Megivern 1981; Milligan 1967).

The Bible's lack of clarity about the subject has meant that, in theory, the religious community's backing was within the abolitionists' reach. And during the period this book focuses on, the ADPM has received at least *nominal* support from most major denominations and national religious organizations — from the American Baptist Church in the USA to the U.S. Catholic Bishops[73] (see National Interreligious Task Force on Criminal Justice 1979). Whereas the NCADP's infrastructure also included civil rights groups, lawyers, and others, its rhetorical and tactical repertoire for most of the decade after *Gregg* was shaped to a large degree by the Catholic, Presbyterian, Quaker, and Brethren criminal justice reformers who found themselves doing death penalty work — often for the first time.[74]

Policy statements from national religious organizations were helpful, but concrete actions were needed. Henry Schwarzschild observed in 1983 that

. . . the churches as a group have been very disappointing on this issue. While they have been generally supportive, they have not made a vigorous commitment, either in terms of staff, program or money. And they have certainly not exercised any sustained or visible moral force on what is essentially a moral issue. This has hurt, and continues to hurt, the public advocacy effort, and undercuts one of its basic premises.[75]

Worse still, whereas national-level religious bodies generally at least had official policies in opposition to the death penalty, local churches were usually not sympathetic at all. Expressed support for capital punishment among self-identified Protestants has roughly equaled that of the population as a whole since 1974, and Catholic support has tended to exceed the national average slightly through the late 1980s (Smith and Wright 1992). When the Presbyterian Church USA surveyed its congregations, it found that roughly three out of every four of their pastors favored abolition of the death penalty, but that more than three-fourths of the *members* of their churches supported its retention. They had never before uncovered a wider split on any social or religious issue.[76] In this and other denominations, the problem seemed to be that supportive clergy were often reluctant to address the issue of capital punishment in more than a passing way or to try to press their congregations into action for fear of alienating them. And when they did try to do so, they were frequently met with little more than uncomfortable silence.

During 1989 and 1990, a major effort to deal with the religious communi- ty's failure to oppose the death penalty in any serious way was undertaken, initially cosponsored by the National Interreligious Task Force on Criminal Justice (NITFCJ) and the National Coalition to Abolish the Death Penalty. They were later joined by AIUSA, the Southern Christian Leadership Confer- ence, and the American Friends Service Committee. The one-year campaign was designated "Lighting the Torch of Conscience," and it was designed both to publicize major religious organizations' opposition to capital punishment and to encourage religious people, especially at the local level, to take more action. The campaign kicked off with a meeting of religious leaders at the Martin Luther King, Jr. Center for Nonviolent Social Change in Atlanta. In a joint statement issued at the conclusion of that meeting, the participants as- serted that they "are here to light the torch of conscience, to rekindle the religious community's long-held opposition to capital punishment, and to pledge anew our active resolve to use all of the resources available to us to abolish the penalty of death in the United States." The statement went on to say that the death penalty is inconsistent with religious values, " . . . which include respect for human life, nonviolence, restoration and reconciliation, and the message of God's redemptive love," that executions violate the inherent worth of each human life, and that they serve no legitimate social purpose that cannot be better attained through more humane policies.

> As we light this torch of conscience, we commit ourselves and our faith communities to do everything within our power to abolish the death penalty. We will use our moral leadership to change attitudes through education and engagement in faithful public witness, service, and advocacy toward that end.
> The religious community's opposition to capital punishment has been on record for years. Now it is time for it to be on fire.[77]

The statement was signed by representatives of 24 religious bodies, includ- ing the American Baptist Churches, the American Friends Service Committee, the Church of the Brethren, the Mennonite Central Committee US, the Na- tional Council of the Churches of Christ in the USA, the NITFCJ, Pax Christi USA, the Presbyterian Church USA, the Southern Christian Leadership Con- ference, the Union of American Hebrew Congregations, the Unitarian Univer- salist Association, and the United Methodist Council of Bishops.

Through October 1990, participants in the "Torch Campaign" carried its message into churches, service clubs, schools, and universities through 36 states. And from May 5 through May 18, 1990, some of them marched 330 miles from the state prison at Starke, Florida, to Atlanta, where the campaign came full circle at the King Center. About 50 completed the entire march, while several hundred took part in at least part of it.[78]

In some respects, "Lighting the Torch of Conscience" was successful. In particular, the march from Starke to Atlanta drew considerable press attention, helped to forge organizational links to the black community through the SCLC, which was not only a cosponsor but also contributed its expertise in march logistics and security, and provided a lasting inspirational "lift" to many of the abolitionists who came from around the country to take part. But it did little to achieve its primary goal of stimulating active involvement by the religious community. Kathy Lancaster, who was instrumental in organizing the campaign, shares this conclusion:

> The people who made the statements and signed the [joint] statement, which sits here on the floor of my office, were deep thinking, really committed people as individuals . . . and did not have, for reasons I understand all too well as a church bureaucrat, did not have the energy, ability, or single focus to be able, then, to carry it back to their denominations in a way that would take. Maybe death penalty is a "Teflon" subject, which is a revolting concept in that way.

But like many of the planners and participants in the campaign, Lancaster looks back on it as an effort that cannot be judged by its results alone.

> I think it was good in and of itself. Maybe some individuals were changed, . . . but I can't see lasting value for it. Perhaps like so many other moral issues—I don't want to sound self-serving here—but we've got to do this because we've got to do it, to be faithful to our calling. To our understanding, those of us who are followers of Jesus Christ, we *can't not* do it. But to be *compelled* to do something is in a way for ourselves. And whether it works or not, is academic and unmeasurable.[79]

Mobilizing Victims' Families

Nearly everyone who has ever spoken out for the abolition of capital punishment has encountered some version of the same response: "All right, but how would *you* feel if someone in *your* family were brutally murdered?" The question is a rhetorical one, because it confidently assumes that regardless of their feelings prior to being touched directly by homicide, *all* victims' families want and need the killers of their children, parents, spouses, or siblings to pay with their own lives. A majority undoubtedly does, although many victims' support groups include members who oppose capital punishment for religious or other reasons.[80] In any case, this assumption amounts to a powerful rebuttal of the abolitionist position because the loss that the victim's family members have lived through gives their views a certain moral primacy. The reality of their suffering tends to silence the voices of those for whom the death penalty is a legal or humanitarian matter.

This puts abolitionists in a very difficult position. If they admit that they, too, might want vengeance should a loved one be murdered, their efforts to take away the state's power to execute smacks of hypocrisy. But if they refuse to acknowledge the revenge motive, they appear detached and unfeeling. Indeed, the stereotype of abolitionists as disproportionately sympathetic to the guilty and deaf to the cries of innocent victims has seriously compromised the legitimacy of the movement. Many activists themselves have recognized this.[81] As put by Bob Gross of the NCADP, "we have let ourselves be characterized as working on behalf of the 2,500 people on death row rather than working on behalf of the whole society—which has a social problem called capital punishment."[82]

To counteract this stereotype, many leaders in ADPM groups have stressed the importance of respecting the feelings of victims' families, and saying so in public. To respond to their calls for vengeance with ridicule or insult is a serious tactical error. It is far better to acknowledge the validity of their feelings, without backing down or apologizing for trying to rid the nation of executions, and to seek common ground. Areas of possible agreement include better treatment of crime victims and their families by the courts, compensation programs to offset the financial crisis that families often suffer in the wake of a homicide, and the need for greater attention to crime *prevention.* Most abolitionists interviewed for this book simply see this effort to reach out as the right thing to do. Sister Helen Prejean, a Louisiana anti-death penalty activist, is among the most adamant on this point. She came to this realization while serving as spiritual advisor to Patrick Sonnier, a death row inmate. Sonnier was convicted of killing two teenagers, David LeBlanc and Loretta Bourque, and was electrocuted on April 5, 1984. The experience had a profound effect on her outlook:

> Ten years have passed since I first met Patrick Sonnier. Over the years I have clarified my perspective. Back in 1982 I was an exuberant activist, having just joined the fray against social injustice, and I see now that I devoted my energies exclusively to Pat Sonnier's plight when I should have shouldered the struggles of victims' families as well. I should have reached out to the Bourques and LeBlancs immediately and offered them love and comfort, even if they chose to reject it. Now, as I befriend each new man on death row, I always offer my help to his victim's family. Some accept my offer. Most angrily reject it. But I offer. (Prejean 1993:32)

In addition to being the right thing to do, building bridges to the families of murder victims helps repair the image that abolitionists are insensitive to the pain of the innocent. But there is an even better means of counteracting the image that abolitionists and crime victims stand at opposite ends of a moral continuum: recruiting and organizing such families to speak out *against* capital punishment. Surprisingly, perhaps, a fairly large contingent of activists within the anti-death penalty movement are the relatives of murder victims. Marie Deans, whose mother-in-law was murdered, headed the Virginia Coalition on Jails and Prisons until it ceased operations in 1993, and worked extensively with death row prisoners in Virginia and South Carolina. The father of the Kansas Coalition's Bill Lucero was the victim of a homicide. Sam Sheppard's mother was murdered when he was seven years old, and his father, a prominent Ohio neurosurgeon, was wrongfully convicted and sentenced to death for the crime. Dr. Sheppard was released after ten years in prison, and his son has been a highly committed abolitionist since the late 1980s (see Hayes

1992). Other prominent activists who have lived through the murders of either family members or close friends include Pat Bane (NCADP, Murder Victims' Families for Reconciliation), Therese Bangert (NCADP), Pat Clark (Death Penalty Focus of California), Mary Dunwell (Amnesty International), Theresa Mathis (Washington Association of Criminal Defense Lawyers), Norman Felton (Death Penalty Focus of California), Bill Pelke (NCADP, Murder Victims' Families for Reconciliation), and Marietta Jaeger (Murder Victims' Families for Reconciliation).

The anger of victims' families is intuitively understandable to most of us. How could one *not* want the killer of one's child or parent to give up his or her own life? How could one live through that uniquely painful experience and then work to preserve the lives of the type of person who could do such a thing? Marie Deans had opposed the death penalty passively since reading Camus' *Reflections on the Guillotine* as a 16 year old. Her husband felt the same way, but the two never even discussed the matter until his mother was killed by a prison escapee from Maine.

> Neither one of us was sure about how the other person felt. We sort of danced around it. We kept saying "what's gonna happen?" and looking at each other. And finally [my husband's] sister said something like "I hope he fries!" Bob and I looked at each other, and I said "Do *you* feel like that? And he said "Hell, no—do *you* feel like that?" And I said "no, I don't!"
>
> I think part of my grieving process was finding a way to put what I was feeling to some kind of use. And [the killer's] sister contacted us. She contacted the sheriff and sent us a message. And I felt a real strong identification with her. I don't remember now exactly what it was that she said, but the sheriff did come to our house and bring her message to us. He ran to her with Penny's blood still all over him, and she turned him in. And I thought, you know, how would I feel if my brother committed a murder like this? And so I really felt close to her. I've never talked to her directly. But I really still feel close to her, like we went through something together. So I wanted to do something with that. I felt *bad* that I had never thought about murderers having families! You know? And I really wanted to do something that addressed the violence in the society. There was this constant question in my mind about "why?" Why had Penny gone through this? Why is this the way it is? Is this the way that we communicate with each other, we shoot each other down? Why are we so good at that? And I really was looking for some way to express that and work on that, to answer that "why?"[83]

Marietta Jaeger's seven-year-old daughter was abducted, abused, and murdered by a man who taunted Jaeger over the phone before the child's body was found. After he was captured, Jaeger insisted that he be imprisoned and treated by psychiatrists rather than charged with capital murder. The killer later took his own life. Jaeger's remarkably charitable stance toward the man who had taken so much from her was motivated by her religious belief and by her sense that revenge is futile:

> As the mother of a victim, I can tell you that no number of retaliatory deaths will compensate me for the loss of my daughter. Her value to me is

inestimable; it cannot be offset by the death of any other person. I have met hundreds of people who have lost loved ones to violence, and I see the deleterious effects of unforgiveness. Legislating the animal desire for revenge that I see in these people would have the same effect on society.

Susie's life was a gift of beauty and sweetness and goodness. I would violate and even profane that gift by condoning the killing of someone in her name. I honor her life and memorialize her far better by insisting that all life is sacred and worthy of preservation. (Boer 1992)

Similar sentiments were expressed in 1985 by Bill Lucero, whose father had been murdered a dozen years earlier, in his testimony against the reintroduction of capital punishment in Kansas:

Revenge! Isn't that why we are really here today? To seek revenge? By this bill you're considering, we are actually proposing to torture a family — I'm talking [about the] victim's family — for nine to eleven years through the trial, appeal, and stay processes — that's how long it takes. And then we're going to end the murderer's life with a little painless injection. Get serious! What will that accomplish? I learned shots don't hurt when I was six years old. Remember we're talking *vengeance* here. Let's think back to the medieval days — like maybe the rack or the whip; remember how they cut off some limbs, broke some bones. Those fantasies were some of my mild ones when I was first confronted with Dad's death. Wanting his murderer's blood or hearing her scream: these thoughts became an obsession. The anger fueled more anger — let her suffer like I have! Am I getting too carried away? I've been told not to talk like this in public legislative committees — it doesn't sound too nice. But then, putting people to death shouldn't sound nice.

But there is only just one problem — it won't bring him back. It won't bring anybody back. No matter what you do to the murderer, it won't make the hurt go away! Life has its pains that all of us have to bear. You can't remove that pain no matter what kind of a sentencing bill you pass.[84]

The symbolic importance of murder victims' relatives who are *against* the death penalty is enormous, second only perhaps to law enforcement officials or prosecutors who might be prevailed on to speak out. Both shatter the illusion that people most directly impacted by violent crime are unanimous in their enthusiasm for use of the electric chair, lethal injection, and the gas chamber. Relatively little effort has been directed at enlisting people from law enforcement into the struggle.[85]

In contrast to law-enforcement people, victim's relatives are rather well represented within abolitionist groups. Soon after her mother-in-law's murder in 1972, Marie Deans founded an organization specifically for such people: Murder Victim's Families for Reconciliation. MVFR is much smaller than the 40,000-member Parents of Murdered Children (POMC), which has no position on capital punishment but which has many outspoken proponents of the sanction on its membership roles.[86] And unlike POMC, MVFR welcomes the families of death row prisoners. Until recently, MVFR was merely a loose network of individuals who were willing to speak out against the death penalty in spite of their loss. The utility of such an organization to the movement was obvious, and in 1987 the NCADP offered to provide Deans with assistance. MVFR later requested and received help from the NCADP in developing the organization further and in staging a highly visible public event to demonstrate that revenge is not a universal impulse among survivors.[87] That event was the 1992 Journey of Hope: 17 days of activities held throughout Indiana and in cities of neighboring states sponsored by MVFR and 17 other groups. About 300 people participated.[88] A core group of MVFR people spent a day in each city – Gary, South Bend, Fort Wayne, and Bloomington, Indiana; Chicago, Illinois; Louisville, Kentucky; and others – staging marches, rallies, concerts, and film showings, planting trees "as living symbols of hope and life,"[89] and speaking with community groups and church congregations. They emphasized their own stories, and stressed the message that healing lies with forgiveness, not revenge. The events were designed to stimulate discussion and awareness. In the words of organizer Bill Pelke, whose grandmother Ruth Pelke was killed by 16-year-old Paula Cooper and her companions: "We're trying to touch hearts, and we think that will change some minds" (quoted by DeAgostino 1993).

The Journey of Hope was deemed a success by MVFR and its supporters. It attracted considerable local press coverage, including more than 60 newspaper articles and 30 broadcast interviews. It was even credited by an Indiana public defender with helping to avoid death sentences in three capital trials that were taking place that summer. Inspired by the experience, the MVFR board conducted a second Journey event in Georgia during October 1992, and have planned others for California (1995) and Virginia (1996). The progress of the ADPM in mobilizing sympathetic families will be greatly affected by the success or failure of MVFR's efforts.

Mobilizing Students

By the time Ronald Reagan was nearing the end of his first term as president, college students had long since relinquished their role as social change agents in American society. The barricades of the 1960s were abandoned as individual concerns such as employment prospects in a changing economy replaced the altruism of an earlier generation. The minority of students in the 1980s who did have activist tendencies seemed more drawn to issues like the struggles against apartheid and environmental degradation. They were conspicuously absent in the movement against capital punishment.

During Jack Healey's term as executive director of AIUSA in the 1980s and early 1990s, the recruitment of students into AI's human rights work was a priority. A special category of local AI group, the *campus* group, was created and pushed by Amnesty organizers. These outreach efforts were given a major boost by the 1988 "Human Rights Now" concert tour that AIUSA organized and staged. Popular musical performers such as Peter Gabriel and Sting spread the message of Amnesty International in packed arenas and sports stadia from Rio de Janeiro to Paris to East Rutherford, New Jersey. While the death penalty was hardly the central focus of these efforts, neither was it absent from them — Magdaleno "Len" Rose-Avila, the director of AIUSA's Death Penalty Program at the time, served as deputy media director for the tour. The result of all of this was a rapid growth in student membership.

To channel as many of these new student members as possible into anti-death penalty work, a National Student Conference on the Death Penalty was held at Northeastern University on November 4, 1989. More than 500 students attended. They were briefed on the death penalty in America and abroad, heard addresses by Jack Healey, former death row inmate Shabaka Sundiata Waolimi and others, and participated in an array of workshops and panels. The atmosphere at the Boston conference was described as "alive" and "riveting."[90]

The long-term impact of AI's outreach to college and high school students for the ADPM is difficult to assess. By 1992, students were the most rapidly growing segment of AIUSA's membership, and over 2,000 college and high school groups had been established. But such campus groups have turned out to be somewhat unpredictable. Some are energetic and active, while some are not. And many alternate between the two extremes: "On any given day a campus group may exist or not exist; on any given day it may be two people or it may be 200 people."[91] It is also difficult to assess how much energy most campus groups devote to the death penalty, as distinct from AI's broader concerns. The best guess is that in most campus groups this issue takes a back seat to more sympathetic cases, such as torture victims and prisoners of conscience. But from AI's point of view, large numbers of young people are at least being exposed to the international human rights dimensions of capital punishment. Time will tell whether this will prove crucial to the debate in coming years.

Mobilizing African Americans

The outreach effort with the most far-reaching potential, at least in terms of the numbers of people that might be brought in, has been directed at minorities. Logic dictates that African Americans would make up the core of the ADPM; after all, the death penalty has historically been applied disproportionately to convicts who are black and poor. And although offender-based discrimination seems to have abated, the hidden message of more recent capital-sentencing patterns in the United States has been that the lives of nonwhite murder victims are worth less than those of whites; killers of African Americans are seldom sentenced to die and even less often executed. Other inequities in law enforcement, especially incidents of alleged police brutality like the Rodney King affair, have spawned tremendous resentment and even violence in black communities. One might reasonably expect the lopsided application of capital punishment to have the same effect. But contrary to expectations, the movement to abolish capital punishment has always been overwhelmingly white and middle class.

The need to diversify the ADPM has been discussed for years by its leaders. As in so many other areas, Amnesty International was the first to follow through. The hiring of Charles Fulwood, an African American with a southern civil rights background, as national death penalty coordinator in 1984, was, in part, motivated by the need to increase the participation of people of color. And when Fulwood moved on to become AIUSA's communications director in 1987, he was replaced with a Mexican American, Magdaleno Rose-Avila, whose strong community-organizing talents had been honed both in the farm workers' movement and as AIUSA's southern regional director. Both men made outreach to people of color and to the poor a high priority.

Fulwood's 1984 strategy paper included minorities as one of the specific population groups to be targeted for public education about the human rights dimensions of capital punishment. Fulwood and Rose-Avila both worked to establish links with African American organizations, especially the Southern Christian Leadership Conference and the National Black Police Association. SCLC and AIUSA jointly sponsored a "Death Penalty Awareness Day" in Atlanta on June 29, 1987, during which more than 200 leaders from religious, civil rights, and abolitionist groups met one another and discussed strategy for working against capital punishment. The event was intended "to merge the civil rights movement with the human rights movement on the issue of the death penalty."[92] The SCLC, whose expertise in organizing marches and demonstrations spanned four decades, was called on for help with planning and logistics for the Starke to Atlanta march in 1990. Rev. Joseph Lowery and Rev. C. T. Vivian of the SCLC and Ronald Hampton of the NBPA have each spoken on behalf of abolition both in the United States and abroad.

The Supreme Court's 1987 *McCleskey* ruling, which struck down the use of statistical evidence of bias in capital sentencing as a constitutional issue, has been used by anti-death penalty organizations as a means of raising the consciousness of the African American community. AIUSA suggested that the death penalty coordinators of its local groups discuss the ruling with minority organizations in their communities and urge them, along with the minority media, to place capital punishment on their agendas. Amnesty International got the National Conference of Black Mayors to pass a resolution calling for a moratorium on executions "while effective alternative measures of dealing with violent crime are researched, selected, and written into law. . . . " The resolution was based, in part, on the "overwhelming evidence that the death penalty is applied in a discriminatory manner against racial and economically disadvantaged minorities . . . ," as well as on international human rights considerations.[93] The Congressional Black Caucus also became quite active on capital punishment in the aftermath of *McCleskey,* especially in terms of pushing for a Racial Justice Act in federal anticrime legislation. Coretta Scott King appeared at a press conference with Rose-Avila and Representative John Conyers to discuss a legislative response to *McCleskey.*

Another aspect of the attempt to mobilize ethnic minority sentiment against executions was AIUSA's "Swainsboro Project," undertaken during AI's worldwide 1989 Campaign for the Abolition of the Death Penalty. The Swainsboro Project focused on one area of Georgia, the Middle Judicial Circuit, chosen to be a laboratory for AIUSA to develop its strategy for changing public opinion on capital punishment in the United States. The circuit comprised four rural Georgia counties—Washington, Candler, Jefferson, and Toombs—"the buckle on the death belt." Support for the death penalty there was known to be overwhelming. There was a history of putting black defendants on trial for their lives before all-white juries and providing them with inadequate defense counsel—almost eight out of every ten death sentences meted out by the state courts there were given to black men—and sentencing juveniles and mentally retarded persons to die.[94]

The project had something of the character of the 1964 Mississippi Freedom Summer, though on a much smaller scale. It began with a "poll," in which residents of the Swainsboro area were canvassed in person and by telephone regarding their feelings about the death penalty. In the months that followed, a constant stream of AI volunteers descended on the area and conducted intensive public education. They met with justice officials, local politicians, religious and civic leaders, and business people. AI staff and members from overseas, including Secretary-General Ian Martin, were brought in for appearances and media events (Minor 1989). Civil rights figure Rev. C. T. Vivian spoke on human rights, racism, and the death penalty. Amnesty members directed letters to local officials and media expressing AI's concerns.

The NCADP also began making efforts during recent years to increase the participation of African Americans and other ethnic minorities in the movement. The coalition's outreach committee was initially formed to find ways to draw law enforcement personnel, prosecutors, sympathetic governors, and celebrities into the movement against the death penalty, but around 1989 its focus shifted toward the ethnic diversification of the movement. In 1992, the coalition adopted the policy that each of its affiliates should be committed to inclusiveness and should seek to diversify along the lines of race, ethnicity, gender, disability, and sexual orientation.[95] And for the first time, the NCADP included a diversity workshop in the agenda of its 1992 national conference.

Some abolitionists, including a few NCADP board members and affiliates, have become concerned that the emphasis on diversity is becoming an end in itself and thus diverting the movement from its primary goal. Most of the dissatisfaction, however, came from those who are frustrated with the lack of progress the movement has thus far made in involving African Americans, Latinos, and poor people in the fight. There are two basic explanations for this lack of progress. One view is that minorities are extremely difficult to mobilize against capital punishment regardless of what sort of recruitment drive the ADPM mounts. They are difficult to mobilize, first, because there are so many competing issues that impact minority communities: poverty, employment, housing, and so on.[96] These issues affect millions of persons, whereas capital punishment affects a relative handful. So in view of the more pressing problems they face, most black, Latino, and poor people and the organizations that represent them are not likely to make the abolition of capital punishment a top priority. In addition, anger about violent crime is just as acute among people of color as anyone else. It *should* be, because, as

Hugo Bedau points out, African Americans are far more likely to be violent crime victims than members of any other demographic category in America:

> Probably the simplest explanation is that blacks throughout this period have also been the principle *victims* of the crimes perpetrated by blacks. Middle-class black Americans and even lower-class black Americans are increasingly convinced of what *white* Americans are convinced of: that the death penalty may not be the first line of defense — the cop on the beat is the first line of defense — but it may be the last line of defense. So attitudes have shifted.[97]

From this perspective then, it is unlikely that massive levels of active minority support for abolition are within reach. The ADPM should continue its efforts in that direction, but not expect too much.

The competing interpretation of low minority involvement is that anti-death penalty groups either haven't tried hard enough to surmount these obstacles or that they have gone about it in the wrong way. This is the perspective of two of the most prominent African Americans in the movement's upper echelons: Charles Fulwood and Ronald Hampton. Fulwood, who left Amnesty International to join the staff of the National Resources Defense Council, believes that there has not been a sustained effort to maintain the links to civil rights groups that he and Magdeleno Rose-Avila forged:

> . . . we had gotten to the point where we could pick up the phone and say "We want Joe Lowery here" or "We want this" or "We want you to give us space on [your agenda]." I got C. T. Vivian, who used to be one of Doctor King's top lieutenants, and I sent him throughout Europe speaking about the death penalty in the U.S. during [Amnesty's] U.S. campaign. That's what *I* mean. Putting Scharlette [Holdman] and a woman from South Africa on the plane to travel with the world [concert] tour. I'm talking about substantive involvement, on their turf *and* on your turf. And on neutral turf. And I don't think that's happening anymore. And it really sort of infuriates me, because I know that Magdaleno and I spent a lot of time on building those relationships. And the fact that they've been dropped, or that they haven't been nurtured properly, really pisses me off! Because that means the movement gets set back. It means it's gonna be doubly hard to do it again![98]

Fulwood also feels that the white-dominated anti-death penalty movement cannot expect civil rights and other minority organizations to participate consistently in strategies they had no hand in designing. He sees many of the abolitionists' overtures to the black organizations and leaders as paternalistic:

> . . . some of the efforts that have been made have been incompetent efforts. Because they have been using old paternalistic approaches — sort of assuming that this is *their* issue, and "I'm inviting you to sort of be involved in *my* issue." Well it's *not* your issue! What are you talking about? You [must] go to people and say "We've been working on this and we've gone as far as we can. And we need another piece to this. We want you to join us in a *partnership*." I know that some of this has been done. To be fair, the black organizations have not responded the way they should have responded. But I think there are ways of holding them accountable, too. Yes, their plate is full and

they've got a lot of issues to take care of. But this ought to be up there. It ought to be up there. And actually, abolitionists give black elected officials an easy way out by just not being consistent, by just making *one* overture — "Would you come and speak on this panel?" or "Would you attend this press conference?" I'm talking about *real relationships*. And that takes time. Don't send around a letter and say "sign this" along with five other organizations and expect them to be in a relationship. Those things have to be built, they have to be nurtured, and they have to be mutually accountable. And I don't think that that's been done. I don't think that that's been done at all. Certain *individuals* [in the ADPM] have hooked up and done some good things. I know Scharlette [Holdman] has, and I know a lot of other organizations around the country have cooperated on various things. But my sense is, and certainly my experience with Amnesty and with the National Coalition, is that its just not happening.[99]

Similar views are held by Ron Hampton, director of the National Black Police Association, who has worked with both the NCADP and AI. Hampton believes a large part of the problem is that many white activists do not feel comfortable working with poor and minority people on the latter's own turf and in their own terms. Magdaleno Rose-Avila agrees. Both applaud the NACDP's decision to hold diversity training at recent national conferences, a step that may help rectify matters.[100] Hampton also contends that AI and the NCADP need to increase the number of African Americans, not just on their boards of directors, but on their *staffs* as well. This is where the real work of fighting the death penalty gets done. And most important, they need to do a better job of raising the priority of the death penalty in the black community by tying it into the whole constellation of issues that matter there: jobs, better education, and recreation for young people, and racial bias in the criminal justice system as a whole — from the police to the courts to the prisons. The National Black Police Association attempts to deal with this broader range of issues, and its stance against capital punishment is in that context. But as we will see in chapter 4, there are structural constraints on the capacity of existing ADPM groups to broaden the context of the issue. In any case, outreach to those communities that are most directly affected by the use of capital punishment in America is of the utmost importance to the ADPM. Hampton is insistent on this point.

We need to go out and organize the people who are disproportionately affected by this thing and then bring them in. And once you wake them up, you have awakened a giant. And *they* will turn this thing around because they are the ones affected by it. So you turn the oppressed into an army and they will march.[101]

Charles Fulwood agrees wholeheartedly with Hampton on the importance of bringing people of color into both the rank-and-file of the abolitionist movement and its leadership:

I honestly think that if abolitionists in these mainstream or human rights organizations think that they're gonna be able to make serious inroads or abolish the death penalty without substantial participation *and leadership* from the black community and Latino community, they're really fantasizing. They're really fantasizing. It ain't gonna happen. It's not gonna happen because there's a certain credibility, and there's a certain amount of expertise that those communities bring to this particular issue. By expertise, I mean organizing expertise and lobbying expertise. . . . [T]here is no change, no social change that has occurred in this country, where people of color have not been on the cutting edge. And if abolitionists think that an issue like this is going to be fundamentally transformed without those communities being a part of the leadership and being a part of the participation, they're really missing the point.[102]

The importance of the African American community was never greater than in the fall of 1992, when a referendum to reinstate the death penalty in Washington, D.C., was introduced. Following the murder of a white aide, Alabama Senator Richard C. Shelby — also white — introduced a bill requiring that the matter be decided by D.C. voters. The U.S. Congress, which has jurisdiction over the District of Columbia, passed the bill only a month before the election. This left opponents very little time to get organized. A "Coalition to VOTE NO on the Death Penalty Referendum" was quickly formed, led by local religious and political figures, and supported by the national anti-death penalty groups headquartered in Washington: the ACLU Capital Punishment Project, the NCADP, and the NBPA. Retired Metropolitan Police Chief Isaac Fulwood, Jr., Congressional delegate Eleanor Holmes Norton, and Mayor Sharon Pratt Kelly spoke out against reinstatement during the short, intense campaign. Preachers railed against it from their pulpits, and "Thou Shalt Not Kill" posters appeared throughout the city.[103]

Washington, D.C., has a very large African American population. It also has the highest murder rate of any city in the nation — 80.6 per 100,000 in 1991 (U.S. Department of Justice, Bureau of Justice Statistics 1992a:372). Polls taken shortly before the election showed a majority of voters in favor of bringing capital punishment back. But on November 3, the measure was defeated by a two-to-one margin. The explanation for this outcome is complicated. Some of the opposition was not so much to the death penalty, but rather to the manner in which it was being "forced down the throats" of local residents by Congress. It is also possible that the voting would have been less lopsided had the referendum not originated with a white southerner, reacting to the murder of another white person, in a city where the killing of young African Americans is a daily occurrence. But significantly, it was in predominantly *black* precincts — both middle-class and poor, high-crime neighborhoods — where the rejection of the death penalty referendum was most resounding. The margin was approximately three-to-one there, while it was much closer in affluent white precincts (McCraw 1992; Sanchez 1992). This was very good news for abolitionists. Capital punishment had been driven back by a popular vote rather than through the "back door" of the courts or the office of a courageous governor. It had been rejected in a city with an extremely high rate of violent crime. And it had been rejected most emphatically by the city's large African American population most threatened by street crime.

4

Framing Disputes in the Movement Against Capital Punishment

Disagreements occur within all social movements over the best way to present issues or the best strategies to employ. For instance, labor activists once fell into two broad categories: those who demanded worker control of the means of production and those who sought only the right to bargain with their employers for better wages and working conditions. In the 1960s, the civil rights movement was torn by questions of whether racial integration or self-determination was the proper objective of African Americans and whether violent tactics were ever justified. Some environmentalists portray the natural environment as "natural resources" to be "conserved"; for others, it is a separate realm over which humankind has no claim of proprietorship. At times, disputes such as these have broken movements apart, whereas in other cases such disagreement has been downplayed in order to preserve at least a modicum of unity.

Robert Benford (1993) has devised a useful vocabulary for understanding internal divisions within movements. Based on the frame alignment perspective, he conceptualized such disagreements as "frame disputes," and identified three major forms they may take. *Diagnostic* disputes are disagreements over the correct way of perceiving the problem that a movement is addressing. The nuclear disarmament groups Benford studied, for example, clashed over whether to focus on nuclear weapons alone or to address factors that increased the threat of military conflict between nations. *Prognostic* disputes have to do with either the solutions a movement endorses or the strategies and tactics it employs. Some of Benford's antinuclear organizations wanted to endorse a moratorium on the installation of medium-range ballistic missiles in Europe, whereas more radical activists saw this as a sellout. The latter would settle for nothing less than stopping further weapons deployment once and for all, and did not balk at calling for the use of illegal forms of civil disobedience to

117

further that objective. *Frame resonance* disputes concern the most effective ways to win over uncommitted people to the cause. Antinuclear activists were sometimes at odds over the need for consistency in their message, the people chosen as spokespersons for the movement, and the most effective ways to make the seemingly distant threat of nuclear weapons relevant to the day-to-day concerns of local audiences (Benford 1993:686–694).

Perhaps because of its relatively small size, the ADPM is characterized by remarkably little infighting. There is almost no open sparring between movement factions. Meetings and conferences rarely erupt in heated arguments. Nevertheless, we have already seen that abolitionists have not been of one mind on a number of key issues. For example, the incremental strategy, which called for chipping away at public support on certain subissues like the execution of the mentally retarded while putting the goal of total abolition on the back burner was the subject of a prognostic framing dispute. So was the matter of how much effort to expend on outreach to African Americans and Latinos. Chapter 4 examines a number of other matters that have been more or less contentious within the anti-death penalty movement at the national level: What should be the proper roles of the lawyers handling particular capital cases and the policy activists battling in legislatures and the press, and which should ultimately call the shots? Should the movement force Americans to confront the inhumanity of capital punishment by "humanizing" death row convicts, or should individual cases be avoided in favor of the larger issues? Must opponents of state-sanctioned killing put their bodies on the line through civil disobedience, as their precursors in other movements have? To have any credibility in a crime-weary society, must abolitionists advocate specific alternatives to the death penalty in cases of first-degree murder — in particular, incarceration for life without opportunity for parole? What types of coalitions should be built to fight the death penalty? And finally, can the ADPM do battle against capital punishment in isolation from other issues, or must it go beyond single-issue politics? The resolution of these issues will shape the movement in the future, and could well determine the ultimate fate of capital punishment in the United States.

Litigators and Abolitionists: Who Calls the Shots?

In recent years, it has made sense to refer to "abolitionists" and the attorneys who specialize in death penalty cases as two distinct groups. This was less true in the 1960s and 1970s, when the litigators in the movement were using test cases systematically in hopes of gradually ending *all* executions. In those days, the LDF lawyers were themselves the leaders of the anti-death penalty movement. But as the federal courts began to reject their broad constitutional claims, lawyers returned to the more modest task of saving the lives of their clients one by one rather than as a class. The broader objective of getting rid of the death penalty — or more realistically, trying to prevent its expansion — now falls to the activist sector of the movement. It is in this sector that AIUSA, the NCADP, and the ACLU operate.

Not that the litigator and abolitionist sectors are *completely* distinct groups. The lawyers and the activists in the movement know each other, they sometimes speak at each other's conferences[1] and work together on projects. They even venture into each other's domains from time to time, as when Death Penalty Focus of California mounted an intense campaign to keep Robert Alton Harris from being the first California convict to be executed,[2] and when attorneys Steven Bright and Bryan Stevenson participated in a debate of the death penalty on public television. The real distinction here is one of focus, not professional training. Several important people on the activist side of the movement are lawyers, but are engaged in public education or lobbying rather than legal representation. These include Ali Miller, director of AIUSA's Death Penalty Program from 1990 through 1993, Richard Dieter of the Death Penalty Information Center, and Diane Rust-Tierney of the ACLU Capital Punishment Project.

Nevertheless, most policy activists and lawyers now differ in their primary responsibilities within the movement as well as in the techniques they use. Although they each recognize the other's indispensability, there remains a residue of tension between the two groups. In the broadest terms, this tension relates to the issue of which objective should take precedence: the short-term goal of preventing and overturning death sentences or the long-term goal of abolition. Nonlegal abolitionists are sometimes impatient with the lawyers and paralegals for failing to see the big picture and for being unable to concede that the law is not the solution to all problems. As Henry Schwarzschild wryly puts it, "it took the ACLU 20 years to figure out that Earl Warren was dead." And other than Anthony Amsterdam and a few others, it took the capital defense bar a very long time to accept fully that the courts will never abolish the death penalty until judges think they have the backing of the American people.[3] For their part, litigators have tended to look at the activists in the movement as relatively unsophisticated second-stringers. But AIUSA's Ali Miller feels that this has been less so since the litigators' successes in court slowed to a trickle.

> . . . for years the strategy was challenging the cases in the courts, taking it to the Supreme Court, getting the Supreme Court to rule, . . . slow[ing] down executions, revers[ing] death sentences. And the litigators' attitude was: "Out of our faces! You're a bunch of do-gooders. You don't have anything to contribute. We've got this one covered!" In the last five years, that has definitely radically shifted, because the Supreme Court has shifted. Now everybody's just touting the death penalty, and the cases are just becoming overwhelming. So even now the litigators are turning and saying "Oops, can you help us with some community organizing? Can you come in here? Can you do this? Can you do that?" Whereas before, the image that I have is of [the abolitionists] sort of running around looking for scraps. That's changing.[4]

The people on the legal side have also accused activists of being indifferent to the real-world carnage of the death penalty, preferring to go on making the same ineffective philosophical arguments they have been making for decades rather than trying to save real human beings from the executioner.[5] And because the requirements of successful litigation and successful policy advocacy can be contradictory, lawyers complain that ill-conceived actions by anti-death penalty activists can be lethal for their clients. Consider the hypothetical case of a mentally retarded African American awaiting execution for raping and murdering a white woman. Imagine further that there are reasons to believe that the man is innocent, and that he now alleges he was coerced by police into confessing to the crime, but that these matters were not raised by his court-appointed defense attorney at trial. Such a case would be enormously useful to abolitionists, illustrating several key themes of their message: racial discrimination, mental retardation, innocence, and ineffective counsel. Activists would certainly wish to use this case to educate the public about the death penalty, and they might also wish to direct a flood of mail to the governor, seeking a new trial. But the attorney for that same inmate might have a very different agenda. She might well conclude that none of these issues stood much chance *in court,* and she might very much prefer to maintain a low profile for her client for fear that attention would lead to the signing of a death warrant or alienate the very judges who will weigh any remaining appeals. Margaret Vandiver, who has fought the death penalty as both a paralegal and an activist, recalls how a well-known defense attorney put this:

> Millard Farmer had a great saying in the early 80s about highlighting individual cases: "If you're trying to smuggle somebody across the border, why would you shine a floodlight on him?" If you focus this kind of public attention on the courts, they're gonna resent it and they're gonna be more stubborn than ever and they're gonna rule against you. You go in quietly. You do as much as you can behind the scenes. You keep the public focus *off* of it, and you settle it that way. And he very strongly argued that in the early 80s, when a lot of us were still trying to spotlight cases.[6]

Furthermore, according to Vandiver, lawyers often fear that the actions or statements of anti-death penalty activists may foul up their carefully crafted legal strategies:

> Suppose the person on death row writes you a tearful letter, and you think to yourself "Wow — I'll release this to the media! This is great!" And you do that, and it turns out that the lawyers' strategy is to claim that the man is mentally incompetent or insane or mentally retarded. Well, maybe he didn't even write that letter! Maybe he paid the guy in the next cell to write it. You don't know. But if you do something publicly, you can contradict precisely what the lawyers are trying to do. An example of that is when Ted Bundy was going through his final warrant. At least one prominent abolitionist stated to the media that Bundy was manipulating the legal system, on the same day that his lawyers were frantically running into court saying that he was mentally incompetent and shouldn't be executed. That kind of clash is really deadly.[7]

In most cases, activists are more than willing to defer to defense counsel when the fate of a death-sentenced inmate may hang in the balance. It is a cardinal rule that no action should be taken to publicize any aspect of a particular case without at least consulting with the attorney in charge. But on occasion, activists ultimately refuse to give the attorney the final say, particularly when they perceive that something much larger than the individual client is at stake. One notable clash between the two arms of the movement occurred in California in the early 1990s. Executions were about to resume in the state, but many sympathetic Californians were complacent. They found it difficult to fathom that the Golden State would go beyond *talking* about capital punishment and join in what was then mostly a *southern* practice — actually killing people. Lest pro-death penalty sentiment appear even more overwhelming than it actually was, Death Penalty Focus, the ACLU, and AIUSA were chomping at the bit to begin large-scale organizing to overcome this complacency. To do so, they needed to be able to talk about Robert Alton Harris, the inmate who was first in line for a seat in the gas chamber. But Harris's attorneys were pursuing a clemency strategy, and they did not want the activists even to mention his name in the press until they gave the go-ahead. From the organizers' perspective, that would be much too late. They could not wait until the last minute to focus the state's attention on important issues the case raised.

The facts about Robert Alton Harris to which the public had access were extremely unattractive ones. On July 5, 1978, only six months after his release from prison for another murder, Harris and his brother Danny abducted two teenage boys from a fast-food restaurant. They needed the boys' car for use in a robbery they were planning. The Harris brothers drove the victims to a nearby reservoir, where Robert shot the boys and then nonchalantly finished eating their hamburgers. Danny Harris testified against his brother and was sentenced to prison. Robert Harris went to San Quentin to wait execution.

Abolitionists wanted to focus attention on unfairness of the death penalty itself, in part by showing Californians a side of Robert Harris that few had seen. Fetal Alcohol Syndrome (FAS) had, in the opinion of many experts, compromised Harris's ability to understand the consequences of his actions, and had contributed greatly to his lifelong pattern of trouble with the law. Additionally, his parents, and later his mother's boyfriend, had subjected him to severe physical abuse when he was a child — he had suffered severe beatings even before his first birthday, and his father once threatened him with a firearm. None of these facts had been introduced either at Harris's trial or on appeal, nor had they been widely publicized by the news media. This information was part of the strategy to persuade Governor Pete Wilson to grant clemency in the case; the attorneys wanted it to be made public, but not until they thought the time was right. Death Penalty Focus leaders saw this as an unreasonable constraint. According to DPF director Pat Clark, "lawyers feel that two weeks before an execution they should be able to call on you and you should be able to get people together and do your thing. It just doesn't work that way!" And the California activists also believed that the information about Harris's background was crucial for setting the tone of the larger death penalty debate there.

Death Penalty Focus did not totally disregard the wishes of Harris's lawyers, but it finally decided to do what its leadership thought was best in the long run. Among other things, this meant using their own timetable, rather than that of the legal team, to publicize details of Robert Harris's life and his diminished capacity for self-control. According to Clark, the very attorneys who had tried to prevent DPF from charting its own course later offered their congratulations for a well-conceived campaign.[8] In the end, the convict was executed — but not before several stays had been ordered by the federal courts and nationwide publicity had been achieved. The Harris case became an important element of the capital punishment controversy, not just in California, but from coast to coast.

The prognostic dispute between the lawyers and nonlegal activists in the ADPM is not likely to go away. Capital defense lawyers are much like primary-care physicians, whose first responsibility is to their sick patients. Activists are more akin to medical researchers whose job it is to develop treatments or cures for the diseases themselves, even though that may require withholding potentially lifesaving treatments from some patients who might benefit from them. The most likely future for the movement is one in which those working primarily in public education and on the legislative front will continue to assert their independence from litigators. This does not mean that death-sentenced inmates will become mere pawns in the larger effort to abolish the institution of capital punishment. Indeed, as we shall see in the next portion of this chapter, a sense of identification with the people on death row shows no signs of abating any time soon. Nor does it mean that activists will resist efforts to *coordinate* their activities with those of the capital defense bar, for such coordination is essential.[9] But after years of domination by courtroom strategists who have apparently failed to make dramatic progress against the death penalty, the policy activists are insisting on a more equal partnership.

"Humanizing the Convict"

Jimmy Lee Gray committed a horrible crime. He molested and killed a three-year-old girl. He did this while on parole from an Arizona prison for killing his sixteen-year-old girlfriend. A lot of people believe the death penalty is designed especially for the person who commits such terrible crimes.

One problem with the abstract notion of eye-for-an-eye vengeance against child molesters and killers is that this notion doesn't consider the fact that the condemned man or woman is still a human being, is still capable of change and growth. However, I feared the image of Jimmy Lee Gray the child molester was frozen in the minds of the public and the politicians. In my visits with Jimmy Lee Gray over the years I found him to be a man of considerable sensitivity and depth. He was deeply troubled by his crimes and freely admitted he needed help. Indeed, he made it clear to his pastor and me that he did not ever want to be released unless he received the psychological help he needed. This soft-spoken man, a writer of poetry and prose, wrestled with the responsibility for his past actions from the perspective of genuine Christian faith. Jimmy Lee was a devout Christian who had committed crimes, who was intensely aware of his responsibility for those actions and the problems

that contributed to his actions, and who sought help in getting the treatment
he needed to keep himself from ever committing such acts again. This was the
man the state of Mississippi wanted to kill. (Ingle 1990:106)

The author of these words, Reverend Joseph B. Ingle, is probably the
foremost among a group of abolitionists for whom the death penalty is a
personal as well as a political issue. Ingle, Marie Deans, Scharlette Holdman,
Margaret Vandiver, Helen Prejean, Michael and Lisa Radelet, and others have
worked extensively with convicts under sentence of death. They have spent
time inside prisons, where issues like capital punishment and habeas reform
are palpable. They have had to say good-bye to men they have become closely
acquainted with, knowing that those men would be led away and killed in a
matter of hours. Some of them, in fact, have witnessed the execution of a
condemned inmate at his request. They have shared the pain of the men's
families and made arrangements for inmates' funerals. But it is Ingle, more
than any other prominent movement figure, who has spoken as openly of his
empathy for condemned human beings as for his hatred of the death penalty
itself.

Other prominent figures in the abolitionist movement, including Henry
Schwarzschild and Hugo Bedau, have met few, if any, death-sentenced inmates. They have chosen to keep their distance from death row for a variety
of reasons, including both temperament and principle. The two segments of
the abolitionist community are hardly enemies. They work together and are
often good friends. They rarely clash openly about the matter, and when
asked, generally state that the movement is strengthened by the presence of
both the Ingles and the Schwarzschilds and the respective styles they represent.
Nevertheless, they have divergent views on how central condemned inmates
should be in their framing of the capital punishment issue.

The difference between these two outlooks is part philosophic, part strategic. The philosophical dimension can be seen most clearly in an ongoing
debate between Ingle and Schwarzschild themselves. Joseph Ingle came to the
anti-death penalty movement via his participation in prison ministry. As director of the Southern Coalition on Jails and Prisons, he started a Tennessee
Death Row Visitation Program in 1976. "Free world visitors" were recruited,
largely through churches, to provide outside contact with men on death row
(Lozier 1976). This was his first experience with the death penalty, and he
came to know many of the men awaiting execution in Tennessee extremely
well. Because the South pursued the resumption of executions with much less
delay than the northern and western regions, Ingle and his colleagues were not
only faced with the need to influence capital-sentencing legislation in that
region, but they were also confronted with the daunting task of finding lawyers to handle the appeals of men who would soon die without them. His
face-to-face encounters with prisoners under immediate threat of execution
had a profound effect on his view of the issue. Capital punishment is not an
abstraction for him, and it is not first and foremost a policy issue. It is a

day-to-day reality, accompanied by the urgent need to help condemned people and their families deal with very immediate needs and fears. Ingle developed deep friendships with persons that most of us perceive, through the cloudy lens of popular culture, as unambiguously monstrous creatures. Like others with extensive death row experience, he sees another side: he knows these inmates as complicated people, frequently the products of tragic lives, who suffer hurts and fears and regrets—and who often agonize over the effect their predicament is having on their loved ones. For Ingle, the message of abolitionism begins with this other side. His position comes through quite clearly in comments he made after being nominated for the 1988 Nobel Peace Prize:

> The death penalty is not simply an issue with me. Rather, I see the faces of friends I have come to know and love over the years in visits to death rows throughout the South. Some of those faces are now tangible only in memory because the state killed them. . . . John Spenkelink—who turned down the prosecutor's offer of second degree murder and who asked me the day before his execution to not forget all the others on "the Row"; Bob Sullivan—an ardent Boston Red Sox fan from Massachusetts whose final words reiterated his claim of innocence . . . ; James Adams—who was innocent and whose greatest crime was to be black and poor in the South; David Washington—convicted of killing three people yet a man who grieved for his victims and never forgave himself for his crimes; four men of the seventeen killed in Florida's electric chair. John Evans and Wayne Ritter—John the braggart yet so vulnerable and Wayne, John's follower, who never actually killed anyone; two of the three men strapped into the yellow electric chair in Alabama. Jimmy Lee Gray and Edward Earl Johnson—Jimmy consumed by guilt for his crime and the victim of childhood abuse from a mother who sought his execution; Edward Earl who was innocent of his charges but who was killed by cyanide gas in the Mississippi gas chamber as was Jimmy Lee. Frank Coppola—who grew weary of life on death row in Virginia and dropped his appeals to end the agony of continued publicity for his family; Morris Mason—a manchild with an I.Q. of 66, diagnosed a paranoid schizophrenic by state doctors three times over an eight year period; Frank and Morris were electrocuted in the electric chair located in the basement of the Virginia State Penitentiary . . . ; Robert Wayne Williams—a black man tried by an all white jury who didn't intentionally kill anyone and who repeatedly lost court appeals by one vote; Tim Baldwin—Robert Wayne's good friend on death row who turned down the prosecutor's offer for second degree murder so he could prove his innocence with a jury trial . . . ; finally, I come to my native state of North Carolina which with poisoned injection has killed three people. Two of the Tar Heel state's victims in the Central Prison death chamber were James Hutchins and Velma Barfield. James, a hot tempered mountain man killed lawmen in a feud and Velma, a woman who still breaks my heart with sorrow when I recall her fate.
>
> So, yes, I am honored by the nomination for the Nobel Peace Prize. But the honor is really for the people I just recalled and the 79 others who have been killed by the state since this grisly practice resumed. And it is for the

almost 2,000 other men, women, and children we have condemned to die in this country. (Ingle 1987)

Identification with condemned inmates also occurs among people in the abolition movement whose contact with those inmates is not so frequent or intimate as it was with Ingle. Newsletters and literary magazines from death row are followed closely by some abolitionists, especially *Endeavor,* a quarterly publication produced collectively by prisoners in several states. The NCADP publication *Lifelines* often carries articles and poetry by death-sentenced inmates. Their paintings and handicrafts are sometimes offered for sale through ADP publications and conferences. And some activists correspond with pen pals on death row, in order to provide them with emotional support in their ordeal. Since 1977, Rachel and Bob Gross of the NCADP have promoted such correspondence through their Death Row Support Project (Gross 1984). The development of an emotional bond with those under sentence of death often happens as a result of encounters that shatter the one-dimensional stereotype of violent offenders, and some movement people are aware of the bind in which this puts them. Margaret Vandiver admits that she and some others in the abolitionist movement occasionally tend

to become so personally involved in the lives of people on death row that we sometimes may emphasize their *good* qualities more than perhaps we ought to. And it becomes particularly easy to do this when the crime happened almost 20 years ago and the person you're dealing with is profoundly different from who he was when he committed the crime. But it's a balance that people have a hard time keeping. I have been taking students from the office up to the lifer's group up at [a nearby penitentiary] and watching them go through it — _____ and _____ are acting like those guys in the Lifer's group are their good friends. They want to go hang out at the prison . . . ! And they're only seeing what is there now. They're not thinking about what happened before. It's very easy for people who are kind of open to thinking the best of people and who are open-minded to go out and meet some of these men and think "Oh, these are great guys!"[10]

Henry Schwarzschild, former director of the ACLU Capital Punishment Project, exemplifies a very different attitude toward death-sentenced inmates. Schwarzschild does not lack compassion. Indeed, he struggled in the final hours of Gary Gilmore, John Spenkelink, Jesse Bishop, and others, supporting the legal battles to save their lives. But Schwarzschild nevertheless sees the death penalty as a social, political, and moral question that is much larger than the convicted killers whose lives it seeks to take (Schwarzschild and Kendall 1985). In 1982, as Texas was preparing to make Charlie Brooks the first victim of lethal injection, Schwarzschild told a reporter

I try to let people understand, and it's hard to get across, that I don't do this [work] because I like these people. I've never laid eyes on Charlie Brooks, and I don't intend to. I never met Gary Gilmore. I'm appalled by who they are and what they've done. . . . I think killing someone is a bad thing to do, whether

Charlie Brooks does it or the state of Texas does it. After Hiroshima and after Auschwitz, after all the blood spilled by governments, it ought to be possible to assert that to give governments the right to kill some people is absolutely unsupportable. (Holley 1982)

Schwarzschild acknowledges that some of the people awaiting execution are undoubtedly victims of miscarriages of justice, and that others are the victims of disordered lives and even pure bad luck. But he insists that the majority are not people for whom abolitionists ought to feel great sympathy. He has expressed irritation with those who romanticize them, and who seem unable "to distinguish between the commandment to love your neighbor, including your neighbor on death row, and . . . the impulse to *like* him."[11]

The abolitionism of Joe Ingle is rooted in Christian faith and in the perception that even the most flawed human beings have some admirable qualities. Ingle would oppose the death penalty even if took only the lives of the most morally reprehensible of beings, but he might do so with less passion. For Schwarzschild, on the other hand, it is simply wrong for the government to destroy a human life, regardless of whether it does so out of tyrannical self-interest or in the name of its citizens. The qualities of those who are led into America's death chambers, their upbringing, the degree of pain and suffering they have caused, even the question of their possible innocence of the crimes they are convicted of, are morally secondary. So, ultimately, are all of the other subissues that proponents and opponents of capital punishment argue about:

We are right in trying to persuade the public, the political leadership, the legislatures and the courts that, on all these questions of deterrence and arbitrariness and error and cost of the death penalty, the evidence suggests that it ought not to be done if it's done that badly and that uselessly. The fact of the matter remains that if it were done better, it would be morally no more tolerable.

The moral issue of the death penalty is the fundamental one. It goes to the question of whether a civilized and enlightened society is entitled to use premeditated violent homicide as an instrument of social policy. Three-hundred years after the Enlightenment, fifty years after the Holocaust, forty years after the end of Stalinist totalitarianism, that notion ought to appall every rational person. (Schwarzschild 1990:499–500)

Franklin Zimring, a legal scholar who has written extensively on the death penalty and other criminal justice issues, agrees. In a 1983 *Los Angeles Times* article decrying the temptation to make heros of death row inmates, he explained his reasoning:

Never mind that condemned prisoners write poems, paint, are good to their mothers or persuasively confide that they were in another town when the execution-style slaying of the grocer and his wife occurred. The central case against state-imposed execution is the offender's humanity rather than his prior good conduct or present inventory of talents. He thinks, feels, breathes, eats, sleeps. Extinguishing humanity is the generic wrong. When not necessary, it arrogates to organized political processes a power they should not have.

It is properly beyond state power whether the accused in the dock is Adolf Hitler, Sir Thomas More or Charles Manson. But seeking out the Sir Thomas More in every Death Row cell undermines this more basic humanitarian postulate. When we search intrepidly for all the good folks on Death Row, it is almost as if we adopt a merit test for the right to escape execution. (Zimring 1983)

There is also a more pragmatic level to the question of whether or not individual convicts should be "humanized" by opponents of the death penalty. On that level, the debate represents a *frame resonance* matter: What is the political impact of statements and actions that attempt to counteract the demonic image of death row inmates? Is the institution of capital punishment weakened when abolitionists throw light on these men and women, or is it strengthened? Here, too, there are two points of view within the movement. One of these, which is probably less widespread now than a decade ago, holds that the human connection with condemned inmates is an indispensable lever with which to pry open the hearts of knee-jerk death penalty supporters. Just as a rather hazy sense of how executions are conducted makes it easier to favor capital punishment,[12] so does the demonization of death-sentenced inmates. That is, it is easier to be in favor of the extermination of convicted murderers if one assumes that they are all at high risk to kill again if freed, that they all lack remorse for what they have done, and that they have no human qualities. But if at least some of the American people can be persuaded to face death-sentenced inmates not as mythical beasts but as human beings, then the moral exclusion underlying capital punishment might be neutralized. This helped keep Caryl Chessman alive for over a decade. It was what led Doug Magee to write *Slow Coming Dark: Interviews on Death Row* (1980),[13] and it underlies the tactics employed by a number of state and local ADP groups in their clemency campaigns for particular inmates, including Robert Alton Harris. Those whose experiences in the movement have taken them behind prison walls are in the unique position of being eyewitnesses to what the vast majority of American citizens neither see nor wish to see.

But the pitfalls of sentimentalizing the issue have become apparent as the years have passed. Professional ethics require diligent defense lawyers to take the side of their clients in public, but most *activists* now seem to understand that any focusing of attention on the sympathetic qualities of inmates must be done with utmost care. Death row inmates are among the most difficult of all human beings to portray in a sympathetic light or to cast in the role of "victim." They are usually poor, are disproportionately members of minority ethnic categories, and have already been found guilty beyond a reasonable doubt of committing crimes that are sometimes so brutal as to nearly defy comprehension. Washington, D.C., political consultant and NCADP board member Earl Bender speaks for those who believe that a great deal of harm can be done when abolitionists come off as overly sympathetic to offenders:

> The movement tends to look at each person on death row as a victim, because they're about to be a victim of state-sponsored killing. That's where the public looks at us and just writes us off as bozos. Because in their view, a good 95% of these people *ought* to be there, and they have very little mercy for what they've done. When you've looked at the crimes that many of these people have committed, they're pretty heinous. And folks say "it doesn't matter that you tell me now that they're victims of Fetal Alcohol Syndrome and this and that and the other thing." And part of our problem as a movement is that by focusing on those individuals, we disconnect from everyone else![14]

In her work with death row convicts, Margaret Vandiver has seen firsthand how the appearance of misplaced loyalty can backfire. She recalls an interview she granted in Florida concerning inmate Willie Darden.[15]

> . . . I thought that I was very calm and dispassionate, and objective. And then the article came out and it said "To some people, Willie Darden is a heroic figure," and quoted me! I don't think I talked to anyone from the media for three or four years after that. I was appalled. I did a similar thing after Bob Sullivan was executed.[16] That does our position no good, whatsoever! It's fine to acknowledge these people's good qualities, but only if you also acknowledge the harm that they have done to other people. And that is a very delicate and sophisticated balance to keep, and it's very hard to keep.[17]

As Vandiver hinted, one way of negotiating the treacherous path of situating the convict in abolitionist frame alignment work is to devote equal time and effort to victims. This is also the approach of Sister Helen Prejean, who was discussed in chapter 3. Prejean, whose organizational base is Louisiana's Pilgrimage for Life, is far less vulnerable to charges of misplaced loyalty than activists like Joseph Ingle. Her close relations with murder victims' families and her active involvement in pursuit of more adequate crime victim assistance programs are enough to convince even her critics that she is neither ignorant of nor indifferent to what murder leaves behind. She does not speak of killers as mere victims of society and she does not absolve them of responsibility for what they have done. As a result, she is more free to speak of her relationships on death row without being dismissed as a sentimentalist.

Another abolitionist who has managed to use individual convicts in anti-death penalty work without exposing herself to the charge of romanticizing them is Marie Deans. Trained as a writer of short stories, she understands the power of a compelling character in driving home a theme. Consequently, her strategy falls between the poles discussed above. Deans does not seek to focus attention on the human face of death row convicts per se; she merely wants to break down the social distance between Main Street and death row. She doesn't avoid discussions of convicts for fear of alienating her audience. Rather, Deans insists on the importance of publicizing selected individual cases to personalize the issues abolitionists are talking about. The cases function as "wedges" to increase the doubts of people whose support for capital punishment is "soft."[18]

Deans did this quite successfully with the case of Joe Giarratano. In 1979, Giarratano was convicted of the murders of a 44-year-old woman and her teenage daughter, in whose Virginia apartment he had been living for several weeks. Giarratano was a drug abuser who suffered from frequent blackouts and hallucinations, and he was under the influence of drugs at the time of the killings. Although he had no recollection of the crime, he assumed he must have committed it and confessed. In fact, he gave five inconsistent confessions during the two days after he gave himself up to Jacksonville, Florida, police. When he discovered a small amount of blood on his own boots while being held in jail, he notified the authorities of this self-discovered "evidence." He later refused a prosecutor's invitation to plead guilty in exchange for a life sentence, waived his right to a jury trial, and asked that a death sentence be imposed. He was sentenced to die at a bench trial.

But while on death row, Joe Giarratano became a changed man in many respects. He changed his mind about wanting to be executed, taught himself the law, and began filing successful petitions on behalf of fellow prisoners who had no lawyers. One of these petitions, *Murray v. Giarratano* (492 U.S. 1, 1989), reached the U.S. Supreme Court. And when his own lawyers brought to his attention the massive inconsistencies in his confessions and in forensic evidence from the crime scene,[19] Giarratano agreed to resume his appeals. But neither the Virginia courts nor the federal courts upheld his motion. This left clemency as the only possible way of saving Giarratano's life. Marie Deans was Joe Giarratano's chief supporter, and she orchestrated the clemency campaign. Deans generated massive nationwide publicity and lined up an impressive list of celebrity support for the Giarratano Review Action Committee. Remarkably, she also won the support of conservatives, especially columnist James J. Kilpatrick, who were normally supporters of capital punishment.

All this placed Virginia governor Douglas Wilder in a difficult bind. Giarratano's case was a very strong one, but Wilder's own political ambitions were threatened by any appearance of weakness on crime and punishment. His office received over 7,000 phone calls and letters requesting that he spare the convict's life (Kaplan 1991), and he finally arrived at what amounts to a political compromise. Eighty-two hours before Joe Giarratano was to be executed, Governor Wilder offered him a deal that canceled his execution on condition that he accept a life sentence. Should he successfully seek a retrial, he could be sentenced to death. Giarratano accepted the offer and appealed to the state attorney general, Mary Sue Terry, for a new trial. That request was denied, and Giarratano will probably remain in prison into the twenty-first century.

The failure to win a new trial for Joe Giarratano was a major disappointment for Marie Deans and the rest of his supporters. But his life was saved. Moreover, Deans's strategy in the clemency appeal had managed to provide not only the citizens of Virginia, but all Americans, with a compelling flesh-and-blood example of the danger of executing the innocent. And Giarratano, despite having lived far less than an exemplary life, was nevertheless something of a self-made man by 1989 — at least by prison standards. Not only was he almost certainly innocent of the crime for which he had been convicted and condemned, but he had turned himself around in prison. This made him a very attractive exemplar of the innocence issue, and woke people up to the fact that new evidence of innocence was inadmissible in Virginia appeals courts unless introduced within 21 days of the original verdict.[20] Joe Giarratano's clemency campaign undoubtedly had more of an impact than a dozen law review articles and scholarly books on the issue could ever have had. Deans believes that support for the death penalty in her state dropped sharply following this and similar campaigns undertaken by the Virginia Coalition.

In any case, the perception that abolitionists are in sympathy with criminals lingers. Activists have a great deal of work to do to overcome this view, and part of their success in doing so will be determined by the finesse with which they manage the presence of condemned killers in the American imagination.

Direct Action and Civil Disobedience

As we have seen in chapter 2, the embryonic anti-death penalty movement took its fight to the streets in the years after the Supreme Court gave states the go-ahead to resume executing killers in 1976. For the most part, they engaged in nondisruptive marches and rallies, as well as vigils outside prisons where executions were taking place. There were also instances of "creative" but legal direct actions during those years, designed to call attention to the crusade against capital punishment. For instance, some activists fasted in protest of executions (Culhane 1988; Ingle 1990), performed mock executions in the streets, and in one case, delivered a "Deathday cake" to the governor of a death penalty state on his birthday.[21]

In a few instances during those early years, death penalty protesters broke the law and were arrested. For example, recall the several acts of civil disobedience by People Against Executions that were described in chapter 2. But as infrequent as it has always been in the ADPM, civil disobedience virtually disappeared from the movement's tactical repertoire after the mid-1980s. There are only a handful of instances of civil disobedience specifically related to the issue since 1980. Three of these occurred in 1985. Eight members of PAX were arrested at the Georgia House of Representatives on February 19, 1985, for attempting without permission to read a prepared statement that asked for a halt to an impending execution and an investigation of alleged discrimination in capital cases (*Lifelines* 1985a). A month later, three PAX members were arrested in the Georgia Pardons and Paroles office, where they were trying to prevent an execution (*Lifelines* 1986). And on May 28, 12 protesters from Open Door Community in Atlanta were taken into custody for demonstrating against capital punishment in a restricted area of the U.S. Supreme Court. Their action was part of a larger multi-issue, multisite protest that resulted in a total of 250 arrests (*Lifelines* 1985b). More recently direct action occurred at San Quentin in connection with the Harris execution, and at the Washington State Penitentiary in Walla Walla prior to the hanging of Westley Allan Dodd. In both instances, small groups of anti-death penalty activists were arrested for leaving the area designated for protesters and crossing onto prison grounds.[22]

As much as anything, the decline in acts of civil disobedience was due to the acceleration of capital punishment's pace in the United States. The abolitionists who had planned and carried out such actions before now found themselves overwhelmed by more immediate tasks, such as locating lawyers to stave off scheduled executions.[23] There was too little time for purely symbolic actions and too little money for bail and legal defense. But the issue of civil disobedience in the ADPM has not faded away entirely. In abolitionist publications and conferences, as well as in informal discussions about strategy on the state level, many still express the opinion that the struggle against the death penalty has to be taken to the street. The theme of the 1993 NCADP conference, in fact, was "Out of the Courts—Into the Streets!" This slogan does not necessarily imply direct actions that violate the law, but such tactics have been discussed annually by members of the organization, and this amounts to something of a low-intensity prognostic dispute in both the coalition and AIUSA. Before assuming the helm of the NCADP, Leigh Dingerson once recommended that activists consider preventing persons who by law must be in attendance at executions—such as wardens, prison physicians, or specific categories of witnesses—from entering the prison (Dingerson 1988). Other activists have suggested that people knowingly trespass onto prison property and force authorities to remove them and disrupt campaign appearances and press conferences by pro-death penalty politicians.[24]

According to more militant abolitionists, one advantage of employing civil disobedience in the struggle against the death penalty is that such methods are essential in increasing the movement's visibility and reversing its defensive posture. Some movement leaders see tactical parallels between the issues of capital punishment and AIDS. Both affect marginalized, somewhat disreputable populations, but militant AIDS activists—especially those in the organization called ACT UP!—have been more successful than anti-death penalty forces in attracting attention to their side of the issue and to their demand for increased funding for the search for a cure for HIV. They have done so by disrupting public events and conferences on AIDS research. Abolitionists in California, where ACT UP! is especially visible, have been impressed by the group's ability to get results with small numbers of highly committed people and have sought its advice on tactics. ACT UP! members made a presentation at the 1992 national conference of AIUSA at the invitation of death penalty activist Claudia King.

> I look at it mainly as attention getting, because it is so hard to get attention on this cause. And when I think of what ACT UP! has done for the AIDS cause! I asked ACT UP! to come [to the AIUSA conference] because they're so angry when they do these actions, and we're always angry too but we don't get that message across that the state is killing in our name. It's fine to just say it, but it makes a difference when you put it into action. That's why I've

always paid attention to what ACT UP! does. Now I'm for their cause, but I also really sympathize with them when they show their anger out there, and *demand* that things change. And that's the way that I would like *our* movement to come across. Instead, sometimes we're seen as these people who are really soft on crime. But instead, we're *angry* about what's happening, we're angry . . . that politicians are using the death penalty as an excuse. So, civil disobedience would just get us out there in a second, would get us into the press in a minute, and instead of our little rallies and demonstrations, these little things that we do, if we did something really dramatic, then it would be an opportunity for us to get the message across.[25]

Another California activist, Pat Clark, echoes King's sentiments regarding the need for highly visible tactics that capture attention.

I would like to see people be a little bit more aggressive than we've been in the past. What I've talked about with their people is that, by and large, the anti-death penalty movement is a very *cerebral* one. People are very much opposed to it and they've thought out the ideas quite well, and they're very willing to, like, go out and hold a sign, maybe. And maybe pass out some information. But beyond that, you know, they're gonna think twice about anything else! Whereas with ACT UP!, you know, we have no problem with doing dramatic stuff with piles of mock corpses, then shouting very impassioned slogans, you know. And I'm not sure that there's not a place for that in the anti-death penalty movement.[26]

Almost no one in the American anti-death penalty movement speaks of civil disobedience as being unjustifiable in and of itself, at least when committed by individuals as an expression of their moral beliefs. But there is widespread disagreement about the wisdom of using such actions to hasten the end of capital punishment. Although many members of the primary ADPM organizations have themselves engaged in civil disobedience as part of the civil rights and anti-Vietnam War movements, they suspect that those tactics are a waste of time in the present political climate. The heyday of nonviolent direct action occurred in a context in which the political center of gravity was much farther to the left than it is now. There was a rather high degree of sympathy for the basic *objectives* of both civil rights activists and, at least by 1968 or so, antiwar protesters. America is now a much more conservative society, with little sympathy for the goal of ending executions. Doug Magee, who was part of PAX during the late 1970s and who argued strongly for the NCADP to venture farther in that direction, now says he would never have predicted the "avalanche of conservatism that we've had in the last decade and the sort of futility of civil disobedience in the face of that." There still needs to be people who feel compelled to put their bodies on the line in protest of executions, he says, but it is unrealistic to do so in the expectation that such direct actions will have much of a concrete impact.[27] Some abolitionists also feel that the appropriateness of civil disobedience on this issue is open to question. To a greater extent than in previous struggles, such actions could put people other than the protesters themselves in jeopardy:

I'm a person that's done a lot of civil disobedience myself, in the peace movement. And I see that there are some built-in problems with doing it on this issue. The main one is that you're dealing with legal stuff to begin with. You're dealing with people that are losing their lives for breaking the law, and . . . you get into some symbolic gray areas about what it means to take that sort of action lightly. I mean, for us to kind of throw ourselves around in a cavalier manner, and cross lines and thumb noses at these authorities, it sometimes gets across the wrong message.[28]

In view of the changed political context of late-twentieth-century America, many leading abolitionists think that for movement groups to embrace civil disobedience on a substantial scale would not only waste scarce resources but would also sap what little popular support they now enjoy. The apparent backlash against the right-to-life movement in the aftermath of protests in Wichita, Kansas, and Buffalo, New York, has fueled these concerns. Eugene Wanger, a Michigan attorney who has served on the board of the NCADP for years, has been outspoken in his belief that participation in illegal protests is a purely personal matter that should never be officially approved by the coalition. This would drive away several important organizational affiliates, discourage new ones from coming aboard, expose the organization and its directors to civil and criminal liabilities they could ill afford,[29] and give "aid and comfort to many of our opponents in spreading the false and pernicious idea that abolition of the death penalty is based on radical left-wing principles."[30] Almost identical concerns were voiced at meetings of Death Penalty Focus's board of directors during the Robert Harris crisis.[31] Proponents of more militant tactics counter that they are not intended to win friends, but rather to force the issue. Only a few years ago, Doug Magee was pushing strongly for confrontational tactics:

In the ten or so years I've been working with the NCADP the one unbreakable tenet of most of our activities has been the need for outreach, for incorporation, for coalition building, for education that will increase the flock. But while there has been turnover and transfusion of new blood in the past years, there has been little increase. The organization has grown well, its work has expanded and its reach increased, but the numbers of people doing the work has remained relatively stable. While it should always be a goal of the organization to multiply its constituents it helps as well to face facts. And facts, as I see them, are that for the foreseeable future we, the people now involved, are the people who must take the responsibility and do the work. If the death penalty is truly to be abolished it won't be because we've first enlisted hordes of supporters who have then organized to bring down the walls. It will be, I believe, because a dedicated group of abolitionists got creative.

. . . [W]e aren't much farther ahead than we were ten years ago and a hundred people have been killed. Now more than ever we need to be making our activism active, we need to be pointed rather than diffuse, we need to be rude rather than polite, we need to be intolerant and insufferable. The focus of our actions should not be to bring new members to the organization but rather to stick it to the powers that be, to put those blithely doing the state's butchery

on the hot seat, to be the strong, competent, and implacable foes of a stink-
ing, virulent cancer.

> . . . [F]or every conference the NCADP sponsors in the next year I would
> like to see it also sponsor some form of confrontational direct action.[32]

For Leigh Dingerson of the NCADP, there would be benefits of a more
complicated sort should civil disobedience take root in the struggle. She thinks
the almost universal politeness of abolitionists at present has *already* made it
easy for opponents to dismiss the movement's simple message as "radical." In
the successful social movements of recent history, the emergence of factions
willing to break the rules has often led to a "radical flank effect" (Haines 1988)
in which the bargaining position of more moderate groups has been multiplied. But such a faction is missing in the ADPM:

> What this movement needs — and has had a various times, but what it desper-
> ately needs now — is the radical fringe! We need folks out there that are, you
> know, lying down in the streets, that are committing civil disobedience, that
> are doing that stuff! . . . I think that's tremendously important for a move-
> ment. The civil rights movement used that so effectively. We don't have that
> in this movement.[33]

For Dingerson, the danger that militant tactics will usher in a backlash of
even greater public support for capital punishment is not great:

> I mean, that's always the fear. But historically I don't think that's really been
> the case. I think that a movement has to be a lot of things. And what you're
> trying to do is get the general public to take sides in the movement. So that
> the public isn't debating whether or not we should have the death penalty,
> [but rather] the public's debating what tactics do we use to get rid of it. That
> should become the debate. That's what happened in the civil rights movement
> and others, and that's where we have to go.[34]

One final source of concern about civil disobedience pertains to the movement's current capacity to support it properly. Not only has the political
climate changed considerably since militant direct action worked so well in the
1960s, say the doubters, but the ADPM is also far weaker than the movements
of that era were. Individual civil rights protesters took great risks when they
went to jail in the South, but their large numbers gave them tremendous
disruptive power. In many instances, most notably the 1963 Birmingham,
Alabama, campaign organized by the Southern Christian Leadership Conference, they could fill the jails and overwhelm the legal control structures of
southern communities. With that level of muscle, it made sense to court arrest.
Moreover, civil rights protesters were usually backed up by substantial organizations like the NAACP and the LDF that could provide legal defense and, if
protesters wanted to secure their release, bail money. The anti-death penalty
movement does not yet have sufficient numbers of activists to mount truly
disruptive protests on that scale, nor do they have the wherewithal to provide
legal representation even for those sent to jail in smaller actions intended
merely to get the public's attention.[35] As Michael Radelet puts it, anti-death

penalty groups have more important things for their volunteer lawyers to do "than to bail out somebody carrying a bunch of flowers and chained to a fence. . . . "[36]

The future role of civil disobedience tactics in the anti-death penalty movement remains to be determined. Discussions continue within the NCADP, though it seems likely that concerns over possible defections by more conservative affiliates will prevent any official policy in support of tactics that violate laws. Amnesty International has never attempted to prevent its members from participating in civil disobedience as individuals, but it has traditionally steered clear of including it in its own approach to human rights issues. In 1992, the AIUSA annual general meeting in Los Angeles resolved to convene a task force to study possible adoption of nonviolent direct action by the organization. After sitting idle for a year, that task force was resurrected in late 1993 and was scheduled to make recommendations at upcoming regional conferences. Discussion of the matter was tabled when the working parties ran short of time and when some within the organization requested more background information on AI's historical position on civil disobedience. Supporters were hopeful that discussion would continue in 1995 and 1996. The approval of civil disobedience by AI would be a very important development in both the death penalty movement and in the human rights movement as a whole, for this is the one organization currently able to produce enough people for dramatic protests against capital punishment.

The Alternatives Minefield

If not the death penalty, then what? The question of how society is to respond to aggravated murder if not with executions is "perhaps the oldest of all the issues raised by the two-century struggle in western civilization to end the death penalty" (Bedau 1990:481). Despite the abandonment of capital punishment in much of the Western industrialized world, as well as the fact that only the tiniest portion of homicides in the United States result in death sentences, high rates of violent crime make this a very serious question for many Americans. The credibility of the anti-death penalty movement hinges on its ability to provide a convincing answer. More than any other single issue, the matter of what that answer should be has the potential to split the movement into pieces.

Until fairly recently, death penalty supporters and opponents alike assumed that the alterative to executing killers was to put them behind bars for the rest of their lives. "Perpetual servitude," in fact, was advocated vigorously by one of the seminal figures in abolitionism, the utilitarian philosopher Cesare Beccaria:

> It is not the intensity of punishment that has the greatest effect on the human spirit, but its duration, for our sensibility is more easily and more permanently affected by slight but repeated impressions than by a powerful but momentary

action. The sway of habit is universal over every sentient being; as man speaks and walks and satisfies his needs by its aid, so the ideas of morality come to be stamped upon the mind only by long and repeated impressions. It is not the terrible yet momentary spectacle of the death of a wretch, but the long and painful example of a man deprived of liberty, who, having become a beast of burden, recompenses with his labors the society he has offended, which is the strongest curb against crimes. (1963:46–47)

The conditions of incarceration in contemporary prisons do not approximate the misery that Beccaria had in mind. Convicts are deprived of a great deal, but they are not transformed into "beasts of burden." And in actual practice, "life" sentences no longer mean that the inmate will necessarily spend the rest of his or her days — or even most of them — in a correctional institution. The reduction of prison terms by parole authorities became something of a scandal as public concern about crime increased in the 1960s, and it continues in the form of "truth in sentencing" reforms at the state and federal levels. Amid the furor, the "true life" sentence, or "life without the possibility of parole" (LWOP), appeared. For most Americans who are willing to consider the abandonment of capital punishment, LWOP seems the most logical and just punishment for persons convicted of first-degree murder.[37]

As a matter of fact, LWOP is widely available to judges and juries in the United States. As of March 1990, 31 states and the District of Columbia had some version of LWOP as a sentencing option for murder. Twenty-four of these states also authorized the death penalty. Eleven others had "life" sentences that deny parole eligibility to the worst category of murderer for a specific number of years, usually 20 or more (Wright 1990; also see Cheatwood 1988; Immarigeon 1990). Laws of the latter type are often referred to as life-without-parole laws, but are actually mandatory minimum sentences for homicide.

LWOP sentences have the potential to affect the fate of capital punishment in the United States. First, as discussed earlier, opinion surveys have consistently revealed that many Americans who otherwise support the death penalty are satisfied when persons convicted of aggravated murder are imprisoned for the rest of their lives rather than executed. Even more appealing is the idea of convict restitution arrangements, in which life-sentenced offenders compensate crime victims with money earned from their prison labor. Americans are outraged not so much by the fact that murderers are allowed to go on living, but rather by their belief that violent offenders are rarely punished in a meaningful way. Thus, the increased availability of LWOP and long mandatory minimum sentences might well drain support from the death penalty. Additionally, abolitionists who line up behind some sort of "meaningful punishment" seem to have more credibility than those who do not. The negative stereotype of death penalty opponents as rehabilitation-minded liberals who are excessively sympathetic to criminals undoubtedly prevents their case from receiving a full and fair hearing. Many of them find that they are taken far more seriously when their condemnation of executions is accompanied by an insistence that killers pay a high price for their misdeeds. And some capital defense lawyers believe that the availability of harsh sentencing alternatives can be an effective weapon against death sentences even in states that retain capital punishment—jurors may be less likely to send a convicted killer to death row when they know that he could be kept off the streets forever.[38] Indeed, interviews with jurors in capital cases have found that those who underestimate the currently available non-death penalty sentences in their states are more likely to impose the death penalty (Bowers 1993:170).

A few anti-death penalty activists and litigators have given their explicit support to LWOP and mandatory minimum sentences as alternatives to the death penalty, if only for strategic reasons. For example, attorney David Bruck told an audience of capital litigators in 1986 that:

> . . . we may need to be less coy about life imprisonment without parole as an alternative to the death penalty. Out of the plus or minus 80 percent who support the death penalty, those who support it primarily out of a fear of individual murderers and a desire to protect society may be the most reachable, as opposed to those whose support is more integrally related to other conservative or religious political views. This is a tough issue, but it's one that can't be evaded. LWOP can be changed and amended later, as crime and public sensibilities that seems [*sic*] to accompany the reinstitution of legalized prisoner-killing may take a very long time to undo.[39]

Similar views are held by American University justice professor Robert Johnson, another critic of capital punishment. Although he would prefer that authorities' hands not be tied entirely by sentences that eliminate parole eligibility,[40] he sees life sentences not merely as a strategic compromise—as the lesser of two evils—but as defensible in principle. In "An Open Letter to the Governors of States with the Death Penalty" (1990b) he wrote:

> A life sentence is a humane alternative to the death penalty. . . . A life sentence is also a just alternative to the death penalty. A life sentence is, in fact, a "civil" death penalty, which takes freedom but preserves life, while categorically rejecting the violence of executions. The notion that a life sentence is a civil death penalty sounds strained at first, but it has merit. True, these prisoners can forge a life of sorts behind bars, but one organized on existential lines and etched in suffering, for at a deeply human level they experience a civil death, the death of freedom. The prison is their cemetery, a six by nine-foot cell their tomb. Their freedom is interred in the name of justice. In effect, they give their civil lives for the natural lives they have taken. No criminal deserves a harsher punishment than this.

None of the national abolition groups have made an explicit call for any specific form of life sentence for aggravated murder, but a few state groups have. The Oregon anti-death penalty coalition, for instance, chose to endorse LWOP,[41] and abolition groups in Utah also threw their weight behind a 1990 bill that substituted life without possibility of parole for capital punishment.[42] But many contemporary anti-death penalty activists are not comfortable with exchanging the death penalty for long prison sentences. And most of them resist coming out in favor of LWOP, which is widely viewed as being nearly as bad as the death penalty itself. They feel that to lock up a convict and take

away all hope that he might earn his release by reforming himself is to resort
to another form of death penalty, and that those who opt for LWOP commit
the same error that underlies executions: they write the offender off as being
fundamentally beyond redemption. This amounts to human garbage disposal.
Joseph Ingle for instance, believes

> [I]t's a real mistake to think that life-without-parole is the alternative to the
> death penalty, because what you're doing is buying into the psychology of the
> people that gave you the death penalty! You're saying that this person is
> basically worthless and needs to be dispensed with forever.
>
> . . . [T]hose of us who are [in contact with death row inmates], you're not
> gonna find us willing to settle for this life-without-parole nonsense. Because I
> think that buys into this whole culture of death we have in this country, which
> is what we're trying to get away from! And I don't think to sell your birthright
> out when you're fighting people from getting killed is the way to do it.[43]

From this point of view, it is better not to become entangled in the search
for alternatives at all, and to reply, when asked, that "the alternative to the
death penalty is *no* death penalty!"

> When the God of Moses passed down His first commandment, He did not
> include footnotes detailing alternative courses of action. Today, we would
> not think to query opponents of mutilation or torture about what they would
> place in its stead for the "really tough" cases. In an area where solutions are
> so hard to come by, some may choose simply to reject the death penalty as
> the worst "solution" without feeling an obligation to discover answers for
> society's most difficult problems.[44]

This point of view was clearly the dominant one among movement leaders
during the decade following the revival of the death penalty. People who
attempted to initiate a discussion at ADPM conferences or in the movement's
newsletters of suitable terms of incarceration for convicted murderers during
those years were often greeted by stony silence.[45] And opposition to LWOP
still holds considerable sway. For instance, there was controversy among those
close to the Death Penalty Information Center when its director, Richard
Dieter, circulated a preliminary draft of DPIC's report on alternatives to the
death penalty (Dieter 1993). The report emphasized survey data on American's
preference for long prison sentences and better victim compensation, among
other things. Several of the readers urged him to "tone down the parts about
life-without-parole" for fear that this would come across as the sentence of
choice.[46]

A few abolitionists resist participating in discussions of LWOP because of
a principled antagonism to punishment of any sort. These are often people
who came to the anti-death penalty movement from reformist religious tradi-
tions. The American Friends Service Committee, the Fellowship of Reconciliation, and the National Interreligious Task Force for Criminal Justice, for
example, have long been associated with the struggle against capital punishment, but each sees executions only as the most extreme facet of the larger

problem of American society's punitive impulse. Some of the members of these organizations take the abolition of prisons to be their ultimate goal. Others merely wish to effect a drastic reduction on the use of incarceration, particularly for nonviolent offenses. But it is thought that even for violent offenders, rehabilitation and reconciliation is usually possible. Confinement in dangerous and dehumanizing penitentiaries is *emotional* violence, akin to the physical violence of execution, and both merely contribute to the cycle of force.[47] Other critics of nonlethal as well as lethal forms of punishment base their views on political rather than religious grounds. The justice system as a whole is widely seen as corrupt and discriminatory against ethnic minorities and the poor, so looking to prisons for solutions is not a viable strategy against crime. As one New York abolitionist explained, America's use of punishment as the primary method of attacking crime ignores the structural roots of violence.

> It isn't just that I oppose harsh punishments. I don't believe that harsh punishments achieve security! I think they are destructive of . . . what it takes to make the world a better place. I think when you can discard [through imprisonment] 60,000 or 70,000 people as we do in New York without a single thought—and I don't say this for dramatics as I suspect some people do—but I think you have accepted the idea of concentration camps! I think that if you don't see the core of criminal behavior residing in the configuration of how people come into the world, how they are treated, how they are raised, how they are socialized, what resources they are given and the extent to which they are able to participate in society, then you don't understand crime![48]

But although mistrust of the justice system is widespread within the movement, the majority of abolitionists are willing to look to prisons for the alternative to executions. The most common viewpoint on alternatives like life without possibility of parole is that they are the lesser of two evils, certainly not goals worthy of enthusiastic pursuit by progressive reformers, but tolerable if they help to stop state killing. Hugo Adam Bedau is one of many who feels this way. He recognizes one huge advantage of *any* prison-based alternative to capital punishment: the moral cost of erroneous convictions is not as severe when the convicted murderer is allowed to live. If a mistake is discovered, at least the inmate can be released to live the remainder of his or her life in freedom. For Bedau, LWOP's major drawback is that it is simply unnecessary from a utilitarian point of view. As a deterrent to murder, it is not demonstrably superior to lesser sentences. And because most offenders do not represent a threat once they grow older, it is neither beneficial nor efficient to keep the vast majority of them confined into old age. Bedau prefers "life without the *probability* of parole" to true LWOP. Under such a system, persons convicted of aggravated murder would receive a minimum sentence of no more than ten years before they become eligible for release. While in prison, they would be required to work and to surrender half of their pay to a victim's family fund. Henry Schwarzschild's opposition to LWOP is grounded more squarely on moral concerns than on utilitarian ones, but he, too, is willing to tolerate it if proposed by others as a trade-off.[49] This type of trade-off can become more than an academic question, as it did in Kansas in 1987. That year the legislature passed a "Hard 40" bill after a long fight over the reinstatement of capital punishment. The statute provided for a "life" sentence for certain types of homicides that prohibited parole for at least 40 years. The idea for such a sentence did nor originate with Kansas abolitionists, but they nevertheless welcomed it as an alternative that helped to delay reinstatement of the death penalty until 1994.[50]

Other abolitionists are much more reluctant to remain silent when harsh but nonlethal substitutes are debated. Different people draw the line at different points. For example, polls in Virginia concluded that large numbers in that state would be willing to give up capital punishment if convicted murderers were sentenced to "life" terms with victim restitution and no parole eligibility for 25 years. Marie Deans, the leading abolitionist in Virginia, is personally opposed to withholding eligibility for that long, because it ignores individual variations among prisoners and because it makes successful adjustment to freedom less likely. She would be willing to accept the 25-year term if it would end capital punishment. But under no circumstances would she be willing to acquiesce to LWOP. In fact, she has threatened to resign from any anti-death penalty or prison-reform organization to which she belongs should it endorse life-without-parole.

> . . . I *accept* the 25 years. I would *not* accept life with no possibility of parole. I *would not* accept that! I have actually said to organizations, including my own, that if that is adopted, I will resign! I feel so strongly about that. I think that's hand-washing.
>   . . . I'll tell you something. You start going to these prisons and seeing these old guys, who are arthritic and can hardly get around, or are in wheel-chairs or in walkers in our prison system. And it makes me want to puke! It just makes me feel so bad for us, about who we are. Are we still afraid of those people? And we haven't prepared them for society, so we can't release them.[51]

In some movements, frame disputes such as this one have resulted in internecine warfare and organizational fragmentation. But abolitionists are keenly aware of their weakness as change agents, their low numbers, and their minuscule budgets, and have sought to avoid such an outcome. They have avoided letting the alternatives issue divide them, first, by choosing not to discuss it very much. This has been easy for AI to do, because its mandate prohibits the organization from taking a position on any issue not directly pertaining to international human rights standards. The appropriate number of years that a convicted murderer should serve in prison is just such an issue. But the NCADP and its affiliates at the state level have had to *decide* whether or not to open the matter up to debate. For the most part, they have chosen not to, because to adopt an official policy on the question would deliver "a potential death blow" to the coalition.[52] The ACLU's overall stance toward prisoners' rights and Eighth Amendment issues makes it highly unlikely that LWOP would even be deemed a matter worth discussing.

Second, nearly all abolitionists are able to finesse the issue by referring to broad public support for the LWOP alternative without endorsing it. This is especially useful in states without the death penalty. In New York, for example, pro-death penalty legislators frequently charged that vetoes by former governors Mario Cuomo and Hugh Carey thwarted the "will of the people." Their opponents responded by trotting out the results of opinion polls like the one conducted by William Bowers and Margaret Vandiver (1991a), which showed that a majority preferred an alternative to the death penalty. The same tactic is in constant use across the country. Broad public support of LWOP or other alternatives undermines the widespread sense that there is something "wrong" with death penalty opponents and suggests to elected officials that they are not playing Russian roulette with their careers when they dare to vote against capital punishment.[53]

But as we have seen, LWOP is frequently adopted as an *additional* sentencing option, rather than as a substitute for capital punishment. In states that already have either LWOP or lengthy minimum sentences for first-degree murder, ADPM groups usually take a slightly different approach. In these states, activists usually attempt to convince lawmakers and the public that the death penalty is not necessary to protect the public because truly dangerous offenders can already be kept off the streets without killing them.[54] Again, abolitionists need not approve of the existing alternatives to call attention to them – but their credibility may rest on not criticizing the existing sentences as well. The biggest challenge sometimes turns out to be convincing the public that tough sentences are already in effect. Members of the Western Pennsylvania Coalition Against the Death Penalty found that not only were many Pennsylvanians unaware that LWOP was already in effect there, but that some state lawmakers were too![55] And there is often widespread suspicion that persons sentenced to 25-year minimums, "Hard 40," or life-without-parole may nevertheless be freed by some legislature or governor in the future. This is a touchier matter, for the case against the death penalty might be strengthened by supporting "tighter" sentencing alternatives. New York's former governor Mario Cuomo offered to sacrifice the clemency powers of his office in order to allay such fears, a move that was criticized by most abolitionists.

A final way to avoid the divisiveness that is inherent in the alternatives issue is to shift discussion away from prison and toward crime-related measures that are more consistent with movement culture. Foremost among these are *crime prevention* – fewer murders mean less demand for capital punishment – and *restorative justice* – responses to crimes that, unlike executions, provide something tangible to victims' families to help them put their lives back together. One of the most ambitious attempts to redirect the discussion of alternatives has some out of the New York State Defenders Association. According to NYSDA's Jonathan Gradess, the idea behind the initiative is to start with well-documented misgivings about various aspects of capital punishment and to "ratchet" the debate down from LWOP to more humane proposals:

> When you ask people the question "do you support the death penalty," they say "yes." If you ask them do they support *LWOP,* they say "yes." When you add restitution to the idea, and you add work, they like *that.* But if you start moving down the list and say "how long do they have to be in prison," they say "well, really, 25 years is an awfully long time for *me.* . . . " Now you move into the range of what you get [for murder] in New York *as it is!* If the maximum for murder were 12 years, people would demand that. What I think they're talking about, in terms of the assessment of sanctions for criminal behavior, is their own fear, their own aggravation, their own desire for security.[56]

From his experience in giving presentations and running workshops in communities around his state, Gradess has concluded that people are less preoccupied with punitive anticrime measures than is commonly supposed. Once the conversations get beyond the death penalty and LWOP, he says, they express approval of measures that would attack the social and economic sources of violent crime. In 1991, NYSDA released an information packet that listed 39 items that it portrayed as alternatives to the death penalty. Among them:

> 1. Early intervention to restore the family in cases of child abuse.
> 3. Training in non-violence.
> 5. Early identification programs.
> 7. Improvement of housing stock.
> 8. Providing drug treatment on demand for every addicted person.
> 11. Providing adequate unemployment compensation, job training and job development.
> 13. The elimination of violence and sadism on television.
> 18. Parental education on Fetal Alcohol Syndrome (FAS), research on FAS, support groups for children with FAS, and a liquor tax to fund these reforms.
> 21. Compensation programs for survivors of homicide victims.
> 25. Community based crime prevention programs.
> 29. Community dispute settlement programs.
> 34. Recruitment of a more inclusive, racially and economically diverse police force.
> 35. The elimination of weapons.[57]

It is unlikely that major ADPM organizations will make specific alternatives to the death penalty a part of their official mission in the near future. Members of those organizations, acting as individuals, will certainly make suggestions for how our nation should deal with violent offenders. Given the current size and fragility of the movement, that might be the wisest course. The issue is indeed a minefield, and abolitionists cannot afford to become divided over their visions of a more adequate criminal justice policy. But nearly every social movement in recent American history has eventually been faced with the demand that its criticisms be augmented with *suggested solu-*

tions. Sooner or later, target audiences who know what activists are against demand to know what they are *for.* Thus, it is unclear whether the anti-death penalty struggle can survive in the long run if its avoids making concrete suggestions for alternatives to the death penalty. Doing so would not require movementwide agreement, any more than all civil rights or feminist organizations had to share the same vision in order for their movements to make progress. But it may mean that practical methods for answering the challenge of homicide without mimicking it will have to emerge from somewhere within the ADPM. The methods used will have to strike a responsive chord across the cultural and political spectrum of the country. We will return to this in chapter 6.

Coalition Work and the Broader Context of Abolition

Capital punishment's opponents in the United States are painfully aware that they are vastly outnumbered. Not only are most of their fellow citizens at least superficially in favor of putting murderers to death, but many of those who are sympathetic to the ADP cause are preoccupied with issues that affect them more directly. To make progress, abolitionists must forge coalitions with kindred movements. This much is beyond dispute. More difficult, however, is the question of which potential alliances should be nurtured most energetically, and what should be the terms of the partnerships that result — in particular, to what extent should anti-death penalty groups be obligated to work on issues other than the death penalty?

Most often mentioned as possible allies in the struggle against capital punishment are civil rights, gun control, and pro-life groups, but there are huge differences in the degree to which abolitionists agree to the idea of working with these movements. Coalitions with African American and Latino civil rights organizations arouse very little resistance, as we have seen. The only internal disputes that minority outreach stimulates are those that pertain to how much effort should be devoted to the task. But the desirability of involving the civil rights community in the cause is doubted by no one. The long-standing racial undercurrents in America's use of the death penalty make working in concert seem perfectly natural, and the human and monetary resources that civil rights groups command would be of enormous benefit to the undermanned and underfunded abolitionists.

The interrelatedness of capital punishment and gun control are nearly as obvious to the vast majority of abolitionists as are the links to civil rights. America's seeming addiction to the death penalty is fueled by its unusually high levels of violent crime and, in turn, by the widespread availability of firearms on its streets. And although there is no hard evidence to back it up, it is probably safe to assume that the rank and file of the ADPM favors strict gun control measures by a wide margin. Nevertheless, some abolitionists see any linking of the two issues in the movement's public education and legislative work as extremely dangerous. This issue presents little, if any, problem with AI, for the organization's mandate prohibits it from speaking to this kind of domestic policy issue, just as involvement in alternative sentencing options is off limits. But the matter has often come up within the NCADP. A few have taken the position that the coalition ought to at least issue a formal call for strong limitations on handguns and assault weapons.[58] On the other hand, one leader of a state affiliate, objecting to an article about an anti-handgun group that was published in the coalition's newsletter *Lifelines,* insisted that the NCADP's policy "should be to publish *nothing* which by *any* stretch of the imagination could be construed as taking sides on other issues."[59] His protest reflected the view that the group was obligated to remain focused on the single issue of capital punishment, and implied that side issues like gun control were controversial enough to drive away members who were not political liberals. Moreover, straying into the weapons controversy can distract abolitionists when they are trying to change people's minds about the death penalty. A Kansas activist, for example, described how mentioning gun control as a method for reducing crime could backfire:

> I'll talk about violence on TV. I'll talk about parents learning appropriate conflict-resolution skills and teaching them to their kids and how we should be doing that in the public schools. You know, I can just come up with lots and lots of different things that deal with violence which I strongly believe in. I can talk about the corporal punishment thing. So we keep pushing noncontroversial subjects. But I don't talk gun control because in this state, the gun lobby is just ferocious. I mean, they think they've just gotta have their guns! I made the mistake one time of mentioning that as an issue. And the next thing I did was debate gun control for 15 minutes. I kept saying "Hey, I'm really not here to talk about gun control, I'm just saying that that's usually the murder weapon of choice. We've got to quit killing people with handguns." But oh, man, did I ever get lectured to![60]

Even more explosive is the possibility of ADPM overtures to right-to-life groups. For some abolitionists, the ethical parallels between the issues of capital punishment and abortion are clear. Both movements are supposedly against the taking of human life, even though they focus on different portions of the life cycle. From this perspective, to decry the destruction of a fetus while standing idly by as a fully developed and fully conscious human being is led to the slaughter is to engage in a very selective form of moral outrage — just as it is inconsistent for opponents of the death penalty to ignore the ethical dilemmas raised by the occurrence of thousands of abortions annually in the United States. Clearly, few on either side now take the inconsistency seriously or even recognize it. But addressing it, say advocates of a dialogue between the two movements, is precisely what is needed. Those antiabortionists who are truly motivated by their belief in the sanctity of life and concern for the unborn, rather than merely by mean-spirited conservative dogma, are not out of reach. They might be brought around if confronted with the experiences that turn an innocent baby into a killer, and made to understand that their pro-life platform would sell better if it were consistently applied. Indeed, there *are* groups that advocate a "consistent life ethic," sometimes called "the seamless garment" (Hentoff 1988). They include Common Ground, The Seamless Garment Network, and until 1993, JustLife.

Even those who don't recognize any ethical equivalence of the antiabortion and anti-death penalty issues sometimes recognize the advantages that would accrue to the ADPM if it were able to tap some of the strength of the right-to-life movement. Among these is Florida scholar-activist Michael Radelet:

> There's *numbers* there. They can mobilize people. For example, in Gainesville [Florida] about three weeks ago they had 1600 people out for an anti-abortion demonstration. They formed a big cross on our two main streets. If *we* had 1600 people show up to protest an execution, we'd never see another one again! Especially if they were fundamentalist Christians who had some power in the community.[61]

A similar position is taken by law professor Bruce Ledewitz, who works with the abolitionists in the Pittsburgh area and has served on the board of the NCADP:

> . . . there is no PRO-death penalty movement in this country. The only reason we have a death penalty is because *we're* so weak! If there were any strong institution that wanted to get rid of the death penalty, we'd get rid of it tomorrow. It doesn't have any staying power on the other side. . . . There's only one institution I know of that's powerful enough to get rid of the death penalty, and that's the Pro-Life movement. If the Pro-Life movement said tomorrow to the Republican Party: "we're pro-life; you've got to be against the death penalty," that would be the end of the death penalty.[62]

But whatever the affinity between the anti-death penalty and antiabortion movements on a philosophical level, and regardless of the enhanced political clout that an alliance would bring to abolitionists, the odds of such a thing occurring are slim at best. In part, this is because the ideological backgrounds of recruits to the two movements are generally worlds apart. *Some* abortion opponents, those in the hierarchy of the Catholic Church, are already on record against capital punishment. The problem lies in the rank and file; the majority of those who participate in the right-to-life movement do not see any equivalence between their issue and that of capital punishment. Their rhetoric is framed around the notion of preserving *"innocent* human life." They tend toward the view that human beings, once born, are fully responsible for their misdeeds. Those that are associated with evangelical Christian groups lean heavily toward an interpretation of scripture that supports executions. For their part, death penalty opponents are drawn disproportionately from liberal and radical backgrounds. It is difficult for them to renounce issues that are part of the civil rights/gender rights/peace constellation, including the pro-choice stance, so it is anathema to work with antiabortion groups other than, for example, the National Catholic Conference. With mistrust and hostility between the two political cultures running so deep, it would be difficult to draw significant portions of the two movements into an active coalition. And it is difficult to conceive of an action by a major national ADPM group — excluding, possibly, vigorous work on behalf of the life-without-parole alternative to capital punishment—that would have the splintering effect of a coalition with groups seeking the recriminalization of abortion. Although the matter has been raised within the NCADP at least as early as 1985,[63] it has always been tabled in order to avoid conflict.

The idea of *individual* abolitionists devoting part of their time to some other issue that concerns them, be it gun control, abortion, or anything else, is perfectly acceptable throughout the ranks. The ADP movement does not demand single-minded devotion from its participants. Leaders of ADPM organizations are eager to tap into the constituencies of the other movements in which abolitionists have contacts.[64] This was done quickly and effectively in 1992 when the death penalty referendum in the District of Columbia was beaten back. For the time being, though, only a few leaders at the national level think that coalition building should include any broadening of the ADPM's goals beyond the elimination of capital punishment. Ronald Hampton of the National Black Police Association and a board member of both AIUSA and the NCADP, is critical of the abolition movement's narrow focus. For Hampton, a critique of capital punishment has to be framed as part of a larger critique of racism and of the cultural and economic sources of violence.[65] Rev. Joseph Ingle hopes that the abolition of capital punishment will become part of a broader political agenda in coming years, an agenda that includes crime prevention, the decriminalization of drugs, serious gun control, improved education and health care for the poor and middle class, and a serious commitment to civil rights. His vision goes beyond the current structure of the ADPM to, perhaps, the creation of a third national political party.[66]

Of course, both the ACLU and AI *already* look at the death penalty as part of a larger complex of issues—civil liberties and human rights, respectively. This is a given. In a real sense, the issue here concerns the agendas of the NCADP and state-level abolitionist organizations. The rest of the movement's leadership, while themselves seeing the death penalty as one part of a much larger complex of social problems, feels that the coalition cannot afford to spread itself too thin. There are simply too few people and too little money to be pursuing other objectives, however relevant those objectives might be to the death penalty. Attacking related issues, like addressing proposals for alternatives to execution, would be divisive.[67] Thus, any overtures that the NCADP makes to other groups must not require any quid pro quo.[68] On the state level, most ADPM groups are too small and weak to seriously consider addressing anything beyond the death penalty itself. Death Penalty Focus of California, one of the larger and richer organizations, elected to remain a single-issue group to preserve the integrity of its coalition and concentrate its resources.[69]

It may well be that the leaders of the ADPM are prudent in not involving their organizations in issues like gun control, alternative crime control strategies, and other questions of social policy. They certainly do not now have the resources to mount an adequate challenge capital punishment even by itself, much less to take part in public education and lobbying on other issues, too.

And the NCADP undoubtedly *would* experience defections if it were to broaden its diagnostic and prognostic framing of the issue. Still, it may well be that the movement is paying a price by fighting capital punishment in isolation. The organizational affiliates and external supporters that the coalition retains by having no formal policy on gun control, LWOP, and television violence, to name only three related issues, may be outnumbered by those who would enlist in a more comprehensive challenge to current criminal justice policy.

5

Abolitionism at the Crossroads

Almost a quarter of a century after its greatest victory in *Furman v. Georgia,* the anti-death penalty movement is often the object of harsh ridicule. Its enemies mock it for being out of touch with the American people, who are sick and tired of crime, and for whining about unfair treatment of lawbreakers. Death penalty opponents are also mocked for having failed utterly in their effort to stem the tide of tough justice. If the news media is one's only window, the movement appears to consist solely of dwindling bands of diehards, bewildered by society's waning interest in their case, holding flickering candles at execution-night vigils.

Much of this ridicule is undeserved. The movement is small, but activity slowly increased in the late 1980s and early 1990s rather than diminished. The nation's surly mood on crime is real enough, but as we have seen in our discussion of opinion surveys, its enthusiasm for executions has been greatly exaggerated. There are indeed many die-hard proponents of capital punishment in this nation, just as there are some who could never be convinced that any execution could ever be justified. But between the two stands a sizable group that seems to be open to persuasion that there are better solutions to illegal homicides than legal ones. And those who write abolitionists off as "failures" overstate their case. Undoubtedly, capital punishment will survive into the twenty-first century. In fact, its use may be on the upswing as the new millennium arrives. But it is also true that far more convicts would be dead today, including at least a few innocent ones, were it not for the efforts of abolitionist attorneys and their supporting cast. Even their detractors recognize this when they lambast the supposedly ineffectual anti-death penalty forces for jamming the machinery of execution. And there would be no public discussion of the social and ethical dimensions of capital punishment if the 200-year-old flame were not kept alive by ADPM groups. Jonathan Gradess thinks that abolition work can be judged only as a cumulative process, not in terms of its immediate impact:

> It's very much like chopping down a tree. It really isn't until the final ax stroke
> that the thing gives. But then it comes thundering down. Up until then you're

148

just chopping, and it seems like nothing's happening. That's what I think this movement is doing. It could do it better, and it could bring the tree down faster, but without it the thing would flourish.[1]

Anti-death penalty activists can also take some of the credit for the fact that fewer states have death penalty laws in effect now than in the past, that capital punishment is now virtually restricted to the crime of first-degree murder, that mandatory death sentences are obsolete, that a wide variety of procedural obstacles now constrain the discretion of sentencing authorities, and that a broad roster of mainstream organizations have officially condemned capital punishment (Bedau 1988). The movement hasn't eliminated executions, but it has helped to make them far less routine than they might otherwise be.

On reflection, it is at least a little remarkable that capital punishment even remains controversial. Americans are justifiably proud of their reputation for humanitarianism and procedural fairness, but our culture also contains an undeniable tradition of using violence to solve problems. There has been little hesitation to turn to lethal force as an instrument of both foreign policy and domestic social control, or to resolve interpersonal and intergroup conflicts. Black activist H. Rap Brown's claim that violence is "as American as apple pie" was perhaps hyperbolic, but it was not groundless. Capital punishment must be seen in the context of this culture of force. It is highly unlikely that activists could bring an end to legally sanctioned executions in a country like the United States even under the most favorable circumstances. Almost everyone close to the movement understands that abolition, if it ever arrives in the United States, is a long way off.

Chapter 5 assesses the struggle toward that objective and discusses the reasons the anti-death penalty movement has had difficulty in mobilizing opposition to capital punishment in the post-*Gregg* era, especially the movement's lack of adequate monetary and human resources. This chapter also briefly restates how the movement has been handicapped by the inhospitable political climate of the United States in the late twentieth century. It suggests, however, that many of the disadvantages that abolitionists face derive from their inability thus far to frame the issue in a politically effective manner. Chapter 6 will present the argument that in spite of the obstacles in the way, abolition *may be* attainable in the long run if the anti-death penalty movement changes the language in which it presents the issue to the American people.

Resources in the Struggle Against Capital Punishment

It has been said that an army runs on its stomach. In like manner, we now understand that social movements function in large part on quite tangible resources like money and manpower. Success is not guaranteed by such resources. But recent history suggests that movements endowed with neither large numbers of participants, significant levels of political influence, nor sufficient funds to employ less member-intensive tactics are unlikely to win many battles for social change. Thus far, the anti-death penalty movement has been severely disadvantaged in terms of such resources.

First, the anti-death penalty movement has never had enough money to mount the type of large-scale, nationwide campaign that would have a reasonable chance of reversing the death penalty's momentum. For example, it has never been able to afford the level of media coverage, such as glossy full-page advertisements in national magazines or 30-second television spots, that has been used in connection with abortion, health care reform, or even animal rights.[2] As was discussed in chapter 3, the death penalty program budget of Amnesty International USA doubled during the mid-1980s, and the funds of the National Coalition to Abolish the Death Penalty more than quadrupled between 1987 and 1991. In spite of these increases, total available funds have been paltry for a national social movement. Hugo Bedau doubts that as much as $1 million was being spent in 1992 to combat capital punishment in the United States.[3] Despite ending 1993 in the black and feeling generally good about its financial picture, the NCADP staff was still seeking donations of office equipment and even paper![4]

Not surprisingly, the need for more funding is a constant source of discussion among abolitionist leaders. A few feel that the scarcity of resources becomes an excuse for inaction, a convenient scapegoat on which to blame the movement's lack of creativity. They do not deny the burden that the movement's poverty imposes, but feel that it is hardly an insurmountable obstacle. Magdaleno Rose-Avila, former director of AIUSA's Death Penalty Program, insists that the architects of the great social movements of our time did not sit around hoping for money to appear. Rather, they made do with what was available. Similarly,

> . . . when Marie Deans and Joe Ingle and Scharlette Holdman started working against capital punishment, *they had nothing!* They did everything with nothing. And that's what people have to learn: you don't need a fat billfold. You don't need that. All you have to do is desire and want to do the right thing. That's why they have to be admired in a special way that can't be expressed.

> . . . You always need money, but you also must have leadership. You have to have a rejuvenation of leadership that is willing to do the impossible. Right now there is going to be even less money [due to the economic recession] — less money for Amnesty, less money for everybody. So what are you going to do, less work? Are you going to say no? We're gonna beg harder, we're gonna stretch money! No more hotels. People's couches! When people started out on doing death penalty work, you'd find four or five lawyers plus a researcher — men, women, and children — in the same room, many in the same bed — they'd take the mattress off and put it on the floor to make more room. People are going to go back to that. People say "Well, I'm not going to that demonstration because I don't have the money to fly there." Get in your car and *drive* there! It may take you a few more hours, but we're gonna do it.[5]

Rose-Avila is probably correct when he says that "no great social movement was started by a foundation." But he nevertheless understands that much of the funding problems for the ADPM derive from difficulties in attracting money from philanthropic sources. A few philanthropies, such as the Veach, MacArthur, and Playboy foundations have supported various abolitionist groups. A three-year grant from the Rockefeller Brothers Fund provided the bulk of the money with which the Southern Coalition on Jails and Prisons began its work on criminal justice reform.[6] For the most part, though, grants have been extremely hard for movement groups to come by.[7] Historically, the contribution patterns of foundations have been rather conservative. Most have preferred to avoid underwriting controversial groups, for fear of arousing public antipathy and increased governmental scrutiny. The pressure foundations endure has increased as a result of changes in tax laws that were enacted during the Reagan administration. But the death penalty has a number of characteristics that make it a particularly unattractive cause, even in comparison to other social controversies. Officials of charitable foundations are drawn to projects that will have a measurable impact on large numbers of people. The direct beneficiaries of abolition, current death row inmates, number about 3,000. And they are not an attractive lot in the eyes of foundation boards of directors. Foundation officials also like to assist organizations that are likely to *win.* The prospects for bringing an end to executions in the short term is slim at best, not just in the nation as a whole but in even a single death penalty state. And finally, foundations may have been leery of the ADPM's inability—at least until recently—to articulate a clear strategic vision. Charles Fulwood, former director of AI USA's Death Penalty Program and a member of the NCADP's board during the mid-1980s, feels that the coalition failed to attract large donations from either foundations or from the religious denominations that are affiliated with the coalition because its leaders didn't really know what they wanted the money for:

> I said you need an organizational development plan. First of all, you need a damn *program!* That's number one! But then you need a *strategy* for the program. You need to revitalize this board, get rid of some of this dead weight, quit preaching to the choir. You need an organizing strategy, a strategy to develop this organization. If you put that kind of a plan together, then you're talking serious turkey! You've shown the funding source that the organization is taking responsibility for itself, that you've given thorough thought to where you're going, that you want to keep the organization alive. You just can't say "give us money." That's not going to work. And they didn't do it, because I don't think that they wanted to think—I don't think they wanted to take the time to think in those terms.

Resources and State-Level Organizing

The lack of clarity and sophistication among abolitionists that Fulwood found so frustrating is less evident now than it used to be, and this may improve the movement's ability to find the resources for its work in the long rum. But for now it remains hamstrung. In addition to limiting the ability of national movement organizations to take their case to the public through the sophisticated use of mass media, lack of funds has prevented the movement from doing intensive grassroots organizing at the state and local level. More than anything else, this has crippled the abolitionist effort to influence emerging legislation. As mentioned earlier, the anti-death penalty movement suffers from a "grassroots deficit"; that is, the network of organizations dedicated specifically to fighting capital punishment at the state level, where the bulk of death penalty politics occurs, is extremely weak. Some sort of anti-death penalty organization exists in every state. But aside from Amnesty International groups, most of which concentrate more of their energy on other issues, state-level abolitionist organizations and coalitions often exist primarily on paper. They are endorsed by an array of religious and policy-oriented advocacy groups and are allowed to use those groups' names on their letterheads. But they almost never have the capacity to call on the memberships of those affiliated groups for any type of coordinated action.[8] And in only a handful of states—California, Massachusetts, New York, and Illinois are the most consistent members of this category—is there even an organization that has paid staff, rather than merely volunteer activists, that concentrates on this issue.[9] Money woes have thinned the ranks of such groups. The Southern Coalition on Jails and Prisons dissolved by 1990, leaving its affiliates in Alabama, North Carolina, and Virginia operating on their own. The Virginia Coalition, headed by Marie Deans, folded in 1993.

Lack of grassroots organization is probably most acute in Texas, which leads the nation in executions. Texas's sheer size makes the organization of an effective network of abolitionists difficult, as does the predominance of unusually strident "law and order" views among elected officials and citizens. Not until around 1986, much later than in other states, did such a network begin to emerge. When AIUSA's state anti-death penalty coordinator, Jude Miller, moved to Austin in 1988, a degree of centralization and outreach finally began. But resistance to capital punishment in Texas is among the weakest in the United States. One of the most prominent activists in the state, Rick Halperin, estimated that there may be fewer than 50 active abolitionists in the state in 1993. The NCADP launched a "Mess With Texas" campaign in the summer of 1994 in hopes of changing the situation. Its goal is to build a stronger abolitionist infrastructure by, among other things, "making contacts with social service providers and those fighting for a share of the state's limited resources for programs in education, child abuse and drug abuse prevention, while Texas spends over $15 million annually on the death penalty."[10]

The presence of salaried organizers at the state level would make an enormous difference in the ADPM's prospects. They would have the time to build or strengthen interorganizational coalitions and coordinate the work of volunteers. They would be more likely than part-time volunteers to develop public speaking and media skills, to build ongoing relationships with legislators, to track cases, and to distribute information throughout abolitionist networks quickly and efficiently. State groups with full-time staff people would be much more likely to achieve 501 (c)(3) or 501 (c)(4) tax status—enabling them, respectively, to receive tax- deductible contributions and to devote a considerable portion of their efforts to lobbying.[11] The importance of increased funding and full-time staff is best expressed by NCADP director Leigh Dingerson:

> What needs to happen is that state-level organizing on the death penalty has to get real sophisticated. And what that means is that in every state, there needs to be a grassroots component, there needs to be a 501 (c)(4) that's doing lobbying full-time. There probably, eventually, is going to need to be a political action committee [in each state]. There's probably less than a half dozen states that have lobbying status. A few other states hook up with someone who does, usually the ACLU. In state after state, we've found that the ACLU folks are just overwhelmed. So the state coalition needs a (c)(4) to do lobbying, and they may or may not need a PAC. And what *that* means is a tremendous infusion of money! Each state coalition needs to be able to hire three and four staff people at a reasonable salary so they get good, experienced folks, to be doing that work effectively.[12]

Along similar lines, movement leaders recognize the importance of well-trained volunteer activists at the *local* level, "in the counties where the death sentences are coming from."[13] The types of proactive work that movement leaders want to do at this level can only be accomplished by local people, people who not only know the abolitionist arguments but know the ins and outs of local politics as well.

Resources and Staff Burnout

The movement's shortage of funds also exacerbates the problem of "burnout" among some of its most active and dedicated participants. Maintaining commitment to the abolitionist struggle is difficult, even without the additional burden of insufficient resources. The reasons for this are fairly obvious. Few causes are as unpopular as this one, and abolitionists often feel a tremendous sense of isolation and public hostility to their work. They sometimes must endure hate mail, harassing phone calls, and the intense animosity of victim's relatives.[14] The psychological toll is even heavier among those who work directly with death row inmates as lawyers or counselors, like Marie Deans, for they often feel that prisoners' lives are in their hands.

> You're working with dysfunctional families, and you're working with guys who are traumatized, who are being horribly dehumanized by the system they're in, who are extremely needy, who are often retarded or mentally ill, or who have been *driven* insane if they weren't before they got there. It's really difficult to deal with! And it's constant.
> You've got to take time away to grieve. I used to treat myself like a robot. Who was *I* to take time off to grieve?! I mean, I didn't feel like I had the right to do it, when there were always more guys, and they were always trying to kill more guys. And they were *there,* and they were hurtin' and they were scared, so who was I to take time off and tell them "don't call me for three days, 'cause I'm gonna be home?" I *couldn't* grant myself that right. And I

should have. Because who I am is the person who needs to be here for them in the *long* run! And I would go down to that death house and go through an execution, and then go to the office the next morning! We kill at 11:00, so I'd be late, you know. But I'd come. And I don't do that anymore. I take days off now, afterwards. But not enough! We need to take *weeks* off, but you can't, because there's somebody always down there who needs you! I went to [a recent NCADP conference in] Chicago [in spite of the fact that one of our prisoners had a scheduled] date of execution. It's the first time I'd ever done that. This poor guy's wondering why he's the first one, and really kind of *asked* me. And I said 'Timothy, it's because there's been somebody down there [scheduled to die] since May! And if I say that I can't leave the state — which is what I said for ten years, that I wouldn't leave the state when somebody has a date of execution — then I'll never leave again! I'll never go to another conference, I'll never go home, I'll never see my family or my grandson. I'll never do any of that ever again!"[15]

The stress and potential for burnout among anti-death penalty people is multiplied by the weaknesses of their organizations and by the fact that those with salaries must often subsist on very low pay and few, if any, fringe benefits. One of these individuals, Leigh Dingerson, expressed it this way:

I think the death penalty is no different from [movements targeted at other social] issues, [but] what does it is the sort of structural stuff, you know — not having enough money for what you want to do, working in single-person offices, and having to cut back to half time because you don't have the funds to go full time, and not being able to pay for health insurance and benefits. I mean, those sort of structural things cause burnout in any organization. With the death penalty, you've got the added pressure of having people die![16]

Resource Mobilization Theory and the ADPM

An earlier chapter raised a number of questions about applicability of the resource mobilization theory of collective action to the anti-death penalty movement. Several of these questions have been answered in this chapter, especially those pertaining to the restrictions that the movement has suffered as a result of unsuccessful fund-raising and low membership levels. But we have not yet determined how much other RMT propositions about contemporary forms of collective action are borne out in the case of abolitionism.

Resource mobilization theory emphasizes how social movements are shaped by resource fluctuations over time, and its adherents generally impute more explanatory power to resource flow than to variation in social discontent. Some (Tilly 1978; Jenkins and Perrow 1977) have asserted that there is always enough discontent to drive collective action, but there are not always sufficient tangible resources and organization to carry it. Others, particularly McCarthy and Zald (1973, 1977) see grievances as the outgrowths of movement enterprise, not as its precondition. In either case, the emergence and growth of social movements should follow, rather than precede, resource inflows (McAdam, McCarthy, and Zald 1988:702).

Firm conclusions as to whether these basic propositions are borne out in the anti-death penalty movement are difficult to reach, because there have not been wide variations in the intensity of ADPM activity since *Furman*. So far, this has been a low- intensity movement. It has managed to survive and even to achieve some limited success with very few resources, but it has not flourished. The entrance of AIUSA, which is large and relatively well funded, has made a difference. Without AIUSA, the nonlitigation arm of the movement would amount to little. But even AIUSA's strength has not been enough to do more than slow capital punishment's advance.

It is also difficult to characterize discontent over the death penalty as being constant in recent decades. Even though overall approval of capital punishment has grown, movement groups have had their greatest success in mobilizing when some external event created a crisis.[17] The most recent example is the rapid development of fairly intense, coordinated anti-death penalty work in New York following the defeat of Democratic governor Mario Cuomo by George Pataki. Among Pataki's campaign promises was a pledge to sign a reinstatement bill as early in his term as lawmakers could deliver one (Golway 1995; Kaufman 1995). He was able to fulfill that pledge, but not until opponents had mounted their most intense lobbying and public education efforts in decades. Another example is the Washington, D.C., referendum of 1992, when ADPM forces were able to make rather dramatic inroads in local minority communities and turn what might have been a major defeat into a rare victory. The impending execution of Robert Alton Harris made the death penalty issue tangible among California liberals and progressives, thus transforming passive opposition to executions into one of the two or three most intense state-level abolitionist campaigns of all time. Fund-raising and attendance at abolitionist meetings and other movement-staged events increased dramatically. So did media coverage and requests for interviews and information by members of the press. The problem, according to leaders in California, was finding a way to sustain the momentum once the crisis had passed.[18] Similarly, the creation of an activist network in Kansas came as an immediate response to a threat of reinstatement there in 1978. That network formed the nucleus of the Kansas Coalition Against the Death Penalty, and it received its greatest boost by the election of a pro-death penalty governor in 1986.[19] In each of these cases, enhanced recruitment and resource mobilization, modest though they were, followed the emergence of a "suddenly imposed grievance" (Walsh 1981, 1988). The ADPM took advantage of these events, put its own "spin" on them, and tried to channel the popular reaction. But as a general rule, grievances have played a more independent role in the movement's history than the resource mobilization perspective allows for. ADP strategists have tried desperately to organize abolitionist sentiment in the various states *in advance* of crises like scheduled executions or reinstatement threats. But as one New York abolitionist laments, they have found that to be quite difficult:

> I have a lurking suspicion that "crisis makes opportunity," that many of these things come together naturally when a crisis occurs. New York is a perfect

example. Whether you *have* to do it that way, I'm not convinced. I have concerns that maybe that's true. I would like to think that it isn't, because I think it's gonna take a hell of a lot longer that way.

[Interviewer: "Whether it has to take this particular form, you mean, or whether crisis makes opportunities?"]

"Whether the only time people can see the necessity for having, you know, full-time people working for manipulating the political system and developing grassroots activities, for getting letter-writing campaigns, for developing telephone trees for communication, for having the resources for high-fallutin' people at a press conference, etc. It seems like whenever we have a crisis in the country — whether an execution is coming or a vote is coming or a referendum is on the table — people put into place those different elements. But they're always *struggling* to put them into place. Otherwise, you know, they either don't have the money or they don't have the big names. . . . My assumption is that it ought to be structured at the outset, that one ought to create models in each state . . . not in the middle of a crisis, but on a routine basis — that allow for, you know, Amnesty and the ACLU and the coalition representatives and the church people to sit down in the same room on an ongoing basis and structure coalitions. So that's the only reservation that I express, that it may not be a doable thing in the absence of crisis. And I think that if it were, we'd be a lot further along.[20]

Resource mobilization theorists have also stressed a change in the relative importance of two types of social movement organizations (SMOs). "Classical" SMOs spring from within oppressed communities and rely on resources supplied from those communities. On the other hand, "professional" SMOs like those of the 1960s and earlier 1970s possessed several characteristics that set them apart from classical insurgency. According to McCarthy and Zald (1973), they were generally led by outsiders rather than members of the groups on whose behalf they worked. They had full-time paid staffs and "paper memberships." Their resources were largely externally derived, often from "conscience" constituents and elites. They attempted to "speak for" the direct beneficiaries of their causes rather than actually mobilize them.

As this investigation has shown, national ADPM organizations have clearly had all of the characteristics of the McCarthy and Zald *professional* movement organization except — at the state level — full-time paid staff. Of the three major groups operating on a national scale, only AIUSA has a large membership base that provides the bulk of its resources and also takes a very direct role in its work. All three national organizations now have full-time paid staff. None mobilize the direct beneficiaries of their efforts, death row prisoners, but focus instead on "conscience adherents and conscience constituents" (McCarthy and Zald 1977:1222). Aside from paid staff, both the AIUSA and NCADP structures rely heavily on the work of volunteers whose occupations provide considerable amounts of discretionary time — especially academics, lawyers and other professionals, and students. But whereas many resource mobilization theorists have suggested that professional movement organizations are as good or better than classical SMOs, the story of the anti-death penalty movement suggests otherwise. Quite likely, the movement would have virtually disappeared by now had it not been for the involvement of the quasiclassical AI.[21]

Finally, other writers in the resource mobilization tradition have suggested that to have their interests represented in the political process, powerless groups must depend on favorable elite intervention. Elites provide "the legitimacy and leverage necessary for critical victories" (Jenkins and Eckert 1986: 812). Clearly, given the disreputability of the ADPM's direct beneficiaries, the only possible source of legitimacy and influence for the anti-death penalty cause would have to come from outside their ranks. Not only are convicted murderers the most despised segment of the American population, but they are too few in number and absolutely without access to the resources and infrastructure necessary to act on their own behalf.

There is no question, then, that a lack of money and manpower has severely limited the strength of the anti-death penalty movement's challenge. But this does not mean that the movement's trajectory fits perfectly with the predictions of resource mobilization theory. Rather than being the main determinant of the intensity of movement activity, the availability of strategic resources is one of a number of variables that account for it. Grievances, based on the ebbs and flows of the politics of crime, have played important and independent roles. So have the strategic and tactical decisions made by abolitionists.

The biggest resource that has allowed the ADPM to struggle on is the intense commitment that is so common among its participants. Considering the obstacles they face, it is remarkable that such commitment remains. Directors do move on to posts in other social movements. People do burn out and withdraw from the movement, but usually only for a short time. Overall, maintaining the enthusiasm of participants seems to be a surprisingly minor problem for the movement as a whole. Anti-death penalty conferences and rallies are rarely marked by any perceptible degree of discouragement or fatalism. AIUSA's Ali Miller contends that this optimism is sustained in part by a form of realism that most abolitionists eventually develop:

> I think people need to have a reasonable understanding of what they can expect to do. Once again, totally as an Amnesty perspective, nobody expects to abolish torture totally by the end of 1995, yet people regularly stand up and give speeches about the abolition of the death penalty in the United States by the year 2000. We understand that our work against torture is the right place to be and that we intend to stop every piece of torture that we can, and ultimately our goal is to do away with it. But there's something about the death penalty . . . because it looks so concrete and discrete — and [it seems somehow that] we should be able to affect it immediately. It's *our* government and *we're* doing it! We know it, we know the date, we know the laws, we can change the laws. Well it's just as much a public expression of pain and anger and complicity in government malfeasance as torture is. But we have a different standard for ourselves on the death penalty, within Amnesty. And I think

that makes it hard for a lot of folks. So I keep trying to work hard on these intermediate goals. And make them clear to people. Because otherwise, you can't survive.[22]

The "intermediate goals" by which Miller and others in the movement have learned to measure their success include the passage of incremental legislation, the defeat of expansion bills, and the reversal of death sentences.

The optimism of many anti-death penalty activists is also sustained by a belief in the historical inevitability of abolition. Henry Schwarzschild is one of those who share this faith:

I think [the death penalty in America will] clearly outlive me and it may outlive you. But I think ultimately it'll be abolished. You're not gonna walk in the opposite direction of the rest of the civilized world forever. For a long time, but not forever.[23]

The Narrow Spectrum of Anti-Death Penalty Activism

If anti-death penalty activists are to begin chipping away at the increasingly entrenched practice of putting convicted murderers to death, they will have to organize more broadly. Their local and state organizations must have as much vitality, if not more, than the national organizations. They must gain at least certain minimum levels of support and participation from sectors of American society that have heretofore either supported capital punishment or have been apathetic about it. And in all likelihood, they must be willing to tolerate—and even encourage—anti-death penalty strategies that are themselves controversial.

But the movement is disadvantaged by its present configuration. It lacks the structures needed to contest the death penalty at the most appropriate level—in the states and counties—and it relies on the participation of a remarkably narrow band of American society. Also, anti-death penalty forces have failed to rally the very groups who might be expected to have the most fundamental objections to capital punishment—especially African Americans, who would bring to the movement much-needed numbers and expertise. These are interrelated problems, for the movement's grassroots deficit is a product of its small constituent base. Unlike self-determination movements, the ADPM's beneficiaries are virtually uninvolved in the struggle. Today's abolitionists are generally motivated not by self-interest, but by either humanitarian principles or by a hatred of what the death penalty seems to them to stand for: racism and class privilege.

Chapter 4 attended to the disagreements among abolitionists over the failure to enlist large numbers of black people in the cause. Some believe that black participation has been low because "their plate is full"; that is, other issues that affect large numbers of African Americans more directly take precedence over capital punishment. Other ADPM personnel feel that movement organizations have made insufficient or incompetent efforts in the black community. It is impossible to say which of the two sides is right. But it may well be that the argument has focused too much on bringing minorities into *existing movement organizations* or enlisting black organizations in *existing strategies.* Doing so would be enormously beneficial for AIUSA and the NCADP. What might be even better in the long run for the movement as a whole, in addition to increased black participation in those groups, would be the appearance of independent black anti-death penalty structures and the elevation of capital punishment on the working agendas of civil rights and other black groups. Involvement in the struggle would thus be increased on black people's own terms rather than in terms of white models for social change. Black abolitionists would be at greater liberty to develop their own critiques of capital punishment, devise their own strategies and tactics, and develop their own resource bases. Some current activists worry that this would lead to disunity within the ADPM. But as we shall see shortly, rhetorical and tactical unity is not always of maximum benefit.

The lack of diversity that has hindered the ADPM is ideological as well as racial. For as long as any living abolitionist can remember, opposition to capital punishment has been seen as a liberal stance. There is no necessary reason why this should be so. If the movement can only succeed in attracting liberal groups and individuals, then executions will go on for a very long time.[24] To slow the death penalty's momentum and ultimately reverse it, activists will have to devise appeals that will work better among those who do not share "progressive" outlooks.

There is also too little strategic and tactical diversity. In particular, the anti-death penalty movement lacks what most relatively successful movements have had: a *street component.* That is, the ADPM has not had the capacity to get relatively large numbers of people involved in highly visible events, be they civil disobedience, demonstrations, rallies, marches, or mass meetings. There have been a few exceptions to this rule, such as the 1977 Witness Against Executions in Atlanta and more recent demonstrations in California just before that state's gas chamber went back into service. But even these events were small in comparison to the rallies and direct actions staged by pro- and antiabortion forces, gay rights advocates, and the like, and they have occurred only sporadically. Prison vigils and poorly attended marches, such as one organized by Texans Against State Killing in 1991, have been about the best that abolitionists were able to muster.

The absence of a street component has meant that anti-death penalty activism has been virtually invisible to the American public, and this invisibility has left the movement's image largely in the hands of its opponents and the press. Again, this was less so for other struggles. It was through direct action in places like Birmingham and Selma that America came to know the civil rights movement, for instance. The most indelible image from that struggle may be Dr. Martin Luther King delivering the concluding lines of his stirring "I Have A Dream" speech on the steps of the Lincoln Memorial in August 1963. But abolitionists as yet have no equivalent symbol, and they are hobbled by their inability to define themselves through dramatic collective events.

A street component, however, implies more than just larger numbers of death penalty opponents. It implies participants with a different orientation, people who are ready, willing, and able to express their opposition to capital punishment in dramatic and highly visible ways. This does not necessarily imply committing civil disobedience. But it does mean public displays of vigorous opposition to execution as a criminal justice policy. The abolitionist cause may well profit from the emergence of different styles of activism that would complement, but not replace, the movement's current reliance on public education, lobbying, and legal work.

Many ADP activists feel that little good would come from this because direct action tactics are no longer as effective as they may once have been. They are also understandably concerned that broadening the tactical repertoire of the movement would only lead to counterproductive disagreements over methods. The development of factions is often thought to doom social movements to failure, but this is not necessarily true. Neither the labor struggles, the civil rights revolution, nor the women's movement, all of which achieved undeniably positive changes for their constituents, spoke with one voice. On the contrary, each was characterized by deep schisms over appropriate objectives and the methods that ought to be used to achieve them. Bitter intramovement conflicts developed. Organizations competed with each other for resources and leaders worried about how the actions of their rivals would hinder or set back their own efforts.

But when victories were achieved, it was often *because* of disunity rather than in spite of it. The struggle of African Americans for their rights during the post–World War II era provides the clearest example. The greatest expansions in civil rights came precisely when "militants" from the Southern Christian Leadership Conference, the Congress of Racial Equality, and other groups were taking their grievances to the streets. Most often they did so over the objections of those who thought that quiet negotiation or litigation was the way to go. And when peaceful demonstrations for desegregation and equal rights gave way to violence and black nationalism, the trend was not reversed. Rather than creating a policy backlash, the escalation of black rhethoric and tactics simply turned up the pressure on decision makers. Most moderate leaders came to realize that the unruly words and deeds of the militants, whom they disapproved of so deeply, actually increased their legitimacy and their bargaining power. When under siege by "militants," white political and economic elites often acquiesced to the demands of "moderates" as a means of damage control. Indeed, the reversal of fortunes for civil rights advocates came when the disintegration of the movement's "radical flank" reduced the pressure to grant concessions (Haines 1988).

It would be unrealistic to suggest that the prerequisites for a more successful anti-death penalty movement are the same as those of earlier struggles. But it does seem likely that the strategic unity of abolitionists, made necessary by the current weakness of movement organizations, deprives them of the creative tensions that were at work in those days. This is a minority view, but one held firmly by the NCADP's Leigh Dingerson:

We need, I think, an arm of the movement — at the national level, but more importantly at the state level — that is the "thorn in their sides." We need a militant arm of the movement that is forcing the debate in public, very visibly, very militantly, and moving the center of the debate to the left. That is what SNCC did for the civil rights community. It's what ACT UP! is for the AIDS organizing. This movement needs a component that is doing that for the issue of death penalty.[25]

Realistically, the anti-death penalty movement is probably too fragile to profit from the emergence of moderate and militant factions. It would first need to get bigger and more secure, and it would need to establish a bit of forward momentum. Thus we are back to where we started: too few resources and too little popular support.

" . . . The Worst of Times": Political Opportunity and Abolitionism

It is easier for collective actors to build support and mobilize resources in some time periods than in others. According to the *political process* model (see McAdam 1982; McAdam, McCarthy, and Zald 1988; Tarrow 1989), social movements are better able to organize and sustain viable challenges either when general social instability is restructuring power relations or when more specific crises are increasing insurgents' bargaining position relative to their opponents and the political authorities. Social movements may be partly responsible for creating such openings, but opportunities are often beyond the immediate control of either activists or their targets. In any case, it is important that movement leaders seize the moment before it slips away. And when opportunities open up, a wide array of movements may benefit simultaneously. We see evidence of "cycles of protest" and "cycles of reform" within societies over time.

The ADPM profited from the cycle of protest that occurred during the tumultuous 1960s. Institutions ranging from metropolitan governments to schools to the family were far more vulnerable to criticism and change than in the years before or after. Abolitionism was pulled along in the draft of that decade, especially by the momentum of the civil rights revolution that America experienced. The death penalty declined and fell not because of any inherent weakness. Nor did it fall because of the organizational strength or the intellectual irresistibility of the case against it. It fell because, as practiced, many people found it to be glaringly inconsistent with the ascendent ideas of the times.

But by the late 1980s and early 1990s, things changed dramatically. Political liberalism declined at all levels and branches of government and in the electorate. A sharp rise in the *visibility* of crime has done immense damage to the abolitionist cause. Violent crime, as measured by victim surveys, has actually fallen from its 1981 peak (Zawitz, et al. 1993). But most people seem to believe that murder, rape, and serious assault are rapidly increasing (Krauss

1994; Lewis 1993; Meier 1993; Nagorka 1993). Real increases in crimes by young people and in gang-related assaults with sophisticated firearms have undoubtedly contributed to misperceptions about crime trends. So has the attraction of the news and entertainment media to drive-by shootings, serial killers (see Jenkins 1994), and other dramatic but relatively uncommon forms of murder. Despite recent efforts, ADPM activists have thus far failed to respond effectively to the discovery, by candidates for political office, that careful nurturing of voters' resentment and terror over crime can be the key to electoral success. Each of these developments has served to mobilize support for capital punishment and to marginalize the ADPM.

Framing the Death Penalty

Given the disadvantages it faces, what would it take to put the movement against capital punishment on a more sound footing? What, if anything, could abolitionists do to arouse more popular opposition, to draw larger numbers of active participants to their cause, and to secure more funding? Does the mood of the American public in the late twentieth century mean that a serious challenge to the death penalty is an impossible dream?

The evidence suggests that the task of reversing the momentum of capital punishment in this country is extraordinarily difficult — improbable but not impossible. The *central* obstacle to the achievement of this objective, the problem that appears to be at the root of most of the ADPM's other problems, is frame alignment. The pages that follow will consider opportunities that abolitionists have yet to seize and resources that may be within their reach, but only if they "repackage" their case against the death penalty.

The Limited Mobilizing Potential of Traditional Abolitionism

The main arguments that opponents of capital punishment have used over the past two centuries fall into two general categories. Their *moral* arguments have rested on the assertion that capital punishment is ethically objectionable, whereas their *pragmatic* critiques have been based on cost-benefit grounds. Both types of arguments have been employed throughout American history, often in an overlapping fashion, but the former have always been dominant. In the eighteenth and nineteenth centuries, the alleged immorality of executions was cast mostly in religious terms. Antigallows reformers portrayed capital punishment as an abrogation of divine authority and spent much of their time putting their spin on the seemingly unambiguous endorsements of the death penalty found in the Old Testament. In more recent times, death penalty opponents have de-emphasized theology, because theological points rarely settle policy questions in a society like the United States. But they have continued trying to convince their fellow citizens that executions are morally wrong. For example, the portrayal of executions as inherently cruel (Amsterdam 1982; Schwarzschild 1990) appeals to humanitarian sentiments, not religious beliefs. So does the claim that capital punishment ignores the sanctity of all human life, and that it is steeped in racial discrimination and caprice (Baldus, Woodworth, and Pulaski 1990; Black 1981; Bowers and Pierce 1980b). The most recent twist in the moral critique of capital punishment is its characterization by Amnesty International and other groups as a violation of fundamental and inalienable human rights that demand recognition in every culture and political system.

Each of these ways of framing the death penalty issue — religious, secular, or human rights-based — is essentially moralistic rather than pragmatic. Each is a particular way of saying that it is *wrong* to put to death those who have been convicted of criminal offenses, no matter how heinous those offenses might be. None of them critiques the death penalty as unwise, ineffective, or counterproductive as an instrument of crime control, or as a waste of time and money.

The ADPM's predominantly moralistic critique has never met with much success the United States, except for a few shining moments between the mid-1960s and 1972. Even then, it worked mostly in the rarefied air of the courtroom. The public and political response has been especially poor during the 1980s and 1990s: fear of crime is very great, and support for capital punishment — crudely measured — is at an all-time high (Gallup and Newport 1991:43). So is anticrime rhetoric; draconian measures like flogging, castration, and summary execution are sometimes endorsed by commentators and office seekers and in letters to the editor. Nevertheless, we have seen, in connection with the more detailed opinion surveys such as those commissioned by AIUSA in 1986, that there is a great deal of unease about the death penalty. Arbitrariness, the risk of executing the innocent, and the practice of putting to death juveniles and mentally retarded convicts continue to trouble many people, and capital punishment is widely believed to be unfair (Gallup and Newport 1991:40). In the years since the first poll in Florida, surveys in other states have produced comparable results on the preference of many Americans for alternative punishments. The most acceptable alternative punishment among people who otherwise favor capital punishment is life in prison without any chance for parole, combined with restitution to the victim's family from the proceeds of prison labor. When "LWOP + R" was presented as an option, majorities in Arkansas (Smith 1993), California (Roderick 1990; Chiang 1992; *cf.* Skelton 1992), New York (Amnesty International USA 1989; Bowers and Vandiver 1991a), Indiana (Leahy 1993), Georgia, Massachusetts, and Nebraska (Bowers and Vandiver 1991b; Thomas and Hutcheson 1986) preferred it to the death penalty. When LWOP was presented alone (that is, without restitution) as a concrete alternative to capital punishment, majorities in New York (Bowers and Vandiver 1991a), Kentucky (Vito and Keil 1989), and West Virginia (Niller 1990) chose it over the death penalty. Smaller but nevertheless sizable percentages in Texas (Fair 1992), Nebraska, Georgia, Maryland, Massachusetts, and Oklahoma (Bowers and Vandiver 1991b:12) deemed it acceptable. Even proposals for 40- and 25-year mandatory minimum sentences for convicted first-degree murders have been found to diminish greatly the expressed support for capital punishment in a number of surveys (see Amnesty International USA 1989; Bowers and Vandiver 1991b:12). Similarly, interviews with capital jurors in California, Florida, and South Carolina revealed a preference for LWOP with restitution rather than death (Bowers 1993). These consistent survey results are important because they show that death penalty support is "a mile wide and an inch deep."

If so many people are uncertain over capital punishment and willing to settle for "tough-but-fair alternatives," then why has it become such a potent political issue? Why have office seekers tried so hard to capitalize on the supposedly overwhelming demand for executions among their constituents? Why, in other words, do people respond to polls in one way and vote in another? The answer may be that they don't. There is little solid evidence that the death penalty, in itself, is really a very powerful determinant of voting behavior after all. Comparisons of survey data and the results of interviews with New York state legislators by Bowers, Vandiver, and Dugan (1994) suggest that there were "reciprocal misperceptions" between the two groups. Voters in the New York survey imagined that their representatives in Albany were even more receptive to alternative punishments than the citizens were. But the lawmakers vastly overestimated their constituents' insistence that the punishment for murder be nothing short of the death penalty. They did so, in all likelihood, because they relied on superficial media reporting of public attitudes and on the mail they received from the minority of fiercely committed death penalty advocates.

Most legislators believed that voting against the reinstatement of the death penalty would hurt their chances of reelection, and they behaved accordingly. Given the widespread oversimplification of public opinion, it is easy to attribute a victory by a conservative candidate to his or her advocacy of capital punishment. It may, in fact, be more the result of the candidate's stance on taxation, welfare reform, or health care. Thus, pro-death penalty voting patterns may be "a self-perpetuating political myth" (Bowers, Vandiver, and Dugan 1994). The striking consistency of opinion survey data makes this the most likely explanation of what otherwise seems to be contradictory citizen behavior.

The important point is that, anecdotal evidence and conventional political wisdom aside, public support for capital punishment is not so solid that the abolitionist movement is doomed to fail.

Moreover, turning the tide against capital punishment would not require a massive proportional shift in sentiment. Attorney David Bruck claimed more than a decade ago that if only a quarter to a third of death penalty supporters changed their minds, the "political potency" of the death penalty would be neutralized (1984).

But it is highly unlikely that framing the death penalty primarily as a moral or human rights issue will suffice to capitalize on the well-documented ambivalence that already exists in the United States. That message resonates poorly with the fear and anger over violent crime that is so widespread at present and that is unlikely to go away in the foreseeable future. To be convinced that executions are morally unacceptable, one must either learn to personify the issue and empathize with the condemned inmate, or to think of it as a matter of philosophical principle. Neither point of view is an easy one for abolitionists to sell. As challenging as it can be to generate identification with groups such as the poor, AIDS victims, and openly gay people, capital punishment presents the greatest challenge of all. Most Americans have great difficulty mustering empathy for persons convicted of aggravated murder. If the actual facts of their crimes are not enough, media- promoted images of subhuman and remorseless killers further reduce the effectiveness of the abolitionists' moral claims. Using the terminology of David Snow and Robert Benford (1988), the traditional anti-death penalty frame is weak in *"experiential commensurability"* (that is, there is a lack of fit with the public's experiences of crime and criminals) and in its *"narrative fidelity"* (that is, it contradicts dominant cultural constructions of crime and justice). Moreover, faith in the reformability of wrongdoers and belief in the sanctity of the lives of deeply flawed individuals — which are perhaps the core values of traditional abolitionism — rank lower in salience than individual responsibility and just desserts. In principle, Americans understand that two wrongs may not make a right. But it is exceedingly difficult to persuade them that murders and legal executions are equivalent wrongs.

Moreover, appearing "soft on criminals" has come to be seen as virtual suicide for incumbents and challengers alike (Applebome 1993; Oreskes 1990). When politicians compete with each other in crime-fighting contests, they generate massive levels of news coverage for the hard-line position. Abolitionists do not command the media muscle to counteract it. Some activists have now come to agree with Charles Fulwood, who believes that moral arguments in general, and not just on issues of criminal justice, have been rendered almost futile by the increasing acceptance of violence:

> There are many things about our culture that make working against the death penalty difficult: we're violence-prone; there's the nature of television, the nature of the local news, the nature of entertainment, motion pictures, films, and our lifestyle in general. If someone says "Don't do that" and the other person says "Why?," and the first person says *"It's not right!"*—people will look at you like *"WHAT?* What are you talking about!?" (laughing) And that's kind of the way the "pure" abolitionists have played this: "Don't do this, because it's not right!" Up against a mountain of facts about the crime! Up against an avalanche of public fear and anxiety about crime! Up against a mountain of media exposure that has demonized the defendant, up against a culture of racism, up against a culture that cares about fairness only in the abstract, and only when it affects you personally.[26]

Another important plank in the predominately moral attack on the death penalty is the problem of racial bias. Discriminatory death sentencing continues to receive a great deal of attention from abolitionists. This was evident, for example, in a nationally televised debate on public television's *Firing Line* on July 1, 1994. The anti-capital punishment team, which included Stephen Bright, Ira Glasser, and Bryan Stevenson, repeatedly steered the discussion back to the tendency of the courts to condemn to death the murderers of white victims, while handing down prison sentences to those who kill blacks. Bright and Stevenson have represented many defendants in capital trials, and they made frequent reference to specific instances of outright racism in the behavior of police, prosecutors, and jurors. Outside of the African American community, concentrating on racial discrimination in the application of the death penalty may well be no more effective than emphasizing its inherent cruelty. Most white Americans do care about racial justice. They would object strongly to a case of overt employment discrimination, for example, in which a qualified, motivated applicant is denied a job because of the color of his skin. But a black man who has been condemned to die for the robbery-murder of an elderly white couple is not likely to be receive much sympathy simply because others guilty of equally brutal crimes go to prison instead of the death chamber. It is the "lenient" prison sentence that many people are likely to see as unjust, not the death sentence. Ernest van den Haag, one of the most vocal in a small band of retentionist academics, captured the feelings of many less eloquent Americans when he suggested that:

> [t]o regard the death penalty as unjust because it is unequally distributed . . . confuses inequality with injustice. The guilt of any one murderer (and the justice of imposing the death penalty on him) is not diminished if other, equally or more guilty, murderers are not convicted or executed, whether because of racial discrimination, accident, or sheer capriciousness. Guilt is personal. That others were spared is no reason to spare you the punishment your crime deserves. Others got away with murder, they were not caught, convicted, or executed, for whatever reason. If these were grounds for not punishing those caught and convicted, we could never punish. (1990:511–512)

The continued existence of documented racial disparities in the application of capital punishment may yet be deemed constitutionally relevant. But as a weapon in the movement's public education arsenal, it may achieve little. Apart from its focused efforts to increase minority participation in the movement, the ADPM may even be making a mistake in highlighting an "imperfection" that, in the end, can be ameliorated through *more,* not fewer, electrocutions and lethal injections.

When all is said and done, American abolitionists have yet to fashion a politically effective case against the death penalty, a case that is powerful enough to turn large numbers of their fellow citizens against the practice of executing murderers. They have many of the pieces of such a case, but they have not yet put those pieces together. How could the death penalty be framed so that its opponents might finally recapture the momentum in their struggle? It is to that question that we now turn.

6

Reframing Capital Punishment: Pragmatic Abolitionism

The beginning of this book posed the question of why the death penalty shows signs of flourishing in the United States when it is disappearing from the rest of the Western democratic world. For various reasons, most of those nations did not require a groundswell of popular pressure before they renounced the state's right to kill lawbreakers. The United States seems to be different in that regard; apparently a vigorous anti-death penalty movement is a prerequisite to any prospects for abolition in the future. Part of the answer to why capital punishment seems to be so well entrenched here is the current weakness of that opposition movement. In a nation where policy advocacy has become a capital-intensive enterprise, death penalty opponents have little money. On an issue that is fought mostly at the state level, abolitionism consists primarily of eastern-based national organizations with weak state affiliates and few local ones. These two disadvantages are linked intimately to a third. In the cynical and angry climate that exists in America, abolitionists have trusted mostly in their ability to bring about not just a national change of *mind,* but a change of *heart.* What has remained underdeveloped within the movement is a more pragmatic vocabulary, capable of more than just preaching to the choir.

Attacking capital punishment as an immoral and inhuman practice is not the only way to contest it. Another is to portray it as an unwise, counterproductive criminal justice policy. This approach has not been completely absent from the movement's repertoire over the years. But moral/humanitarian claims have dominated abolitionism from the beginning, and pragmatic arguments have generally played no more than a supporting role. They have also taken what might be called the "weak form": abolitionists have usually limited them-selves to claiming that executions are *no better* than less extreme punishments as a means of addressing violent crime. Before the rise of post-*Gregg* "super due process" provided them with a stronger case, for example, ADPM activists used to assert merely that the death penalty *probably wasn't less expensive*

167

than life in prison, as many believed at the time. They vehemently denied the retentionists' assertion that nothing less than the dread of the hangman's noose would prevent a tidal wave of homicide. Long before empirical investigations of punishment and deterrence were conducted, reformers insisted that most killers were either too mentally disordered, too overcome by passion, or too sure of their own ability to avoid capture to worry about the price they might later have to pay. The lack of a unique deterrent effect has been much easier to demonstrate in the years since Thorsten Sellin conducted the first reasonably sophisticated studies of the matter in the 1950s (see Sellin 1959, 1967).

But weak pragmatic objections to executions, like moralistic ones, are somewhat limited in their effectiveness. When people face two options that appear to have roughly equal utility, they will generally choose the one that "feels good." The death penalty feels very good, very just, to tens of millions of ordinary Americans in the late twentieth century. So if it is merely "no better" than lesser punishments, people are apt to favor it on retributive grounds alone.

Stronger forms of pragmatic reasoning have been rarer in the historical struggle against executions. One instance was the nineteenth-century objection to *mandatory* death sentences on the basis of "jury nullification." It was claimed that jurors, faced with the realization that conviction on certain charges would mean death, sometimes chose to acquit defendants who they knew were guilty. Rather than achieving justice, then, the death penalty was allegedly multiplying injustice by providing offenders an undeserved means of escape. More recently, the "brutalization hypothesis" represented a potentially strong claim, but one that has not been utilized by activists as extensively as it appeared it might. The brutalization hypothesis refers to the possibility that the use of death as a punishment by legal authorities legitimizes the use of violence and thus *increases* the violent crime rate rather than diminishing it. This was proposed as early as the eighteenth century in America (Mackey 1976), but there was no clear evidence to back it up until William Bowers and Glenn Pierce (1980a) examined it systematically. The ADPM has nevertheless refrained from making the possibly criminogenic effects of capital punishment into a major issue, and pragmatic claims pertaining to the effect of capital punishment on crime and crime control efforts have been largely owned by death penalty advocates.

We return, then, to a crucial question: *is* there a case against the death penalty that might work in the United States? Is there a manner in which the issue might be framed that would lead large numbers of people to rethink their support for the sanction? The experiences of at least some anti-death penalty activists, lawyers, and sympathetic public officials suggest that there might be. What could well be more effective than traditional strategies would be for at least a segment of the movement to attack the death penalty on the basis of three interrelated pragmatic claims: (1) the crippling expense of maintaining a criminal justice apparatus that includes capital punishment, (2) the demonstrable failure of the death penalty to enhance the safety of law-abiding citizens, and (3) the availability of numerous alternative measures for addressing violent crime that are both just and cost-effective (although these measures will remain unaffordable so long as "extravagances" like the death penalty are allowed to drain scarce resources from the system). Characterized in this way, the restriction or elimination of capital punishment could be "marketed" as not merely a humanitarian reform, but an intelligent step toward a realistic crime control policy. This is a message with broader appeal, capable of being taken more seriously by people who are deaf to the primarily moral claims of traditional death penalty opponents.

The Costs of Capital Punishment Systems

The cornerstone of a more effective assault on the death penalty would most likely be its crippling cost. The money it takes to prosecute a capital case and to sustain it through the mandated appeals has been shown to be enormous in state after state. Estimates of the cost per case to taxpayers have ranged from $1.8 million in New York[1] (New York State Defenders Association 1982) and $3.2 million in Florida (*Miami Herald* 1988) to $15 million for California's earlier post-*Gregg* cases (Magagnini 1988). The California estimate includes the costs of unsuccessful capital prosecutions, that is, cases in which charges of capital murder are brought by prosecutors but which end in either life sentences or successful appeals. Studies in other states have also found that efforts to execute prisoners are considerably more expensive than simply putting them behind bars for the rest of their lives (Cook and Slawson 1993; Dieter 1992; *Houston Post* 1986; Simon 1993; Spangenberg and Walsh 1989).[2]

A sense of why these expenses accrue is given in a "Model for Determining Death Penalty Costs" that the National Center for State Courts devised several years ago (U.S. General Accounting Office 1989: Appendix II; Tabak and Lane 1989). The model hypothesizes that, when compared to homicide cases not involving the death penalty, the decision to seek a death sentence will produce:

- More intensive investigations;
- More extradition proceedings;
- More pretrial motions filed, more motions heard, and longer hearings;
- A greater likelihood of requests for psychiatric and/or medical evaluations of defendants;
- A greater proportion of cases going to trial;
- More complex jury selection procedures;
- More expert witnesses and consultants during pretrial, trial, and sentencing stages;
- Longer trials, more frequent use of sequestered juries, more witnesses, lengthier interrogations, and lengthier deliberations;
- Longer sentencing proceedings;
- More extensive presentence investigations;
- More motions for new trials, lengthier motion hearings, and more motions granted;

- Higher proportions of appeals, longer appellate proceedings, and longer opinions on appeal;
  - More state and federal postconviction petitions;
  - More requests for clemency;
  - Purchase and maintenance costs for execution equipment, unique training and personnel costs for execution staff, and special facilities for witnesses;
    - Higher presentencing security arrangements;
    - Higher postsentencing custodial costs, and loss of prisoner labor; and
    - Higher prosecution and defense attorney costs.

Heightened costs seem to occur in all cases where a death sentence is sought, whether successfully or unsuccessfully. Thus, when defendants' lawyers are able to convince the jury (or in a few states, the judge) to send their clients to prison rather than to the death chamber, the taxpayers have already picked up the check for a very costly trial. And when a death sentence is overturned on state or federal appeal, prior appellate expenses must be added to the trial costs. The fiscal impact of the death penalty is determined by the number of people a state *attempts* to execute, not the number of executions that actually take place. Community outrage at high-profile crimes combined with the political payoffs of a "tough-on-crime" image make prosecutorial restraint less likely. The ADPM must show that the very existence of capital punishment as part of a state's justice system, not simply the number of executions that actually occur, leads to massive drains on a state's resources. The availability of the death penalty seems to generate a pressure toward its use that is difficult for judicial decision makers to resist. How is a prosecutor to explain to grieving family why she decided to seek death for another accused murderer but not for the killer of their loved one? How is she to apply it sparingly, knowing that her opponent in some future election will accuse her of being soft on criminals? Elected officials striving to appear moderate sometimes call for limited death penalty laws intended only for the "worst of the worst" killers. But limited death penalties beg to be expanded, especially in election years. Capital punishment, then, often seems to have a built-in momentum that demands that it be used and drives up its cost. It was once estimated, for instance, that California might save as much as $90 million per year by abolishing capital punishment (Magagnini 1988). At the time that estimate was made, the state had not put a convict to death since 1967. As of 1995, it has executed only two. Florida spent approximately $57 million administering its death penalty from 1973 to 1988, during which time there were only 18 executions. The Death Penalty Information Center estimates that criminal justice expenses nationwide ran about a half billion dollars higher since 1976 due to the expenses associated with capital punishment.

The fiscal impact of capital prosecutions is split between states and counties. Counties normally pay for the prosecution of criminal trials, and because the vast majority of murder defendants are indigent, they often foot the bill for the defense as well. The strain on budgets can be overwhelming. Some counties have had to cut basic services—including, paradoxically, police protection—in order to meet the demands of a single capital murder trial. Two adjacent counties in Mississippi became embroiled in a dispute over the precise location of a murder, each fearing it would have to assume responsibility for the prosecution. The loser, Kemper County, faced the necessity of a tax increase (Dieter 1992:6). Until 1990, the state of California reimbursed counties for their share of defense expenses in death penalty trials. But that aid was eliminated in the midst of a state budget shortfall, and counties in which prosecutors initiated capital prosecutions found themselves in dire straits (Tugend 1993; Uelmen 1992). Orange County tried unsuccessfully to sue the state to recover the funds. Similar crises occurred elsewhere, and some counties were driven to near bankruptcy. County officials in Kentucky and Georgia have been jailed for contempt after having refused to allocate funds for expert defense testimony in murder cases (Gerth 1994; Lindner 1993; Weir 1993).

In recent years, some litigators have used the prospects of high cost in their pretrial negotiations. They have discussed the anticipated trial expenses with prosecutors while negotiating pleas, provided cost estimates to the local press, and, in general, made the case that aiming for a death sentence might not be the wisest use of the county's resources (*Capital Report* 1989a). This is especially effective in smaller counties, but it has sometimes worked in larger metropolitan areas as well. For example, prosecuting attorneys in Marion County, Indiana, which surrounds Indianapolis, elected not to seek the death penalty in a 1993 double rape-murder case because they had already spent $481,433 in three unsuccessful capital trials that year (Williams 1993). Statewide, the death penalty was sought only nine times in Indiana during 1993, down from 24 in both 1990 and 1991 (French 1994).[3] In Tennessee, cost considerations drove the number of death sentences down from 20 to 11 between fiscal 1991-1992 and 1993-1994 (*Memphis Commercial Appeal* 1994).

The danger in introducing anticipated costs during pretrial negotiations, from the perspective of defense lawyers, is that it may be perceived as a threat to overlitigate a case. At the same time, they must avoid underlitigating and allowing the county to conduct trials at bargain prices, with their clients being the ultimate losers. Bruce Ledewitz, a Duquesne University law professor who also handles death penalty cases, complained that Pennsylvania attorneys have let the counties off the hook:

> The problem is, it's *not* that expensive [in Pennsylvania]! We haven't made it expensive enough. I mean, a lot of our cases are in Philadelphia, so many that if we really litigated each one *right,* we would bankrupt the county. We haven't done it. So really, that's the problem. We could win that argument by making a lot of fiscal problems. But we *haven't* made the fiscal problems. We're prepared in Allegheny County to make the fiscal problems, but they haven't sought the death penalty often enough![4]

Anti-death penalty activists have also pointed out that not all the costs of the death penalty can be measured in dollars and cents. Capital cases also gobble up tremendous amounts of criminal court time, thereby delaying the processing of other important cases. This problem was recognized even before bifurcated trials and super due process became common, and was one reason that some members of the American Law Institute favored an abolition resolution in the late 1950s (Epstein and Kobylka 1992:40). State Supreme Court personnel may have to devote as much as half their time to death penalty appeals (Lindner 1993), and the burden on the U.S. Supreme Court has also been considerable.

When abolitionists raise the inherent tendency of capital cases to use up the time and money of the judicial system, defenders of capital punishment sometimes counter that the high price tag is the result of both unjustifiable defense costs at the trial stage and frivolous appeals. They portray defense lawyers as the villains, and claim that more responsible conduct would cause the expense of capital punishment to plummet to affordable levels. Private lawyers who are appointed to handle the trials and appeals of murderers are particularly vulnerable to the charge of fee gouging. The Superior Court in San Diego, California, imposed a flat-fee bidding system for capital defense services in 1994 to bring down costs. The attorneys whose fees were limited countered that the new system would damage the quality of representation in the most consequential of all criminal cases. Moreover, they claimed that the fees they had received, which seemed high to laypersons, were entirely justified—for the demands of life-and-death cases practically wipe out an attorney's regular practice (Callahan 1994). Capital Resource Centers, which are federally funded offices designed to handle the appeals of condemned inmates, have also come under fire.[5] Texas prosecutors charged that the two centers in their state were trying to abolish the death penalty at the citizens' expense and clogging the courts with groundless appeals. A bill in the House of Representatives that would have eliminated all funding for the resource centers failed in 1993 (*National Law Journal* 1993; Warren 1993).

The complexity of the legal machinery of capital punishment makes these charges difficult to counter, and there has been some reluctance within the movement to try.[6] This issue can get very technical, and most anti-death penalty activists are more comfortable with less complicated moral appeals. But the future viability of the abolitionist movement in the United States may depend on its articulation of the message that the death penalty is expensive because of trial costs, not appeals. Further, abolitionists must try to convince the public that there is no practical way either to reduce trial costs or to streamline the appellate process without multiplying the rate of Type II errors—that is, convictions and executions of the innocent. Most people, if they believed such errors to be likely, would find this unacceptable (Moran 1989). To bolster this claim, ADPM groups would need to continue focusing attention on recent cases of innocent people *belatedly* released from death row. These cases prove that mistakes can be made in spite of the safeguards that currently exist. Streamlining would exact a tragic cost in exchange for financial savings.

The second and more difficult response to the issue of the death penalty's high cost is the assertion that "you can't put a price tag on justice," that some murders are so heinous that we cannot allow fiscal considerations to prevent the application of the only penalty that fits the crime — death (for example, see Chen 1992; Lehr 1993). But even if one grants that murderers deserve to die for what they have done, one faces the burden of demonstrating that executions achieve some collective good that is great enough to justify the cost. This burden is not limited to the issue of capital punishment. In the policy arena, the real world of government, we encounter many desirable objectives that are deemed unaffordable. Most people would agree that every hungry child ought to be fed, that every illiterate adult ought to be taught to read, that every American ought to have access to affordable health care. Most people who consider themselves rational and realistic understand that however much these things *ought* to be so, there are practical barriers to realizing them. There may be disagreement as to the precise nature of those barriers, the exact point at which a desirable end becomes too expensive to achieve, but nearly all of us recognize that the cost of any social policy *is* an issue. The death penalty is no exception, and the fact that its strongest supporters are often fiscal conservatives leaves them vulnerable when they propose to write the executioner a blank check.

The costliness of maintaining capital punishment as a part of our law-enforcement apparatus is, then, a potentially powerful tool that has yet to be fully exploited by the anti-death penalty movement. It has the advantage of resonating with the vocabulary of "investment" that seems to be so much more persuasive in the United States than the humanitarian language of the "do gooder." It appeals to the "hard-headed," "practical-minded," "realistic" character traits that our culture encourages. Further, the cost issue provides those who fear being ridiculed as liberals with a socially acceptable reason to be skeptical about the death penalty.[7]

The Ineffectiveness of Capital Punishment

Convincing people that it costs a lot of money to put convicted murderers to death does little to advance the abolitionist cause if they feel executions are worth it. It is extraordinarily difficult to portray capital punishment as cost ineffective to those who support it primarily on retributive grounds. And retribution *is* a common basis for support; majorities of those in favor of capital punishment have been telling opinion researchers for years that they would continue to support it even if they were convinced that it did not have a deterrent effect (Paternoster 1991:246).

But many people want more from capital punishment than retribution alone. Hope remains that the prospect of being strapped to a chair or gurney and killed makes at least some people think twice before committing murder. But this is one argument, at least, that anti-death penalty forces have won. Retentionists are guilty of exaggeration when they claim that the evidence on the deterrent effects of capital punishment is "mixed." In fact, the evidence from nearly 40 years of research runs overwhelmingly against the proposition that the death penalty deters any more effectively than other severe punishments. A brief review of that research is in order, because when translated into lay terms, it is indispensable to the pragmatic abolitionist's case.

Some of the earliest systematic research on the possible deterrent effects of capital punishment was conducted by Thorsten Sellin (1959). Sellin's method consisted of comparing the rates of willful homicide in contiguous death penalty and non-death penalty states. His underlying assumption was that geographically proximate states would also be more or less alike on various social, economic, and historical factors that might also effect crime. Sellin was able to conclude that homicide rates in states with capital punishment were generally not lower than those of neighboring states without the sanction. Sellin's data were limited to the pre-*Furman* era, but similar conclusions were later drawn by Ruth Peterson and William Bailey (1988) for the post-*Furman* years.

The contiguous states method for investigating deterrence is vulnerable to a number of criticisms. First, the mere physical proximity of two or more states is no guarantee that they are truly comparable. They might differ in a number of ways, such as in their poverty rate or urban-rural ratio, and these differences might affect the homicide rate independently of punishment policies. This criticism was muted somewhat after David Baldus and James Cole (1975) were able to confirm that the states Sellin had matched were indeed comparable as to the probability of arrest and conviction and on an array of relevant socioeconomic variables.

Other researchers turned to more sophisticated statistical techniques to improve on Sellin's methods. Isaac Ehrlich, an economist, was among the first to do so. Ehrlich maintained that the contiguous states approach was statistically inadequate, and that most previous studies had failed to consider the *certainty* of punishment as well as its severity. Merely having the death penalty on the books did not make it a credible threat. In his own work, Ehrlich employed multiple regression analysis and applied it not to state-level crime data, but to aggregated data from the United States as a whole from 1933 through 1969. He concluded that a high risk of execution significantly suppressed the murder rate; each execution during that period, he claimed, prevented an average of seven to eight murders (1975). Although this finding contradicted virtually all previous research, it was taken very seriously at first. It even figured prominently in Supreme Court deliberations in the *Fowler* and *Gregg* cases, as we saw earlier. But Ehrlich's intriguing work was soon discredited. When data for 1962 through 1969 (when crime as a whole was increasing) were removed, the apparent effect of capital punishment on homicide reversed direction—that is, the evidence suggested a "brutalization" pattern (Bowers and Pierce 1975). Ehrlich's research was also criticized for having ignored important factors such as the effects of gun ownership on murder rates (Kleck 1979).

Other than Ehrlich, only three investigators have published findings supportive of the deterrence hypothesis. David Phillips (1980) concluded that well-publicized hangings of London murderers between 1864 and 1921 produced short-term drops in homicide, but that there followed equally large increases in murders five or six weeks later. Steven Stack (1987) presented evidence that month-long dips in homicides occurred following highly publicized American executions between 1951 and 1971. Stephen Layson, a student of Ehrlich, went even further than his teacher. Based on a multivariate analysis of homicide between 1933 and 1977 (1985), he claimed that every execution deterred 18 murders. However, the work of Phillips, Stack, and Layson has proved vulnerable to the types of methodological criticism that greeted Ehrlich's work (Fox and Radelet 1989).

Other than the investigations by Ehrlich, Phillips, and Stack, efforts to identify a unique crime-prevention effect of executions have failed. Executions have been found to either increase the numbers of killings of police officers (Bowers 1988) or to have no effect on these crimes (Bailey and Peterson 1987). The vast majority of investigations using either state or national data have found no evidence of short- or long-term suppression of aggravated murder based on execution risk.

Due to the overwhelmingly negative results of research, as well as of commonsense interpretations of current crime rates from state to state and year to year, death penalty supporters no longer use deterrence as a debating point very often. When the issue is raised, it is often in the following form: perhaps there is no evidence *at present* that the fear of capital punishment makes criminals think twice about killing, but that is only because the risk of actually being executed is so low. Criminals know that they are unlikely to wind up in the execution chamber even if they are caught and convicted. But if capital punishment were imposed on a larger scale, it would, in fact, produce a deterrent effect. The ability of death penalty opponents to respond to this change is important, because they are frequently held responsible for the delays and loopholes that make executions rare events.

It is entirely possible that some effect *would* be felt if hundreds of executions were carried out in the United States each year, especially if those executions took place within a few months of the crimes they were intended to punish. It is unlikely that the benefits would be very great, because many of the studies that have failed to uncover a deterrent effect used homicide data from the era when executions were quite common in this country. But in any case, the movement against the death penalty is not seriously challenged by this line of reasoning. Abolitionists need not become diverted into academic arguments over what would happen under a system their opponents regard as ideal. Rather, they can best respond by returning to the matter of cost. As things now stand, hundreds if not thousands of murders occur in death penalty states every year that could be made into death penalty cases if prosecuting attorneys elected to do so. The only way costs have been kept from reaching truly outrageous levels is by seeking the death penalty in only a very small percentage of those cases. Staging the number of executions that would be required in order to achieve even a small deterrent payoff would require a massive outlay of public funds, one that would dwarf the already crippling costs experienced by some counties and states. Consider the case of New York, where only a long series of gubernatorial vetoes prevented the reactivation of the state's electric chair for almost two decades — and where the state legislature avoided confronting the fiscal impact of reinstatement. About one-third of the homicides that occur in the state are felony-murders — that is, homicides committed in the course of other serious crimes like robberies or rapes — and are thus potentially capital offenses (Acker 1990:582). Under the original reinstatement bill, then, approximately 800 of New York's 2,397 murders in 1992 (U.S. Department of Justice, Bureau of Justice Statistics 1994:359) *could* have been tried as death penalty cases had capital punishment been in effect that year. Using the New York State Defenders' Association 1982 estimate of an average cost of $1.8 million per case, the cost to the state and its counties could have come to around $1.44 billion for felony-murder cases alone. In reality, it is most unlikely that a billion and a half dollars would be spent for that purpose. Rather, the lottery-like system of sentencing that now operates in other states — in which the selection of homicides as capital cases is quite arbitrary — would reduce capital charges to an affordable number, simultaneously demolishing any hope of the long-sought deterrent effect.

Although most defenders of capital punishment seem to have conceded defeat on the question of general deterrence, they often cite *specific* deterrence — "incapacitation" — as a benefit. That is, they claim that executing convicted murderers at least insures that those individuals will not take another innocent life. This point is an effective one, far more difficult to contend with than general deterrence. It is self-evidently true, and it has a commonsense appeal that the other side's complicated statistical arguments lack. The real issue, of course, is whether the death penalty is so superior as a means of incapacitating killers that it is an absolutely necessary part of our anticrime arsenal. Abolitionists usually contend that we can control truly dangerous convicts well enough by simply incarcerating them. But prison cannot provide *absolute* assurance that violent convicts are neutralized. They may be released too soon. They may injure or kill other convicts (although the safety of prison inmates is not of utmost concern at present). Worse, they may injure or kill prison staff, especially if they are already "lifers" with nothing else to lose. And worst of all from the point of view of most people, convicts may escape from prison and wreak more devastation on the innocent.

By most accounts, typical death row inmates are far less of a threat than one might suppose. Research on the inmates whose sentences were commuted by the *Furman* decision found that a majority "served out their sentences with few instances of serious institutional misconduct" and that only one of the 239 who were paroled committed a subsequent homicide (Marquart and Sorensen 1989). Anecdotal accounts from prison superintendents generally reinforce this. Donald Cabana, a former corrections commissioner and prison warden who has overseen executions at Mississippi's Parchman Prison, told NCADP conferees in 1992 that he would much prefer being responsible for a death row population than for a group of short-sentenced property offenders in their 20s. But neither scholarly investigations nor the testimony of wardens is likely to put people's concerns about recidivism to rest. And that is quite understandable; it takes only one person to produce a tragedy. Appropriate classification of inmates and appropriate security precautions for the predictably violent ones may reduce these risks considerably, but it is unlikely that they can be eliminated altogether. And for some people, nothing less than 100 percent certainty is enough when it comes to public safety. Death provides the only method to achieve that level of certainty.

In the end, neither the surprisingly high cost of capital punishment nor its ineffectiveness as a deterrent are by themselves likely to help the anti-death penalty movement turn the corner. Both are probably necessary, but not sufficient. Most successful social movements have found that it is not enough to be against something. It is helpful, and perhaps necessary in most instances, to be *for* something else. The vision that activists put forth must be true not only to their own principles, but to those of the uncommitted. It is to this element of a pragmatic anti-death penalty frame that we now turn.

The "Abolition Dividend" and Realistic Crime Control

Whereas capital punishment is demonstrably ineffective in bringing down rates of violent crime, there are other policies that offer far more promise. This subject alone is enough to fill a book. For present purposes, we need only look briefly at alternatives to capital punishment that are both potentially useful in dealing with the plague of violence in our streets and consistent enough with prevailing views on justice to stand a reasonable chance of being taken seriously. Arguably, the best measures we could take have little to do with criminal justice per se. These include such things as full employment policies and greater attention to the needs of families.[8] It is doubtful that most of these proposals would be very helpful by themselves in undermining support for the death penalty, however. Attacking the roots of crime is a long-term remedy that would produce gradual and undramatic results. People prefer more immediate solutions. Striking at crime as a symptom of deeper social maladies is so widely associated with liberal "social engineering" that it stands little chance of being seriously discussed at present.

To be credible, a pragmatic attack on the death penalty must appear more focused on the needs of the innocent than those of the guilty, but as things now stand, the loyalties of death penalty opponents are widely perceived as misplaced. It is thought that anyone who is against the death penalty sees murderers merely as victims of poverty, racism, and a brutal law enforcement system, and is blind to the carnage those criminals have caused. Some abolitionists are guilty of these things. But they are hardly typical of their movement, certainly no more so than the intoxicated celebrants chanting "Fry the Nigger" on the night of an execution are typical of death penalty supporters. Both represent little more than caricatures. But activists stand little chance of being heard so long as this image prevails, and sympathetic people outside of movement organizations are discouraged from speaking their minds by the fear that they will be viewed in the same manner. Opposition to the death penalty, in short, has failed to achieve "respectability." As a result, not only do capital prosecutions and ever more draconian "wars" on crime and drugs draw off scarce funds that could be better spent, but the punitive mindset in which they are grounded so completely monopolizes public discourse that rational alternatives rarely receive the serious discussion they deserve:

> . . . the death penalty continues to monopolize center stage in the current debate over violent crime control. The emotional heat it gives off leads to a polarization of views which prevents consensus and compromise on other law enforcement fronts. Other anti-crime initiatives — criminal sentencing and bail reforms, victim assistance programs, and renovation and construction of prison facilities — are all forced to take a back seat to what has become the litmus test of a politician's commitment to safe streets. (Feinberg 1984)

The author of these words, Kenneth Feinberg, a former assistant U.S. attorney and special counsel to the U.S. Senate Judiciary Committee, was reacting to the election-year posturing that doomed a bipartisan crime bill in the 1984 congressional term. Had it passed, the bill would have revised federal sentencing laws, reformed bail provisions and the federal insanity defense, and enacted a number of other measures, many of which were still being debated a decade later. Not all of the provisions of that bill would have protected us better, and some had troubling civil liberties implications. But the point is that even those imperfect proposals ran aground because of the contaminating effect of capital punishment. Continuing, Feinberg explained that:

> The inability of our elected officials to put capital punishment aside and focus on other more important crime-control initiatives is the reason I oppose the death penalty. Unfortunately, however, the critics of capital punishment have largely failed to pick up on this point and use it to their advantage. Instead of pointing out how the death penalty impedes badly needed law-enforcement reform, these critics offer the same . . . traditional justifications for abolition, each seriously flawed and unconvincing. (Feinberg 1984)

The rhetoric of the ADPM remains much the same as when Feinberg expressed these sentiments. Connecting the shortcomings of capital punishment with the anticrime frame that has dominated public discourse since the late 1960s may be the only way for abolitionists to capitalize on the public's ambivalence. To do this, some significant and visible faction of the movement will probably need to endorse alternatives that are acceptable to a major segment of American society, and it must propose that those alternatives be financed in part with the funds currently squandered on the death penalty.

What rational anticrime proposals might be discussed if the death penalty did not get in the way? What might the dollars saved by abolition purchase? The most politically potent alternatives would be those that are "tough," that accommodate the public's anger about crime. They would also be the most difficult for the ADPM, as it currently constituted, to take on.

Mandatory Sentences and Parole Limitations

Like it or not, the only proposal that strikes large numbers of death penalty supporters as a viable sentencing option in aggravated murder cases is life in prison without any chance of parole, preferably combined with some form of restitution to victims' families. Some anti-death penalty groups, most notably in Oregon, have *endorsed* life-without-parole as a specific alternative. In terms of overcoming their negative image and becoming more serious players in state-level politics, this is probably the most promising course to chart. But as we have already seen, proposing specific alternatives—and "tough," prison-based alternatives in particular—is a "minefield" that most ADP organizations have chosen to skirt. Imprisonment without any hope of eventual freedom is little more than a slow form of death penalty, according to many abolitionists.

With or without the blessing of abolitionists, LWOP is increasingly a fact of life in the United States. It already exists in most states, usually alongside capital punishment, but occasionally by itself. Abolitionists do not really have to endorse LWOP in order to put it to strategic use. It may be enough in some states merely to point out that LWOP is already on the books and to try to convince the people and their elected officials that it makes the death penalty unnecessary and superfluous.

But there is another problem: even though very large numbers of people say they would be satisfied with LWOP rather than capital punishment, many of them lack confidence that convicts receiving that sentence will really spend the rest of their days behind bars. Someday, they fear, a group of softhearted legislators will change the law and nullify the true life sentences handed down in past years. Or perhaps a future governor will do what New Mexico's Toney Anaya and Ohio's Richard F. Celeste did: commute the sentences of convicted killers as a final act before leaving office. In these instances, death sentences were reduced to life-without-parole.[9] But citizens feel no certainty that a prisoner serving a LWOP sentence might not someday have that sentence reduced to a term of years and end up on the streets again. Execution often seems to be the only way to make absolutely sure that justice is done.

If there were an anti-death penalty group or coalition not philosophically opposed to such things, it might consider forcing the issue by offering anti-crime hard-liners a deal: you work with us to end the death penalty, and we'll work with you to tighten up parole and commutation laws. The opposition would most likely refuse such a compromise. But even so, they would nevertheless be placed on the defensive, having to explain why they opposed saving their state millions of dollars by adopting a truly ironclad life sentence. This might be termed the "Cuomo strategy," for it is quite like the tactic New York's governor Mario Cuomo used in trying to seize the high ground in his long war with the state's lawmakers. Years ago, Cuomo began calling for LWOP instead of the death penalty, and he offered to sign away his clemency powers in the bargain. The governor was made vulnerable by his principled opposition to reinstatement, and it undoubtedly was a factor in his defeat in the 1994 election. But the legislators were never able to muster enough votes to override his veto.

In both LWOP states and in states that have not enacted life-without-parole statutes, enthusiasm for the death penalty is also nurtured by misunderstandings about how much time convicted murderers actually serve when they are sent to prison. For decades, the belief has flourished that killers are back on the streets after only a few short years. William Bowers (1993) found that about half of the people he surveyed in New York and Nebraska thought that convicted murderers who were not sentenced to die would serve 15 years or less behind bars. A quarter of the New Yorkers and a fifth of the Nebraskans thought the convicts would be free in less than 10 years. In reality, then-current laws in those two states required mandatory *minimum* sentences of 15 years and life (without parole eligibility), respectively. Relatively early releases of killers did, in fact, occur in the past, but they are now virtually impossible in the United States for people found guilty of first-degree murder. Bowers attributes the widespread misperceptions about sentencing to "selective media reporting of crime by previously incarcerated inmates and the absence of statistics that distinguish persons convicted of the kinds of murder that might be punishable by death from other lesser forms of criminal homicide" (1993: 168). Additionally, most convicted murderers are also faced with other charges, such as robbery or even parole violation, which add to already stiff sentences. The greatest irony of this entire controversy is that such a large proportion of citizens say they are willing to trade the death penalty for alternatives *that are already in place where they live.* A more effective pragmatic strategy would have to include wider publicity about actual sentences under existing law, because public support for capital punishment is so dependent on the belief that no other meaningful punishments are available.

To make their case more attractive to an angry nation, abolitionist organizations would also be well advised to stress the retributive value of prison. At present, myths abound about life behind bars. People are aware that tax-supported educational programs and recreational facilities like basketball courts, weight-training equipment and cable television are available to convicts. Prison life sometimes sounds almost inviting, and all the more so when we take into account the urban squalor in which so many inmates have lived before they were incarcerated. If one imagines America's penitentiaries to be almost resortlike, then even life-without-parole may seem too mild a punishment. But maximum security prisons are not resorts. They are dangerous, violent, highly regimented places with few creature comforts. They are populated to a large extent by people whose appetites for such comforts are ravenous and who do not like to live within constraints imposed by others. It is a rare convict who feels very comfortable behind bars for a long period of time. Awareness of these things makes it rather difficult to think of the long prison sentences now imposed on murder convicts as "letting them off easy." Abolitionists need not *celebrate* the pains of imprisonment, nor join in current efforts to intensify them.[10] But greater public awareness of the realities of incarceration may help them in achieving their goal.

If people became convinced that LWOP was a viable sentence, immune to commutation except perhaps where an obvious miscarriage was discovered, and that a lifetime in prison is a harsh enough fate for aggravated murder, then it might enable death penalty opponents to hold off reinstatement and perhaps even get rid of the death penalty in a state or two. Most of the remaining non-death penalty states have provisions for life-without-parole. A law that withholds parole eligibility for 40 years helped hold off capital punishment in Kansas for several years. Existing LWOP laws have also figured prominently in debates over restoration in Alaska (Mader 1994) and Wisconsin (Doege 1994). The full potential of lengthy mandatory sentences to effect capital punishment in the legislative arena is yet to be tested because abolitionists have yet to mount a full-scale assault using this weapon.

As we have seen, LWOP has already become more common as an *addition* to the death penalty, as another choice available to jurors, than as a replacement. But even where solid, well-publicized LWOP statutes do not lead states to abandon executions, they may at least slow them down. Where LWOP exists, some prosecutors have been able to satisfy their constituents' demand for toughness without seeking many death sentences. Texas provides a case in point. Harris County, where Houston is located, leads the nation in death sentences and executions. In 1992 alone, 21 death penalty trials were held there, and the county was expected to top that mark in 1995. The high volume of capital prosecutions is due to the aggressive efforts of the county's popular prosecutor, John B. Holmes. Dallas County, on the other hand, staged only three such trials in 1992, one in 1993, and one in 1994—because prosecutors there have decided that life sentences usually make more sense. Each capital prosecution in Texas costs in the neighborhood of $2 million (Taylor 1994). Officials outside of Harris County have been reluctant to spend that kind of money, and a law that took effect in September 1993 makes it possible to sentence a convicted killer to life in prison with no parole eligibility for 40 years—a de facto LWOP sentence. Even former Texas attorney general Jim Mattox, who during an unsuccessful campaign for governor boasted of having presided over 36 executions, has become less enthusiastic about the death penalty and now preaches prosecutorial restraint (Mattox 1993; Dieter 1994). LWOP has apparently saved lives—and dollars—in the Lone Star State.

Awareness of a life-without-parole option also seems to have an impact on juror behavior during the penalty phase. In Dallas County, Texas, recently, three of six capital prosecutions resulted in life sentences rather than death penalties (Scott 1993). Similar trends have been noted elsewhere (*Daily Oklahoman* 1992), and they might be even more pronounced were jurors not so frequently unclear about what a "life" sentence would mean if they imposed it. Bowers has found that jurors are often as confused as the general public about how long a convicted murderer will stay confined if not sentenced to die. When his research team interviewed capital jurors from California, Florida, and South Carolina, they found that the jurors' understanding of "life" sentence was a little more accurate than the general public's, but that a third of them still thought convicted murderers were usually freed in 15 years or less. Those who were the most misinformed were also the most inclined to impose the death penalty (Bowers 1993:169–170; also see Paduano and Smith 1989; Stark 1994). Apparently the jurors' reasoning was that they would be responsible for turning a dangerous individual loose after a short time if they didn't have him executed. In many states, judges are expressly prohibited from discussing parole with the jury, even if its members ask how many years must pass before parole can be considered. Thus, juries that are leaning toward a life sentence but are concerned about when, if at all, the convict might be eligible for release, are often unable to get an answer to that simple legal point. According to Dieter (1993:16), this is the case in 23 of the 29 states where the jury imposes sentence.

Beyond Murder: Sentences for Other Violent Offenders

Coming to terms with life-without-parole for murderers is not the only way that the ADPM might align opposition to capital punishment with a crime control frame. It is not just the crime of murder that angers the public, but other violent offenses as well: rape and other predatory sex offenses, robbery, and assault. About four out of every five Americans feel that the sentences currently imposed on criminals are insufficient, and the same proportion either "favor" or "strongly favor" making parole more difficult for prison inmates to achieve (U.S. Department of Justice, Bureau of Justice Statistics 1994:192). The popular respectability of the abolition movement's objective might grow if a major movement oganization acknowledged the legitimacy of these views and suggested that the *abolition dividend*—the millions or tens of millions of dollars a state might save by discarding capital punishment—be used to keep a wide range of violent predators behind bars long enough to protect law-abiding citizens adequately. Violent predators are the figures who dominate the popular imagery of crime. They include career violent offenders, serial killers, and habitual sex offenders. They are the Ted Bundys, the Jeffrey Dahmers, the Willie Hortons, and the thousands of other villains whose notoriety is local rather than national.

The "incapacitation" of criminals, that is, the strategy of suppressing crime by removing habitual offenders from the streets, has garnered enthusiastic support in recent years, but the most formidable obstacle in its path is expense. New York's prisons, for instance, are full. The only ways to get more offenders off the streets are to release current inmates to free up space, to further increase overcrowding and thereby increase security risks, or to build more prisons. It costs the state about $100,000 to construct a prison cell, according to corrections officials, and another $25,000 per year to operate it (Fisher 1994b). But although the corrections system is still in crisis, New York has built thousands of those expensive cells over the last dozen years or so. The state has been able to afford them in part because of its tardiness in reinstating capital punishment. In states that already have the death penalty, a strong point for either dropping it or imposing it sparingly might be that the prison system's capacity to hold serious felons could then be stretched. In a more perfect world, people might wish to direct the abolition dividend toward education or health care. But in America in the mid-1990s, there is currently more support for new penitentiaries.

There are many practical problems with the "selective" incapacitation of offenders, including the surprising difficulty of making reasonably accurate predictions about the future behavior of today's wrongdoers (Chaiken and Chaiken 1990:358–364; Visher 1987). But in principle, it is an attractive and defensible idea. Complaints about insufficient sentences for violent offenders *other than first-degree murderers* are not unfounded. The median prison sentence imposed by state courts in cases where the most serious offense is murder or nonnegligent homicide is about 20 years. For forcible rape, it is about 10 years, and for robbery and aggravated assault, it is 6.0 and 4.25 years, respectively. Probation rather than prison time is imposed on 14 percent of rapists, 10 percent of robbers, and 28 percent of those convicted of aggravated assault (U.S. Department of Justice, Bureau of Justice Statistics 1994:537). Most of those who are sent to prison actually serve far less time than their sentences seem to call for, thanks to the use of parole and work release to relieve prison overcrowding.

It is probably true that prison sentences in the United States are already harsh by comparison to comparable nations, and it is beyond question that we incarcerate a larger proportion of our population than any other nation in the world except Russia. It is also true that our violent crime rates continue to soar above those of other Western industrial nations. Obviously, our reliance on punishment is not solving the problem. If long prison sentences are justified for anyone, though, surely they are justified in case of violent offenders. Abolitionists who acknowledge this publicly would be taken far more seriously than those who appear to shy away from any discussion of fair and just punishment. Equally important is exposing the death penalty as an impediment to financing the correctional facilities we need to keep violent felons securely confined.

Enhanced Local Law Enforcement

Still another "tough" utilization of the abolition dividend would be the strengthening of law enforcement at the local level. From a deterrence standpoint, the core failure of America's crime-control efforts is not the severity of the penalties we impose, but rather the certainty of capture and conviction. The procedural restrictions the United States has traditionally placed on the police, combined with the sheer volume of crime our law enforcement personnel confront, make the risk of capture and conviction for American lawbreakers lower than most of us would wish. This is not something that can be overcome simply by putting more police on the street or by equipping them with more sophisticated hardware and weaponry. Still, both ideas are popular. One of the least controversial features of the federal crime bill that finally passed during the 1994 session of Congress was the provision of funding for 100,000 more police officers. The only substantial disagreement concerned whether or not the appropriations would be sufficient to that objective.

But as part of a comprehensive anticrime program predicated on savings from wasteful policies like capital punishment, the enhancement of law enforcement could take other forms. For instance, justice reform organizations might call for more widespread use of "community policing." The term has come to mean different things in different cities. But, in general, it implies preventing crime by making the police a visible part of community life, not anonymous social control agents from outside the neighborhood. Closer ties with the community are encouraged through foot patrols, consistent assignment of the officers to the same "beats," an emphasis on proactive crime prevention rather than emergency response, and the encouragement of police-citizen partnerships in keeping neighborhoods safe (Mastrofski 1992; *National Institute of Justice Journal* 1992). The transition from traditional styles of law enforcement has not been easily accomplished in all departments where the new philosophy has been adopted. But research on the results of community policing have been promising. Studies of its use in Baltimore, Houston, and Newark, New Jersey, suggested that it reduced the fear of crime in communities. And declines in crime in New York, Boston, and Prince George's County, Maryland, have been attributed, in part, to experimentation with the new approach (Dieter 1992).

Approaches to crime control that rely on the apprehension of lawbreakers and the imposition of tough, meaningful punishment, such as those suggested here, would help to neutralize the widespread view that opposition to death penalty can only be based on a "softness" toward crime. It would help to broaden the mobilization potential of the anti-death penalty movement, bringing in allies and funds from new directions. In fact, reframing capital punishment opposition in this manner would likely make it possible to attract political conservatives to the cause. Franklin Zimring and Gordon Hawkins find this rather far-fetched, because they see support for capital punishment as a symbolic phenomenon that is not really about crime control at all:

> The idea that there might be some kind of reluctant accommodation between hard-liners and liberals, with the former relinquishing the death penalty in exchange for liberal support for other harsh crime control measures, might seem plausible in the abstract. But its plausibility rests on the false assumption that the real issue is crime control rather than the feelings of potency and security that accompany the use of governmental power in its ultimate form. On this deeper issue, there is no room for compromise. (1986:150)

But the prospect of at least reducing the virtually unanimous support of the death penalty by the political right is less outlandish than it might seem, and far less so than creating a working alliance with right-to-life groups based on ethical parallels between the two issues. Proposals for the decriminalization of drugs, once considered the sole property of the fringe left, has attracted several well-known conservative spokespersons based on pragmatic grounds. These include George Schultz, William F. Buckley, and economist Milton Friedman. It is also worth noting that Marie Deans was able to persuade conservative columnist James Kilpatrick and members of Virginia's Republican party to support the commutation of Joe Giarratano's death sentence.[11]

In addition to the possibility of bringing some portion of America's conservatives into the struggle against capital punishment, a pragmatic emphasis on crime control also has the possibility for mobilizing law enforcement groups.

Police and prosecutors have overwhelmingly supported capital punishment in the past. But as we have seen earlier, there are district attorneys and state attorneys general who once manipulated the issue opportunistically, but who now — without necessarily disavowing their sense of its retributive value in some cases — have moved toward supporting long, no-parole sentences instead. Some prosecutors and police are capable of being persuaded that it would be in their interest to reallocate time and money that the capital punishment process consumes. And the importance of even a small handful of outspoken converts from their ranks would be most significant. Moreover, politicians who are sympathetic with the abolitionist position, but apprehensive about the damage that might be done to their careers if they said so out loud, need to be given an acceptable vocabulary with which to explain their position to constituents. The abolition dividend might well provide that vocabulary.

But despite its advantages, there is much that prevents current ADPM organizations and leaders from using tough alternatives to undermine capital punishment. Foremost among these is the movement's culture and the political background from which it has heretofore recruited members. Opposition to capital punishment in this country has always been associated with political liberalism, and the movement has been populated almost exclusively from those ranks. There are exceptions, but they are relatively few in number. The organizational affiliates of anti-death penalty coalitions at the state and national levels have also been mostly liberal and progressive groups. Coming from the ideological left, abolitionists are not favorably disposed toward punishment and have little faith in the ability of the law enforcement and judicial systems to deliver it fairly. Nancy Otto, a member of the ACLU of Northern California, points out that many of the arguments against capital punishment are really about more fundamental flaws in the criminal justice process itself:

> With more African Americans, or people of color, being sentenced to death, that's not so much a problem with the death penalty . . . as it is an argument against our justice system. I mean, the unfairness of the system itself. And that unfairness would still exist if you're pursuing life without the possibility of parole.[12]

In a similar vein, Michael Radelet believes that the motives of most abolitionists are broader than they appear:

> The death penalty so far has only taken 184 lives in the last twenty years! That's not very many. That's like half a plane crash. Why all this attention devoted to those lives? The reality is that what a lot of abolitionists are fighting against is not the death penalty per se. We're fighting against rich white people pushing around their power against poor scapegoats — rich white men making political careers from killing black people![13]

There are other credible elements of a broader anticrime platform that are less punitive than longer prison sentences, greater restrictions on parole, and expanded police protection. Wider use of alternative sentences like intensive probation and electronic monitoring for nonviolent offenders would also free up scarce resources for use against the worst kinds of predatory offenders. So would rethinking the nation's strategy to combat drug abuse. The savings from these reforms could be applied to more adequate victim assistance services and broader crime prevention efforts. And stricter gun control policies could be offered as a more effective means of preventing homicide than the execution of two percent of convicted killers. Though many of these measures are controversial in their own right, they are less objectionable to traditional abolitionists, and they provide a more supportive context for opposition to the death penalty than the movement's current single-issue orientation.

Crime-Prevention and Rational Criminal Justice Reform

If one or more anti-death penalty movement organizations were to make the case that abolition would free up tax dollars for tough but fair sentences for violent predators, it would be advantageous to tie that message to a broader critique of current sentencing practices. In recent years, approximately 31 percent of prison inmates are people convicted of property offenses. Drug and public order offenders account for another 13.8 percent (National Council on Crime and Delinquency 1992:14). As a result of nearly two decades of "getting tough" on criminals in a rather indiscriminate way, the nation's prison population has more than tripled. Corrections spending grew 65 percent in the 1980s alone. Abolitionists might augment their case against the death penalty by calling more broadly for a rational criminal justice strategy, one that would entail wiser use of existing prison space. This would make it possible to give the most dangerous offenders the sentences they deserve and to protect the law-abiding public *without the massive new expenditures that prison expansion requires.*

If prison space were reserved for truly dangerous criminals, less serious offenders could be better handled through various alternative sentences that do not rely on incarceration. At the very least, the severity of sentences for many property and drug offenders might be reduced. Traditional probation might be used more widely, reversing the trend that boosted imprisonment rates so dramatically during the 1980s and that raised the cost of corrections in the United States to $25 billion per year (National Council on Crime and Delinquency 1993:23). *Intermediate sanctions* could be used for many convicts who present little risk of physical violence. Intermediate sanctions lie between prison and probation in intrusiveness. Examples include: day fines, in which the amount is determined by both the seriousness of the offense and the defendant's ability to pay; intensive supervision probation, which imposes rigid restrictions on the offender's behavior and subjects him or her to close surveillance by officers with low caseloads; electronically monitored house arrest; and "shock incarceration" for maximum periods of three to six months[14] (Gowdy 1992; Morris and Tonry 1990). Greater use of these alternatives would free up prison cells that should more properly hold violent offenders.

Calling for the use of alternatives to incarceration for nonviolent offenders is far less distasteful for the vast majority of abolitionists than lining up behind life-without-parole and other punitive measures. Alternative sentencing is much more difficult to sell to the general public, however. In large part, this is due to the widespread habit of basing one's view of offenders almost totally on high-profile cases. People forget that the vast majority of the crimes that occur in our society are *not* crimes against persons, but rather property offenses and what were once called "victimless" crimes — acts of illicit but consensual sex, the use and sale of illegal drugs, and the like. It is true that many nonviolent offenses are committed by persons who also employ force in other settings. But popular views are nevertheless based disproportionately on overgeneralizations from spectacular cases. The first step in generating support for more cost-effective responses to crime is correcting some of these misperceptions. Not all lawbreakers are so threatening that they must be locked in a cage, nor is justice always served by doing so. The second step is encouraging people to see this as a pocketbook issue. Crime control — or more accurately, our belief that crime can only be controlled through the most costly forms of punishment — is hurting each and every taxpayer in very tangible ways. As Delaware governor Michael Castle put it when addressing a conference on intermediate punishments, "[t]hink about how your dentist, your auto mechanic, or your child's teacher would react if you told them how much money is being taken out of their pockets to build prison beds and take care of criminals" (Castle 1991).

There is also a logical link between pragmatic abolitionism and antidrug strategy. For one thing, illicit drugs and criminal violence are interconnected problems. Drug or alcohol intoxication often precedes homicides and other violent crimes. And the business of distributing illegal substances is one that generates a great deal of violence, with dealers often killing each other over territory and unpaid debts. A reduction in illegal drug use would almost certainly help to reduce the incidence of criminal homicide in the United States. But there is another connection between the issues of capital punishment and drug policy: the strategy for curtailing drug use that has been in effect in the United States since the early 1980s has emphasized deterrence over treatment, and has thus been instrumental in the overfilling of the corrections systems. Legislation that set mandatory minimum sentences for drug offenders has dramatically driven up the population of the nation's penitentiaries. In 1981, drug offenders made up fewer than eight percent of all admissions; by 1989, the proportion had risen to just under 30 percent (U.S. Department of Justice, Bureau of Justice Statistics 1991:14). Drug offenders make up more than half the inmate population in the federal system (Nadelmann 1992:210), and 15,000 to 20,000 of them have minimal criminal backgrounds (Edwards 1994).

The decriminalization of drugs, of course, would be the most direct way in which to combat most drug-related violence. In theory, it would drive down the spectacular profits that drug distribution offers in a climate of illegality, drive the criminals out of the business, and thus remove the incentives to eliminate one's competition. But whether drug decriminalization would have these beneficial effects or merely create untold new problems, it is not a proposal that would be easy to popularize. A more "marketable" critique that would better complement a pragmatic attack on the death penalty would call merely for the reallocation of resources from the demonstrably futile "zero-tolerance"/deterrence approach to a public health/drug treatment paradigm. Even this would be politically difficult, as the fate of the 1994 crime bill again demonstrates. President Clinton's efforts to shift a greater portion of federal antidrug funding from enforcement to education and treatment ran headlong into the resistance of congressional hard-liners from both parties. Nevertheless, the electorate may not be as opposed to this change in emphasis as those it elects to the Senate and House. A Media General/Associated Press poll in 1989 revealed that 57 percent of those surveyed thought that putting users into treatment programs would be the most effective way to reduce drug use, whereas only 33 percent favored punishing them (U.S. Department of Justice, Bureau of Justice Statistics 1992a:242).

One of the most appealing proposals for utilizing an abolition dividend and savings from sentencing reforms is crime victim assistance. Were ADPM groups to address this in specific ways, the movement might experience the closest thing to a public relations coup in its history. Most abolitionists already know that retributivists have gained virtual ownership of the victims movement. The needs of victims have come to be thought of almost solely in terms of the need to see offenders punished severely. This emotional need for retribution is common among victims and their families, and anti-death penalty activists understand how unwise it is to deny its validity — except where it is used to justify an execution. But to establish any momentum whatsoever, opponents of the death penalty need to be strong advocates of meeting other equally important needs of murder victims' families and other crime victims. They need to be out ahead on this issue, not playing catch-up and merely *responding* to angry victims and their advocates. Victim assistance programs, counseling services, and victim compensation arrangements already exist around the country. Existing compensation programs usually aim to cover medical bills and lost wages for people against whom crimes have been committed. But such programs are generally funded out of already overburdened state budgets, and their adequacy varies. Victims of violent crimes must often show financial need in order to qualify, and maximum awards rarely exceed $25,000 (U.S. Department of Justice, Bureau of Justice Statistics 1988:36–37).

Here is where LWOP *with restitution* could play an important role. Despite the attractiveness of the idea of LWOP + R as revealed in opinion surveys, few efforts have been made by anyone — neither abolitionists, victim advocates, corrections officials, nor elected officeholders — to work out the details of how such a program might work. The major obstacle at present is the low rate of pay for labor in prison industries. The average hourly wage received by inmates in 1985 was between 21¢ and $1.02 (U.S. Department of Justice, Bureau of Justice Statistics 1988:123), and it is unlikely that it has risen much since then. A convicted killer cannot possibly make much of a contribution to the daily financial needs of his victim's family on such wages, much less toward future educational costs and other expenses that his crime may have made a family unable to meet on its own. Ideally, some mechanism ought to be found for increasing the wages of those inmates who have financial obligations to their victims. If the funds for higher wages came from the prison system itself, critics would undoubtedly charge that the taxpayer, not the offender, was compensating victims. They would have a point. But there are few uses for the abolition dividend that would be more in keeping with popular views. Also, a measure of symbolic justice would be achieved: a convict required to make restitution would at least labor in the knowledge that most, if not all, of the proceeds were going not to the prison commissary for cigarettes and magazines, but to persons whose lives he had shattered. The gesture of writing a weekly or monthly check might help to drive that point home. There are many obstacles to making prison-based restitution a working reality, but there is no inherent reason why such programs could not be tried. ADPM groups need to be involved in designing concrete proposals to overcome those obstacles. If they were, death penalty opponents would be less vulnerable to the charge of misplaced sympathy.

Crime prevention efforts also deserve more specific attention from the ADPM. Abolitionist organizations need to tell the American public that the death penalty deals with crime at the wrong point — after it had already taken place. Society needs to invest its resources in preventive measures that will help stop crimes before they occur. The National Council on Crime and Delinquency has gone further in this direction than ADPM organizations. Although it is neither specifically an anti-death penalty organization nor even a membership group, the NCCD has made rather detailed recommendations concerning the steps the United States needs to take to deal aggressively with its crime problem (1993). To name only a few, these include:

- linking drug treatment to job training and placement programs;
- reducing unwanted pregnancies through aggressive family planning, so as to help create stable families and better-functioning young people;
- increased funding for Head Start and other early learning programs; and
- adoption of a year-round school year, class-size limits, and new programs for young people with learning disabilities.

Some of the proposals the NCCD recommends would be difficult to portray as wise crime prevention policy, others less so. But the point is that the council has at least taken the initiative by advancing *specific programmatic steps* to come to grips with the problem of American crime over the long haul. Organizations engaged in fighting capital punishment might well benefit by doing more of the same — not just paying lip service or voicing moral support, but talking very concretely about more adequate crime policies. Given the level to which discourse about crime sometimes sinks in this country, it might seem that this strategy would hold out little hope. The alternatives to the death penalty most likely to be taken seriously at present seem to be those that are harsh, punitive, consistent with a just desserts perspective, and, given recent experience, least likely to have much measurable impact on crime. Still, the

American public may not be as unwilling to consider nonpunitive policies as it often appears. Sixty-one percent of the respondents in a 1989 Gallup poll favored lowering the crime rate by attacking social problems, whereas only 32 percent thought that improving law enforcement offered the most hope (U.S. Department of Justice, Bureau of Justice Statistics 1992a). The split was 52 percent to 38 percent in favor of the social reform strategy when the *Los Angeles Times* put the same question to a nationwide sample in 1994. Sixty-four percent of the respondents believed that at least some lawbreakers could be rehabilitated if referred to an appropriate program early enough, and only 49 percent gave unequivocal support to increased punishment alone as the best societal response to crime (U.S. Department of Justice, Bureau of Justice Statistics 1994:191, 196). To be sure, there are contradictory findings about crime attitudes; most polls also report high levels of support for harsher punishment. The important point, however, is that the public's anger does not totally preclude discussion of measures to control crime through the amelioration of the social conditions that contribute to it.

Finally, there is one specific approach to crime prevention that is especially salient at present: gun control. The waiting period for firearm purchases that the "Brady Bill" imposed is as popular as the death penalty, which is no mean feat. Eighty-six percent of the public supported it in 1993. Smaller majorities favored banning the sale of guns to minors, banning assault weapons, requiring safety classes for all gun owners, banning inexpensive handguns, limiting gun purchases to one per month, and imposing a high tax on ammunition (U.S. Department of Justice, Bureau of Justice Statistics 1994:208–209). The anti-death penalty movement could afford to be much less cautious about endorsing measures such as these.

There is, of course, a very substantial danger that if existing ADPM organizations tried to add drug policy reform, gun control, or other alternative crime-control measures to their agenda, their work against the death penalty itself would be lost in the shuffle. We have already seen that there are not even sufficient resources to support the narrow anti-death penalty focus adequately. But pragmatic framing does not require organizations to lose their focus on capital punishment. It merely requires that they adjust their message. There are other organizations and coalitions that have been formed to pursue specific crime-control objectives: for example, the Sentencing Project, the Drug Policy Foundation, and Handgun Control Inc. Abolitionists could integrate an alternative vision of crime policy into their case, yet still direct their activism squarely at capital punishment. A more potent objection to a broader pragmatic approach is that if sentencing policy and drug strategy were reformed along rational lines, the nation might find that it *could* afford to pay the bills for the death penalty. Nevertheless it remains unlikely that great progress against capital punishment is going to be made by a single-issue movement alone.

In any case, it is highly improbable that any existing national abolitionist organization will reframe opposition to the death penalty as part of a broader, pragmatic package of anticrime measures—even the types of alternatives that do not clash with the sensibilities of traditional abolitionists like the "tough" policies discussed earlier. A further obstacle to pragmatic frame alignment lies with the current organizational structure of the anti-death penalty movement.

The American Civil Liberties Union has in fact made practical crime-control alternatives an element of its case against the death penalty. In its publications, the organization has advocated alternative sentences for nonviolent offenders; the decriminalization of drugs and the provision of greater resources for drug treatment and rehabilitation; community policing; more adequate victim services, including compensation, counseling, and the right to be kept informed about the prosecution of offenders; and the redirection of funds from prison construction to educational, housing, and employment programs that will help to reduce crime. It has even referred to incapacitation of dangerous offenders through very long prison sentences as an alternative to the death penalty.[15] But the ACLU also decries "get-tough" strategies, including prison expansion and pretrial detention, and this tends to drown out its statements about incapacitation. The cornerstones of the organization's Capital Punishment Project continue to be moral claims such as racial discrimination in sentencing and the cruelty of the death penalty. Moreover, the ACLU's image as a left-wing organization habitually drawn to unpopular causes constrains the impact of its otherwise promising way of framing the issue.

The remaining two major groups that make up the ADPM on the national level are effectively blocked from endorsing specific alternatives to the death penalty as parts of their official policies. In the case of Amnesty International, the barrier is the mandate. AI has established itself as a nonpartisan, nonideological, and highly respected human rights organization by limiting itself to *human rights issues.* It has avoided becoming embroiled in domestic policy questions except where a nation's internal policies violate the fundamental and internationally recognized liberties. The death penalty is regarded by AI as a violation of the right to be protected from inhuman and degrading punishments, and thus it is considered to be within the organization's mandate. So is the incarceration of persons for political reasons without trial. So is torture or official persecution of citizens for their religious beliefs. But life-without-parole, intermediate sanctions for nonviolent offenders, gun control, and the like are not directly related to any recognized human rights principles. Rather, they are domestic policy matters and are thus off-limits for Amnesty International to take an official position on. Individual AI members can pursue these or other preferences as private individuals, but AI must remain silent as an organization.

With respect to the National Coalition to Abolish the Death Penalty, the barriers to pragmatic frame realignment are a bit different. NCADP is unable to broaden the context of its opposition to capital punishment largely because it is so fragile. Its affiliates share one thing in common and one thing alone: their opposition to capital punishment. Consequently, adopting an official policy on virtually any other issue would lead to defections. Some of these would be devastating. AIUSA's involvement, for instance, is predicated on the fact that the NCADP is a single-issue coalition and that the issue it addresses falls within AI's mandate.[16] Consequently, NCADP cannot even formally endorse gun control, a very popular idea and one with which the vast majority of abolitionists agree. State anti-death penalty coalitions that are part of the NCADP structure, like other affiliates, are autonomous and may endorse specific alternatives if they wish, so long as they subscribe to all NCADP policies. But many state coalitions are under the same constraints as the NCADP itself. They are composed of representatives from groups as diverse as the Catholic Church and local AIUSA groups,[17] and this discourages potentially divisive stands on related issues. The only ADPM organization that has been ideologically and structurally free to venture into pragmatic, multi-issue reframing has been the Death Penalty Information Center. Several of its recently published reports have featured the damage the death penalty does to the judicial system, its expense, and the uses to which the money might otherwise be put (Dieter 1992, 1993, 1994).

Most of the activists interviewed for this book believe that movement groups, especially the NCADP, are currently too fragile to take formal positions on *any* specific issues beyond the death penalty itself. As a substitute for organizational policies, they suggest that individual activists should address various alternatives as the need arises, without implying that their views represent their organizations as a whole. One NCADP board member and strategist, for example, put it this way:

> . . . we are in fact a true single-issue organization. There are many groups whose *only* commonality is their opposition to the death penalty. If we were to have any other stated policy, we would narrow our coalition. [But] why can't I advocate [an alternative to the death penalty] in a particular position as a solution to a particular problem today without getting into a policy question that threatens my institution or movement? Why can't I point out that these nuts in New York who want to impose the death penalty out there, the senators and the assemblymen who wish to do that, are in fact blind to all the alternatives? And in New York, if we just had a variety of different alternatives, people would be quite supportive of it and we wouldn't have to impose a death penalty in that state in which there is none. Why couldn't, you know, we find a coalition in Georgia led by a strong governor perhaps who would come along at some point in the future and lead the state toward certain incarceration, and all abolitionists advocate abolition of the death penalty and be willing to accept—as a *step today*—something that stops state killing?[18]

Clearly, this approach would have its advantages. If it would suffice for activists to speak for specific alternative anticrime measures on an ad hoc basis, movement organizations would be spared the necessity of bitter disputes over binding policy decisions. But it remains to be seen whether ADPM groups are capable of raising the social acceptability of abolitionism while sidestepping concrete alternatives. A more consistent and concentrated message may be required, regardless of the costs. Intraorganizational unity is important, but the movement as a whole does not have to speak with one voice to have an impact. To redirect the debate, it may be necessary that at least one substantial organization, probably at the national level but with arms in key death penalty states (for example, California, New York, and Texas) and states where reinstatement threatens (such as Wisconsin and Iowa at present), come forward as a forceful *anticrime* abolition group. And that organization may not yet have been formed.

Prospects for the Future

Charles Fulwood no longer holds a formal position in the abolition movement. He speaks more openly of unconventional approaches than he could as AIUSA's Death Penalty Program director and NCADP board member:

> I think that's the kind of campaign that's needed now, a campaign that's a coalition of all the groups that are connected to this philosophically or morally or what have you. But I think that the focus of it has to be what will really control crime. What will really reduce crime and what will really reduce the taxpayers' burden. And then around the edges you can do the human rights number and the moral outrage number. Not at the center of it. Others may disagree, but that's where I am on it. I don't think that our culture responds to morality first. That's not at the top of the hierarchy. That's further down. You know, we are a lot more pragmatic, or at least we think we are. But you've got to dig real deep to get to the moral paydirt. Real deep.[19]

If the future of capital punishment in America is in the hands of an anti-death penalty movement alone, then executions will most likely continue for a long time indeed. This does not reflect any lack of dedication or talent within that movement, but rather the symbolic role that the death penalty will continue to play. If its future is to be shortened, what will probably have to happen is for abolitionism to become an integral part of a much larger and broader movement for rational criminal justice policy. This means that new organizations will be needed, organizations that have as their goal reducing America's leadership of the industrialized world in violence. They will have to transcend the liberal-conservative dichotomy that has defined the issue in the past.

A new crime-control movement that dealt less in ideology and more in the practical assessment of what works and what does not, what merits the expenditure of public funds and what does not, would of necessity condemn the death penalty. For in *instrumental* terms, the death penalty makes little sense. Its fatal flaw is not its immorality, about which there is vast space for disagreement, but rather its enormous lack of cost-effectiveness. Executions deliver no more than brief emotional satisfaction. Coming to grips with American crime in the twenty-first century will almost certainly require their elimination, or at the very least, severe statutory constraints on their use.

If such a larger movement emerged, what would be the relationship of today's anti-death penalty organizations to it? For those activists whose commitment is traditional and "pure," the partnership would be an uneasy one.

They would find it difficult to be involved, however indirectly, in the pursuit of relatively harsh societal responses to violent crime. Some might also object that generating opposition to the death penalty on the basis of its poor return on the dollar avoids the more fundamental issue: America's habit of trying to solve problems through force. They are right that faith in violence is an important source of the death penalty's popularity. It is less clear that theirs is the wisest strategy. The *strength* of a broad and pragmatic anticrime movement would be that it would undermine the death penalty without first requiring ordinary people to change their fundamental feelings about crime and justice. While other views on human affairs might be desirable, they could only come about slowly. Ridding ourselves of the death penalty may be a prerequisite to coming to grips with that deeper cultural problem, not its result. If so, it is wiser to seek abolition *by whatever method works*. For others now involved in the movement, the deciding factor would be the overriding importance of bringing an end to judicial killings. Misgivings about limitations on parole, or about channeling more money into police departments rather than school districts, could be left for another day.

Will the anti-death penalty struggle end if it does not merge into a broader and more pragmatic reform movement? Certainly not. The spirit of abolitionism has survived for more than two centuries, through even tougher times than these. Rather, the most realistic objective of the ADPM in coming decades, if it continues in more or less its present form, may turn out to be not *abolishing* capital punishment but rather slowing its advance. A return to the "taken-for-grantedness" that capital punishment once enjoyed, not merely the continuation of executions, would signal the ultimate defeat of the movement. It might seem unlikely that the controversy could ever fade away, that a society without executions could become truly unimaginable again. But then, it was not long ago that the Balkan city of Sarajevo was admired as a center of religious and ethnic tolerance. "Progress" can be fleeting.

One of the most honored veterans of the anti-death penalty struggle, Henry Schwarzschild, is well known for his pessimism. He does not expect victory to come during his lifetime, and fears that the death penalty will outlast most younger activists as well. Nevertheless, Schwarzschild insists that abolitionists must do two things as matters of moral obligation. First, they must be obstacles to society's deadly "justice," making executions as procedurally difficult to carry out and as costly as possible. And second, they must keep the issue alive so that others will be able to build on their efforts when political opportunities improve.

> I don't know if you ever saw that wonderful documentary that was made about I. F. Stone, the great radical journalist, probably about ten years ago. He was about ready to speak in the middle or late Vietnam war at the University of Virginia, as I remember it. And he spoke at great length about the horrors of the war and the machinery of the society and the economy and the military-industrial complex that kept it going. And then some kid got up in the audience and said "Well, Mr. Stone, if everything is as hopeless as you say

about ending the war, what do you want us to do? What should we be doing?"
And he stood up there on the platform, with his finger on his nose for about
thirty seconds, and finally he said "Keep on screaming!"

There is really a sort of moral obligation to do that. And what I've said in
public on occasion about that is that the reason we admire the William Lloyd
Garrisons or the Charles Sumners or the Frederick Douglass' of the 1840s is
not because they worked at something they could win. The Constitution was
against them and the law was against them and the economy was against
them. Politics was against them. It was an utterly, utterly hopeless battle. But
they *couldn't not* fight it, you know. Now without arrogantly saying that
those are entirely analogous, the social and moral principles are the same. It's
a nasty thing for a society, for one's own society to use homicide as an
instrument of social policy. And one ought to object to that.[20]

At present, the future of the death penalty in the United States looks
secure. But as Schwarzschild notes, so did the future of slavery once upon a
time. So did unquestioned male supremacy in the workforce, the industrial
practices that turned the Hudson River and Lake Erie into lifeless sewers, and
dozens of other conditions that were ultimately changed. Perhaps the practice
of executing killers is different, but its current popularity does not prove it so.
As long as at least a few keep objecting, the death penalty may someday fall
under its own weight.

Afterword—Spring, 1999

In the three years since *Against Capital Punishment* first appeared, the death penalty has continued to entrench itself ever more deeply in the United States. This surprises almost no one. Even the most optimistic of abolitionists acknowledge that matters will get worse before they begin to get better, and from their viewpoint, things are indeed getting worse. In 1997, a record-high 74 convicts were put to death, the most since 1955 (Snell 1998). The total for 1998 slipped to 68, but the last of the year's executions was a milestone: 38-year-old Andy Smith, lethally injected in South Carolina on December 18th, was the 500th execution of the post-*Gregg* era.

This book has concentrated primarily on a time period that extends from 1972, the year that the Supreme Court struck down capital punishment in its narrow *Furman* decision, through 1994. It has described the slow development of anti–death penalty organizations and has offered an explanation of their victories and defeats during those years. In the following pages, I will not attempt to provide a complete account of anti–death penalty movement (ADPM) activities during the late 1990s, tempting as it might be to do so. Instead, I will only focus on events and trends that bear directly on what I have identified as the movement's strengths and weaknesses and the prospects for a pragmatic framing of the issue. These include continuing efforts to curtail appeals of death sentences, the attention-grabbing capital cases involving convicts Mumia Abu-Jamal and Karla Faye Tucker, and the rapid proliferation of life-without-parole sentences in death penalty and non–death penalty states alike.

Habeas Reform

The momentum toward reducing the legal avenues open to death-sentenced inmates and shortening the span of time between trial and execution has continued, though not without a hitch. In the aftermath of the 1995 bombing of the Alfred Murrah Federal Building in Oklahoma City, President Clinton signed into law the Anti-Terrorism and Effective Death Penalty Act of 1996, which included "the most far-reaching assault on habeas corpus since its expansion to the states in 1867."[1] The death penalty provisions of the new law impose a one-year time limit for filing petitions for habeas corpus following the completion of condemned inmates' appeals in state court—a period potentially as short as six months. The Act requires the approval of a three-judge panel of the U.S. Court of Appeals before a second habeas petition can be filed in federal court, and the Supreme Court is not empowered to review the panel's decision. To have a chance of approval, such "successor" petitions must rely on either new law established by the Supreme Court or new evidence of innocence so convincing that no reasonable juror would have found the petitioner guilty had it been presented at trial. Attorneys representing death row inmates have argued that these standards are so high as to be practically impossible to attain. Finally, the 1996 Act prohibits federal judges from overruling state court judgements in death penalty cases unless those judgements either flatly contradict or unreasonably apply clearly established rulings of the U.S. Supreme Court.[2] Taken together, these reforms sharply limit the much-maligned appeals process which has resulted in the reversal of more than half of the death sentences imposed by trial courts since the 1970s and has bought precious time for the dozens on death row who eventually demonstrated their innocence and were released.

Habeas reform clearly puts a premium on the availability of qualified legal counsel early in the appeals process, since the clock begins ticking earlier and faster than in the past. In order for the new time limits to apply, the 1996 law requires states to come up with satisfactory mechanisms for certifying, appointing, and compensating qualified lawyers for state court appeals of capital cases. Paradoxically, Congress made this more difficult when it withdrew the funding of the twenty Post-Conviction Defender Organizations—formerly known as Capital Resource Centers—that had been providing appellate representation to many death-sentenced inmates. Some of these centers have obtained enough private funding to struggle along on a reduced scale. But the inability of inmates to find lawyers to handle their appeals has proved to be an obstacle to the goal of reducing delays in the administration of the death penalty. As of early 1999, no state has yet been able to devise a system that satisfies the Anti-Terrorism and Effective Death Penalty Act's prerequisites for the imposition of the shorter deadlines (Dieter 1998).

As Congress tries to speed up the appeals process, evidence continues to mount that the danger of executing innocent persons by mistake is greater than ever. The number of inmates released from death row after being found innocent has risen to seventy-five. In Illinois alone, which had executed only seven men as of 1998, nine death-sentenced inmates have been exonerated. Two of these, Rolando Cruz and Alejandro Hernandez, served eleven years on death row before the cases against them unraveled. The pair were convicted and sentenced to die in 1985 for the rape and murder of Jeanine Nicarico, a ten-year-old Naperville, Illinois girl. It was later revealed that prosecutors knew at the time of the trial that another man, Brian Dugan, had confessed to the Nicarico murder as well as to two other similar crimes, but withheld the information in order to obtain the conviction of Cruz and Hernandez. In addition, law enforcement officers testified that Cruz had described to them a dream containing details only the killer could have known. No record of this "dream statement" was made, and the episode was not revealed until shortly before the trial began. The story turned out to be fabricated. Ultimately, three DuPage County prosecutors and four deputy sheriffs faced trial for misconduct, including perjury and withholding evidence. DNA testing showed that the semen found at the crime scene did not match Cruz and Hernandez, and they were finally released in 1995. The men owe their lives to the very delays that are targeted by habeas reform. Two years later, a coalition of attorneys, judges, and legal organizations petitioned the Illinois Supreme Court for a year-long moratorium on executions in the state until the rash of near-misses was investigated and remedial steps taken (Drell and Forte 1997; Henderson 1997). The American Bar Association in 1997 called on each death penalty jurisdiction to forgo further executions until numerous procedural flaws in the death penalty are remedied. And death penalty opponents also succeeded in attracting a great deal of public attention to the danger of executing the innocent when a three-day National Conference on Wrongful Convictions and the Death Penalty was held at Northwestern University in November of 1998. The gathering attracted approximately 800 lawyers and activists, as well as thirty death row survivors, and received widespread press coverage in the United States and abroad.

Rising numbers of executions and vanishing legal safeguards are not the only challenges confronting the anti–death penalty movement at the end of the twentieth century. The movement is also faced with the constant task of preventing the reinstatement of capital punishment in the handful of states that still do not have it. When *Against Capital Punishment* first appeared, Kansas and New York had just become the thirty-seventh and thirty-eighth states to bring back the ultimate sanction. No more states have been added to the list so far, but reinstatement elsewhere remains a constant threat. The Massachusetts legislature came within one vote of passing a death penalty bill in 1997. A last-minute change of heart by Representative John Slattery resulted in a tie vote, ending the matter for the time being. Death penalty advocates in Massachusetts have vowed not only to try again, but to unseat Slattery and others who, in their view, thwarted the will of the Commonwealth's citizens. Abolitionists also had to scramble to prevent less serious reinstatement efforts in Michigan, Iowa, and the District of Columbia over the past two years. Similarly, lawmakers attempt to expand existing death penalty laws almost every year—to make new crimes like drive-by shootings or killings of children punishable by execution, to lower the age of eligibility, and the like. The limited resources of national abolitionist organizations and the scarcity of well-funded and -staffed coalitions at the state level make it extremely difficult to put out these brush fires when they are ignited.

High Profile Capital Cases

Throughout this nation's history, the rise and fall of capital punishment in particular states has tended to rest on highly publicized capital murder cases. Abolition has often followed on the heels of botched executions or alleged miscarriages, while reinstatement and expansion has usually occurred in the aftermath of particularly notorious or heinous crimes. Since the initial publication of this book, two capital cases have attracted levels of national and international attention that far exceed the norm in recent years. Both could have implications for the ADPM's strength and diversity, which have been so limited during this fourth historical era of abolitionism. These are the cases of Mumia Abu-Jamal and Karla Faye Tucker.

"Live from Death Row:" Mumia Abu-Jamal

On December 9, 1981, police arrived at 13th and Locust Streets in Philadelphia in response to a reported shooting. There they found a fellow officer, 26 year-old Daniel Faulkner, dying on the ground with 38-caliber bullet wounds in his back and face. Mumia Abu-Jamal was lying nearby, wounded in the chest by a bullet from Faulkner's gun. Abu-Jamal's handgun, from which five shells had been fired, was found at the scene. At his subsequent trial, prosecutors charged that the former Black Panther and local radio commentator shot Faulkner after happening onto the scene where Abu-Jamal's brother, William Cook, had been pulled over at a traffic stop. Seeing his brother struggling with a policeman, he allegedly stopped the cab he was driving, got out, and shot the officer. Two witnesses—another lawman and a security guard at the hospital to which both men were taken—testified that Abu-Jamal had admitted shooting Faulkner and had stated that he hoped the officer died (Ditzen 1998; O'Reilly 1998).

Mumia Abu-Jamal was convicted of capital murder in 1982 and sentenced to death by Common Pleas Judge Albert Sabo. According to supporters, the trial was marred by an inept legal defense and by the biased conduct of Sabo, known in legal circles as "the king of death row" (Norman 1998) for having sentenced more defendants to die than any other judge in America. The State of Pennsylvania was still many years away from its first post-*Gregg* execution when Abu-Jamal was sent to death row, and in the years since his trial, his case has gradually attracted widespread attention on both sides of the Atlantic. Unlike the majority of death-sentenced inmates, Mumia Abu-Jamal is an articulate, well-read, and charismatic figure. Both before and after going to prison, he has spoken eloquently on the politics of race and criminal justice in America. His prison writings have attracted the attention of several groups on the political left, including the Partisan Defense Committee in New York City and the Quixote Center, which advocates liberation theology. By the 1990s, his ideas began to reach a wider audience through publications like *The Nation* and the *Yale Law Journal* (Kaufman and Morello 1995).

Abu-Jamal's fame was multiplied when, despite his legal status, he nearly succeeded in becoming a nationally syndicated radio commentator. A San Francisco radio producer, Noelle Hanrahan, began taping his death row commentaries in 1994 for broadcast on California radio stations. Hanrahan submitted a demonstration tape to producers at National Public Radio (NPR), who decided to make Abu-Jamal a regular contributor to its daily news and public affairs program "All Things Considered." NPR later reversed itself under pressure from groups including the Fraternal Order of Police, which objected to giving a convicted cop-killer a national forum. The network maintained that the decision was based on legitimate programming considerations, not external pressure. Abu-Jamal filed an unsuccessful lawsuit against NPR, alleging censorship and violation of the his First Amendment rights (Vulliamy 1997). Even though the controversial essays never reached the airwaves, several of them became the basis of a 1995 book, *Live from Death Row*, a scathing critique of the dehumanizing conditions in prison and the racism of the death penalty. It was followed by a second book, *Death Blossoms*, in 1997. Abu-Jamal's writings, like those of Caryl Chessman four decades earlier, helped transform Mumia Abu-Jamal into a folk hero among many on the political left and attracted many celebrities from the entertainment and academic worlds to his cause. Protesters have taken to the streets in New York, Paris, Berlin, and other cities around the world to demand that Abu-Jamal be freed. The presidents of France and South Africa, as well as the foreign ministers of Germany and Belgium, have urged that he be granted a new trial. Support has also come from the Netherlands and from Italy, where 100,000 Romans signed a petition to stop his execution. Dozens of web sites now plead his case.

Mumia Abu-Jamal's legions of supporters claim that he is innocent of the Faulkner murder. Neither Mumia nor his brother have offered an alternative account of what happened on December 9, 1981 other than to assert that the wrong man is on death row. But the "Free Mumia" movement contends that he was framed because of his radical political views, his long-standing and outspoken criticism of Philadelphia police, and his involvement with the Black Panthers and the local radical group MOVE. His current defense team, headed by famed attorney Leonard Weinglass, has accused Judge Sabo of judicial misconduct in both the original trial and in a post-conviction hearing that took place in 1995. The attorneys have also alleged that prosecutors withheld evidence, intimidated potential defense witnesses, and made deals involving lenient treatment of prosecution witnesses in exchange for testimony damaging to the defense. Each of these points was rejected by the Pennsylvania Supreme Court in October of 1998, and Abu-Jamal's attorneys are preparing a habeas corpus petition to federal court as of this writing (Ditzen 1998).

Many abolitionists hope that Mumia Abu-Jamal will become the catalyst that will either draw large numbers of African-Americans into existing ADPM organizations or lead them to form their own groups. To be sure, it is hardly unusual for a black man to be condemned to die for killing a white man—nearly half of death row inmates are black, and a large proportion have been convicted of interracial homicides. But Abu-Jamal is hardly the typical African-American facing a date with the executioner. He possesses great charisma and rhetorical skills. And he is defiant. Not only is he seen by sympathetic observers as a black man railroaded for a crime he did not commit—indeed, a widespread belief in the black community is that such injustices are commonplace—but as a man who refuses to bow down before his oppressor even in the face of imminent death. A strong, handsome man, bearded and dreadlocked, who will not allow his psyche to be imprisoned along with his body, Mumia Abu-Jamal touches much the same nerve that Malcolm X touched in the 1960s.

On the other hand, the uniqueness of Mumia Abu-Jamal seems to limit his "usefulness" to the anti–death penalty movement. Many of the thousands who have been drawn to the "Free Mumia" campaign are attracted more to the man himself than to the larger issue of capital punishment. They are primarily affiliated with an array of organizations and groups on the political left, like MOVE and the Socialist Workers' Party, rather than to the ADPM. And those affiliations represent potential problems for some mainstream abolitionists. Abu-Jamal's supporters have often been portrayed in newspapers and on television as naive outsiders driven not by familiarity with the facts of the case, but rather by radical fervor. Some ADPM activists have been reluctant to work closely with the Mumia people, fearing that they would find themselves subjected to the same caricatures. The result has been that the two movements have remained separate rather than united.[3] It remains to be seen how many of the Mumia activists will take on capital punishment as an issue in and of itself once the case is settled one way or the other. Some of them may. But most will probably continue to focus on the causes they were devoted to before they began struggling to save this unusual man.

A Human Face in the Death Chamber: Karla Faye Tucker

Executions have become so commonplace in this country that they often pass with little media attention and even less visible protest. But the scene in Huntsville, Texas on February 3, 1998 was unlike anything that had been seen since the execution of Gary Gilmore two decades earlier. Outside the Walls Unit, where the busiest death chamber in the nation is housed, hundreds of demonstrators and reporters gathered to await the first of the Lone Star State's 20 executions of the year. What made this particular lethal injection so eventful was that the person about to die was a born-again Christian woman, 38-year-old Karla Faye Tucker, who had by nearly all accounts undergone a dramatic and positive transformation during her fourteen years in prison. She was to be only the second female put to death since *Gregg*, and the first in Texas since the Civil War. The numerous media representatives from various European countries who were on hand had much to report, not only about the execution itself, but also about the surreal mixture of mournful abolitionists and pro–death penalty celebrants outside the prison. The competing sentiments were evident from the signs they carried: "Jesus Loves Karla," "Die Like a Man," "La Execucion No Es La Solucion," and "God Bless Karla Faye—But Kill the Bitch Anyway." Cheers drowned out the sound of sobbing when prison officials announced that Ms. Tucker had been pronounced dead at 6:45 p.m.

Karla Tucker had been convicted of a particularly ugly crime. Along with Daniel Garrett, her boyfriend at the time, Tucker broke into the apartment of Jerry Lynn Dean on June 12, 1983 to steal some motorcycle parts. Both Garrett and Tucker were high on drugs. The two found Dean in bed with Deborah

Thornton, a married woman that he had met at a party that evening. Garrett struck Dean in the head with a hammer, then Tucker took up a pickax that she found nearby and buried its blade in Dean's chest. Tucker next attacked and killed the terrified Thornton with the same weapon. Between them, the two victims' bodies bore the marks of at least 35 blows (Verhovek 1998a; Hewitt et al. 1998). A witness testified that Tucker claimed she had experienced a sexual climax with each swing of the ax. Both assailants were sentenced to die for the crime, but Garrett succumbed to liver disease before his sentence could be carried out.

On the day Tucker died, the U.S. Supreme Court twice rejected requests by her attorneys to stay the execution pending a challenge to the state's unique clemency process. The Texas Board of Pardons and Paroles, which operates in virtual secrecy to insulate the governor from making difficult clemency decisions, and which had denied all 76 requests in death penalty cases that had been put before it, had already voted unanimously not to recommend that Governor George W. Bush commute her sentence to life. Bush was empowered to issue a 30-day reprieve, but chose not to do so (Verhovek 1998b; Hewitt et al. 1998).

As the likelihood increased that Karla Tucker might become only the second woman to die at the hands of the state in decades, her case began to attract considerable attention and sympathy. From an anti–death penalty perspective, a sympathetic death row convict couldn't have appeared at a more opportune time. The previous year, the nation's attention had been riveted to the trial of Timothy McVeigh for his part in the Oklahoma City terrorist bombing that killed 168 people and injured over 500. The unrepentant McVeigh had become a virtual poster boy for capital punishment, a living symbol for why, in the eyes of many Americans, the death penalty is necessary. Suddenly Tucker's story burst into the news, and it attracted a large and unusually broad group of supporters who wanted to save her life. Among these supporters, of course, were dedicated death penalty opponents, many of whom wanted in particular to draw attention to the shocking details of the woman's upbringing. Death-sentenced inmates are often the products of horrific childhoods, and Karla Tucker was no exception. She was smoking marijuana and using heroin by the time she turned 10. She became sexually active at 11 or 12, and soon learned to take money in exchange for sex. Both her drug abuse and prostitution occurred with her mother's encouragement. As a teenager, Tucker became involved in the local motorcycle subculture and earned a reputation as a girl who could keep up with the guys, whether the activity was drinking, taking drugs, or even fighting (Lowry 1992).

As a symbol of capital punishment, in fact, Karla Tucker underscored *several* issues that abolitionists often raise. In addition to the role of childhood pathology in the origins of violent crime, she also drew attention to gender bias in capital punishment. Few Americans were aware of how unlikely it had become for women to face execution until the Tucker controversy arose. Although aggravated homicides by females are relatively rare, the apparent reluctance of prosecutors and juries to sentence women to die nevertheless raises fundamental issues of fairness. Tucker's case also pointed indirectly to the matter of race, in that many commentators questioned whether people would be paying much attention to her if she were a born-again *African-American* rather than a born-again white (Verhovek 1998c).

What was most unprecedented about the effort to save Karla Tucker, however, was that the usual band of death penalty opponents was joined by a substantial contingent of Christian conservatives who generally support capital punishment. Jerry Falwell, founder of the conservative organization Moral Majority, was among these. So was Pat Robertson, head of the Christian Broadcasting Network, host of the CBN television program "The 700 Club," and former candidate for the Republican presidential nomination. A taped interview with Tucker was first broadcast on CBN in 1993, and a survey conducted on the network's web site found that 34 percent of viewers reported a change in their feelings about the death penalty after they heard her story (Verhovek 1998b). Weeks before the execution, Robertson told his television audience that "There are times that mercy overwhelms justice, and that's what's called for here" (Hewitt et al. 1998). Karla Tucker's capacity to cause Evangelical Christians to rethink their normally pro–capital punishment views rested on the fact that she was one of them. In 1983, Tucker stole a Bible from a prison ministry program. Reading it, she underwent a profound spiritual transformation. By her own account, she felt true remorse for her misdeeds for the first time and committed herself to spreading her newfound Christian faith to other inmates. From that time forward, she was a model prisoner. The exposure she enjoyed in the Christian media meant that Tucker put a human face on the death penalty. She demonstrated that in America's prisons, which few of us have direct experiences with, there are people who have done terrible things but have changed. When those people are mere abstractions, it is easy to say that their conversion is too little and too late to affect their just deserts. But when their faces are seen and their voices are heard, when they are revealed to be *like us* in some way, then things may be seen in a different light. Religious conversions on death row are hardly rare, but hers was taken seriously by many fellow Christians as a result of her exposure on CBN and the Larry King television program.

In chapter four, death penalty opponents Bruce Ledewitz and Michael Radelet commented on how tremendously important it would be if pro-life activists and/or conservative Christians could be won over to the cause of abolishing the death penalty. Not only would this diminish some of the staunchest political support on the other side, but it might also bring an infusion of desperately-needed resources from those groups. This seemed like an impossible dream until Karla Tucker came along. Then, in 1997 and 1998, many abolitionists saw a golden opportunity to make inroads on the right. If politically active televangelists like Robertson and Falwell could be moved by sympathy for a convicted murderer, then perhaps her case could be used to crack the hard shell of apparent conservative unanimity and open a dialogue on this issue.

A year later, it is still unclear how much difference the Tucker story made. There is anecdotal evidence to suggest that the impact was profound. The Christian Broadcasting Network, which produces Pat Robertson's *700 Club* and other programs, approached the Death Penalty Information Center (DPIC) seeking information on a broad array of abolitionist concerns and used the information DPIC provided in its programming. CBN had exhibited no interest whatsoever in DPIC's services before the Tucker case.[4] An editorial in a prominent evangelical journal (*Christianity Today* 1998) two months after her death endorsed traditional abolitionist arguments concerning the arbitrary and discriminatory nature of death sentencing in America, the danger of false convictions in capital cases, and the failure of executions to serve as either a deterrent to the violent or a consolation to the bereaved. It encouraged evangelicals to engage in "prayerful conversation" about the death penalty, and to bear in mind that there are "two parallel streams of biblical thought about crime and punishment"—one focused on justice, one on ending violence, but both "designed to break the cycle of vengeance." There have also been scattered press accounts of deep divisions among Christians soon after the execution (Niebuhr 1998, Jones 1998). But there is as yet no hard evidence of a measurable change in outlook among those believers traditionally most supportive of harsh justice.

Lacking firm evidence about the long-range impact of Tucker's execution, ADPM activists' opinions are somewhat divided. Some feel that it may have helped encourage persons on the other side of the issue at least to pay more attention to the details of the death penalty's administration, to soften their attitudes and enter into less heated dialogues with critics of capital punishment.[5] Much the same conclusion was reached by a policy analyst for the National Association of Evangelicals, which since 1973 has officially supported the execution of convicted murderers:

> at least it is prompting organizational people such as myself to suggest to our leadership that we need to begin a closer examination of the issue of the death penalty. . . . [W]hen ABC, I think it was, last night carried a whole story on the subject of one man's execution, I, for one, watched it. And I maybe wouldn't have [watched] a year ago. And I know, for example, that there are some people in our circles that are watching the movie "Dead Man Walking." In other words, if they're not changing their view, they're at least paying attention to the subject in a way [they] never [did] before.[6]

According to this same individual, the Tucker case has amounted to more than just food for thought for some conservative Christians. It has also caused anger and a willingness to take political action:

> No one will forget it. When George [W.] Bush, when he runs for President (pause), none of us is ever going to forget. The fact that he can say that the Board of Pardon and Paroles is the determining factor, and that he is obligated to do what they recommend—which was his excuse—at least *some* of us, some of us won't forget Karla Faye Tucker![7]

However others in positions of ADPM leadership are not optimistic about lasting shock waves on the right. The impact of Karla Faye Tucker on conservative Christian thought, they suggest, was intense but short-lived. In part, this is because ADPM organizations were poorly positioned to exploit the case and had little credibility among fundamentalists when the story broke.[8] More importantly, they say, Tucker was an anomaly. That is, a common view among death penalty opponents is that it was actually the rare combination of her religious status (born-again), her gender (female), her race (white), her relative physical attractiveness, and her ability to express herself in an articulate manner on television that moved people—along with the fact that the brother of one of her victims became an outspoken ally of the people who struggled to save her life during the last weeks and days. It will almost certainly be a long time before another convict comes along with several of these features in combination.[9] Individually, none of Tucker's attention-grabbing characteristics can arouse the passions that she aroused. Barely a month after she died, for instance, Florida electrocuted a woman, Judias Buenoano, with little fanfare. There has even been speculation that the ultimate significance of Karla Tucker may be that her execution will ease the pressure on states *not* to carry out the death sentence on women—that "if they can kill *her* they can kill *anyone!*"

Life without Parole—What *Sort* of "Alternative?"

In this book, I have argued that for the anti–death penalty movement to reverse the momentum of capital punishment in America, it may need to adopt a more *pragmatic* strategy, one that places less emphasis on moralistic appeals and more emphasis on tangible costs and on policy alternatives that resonate with widespread cultural sentiments. And while any number of social, economic, or criminal justice policies might well be marketed as viable alternatives to the death penalty, I have suggested that only some form of life-without-parole (LWOP) is likely to be seen by the largest segment of the American public as capable of making executions unnecessary. Murderers represent *perpetual threats* to the innocent in the popular imagination. If the state is not going to exterminate them, then few will be satisfied with anything short of permanent confinement in a secure facility.

Ten out of the 12 states that have not yet reinstated the death penalty have provisions for release-proof life imprisonment.[10] Taken by itself, this observation would seem to support the appeal of life-without-parole as a *statutory* alternative to the death penalty. It seems to suggest that where LWOP is in place, efforts to resume executions garner less support. But matters are actually less clear. As of early 1999, LWOP and the death penalty *co-exist* in 33 states, the federal government, and the U.S. military. Only five death penalty states—Kansas, New Jersey, New Mexico, Oregon, and Texas—make no provision for true life sentences. This is a significant change from 1990, when only 24 death penalty states had life-without-parole and 12 did not. What does this mean in terms of the potential efficacy of pragmatic abolitionism and explicit endorsements by ADPM organizations of specific alternative sanctions? Does it indicate that this avenue is a blind alley, that LWOP merely widens the net—adding another draconian sanction to the mix rather than helping to reduce the demand for executions?

It goes without saying that the rapid proliferation of life-without-parole laws has not led to a corresponding wave of death penalty abolition. In fact, no state legislature has voluntarily abandoned an existing death statute, for *any* reason, in over thirty years. But the co-existence of LWOP and capital punishment does not mean that the former has no place in the arsenal of pragmatic abolitionists after all. For one thing, there is the matter of sequence. Had the ADPM been able to aggressively endorse life-without-parole before so many states had reinstated the death penalty, then they might have been better able to frame capital punishment as unnecessary and wasteful. As this book has shown, however, the aggressive endorsement of LWOP or any other specific alternative by existing ADPM organizations was impossible for a variety of reasons. But securing the enactment of a life-without-parole statute in the two states that currently have neither LWOP nor the death penalty might be a wise proactive strategy to head off future reinstatement campaigns there.

While life-without-parole has not functioned as a *statutory* alternative capable of bringing abolition about, activists are virtually unanimous in their view that LWOP statutes have worked as a *sentencing* alternative.[11] That is, LWOP has helped minimize the number of death sentences sought and achieved. Prosecutors frequently use it as a bargaining chip, offering life in prison to defendants as an inducement to plead guilty and avoid the danger of winding up strapped to a gurney. When given the choice, juries often opt for it. According to District Attorney John Holmes of Harris County, Texas, "You're not going to find 12 people back-to-back on the same jury that are going to kill somebody when the alternative is throwing away the key."[12] As a matter of fact, it is probably no accident that Texas leads the nation in executions. Its criminal code requires a determination of future dangerousness as a necessary aggravating circumstance in capital cases but has no LWOP option for jurors to fall back on should they want to spare an offender's life *and* ensure that (s)he never kills again. In short, the rapid spread of life-without-parole is almost certainly keeping the number of new death sentences far lower than it would otherwise be. Until the actual abolition of the death penalty again becomes a realistic objective, this may be the most sensible goal for the ADPM to seek.

The time is probably not yet right for abolitionists to make much public education and lobbying headway by stressing the redundancy of capital punishment in states that already have severe mandatory minimum sentences for murder, and few of their organizations have yet done so. One exception to this rule on the national level is CUADP (Citizens United for Alternatives to the Death Penalty), founded in 1997. CUADP "recognizes and upholds the responsibility of society to protect everyone from people who are dangerous, in particular, those who are convicted murderers." The organization advocates that persons convicted of aggravated murder "should serve a minimum of 25 years in prison before the possibility of consideration for parole" and [i]n certain cases, imprisonment should be for life, with no possibility of parole—ever."[13] At least one state group, Virginians for Alternatives to the Death Penalty, has organized itself around the advocacy of nonlethal responses to homicide. The Virginia organization has experienced an improvement in its public image as a result of offering concrete proposals rather than criticism alone. Moreover, the reluctance to address incapacitation that was so evident in the 1972–1994 period is fading in the face of harsh political reality. Pragmatism is beginning to find a foothold.

Although the redundancy issue, like other pragmatic arguments against the institution of capital punishment, may be unlikely to meet with much success in the short run, abolitionists will most likely hammer it home with increasing frequency and forcefulness. Should violent crime rates continue to decline, and criminal justice expenditures continue to put the squeeze on other important budget items like education and health care, it may soon become possible for officeholders to voice doubts about wisdom of our continued reliance on the expensive "luxuries"—in both the financial and moral senses—that executions have become.

Notes

Introduction

1. Throughout this book, the terms "capital punishment," "the death penalty," and "executions" refer to *judicial* executions, that is, legally sanctioned killings by state agents of persons who have been convicted of criminal offenses. It is this form of above-board, "legitimate" execution that is in decline worldwide. Regrettably, the same cannot be said for *extrajudicial* executions, which are carried out by clandestine state agents, such as "death squads," acting outside of legal systems.

2. For the most part, surveys have measured support for capital punishment only at an abstract level. Since 1986, a number of polls have found that very large numbers of death penalty supporters actually prefer nonlethal alternatives for convicted murderers, especially life sentences without possibility of parole. This issue will be discussed in detail in later chapters.

3. Interview, November 18, 1992.

4. Not all these elites were absolute "abolitionists" in the contemporary sense: they did not all wish to banish the gallows from the American landscape altogether. Clearly Rush assumed such a stance, and Franklin probably agreed. The extent of Jefferson's opposition to capital punishment is less clear. He admired Beccaria and his writings on crime and punishment, but had proposed only the reduction of the number of capital crimes when he drafted a Virginia criminal code during the Revolution. John Jay and James Madison also sought the reform of criminal laws and the limitation of the death penalty (Masur 1989).

5. Among the recommendations in the commission's report were that hanging be retained as the method of execution in Great Britain, that juries be given the discretion to decide between the penalties of death or life imprisonment, as in the United States, and that the crime of murder *not* be subdivided into degrees. Although the report of the Royal Commission helped revive the American anti-death penalty movement, British abolitionists were not at all enthusiastic about it. For example, the Howard League, one of the leading abolitionist organizations in that country, only reluctantly and belatedly endorsed the report (Cristoph 1962:85–90).

6. *Gregg v. Georgia,* 428 U.S. 153 (1976); *Jurek v. Texas,* 428 U.S. 262 (1976); *Proffitt v. Florida,* 428 U.S. 242 (1976).

7. Some of these organizations, such as the National Coalition to Abolish the Death Penalty and Law Enforcement Against Death, are dedicated exclusively to the abolition of capital punishment. Many others include ADP work as only one of many goals. These

include the American Civil Liberties Union, the Fellowship of Reconciliation, and the National Council on Crime and Delinquency.

8. See Diani 1992 and Burstein 1991b for discussions of this issue. Diani concludes, as I do, that "anti-institutional styles of political participation" should not be taken as a defining characteristic of social movements (1992:17). Similarly, Burstein argues that *most* social movements employ conventional tactics like litigation to some extent, especially as they begin to achieve a measure of success (1991a:1203–1024, 1991b:513).

Chapter 1

1. Although saved from the electric chair, the Scottsboro defendants were nevertheless reconvicted, and five of the eight spent between 10 and 20 years in prison. It is now generally accepted that the charges in the case were fabricated. The Scottsboro case also resulted in another Supreme Court decision, *Norris v. Alabama* (294 U.S. 587, 1935), dealing with the improper exclusion of blacks from a jury (Wolfe 1973:81–82; Radelet, Bedau, and Putnam 1992:116–118).

2. In 1993, a federal judge was asked to prohibit the state of California from carrying out its second gas chamber execution of the 1990s on grounds that lethal gas "is an unnecessarily painful and slow method" (Chiang 1993). She did so on October 4, 1994, ruling that the state would have to conduct future executions by lethal injection (Holding 1994).

3. Since the purpose of this section is to set the stage for a detailed account of the post-*Furman* era of anti-death penalty activism, it will necessarily be brief and will merely scratch the surface of the events of that period. Other writers have described much more fully the era of abolitionist history during which the battle moved into the courtroom. The main source for readers wishing to delve more deeply into these events is Michael Meltsner's *Cruel and Unusual: The Supreme Court and Capital Punishment* (1973), written by an insider who—at least in relation to the third wave of American abolitionism—was "there at the creation." Useful companions to Meltsner's book are Burton Wolfe's *Pileup on Death Row* (1973) and portions of Roger Schwed's *Abolition and Capital Punishment: The United States' Judicial, Political, and Moral Barometer* (1983). Eric Muller's 1985 article in the *Yale Law and Policy Review* clarifies certain points of chronology and adds some organizational detail. Other useful sources of information on the legal issues of the period are Bedau (1977, 1987) and Bowers (1984) and, on related developments outside the courtrooms, Bedau (1967, 1980) and Cobin (1967).

4. These include *Hampton v. Commonwealth* (190 Va. 531, 58 S.E.2d 288, 1950), *Jones v. State* (209 Ga. 685, 75 S.E.2d 429, 1953) the Groveland case (*Irvin v. Chapman, cert. denied,* 348 U.S. 915, 1955), and *Hamilton v. Alabama* (270 Ala. 184, 116 So. 2d 906, 1960, *cert. denied,* 363 U.S. 852, 1960, 368 U.S. 52, 1961).

5. The notion of "evolving standards of decency" was grounded in a previous decision, *Trop v. Dulles* (356 U.S. 86, 1958), in which the Court ruled that the revocation of citizenship for military desertion constituted a cruel and unusual punishment. In his opinion of that case, however, Chief Justice Earl Warren wrote specifically that capital punishment was too commonly used in the United States to be the target of the same charge.

6. Privately, Justice Black believed that the moratorium strategy would be victorious in the U.S. Supreme Court. Black had no doubts as to the constitutionality of the death penalty, but predicted that reluctance to initiate a sudden wave of executions would eventually persuade the justices to abolish capital punishment. In 1972, Potter Stewart literally lost sleep over the prospect that his vote in the *Furman* case might be the one that sent over 600 people to their deaths (Woodward and Armstrong 1979:207–209).

7. The man at the top of the Legal Defense Fund, Jack Greenberg, wasn't certain that the plan would work. He reasoned that "[t]hose who approved executions were generally not fazed by having huge numbers of people put to death" and might even "be more pleased by many than by few" (Greenberg 1994:446).

8. The apparent victory was all the more impressive because it was retroactive. If anyone who had been tried by a jury whose selection did not meet *Witherspoon* standards was entitled to a new trial, then capital punishment would seem to have been dealt a major blow. But subsequent lower court rulings diluted *Witherspoon's* impact by restricting its application to the most egregious and systematic instances of exclusion, by placing resentencing in the hands of judges rather than juries and the like (Meltsner 1973:124–125). And in some states, the judgment was simply ignored.

9. In his brief for the *Boykin* case, Amsterdam developed an Eighth Amendment theory considerably more sophisticated than that envisioned by Gerald Gottlieb in 1963. Amsterdam explained that whereas contemporary public opinion might very well support the *threat* of execution as an element of the criminal law, society had clearly become far less comfortable with the actual *use* of the death penalty, except for a tiny proportion of persons—usually members of despised minorities—convicted of capital crimes. That is, the public approved only of a death penalty that was so unfairly applied as to violate the doctrine of equal protection. To carry out the threat of execution only on this fraction of humanity, Amsterdam reasoned, cannot be seen as anything but cruel and unusual (Bedau 1977:86–87).

10. Woodward and Armstrong, in *The Brethren* (1979:205–206) report that in 1968 the justices had secretly voted six to three to strike down the Arkansas death penalty. But Justice Harlan changed his mind, and the arrival of Warren Burger changed the likely outcome to five to four to uphold.

11. Undated letter, Hugo Adam Bedau to Spencer Coxe. Papers of Hugo Adam Bedau.

12. Before the Supreme Court rendered its judgment on Aikens's appeal, the California Supreme Court struck down the death penalty as a violation of the *state* constitution. Aikens's sentence was commuted to life imprisonment and the appeal was dropped.

13. The hanging of Louis Jose Monge by the state of Colorado on June 2, 1967, was the last execution before the de facto moratorium. Executions resumed on January 17, 1977, when Gary Gilmore was shot by a firing squad in Utah.

14. Aryeh Neier, executive director of the ACLU from 1970 to 1978, believes that a concerted legislative strategy might well have succeeded in the mid-1960s. He notes that legislatures in New York, Iowa, Vermont, and West Virginia abolished or virtually abolished capital punishment in 1965 despite the lack of a strong abolitionist lobby. Moreover, public opinion briefly favored abolition in 1966, and Oregon voters passed an abolition referendum in 1964. Thus, he reasons that had the ACLU, whose tax status and nationwide structure of state affiliates would have allowed for coordinated lobbying, taken the lead in abolition efforts, the movement "might well have been as heavily legislative as litigative." Had the ACLU devoted the same proportion of its resources to the effort as did the Legal Defense Fund, such a strategy might well have paid off (Neier 1982:198).

15. Among the most important of these were rulings expanding the right to education regardless of race (*Brown v. Board of Education,* 347 U.S. 483, 1954; *Bolling v. Sharpe,* 347 U.S. 497, 1954; *Green v. County School Board,* 391 U.S. 430, 1968) and safeguarding the rights of African Americans to vote (*Harper v. Virginia State Board of Elections,* 383 U.S. 663, 1966; *South Carolina v. Katzenbach,* 383 U.S. 301, 1966).

16. "The Case Against the Death Penalty" first appeared in the late 1960s. A revised version was released in 1992.

17. Citizens Against Legalized Murder, at its height, listed as many as 5,000 members

and boasted a celebrity-studded advisory board. But contrary to appearances, CALM was essentially a paper organization. Lyons himself, the son of a prominent newspaper columnist, did all the work.

18. Interview with Hugo Bedau, April 27, 1992. Letters: Lyons to Mrs. William F. Conant, October 25, 1965; miscellaneous correspondence, Lyons to Sara B. Ehrmann, 1968, Sara B. Ehrmann Collection. Bedau met Mrs. Ehrmann in New York during the fall of 1958, after he helped to organize Princeton Citizens Against the Death Penalty. Lyons met her in 1964 or 1965.

19. Interview with Hugo Bedau, April 27, 1992; interview with Henry Schwarzschild, March 10, 1992. The sense that the death penalty had become a legal issue rather than a policy matter can be seen in the rejection of a proposal from Florence Robin, of the Georgia ACLU affiliate, in 1968. Robin wanted to use Field Foundation money to create an ACLU Capital Punishment Information Project. The proposal was opposed by none other than Henry Schwarzschild, whose name would become synonymous with such a project years later. But at the time, Schwarzschild feared that "there may be a great danger in a new public campaign": the death penalty was already "withering away," and such a campaign threatened to "unleash a massive backlash." (Memorandum, September 12, 1968; papers of Henry Schwarzschild)

20. On February 18, 1972, several months before the U.S. Supreme Court had acted, the California Supreme Court had declared capital punishment to be cruel and unusual punishment in violation of the *state* constitution (*People v. Anderson,* 6 Cal. 3d 628). The vote was six to one, and the majority opinion was written by Donald Wright, a Reagan appointee. According to Burton Wolfe (1973:383), the California justices referred to the state rather than the federal Constitution in order to render their decision immune to being overturned by the U.S. Supreme Court.

21. A few cases of mandatory death penalties for unusual crimes did exist in the post–World War II era. Massachusetts passed a law in 1951 requiring execution for persons found guilty of rape-murders. Laws requiring death for certain persons who committed murder while in prison were on the books in Rhode Island and New York (Bedau 1987:187–216).

22. Those whose activities actually took them inside southern prisons were less sanguine than most of those who encountered capital punishment in a courtroom. Joe Ingle, a Tennessee minister, told me that "Everybody thought we'd won[, but] *I* didn't think we'd won, 'cause I kept seeing people on *death row!* My Yankee colleagues were telling me we'd won this fight, but I kept encountering men and women behind barred doors with execution dates! Something didn't jibe with this picture" (interview, March 28, 1992).

23. Hugo Bedau, "The Future of Capital Punishment—A Problem for Law and the Social Sciences." Project Statement submitted to the Russell Sage Foundation, January 1973, p. 7–8. Papers of Hugo Adam Bedau.

24. Participants in the conference were Amsterdam, Bedau, Derrick Bell (Harvard Law School), Egon Bittner (Sociology, Brandeis), Edward Bronson (Political Science, California-Chico), Leroy Clark (New York University Law School), Samuel Dash (Institute of Criminal Law and Procedure), Alan Dershowitz (Harvard Law School), Bernard Diamond (California-Berkeley), Harold Edgar (Columbia Law School), Michael Edison (Louis Harris and Associates), Jerome Falk, Jack Greenberg, Elaine Jones (LDF), George Jurow (City University of New York), Douglas Lyons, James McCafferty, Philip Mackey (History, Rutgers), Michael Meltsner (Columbia Law School), Sheldon Messinger (California-Berkeley), Kellis Parker (Columbia Law School), Milton Rokeach (Sociology, Washington State), Thorsten Sellin, Jerome Skolnick (California-Berkeley), Terence

Thornberry (Pennsylvania), Neil Vidmar (Western Ontario), James Vorenberg (Harvard Law School), Lynn Walker (LDF), Welsh White (Pittsburgh Law School), Leslie Wilkins (SUNY-Albany), Marvin Wolfgang (Pennsylvania), Hans Zeisel (University of Chicago Law School), and Franklin Zimring (Yale Law School). Memorandum, Jack Himmelstein to participants, November 14, 1972. Papers of Hugo Adam Bedau.

25. Memo, Hugo Bedau to Jack Himmelstein and Tony Amsterdam, January 6, 1973. Papers of Hugo Adam Bedau.

26. The 1973 research conferences were held at the Center for Studies in Criminology and Criminal Justice, University of Pennsylvania; the Center for the Study of Law and Society, University of California, Berkeley; the Center for Research in Criminal Justice, University of Illinois, Chicago Circle; the Department of Criminology, Florida State University; the Center for the Study and Reduction of Violence, UCLA Medical School; the Center for Criminal Justice, Harvard Law School; Yale Law School; and at the offices of the Russell Sage Foundation in New York (Bedau 1977:93).

27. Interview with Hugo Adam Bedau, April 17, 1992; interview with Henry Schwarzschild, March 10, 1992.

28. Interview with Hugo Adam Bedau, April 27, 1992.

29. The New York Committee to Abolish Capital Punishment, for example, was advised by the LDF not to go through with plans to disband after the *Furman* decision was announced. One of the few viable state abolitionist groups at the time, NYCACP was characterized as "uniquely able to rally the kind of citizen and organizational support that alone can beat back legislative attempts to reimpose capital punishment." Memorandum, New York Committee to Abolish Capital Punishment, July 14, 1972. Papers of Hugo Adam Bedau.

30. Memorandum, Jack Himmelstein to Aryeh Neier, Sanford Rosen, Ken Norwick, Ruth Teitelbaum, and Doug Lyons, December 18, 1972. Papers of Hugo Adam Bedau.

31. Letter, Hugo Adam Bedau to Aryeh Neier, August 30, 1973. Papers of Hugo Adam Bedau.

32. Levine, memorandum, August 22, 1975; Leavy, memorandum, January 9, 1976. Papers of Hugo Adam Bedau.

33. Letter, Levine to Himmelstein, May 22, 1974.

34. Letter, Levine to Himmelstein, May 22, 1974; letter, Levine to Lyons, May 22, 1974; Deborah Leavy, "The death penalty" (1976).

35. Memo from Jack Himmelstein to Aryeh Neier, Sanford Rosen, Ken Norwick, Ruth Teitelbaum, and Douglas Lyons, December 18, 1972. Papers of Hugo Adam Bedau.

36. At least one Supreme Court justice, however, thought initially that abolition was the logical next step. Woodward and Armstrong (1979:432) write that Lewis Powell believed that the pressure from the abolitionists and the dread of ending the nine-year-old moratorium would lead either Stevens or Blackmun to join the four remaining members of the *Furman* majority. He assumed that Stewart and White, who had voted with the majority in both *Furman* and *McGautha* would be able to find no alternative to striking down capital punishment in all its forms.

37. Ehrlich's investigation (1975) suggested that an examination of executions and murder rates in the United States from 1932 through 1969 showed that each time a convict was put to death, seven or eight innocent lives were saved. Almost from the moment of its publication, Ehrlich's work was subjected to intense scrutiny (especially see Bowers and Pierce 1975). His study is generally acknowledged to have suffered from methodological errors severe enough to undermine its central conclusions. For a useful overview of the critiques of Ehrlich's investigations and those using similar research designs (Layson

1985; Stack 1987), see J. A. Fox and M. L. Radelet, "Persistent flaws in econometric studies of the deterrent effect of the death penalty," *Loyola of Los Angeles Law Review* 23:28–44 (November 1989).

38. Capital Punishment Project, memo, June 17, 1976. American Civil Liberties Union Archives, Princeton University.

39. Letter, Henry Schwarzschild and Deborah Leavy to Hugo A. Bedau, June 23, 1976. Papers of Hugo Adam Bedau.

40. Deborah Leavy, "The death penalty." Paper prepared for American Civil Liberties Union Biennial Conference, Philadelphia, June 10–13, 1976.

41. Upholding the constitutionality of capital punishment is not the same thing as asserting its morality. Among the justices who sided with the majority in the *Gregg* ruling, at least four—Potter Stewart, Lewis Powell, Harry Blackmun, and Chief Justice Warren Burger—felt some degree of personal repugnance for the death penalty (see Woodward and Armstrong 1979:206–226). Burger probably captured the feelings of the others when he wrote in his dissenting opinion in *Furman* that "If we were possessed of legislative power, I would either join with Mr. Justice Brennan and Mr. Justice Marshall or, at the very least, restrict the use of capital punishment to a small category of the most heinous crimes. Our constitutional inquiry, however, must be divorced from personal feelings as to the morality and efficacy of the death penalty, and be confined to the meaning and applicability of the uncertain language of the Eighth Amendment" (408 U.S. 375, 1976). Blackmun was even more graphic in his *Furman* dissent: "I yield to no one in the depth of my distaste, antipathy, and, indeed, abhorrence, for the death penalty. . . . For me, it violates childhood's training and life's experiences, and is not compatible with the philosophical convictions I have been able to develop" (408 U.S. 405, 1972).

Chapter 2

1. "Background paper on the Supreme Court's death penalty decisions." Unpublished document, American Civil Liberties Union Archives, Princeton University. Emphasis in the original. The anonymous author of this document predicted that Georgia, Florida, and Texas would probably be executing between 10 and 20 people each year.

2. Pessimism wasn't universal within the anti-death penalty community, however. One activist who became involved in 1977 and wrote a book about death row convicts (Magee 1980), confessed to having been somewhat concerned that capital punishment would be abolished once and for all before the book came out. He was among a segment of the movement that still had faith that once people understood the realities of the issue, they would see the light. But the faith was short-lived. "[W]e hadn't had an execution at that point in some 10 or 12 years in this country. And we really just felt that education would in fact have an effect. And then the first couple of executions splashed—they were well covered and everything. And after that started to not have an effect, then you'd get botched executions where somebody would be, you know, cooked to death. Those didn't have an effect. You had executions of possibly innocent people, and those didn't have an effect" (Interview with Doug Magee, October 9, 1992).

3. In a sense, the *Lockett* decision seemed to compromise the Court's earlier reasoning, because it allowed for apparently unguided discretion *on the side of mercy* (Weisberg 1983:328).

4. For fuller accounts of the events leading up to the execution of Gary Mark Gilmore, see Neier (1982:207–210) and Mailer (1979).

5. Interview with Joe Ingle, March 28, 1992; Ingle 1990:34–39. Although the South-

ern Coalition organized demonstrations and worked with the press, most of its activity involved counseling death row inmates, locating lawyers to handle their appeals, and ministering to the needs of their families.

6. Interview with Doug Magee, October 9, 1992. Magee was one of the early members of PAX and a participant in the 1979 protests.

7. "Background paper on the Supreme Court's death penalty decisions"; Memorandum, Capital Punishment Project to affiliates, July 13, 1976. American Civil Liberties Union Archives, Princeton University.

8. Memorandum, Hugo Bedau to Aryeh Neier, August 4, 1971. Papers of Hugo Adam Bedau.

9. Minutes of the Interorganizational Meeting on Capital Punishment, July 8, 1976. Papers of Hugo Adam Bedau.

10. Interview with Henry Schwarzschild, March 10, 1992. In addition to Schwarzschild, Howard Maxwell of the United Presbyterian Church and John P. Adams of the United Methodist Church worked to bring out the religious denominations against the impending execution of Gary Gilmore, and hence into the abolitionist camp (telephone interview with Kathy Lancaster, July 27, 1993; Mackey 1993).

11. Miscellaneous financial documents, files of the National Coalition to Abolish the Death Penalty, Washington, D.C.; telephone interview with Kathy Lancaster, July 27, 1993.

12. As of June, 1978, the following organizations had become NCADP affiliates: American Civil Liberties Union; American Ethical Union; American Friends Service Committee; American Orthopsychiatric Association; Catholic Committee on Urban Ministry; Central Conference of American Rabbis; Committee of Southern Churchmen; Episcopal Church; Fellowship of Reconciliation; Fortune Society; Friends Committee on National Legislation; Jewish Peace Fellowship; Martin Luther King, Jr. Center for Nonviolent Social Change; Law Students Civil Rights Research Council; Legal Action Center; Lutheran Church in America (Division for Mission in North America); National Alliance Against Racist and Political Oppression; National Association for the Advancement of Colored People; National Bar Association; National Committee Against Repressive Legislation; National Committee to Reopen the Rosenberg Case; National Conference of Black Lawyers; National Council of Churches; National Council on Crime and Delinquency; National Jury Project; National Lawyers Guild; National Legal Aid and Defender Association; National Ministries, American Baptist Church in the USA; National Moratorium on Prison Construction; National Urban League; Network; Offender Aid and Restoration, USA; Prisoner Visitation and Support Committee; Southern Christian Leadership Conference; Southern Coalition on Jails and Prisons; Southern Poverty Law Center; Southern Prison Ministry; Team Defense Project; Union of American Hebrew Congregations; Unitarian Universalist Association; United Church of Christ; United Methodist Church (Board of Church and Society); United Presbyterian Church in the USA; U.S. Jesuit Conference; War Resisters League; Women's Division of the United Methodist Board of Global Ministries; Women's International League for Peace and Freedom.

13. Memo, Leavy to NCADP affiliates, March 7, 1977.

14. Amnesty International, International Secretariat, *Death Penalty Handbook* (1986 ed.), Part 4; AIUSA, *Death Penalty Coordinator's Handbook,* July 1981, p. 1.

15. Amnesty International Conference on the Abolition of the Death Penalty, "Declaration of Stockholm, 11 December 1977."

16. Telephone interview with Larry Cox, October 1, 1992.

17. As of 1992, the U.S. section of Amnesty International consisted of approximately 400 local groups and over 2,000 high school and college groups. There were about 350,000 dues-paying members in AIUSA (Interview with Ali Miller, March 12, 1992).

18. In 1984, Charles Fulwood, then the director of AIUSA's campaign against the death penalty in the United States, argued that treating the matter as a human rights struggle "broadens the context for organizing diverse groups . . . " and "adds more prominence to the fact that the U.S. remains as the only western industrial democracy that still imposes the death penalty." But he acknowledged that there are inherent tensions between this approach and the more established sociolegal arguments. "Constitutional arguments may be just as, and in some cases more, persuasive than the international human rights approach," he wrote. Thus, it was necessary for AI's critique to be flexible and to go beyond human rights considerations alone (Charles Fulwood, "Strategy against the death penalty approved by the board of directors, Amnesty International USA," November 18, 1984).

19. Memorandum, Arthur Michaelson to the executive committee, January 27, 1978.

20. Arthur Michaelson, memorandum to the executive committee, January 27, 1978.

21. Arthur Michaelson, memorandum to AIUSA board of directors, August 17, 1979. In addition, Michaelson stated in an interview on October 6, 1992, that he felt Amnesty's International Secretariat in London may have had a hidden agenda in pursuing the death penalty vigorously—it was an issue on which the United States could be targeted. "The Europeans would be very interested in being able to point out that the great power of the United States was a violator of human rights, and I felt that getting into the death penalty, which was the one place where our system could be faulted, did have to do with that."

22. Interview with Barbara Sproul, October 7, 1992.

23. Arthur Michaelson, memorandum to David Hinkley, Gerhard Elston, and Barbara Sproul, August 16, 1979.

24. Report of the Death Penalty Committee, June 1980.

25. "Report of the discussion group on the death penalty at the 12th International Council, 1980, Vienna, Austria," December 5, 1980 (AI Index: ACT 057357). Sandy Coliver, memorandum to Death Penalty Coordinators, et al., August, 1980; AIUSA, *Death Penalty Coordinator's Handbook,* July 1981, p. 13.

26. "The death penalty: A question of human rights." Delivered at the Amnesty International USA annual general meeting, June 23, 1984, Chicago, Ill.

27. Interview with Arthur Michaelson, October 6, 1992.

28. Dissent over the death penalty was not limited to U.S. section. Eric Prokosch, who directed international ADP efforts out of the International Secretariat in London, referred to membership misgivings in this "Report of the discussion group on the death penalty at the 12th International Council meeting, Leuven, Belgium, 6–9 September 1979."

29. Interview with Barbara Sproul, October 7, 1992.

30. Telephone interview with Larry Cox, October 1, 1992; interview with Barbara Sproul, October 7, 1992; interview with Charles Fulwood, May 29, 1992. At Amnesty's annual international conference in 1981, the American section opposed a resolution that would have required Amnesty groups to work on death penalty issues. "It was felt that to require groups to do DP work at this point in the US might be disastrous as well as running contrary to instincts of voluntarism." Death Penalty Committee Minutes, June 12, 1981.

31. Amnesty International Campaign and Membership Department, "Guidelines for section activities concerning violations of human rights in their own countries—discussion paper" August 15, 1986.

32. Interview with Ali Miller, March 12, 1992.

33. Interview, March 12, 1992.

34. Letter, Maggie Bierne (Campaign and Membership Department, International Secretariat) to Susannah Sirkin, September 8, 1983; letter, Erik Prokosch to the author, January 26, 1993.

35. Interview with Ali Miller, March 12, 1992; undated 1989 letter, Magdaleno Rose-Avila to Jack Healey and Curt Goering.

36. Interview with Ali Miller, March 12, 1992; interview with Barbara Sproul, October 7, 1992.

37. Memorandum, Henry Schwarzschild to Ira Glasser, October 7, 1983.

38. American Civil Liberties Union, "Proposed draft amendments for capital punishment statutes." Mimeographed document, February, 1977.

39. Amnesty International USA Southern Death Penalty Newsletter, May 1982.

40. Telephone interview with Bob Gross, January 27, 1993.

41. During 1979, the first year of Amnesty International's focused death penalty work, nine targets were selected for pressure: China, Trinidad and Tobago/Jamaica, France, Iraq, Japan, Nigeria, South Africa, the United States, and the Soviet Union. The precise strategies used were tailored to political and cultural conditions in each country. "The death penalty program," mimeographed document, 1980; "Report on the death penalty program, 1979–80," June 24, 1980.

42. "Report on the death penalty program, 1979–80," June 24, 1980.

43. Amnesty International, "Proposal for a presidential commission on the death penalty in the United States of America," April 1980; letter, Larry Cox to Michael Nelson, August 25, 1980.

44. Anthony P. Dunbar, "A presidential commission on capital punishment," January 23, 1980; letter, Sandy Coliver and Ira Mazer to Death Penalty Coordinators, et al., March 10, 1980.

45. Telephone interview with Larry Cox, October 1, 1992.

Chapter 3

1. The lawyers for the appellant in this case, Roger Keith Coleman, had inadvertently missed by one day the deadline for filing his petition for appeal. According to Amnesty International, the Supreme Court's ruling meant that "almost any failure by a state prisoner to meet the state court system's procedural requirements, for almost any reason, will result in forfeiting the right to appeal to the federal courts . . . even if the inmate, through a lawyers's mishandling of the state appeal, has not been able to bring any of his constitutional arguments before the state courts" (Amnesty International USA, "United States of America: Death penalty developments in 1991," AI Index: AMR 51/01/92). Coleman was later executed.

2. In June 1988, Chief Justice William Rehnquist appointed an Ad Hoc Committee on Federal Habeas Corpus in Capital Cases, headed by Lewis Powell, who had by then retired from the Supreme Court. The committee's charge was to look into "the necessity and desirability of legislation directed toward avoiding delay and the lack of finality in capital cases in which the prisoner had or had been offered counsel." In its 1989 report, the "Powell Committee" recommended that the existing federal habeas corpus law be amended to eliminate the delay in carrying out death sentences. Separate procedures for capital cases were called for. Competent lawyers would be provided for death-sentenced inmates in *both* state and federal appeals, but capital cases would be limited to "one complete and fair course of collateral review" under strict time limits. Federal habeas corpus proceedings on new claims that had not been raised earlier in state courts would be prohibited, "absent extraordinary circumstances and a colorable showing of factual innocence" (Ad Hoc Committee on Federal Habeas Corpus in Capital Cases 1989:7).

The recommendations of the Powell Committee were submitted to Congress in 1989.

During congressional action on the Omnibus Crime Control Act of 1991 (H.R. 3371), a House-Senate conference committee reached a compromise on the issue that made successor habeas corpus petitions more difficult, and placed time limits on the filing of such petitions that were not as restrictive as those recommended by the Powell Committee (*Congressional Digest,* April 1992). The federal crime legislation, however, became stalled due to Congress's failure to reach compromise on gun-control provisions.

As this book goes to press, the recommendations of the Powell Commission are nearing realization. A Republican-sponsored amendment to the Comprehensive Terrorism Prevention Act of 1995, passed by the U.S. Senate on June 7, 1995, seven weeks after the bombing of a federal building in Oklahoma City, limits most death row prisoners to one appeal in federal court and gives them one year from the time of their conviction to file it. Although he initially opposed the inclusion of the seemingly unrelated *habeas* provisions, President Clinton has now promised to sign the bill, and passage by the House of Representatives—which passed similar *habeas* reform legislation earlier— is likely (Gray 1995).

3. The partial-regression analysis utilizing 39 variables was the "centerpiece" of the *McCleskey* evidence, although other analyses by the same researchers utilized as many as 230 control variables. The researchers "selected these thirty-nine variables because, from both a theoretical and statistical standpoint, they appeared to exercise the greatest influence in determining which defendants indicted for murder would actually receive a death sentence" (Baldus, Woodworth, and Pulaski 1990:316).

4. The importance of the case was clear. One Supreme Court clerk revealed that "Around the [Supreme Court] building, . . . everyone saw *McCleskey* as the biggest case of the year. It was an all-or nothing case" (Savage 1992:83).

5. *McCleskey v. Kemp,* 478 U.S. 1019 (1986).

6. Since handing down their ruling in *McCleskey v. Kemp,* the justices of the U.S. Supreme Court have been increasingly unwilling to incorporate the findings of empirical social science research in their death penalty decisions. This is an unfortunate development for anti-death penalty litigators, because the vast majority of such research has produced findings that bolster the anti-death penalty side, and because social science evidence was cited in a number of earlier high court decisions that went their way. But since 1986, the justices have cited empirical research less frequently and have moved in the direction of dismissing it as irrelevant in assessing the constitutionality of the death penalty (see Acker 1993; Zimring 1993).

7. AIUSA, "Campaign mailing #5, May 6, 1987," pp. 3, 10–12; NCADP Executive Committee minutes, May 24–25, 1987.

8. Unpublished ACLU document, "Questions and answers about the Racial Justice Act," 1991.

9. *Source:* "Death penalty program budget: 1982–1983 (Revised April 2, 1982)"; memo from Magdaleno Rose-Avila to "Jack Curt, and Hans," April 12, 1988. These figures understate the budgetary commitment to the issue by AIUSA, however, because each of the four regional offices has the authority to shift part of its allocation into death penalty work (Interview with Magdaleno Rose-Avila, June 26, 1992).

10. Interview with Ali Miller, March 12, 1992; telephone interview with Rick Halperin, August 12, 1992.

11. Telephone interview with Bob Gross, January 27, 1993.

12. Bob Gross, staff report, November 1985; Executive Committee minutes, June 10, 1986.

13. "NCADP affiliation: Relationships and expectations." Working draft, November 1988.

14. Memorandum, Schwarzschild to Ira Glasser, September 27, 1979.

15. Michael Kroll, then with the National Moratorium on Prison Construction, strongly recommended that the Capital Punishment Project be moved from New York to Atlanta or some other southern city, and that the ACLU hire "a new director whose skills are those of an organizer." Letter, Kroll to Chan Kendrick, September 11, 1979. American Civil Liberties Union Archives, Volume V, Princeton University.

16. According to Florida activist Scharlette Holdman, the Capital Punishment Project was being "treated as the bastard project of the ACLU. ACLU leadership has failed to set priorities for the project, to examine its effectiveness or goals, to fund the project adequately—in sum, ACLU has failed to have a *campaign* against the death penalty. It has an excellent *spokesperson* against the death penalty [Schwarzschild], but that's about it." Letter, Scharlette Holdman to Chan Kendrick, September 8, 1979. American Civil Liberties Union Archives, Volume V, Princeton University.

17. "Capital Punishment Project: A review by the Capital Punishment Project Review Committee." American Civil Liberties Union Archives, Volume V, Princeton University.

18. Memorandum. Schwarzschild to Ira Glasser, October 7, 1983. The Capital Punishment Project's total budget, according to Schwarzschild, was in the neighborhood of $60,000 at that time.

The ACLU decided to fund Litigation Centers in the 5th and 11th circuits in 1986 at a cost of $90,000, but the public education budget for the Capital Punishment Project—its traditional focus—remained virtually unchanged. Of the total public education budget of $68,000, $27,000 came from earmarked grants and the remainder from general funds (Memorandum, Ira Glasser to ACLU board of directors and ACLU foundation board of directors, January 15, 1986.

19. Memorandum, Schwarzschild to Ira Glasser, October 7, 1983.

20. NCADP Executive Committee minutes, September 8, 1990; Letter, Hugo Bedau to Ira Glasser, February 14, 1991; letter, Ira Glasser to Hugo Bedau, February 22, 1991 (Papers of Hugo Adam Bedau).

21. Interview with Damaris Walsh McGuire, statewide coordinator, November 8, 1992.

22. The annual maintenance cost for one inmate in New York in 1978, $15,050, was used as the basis for this estimate. Assuming an average age of 30 for persons convicted of first-degree murder and a life expectancy of 70, a life-without-parole sentence was expected to last, on the average, 40 years. The annual cost estimate was multiplied by 40 to yield the estimate of $602,000 for a sentence of imprisonment for life (New York State Defenders Association 1982:23).

23. See Cook and Slawson 1993; *Houston Post* 1986; Magagnini 1988; *Miami Herald* 1988; Spangenberg and Walsh 1989. For an overview of the cost issue, see Dieter 1992.

24. Death penalty reinstatement bills were passed by both the state senate and the assembly in New York every year since 1979, only to be vetoed by governors Hugh Carey and Mario Cuomo. The bill's sponsors were never able to muster quite enough votes to override those vetos, but the election of George Pataki in 1994 ended the 16-year standoff. The death penalty took effect in New York in September, 1995.

25. The possibility that the financial burden posed by the death penalty might be used to fight it had, in fact, been raised a decade earlier at the October 1972 Columbia University conference mentioned in chapter 1. But at that point, the participants were anticipating an effort by the states to enact *mandatory* death penalties in order to overcome the problem of arbitrary and capricious sentencing. This seemed likely to produce a high rate of acquittals and reduced sentences. (Minutes, "Capital Punishment Conference, Columbia University, October 7, 1972," Papers of Hugo Adam Bedau).

26. Telephone interview with Jonathan Gradess, November 23, 1992.

27. Interview with Bill Lucero and Sister Therese Bangert, Kansas Coalition Against the Death Penalty, April 3, 1992. Telephone interview with Donna Schneweis, Kansas Coalition Against the Death Penalty and Amnesty International, August 17, 1992. Telephone interview with Jonathan Gradess, November 23, 1992.

28. Governor Joan Finney, "Message to the House of Representatives of the State of Kansas," April 22, 1994.

29. Telephone interview with Jonathan Gradess, November 23, 1992; AIUSA Monthly Death Penalty Mailing, January–February 1991.

30. AIUSA Monthly Death Penalty Mailing, September–October 1991.

31. As noted in the Introduction, the ALACP had its origins in the notorious case of Sacco and Vanzetti, who were suspected by many of being innocent and were eventually granted a posthumous pardon by Massachusetts governor Michael Dukakis. The ALACP continued to emphasize the cases of possibly innocent death row inmates as long as the organization existed. For example, *League News,* April 25, 1934; ALACP *Bulletin,* April 1953; ALACP/MCADP *Bulletin,* November 1954; ALACP *Bulletin,* July 1961.

32. Bedau and Radelet studied "potentially capital cases" rather than only those cases in which possibly innocent persons were actually sentenced to death because doing so "would exclude several types of cases, involving defendants also convicted 'beyond a reasonable doubt,' that shed light on how our criminal justice system has treated the most serious felony defendants during this century" (1987:31).

33. James Adams, executed in Florida on May 10, 1984. See Radelet, Bedau, and Putnam 1992:5–10. Since the book was published, there have been two more executions of persons who had credible and widely publicized claims of innocence: Leonel Herrera and Roger Keith Coleman.

34. For an overview of the Gary Graham case, see Elliot 1993; Elliot and Ballard 1993; Hensel 1993; Hoppe 1994.

35. Interview with Charles Fulwood, May 29, 1992.

36. "Strategy against the death penalty." Unpublished document, Amnesty International USA.

37. Interview, June 26, 1992.

38. Interview with Margaret Vandiver, April 27, 1992. The implications of this fact will be discussed in the final chapter.

39. Interview with Charles Fulwood, May 29, 1992.

40. Interview with Magdaleno Rose-Avila, June 26, 1992; interview with Pam Tucker, August 20, 1992; telephone interview with Rick Halperin, August 12, 1992.

41. Interview with Charles Fulwood, May 29, 1992; letter, Erik Prokosch to Herbert Haines, January 26, 1993. According to Prokosch, London was also concerned about the propriety of AIUSA opposing legislation to substitute lethal injection for other execution methods.

However, a point that is frequently overlooked is that AI had briefly toyed with a type of "incrementalism" on the international level even before Fulwood took over the U.S. program. AI's earliest death penalty campaigns called for targeting particular nations and identifying subissues to attack. It was understood at the outset, for example, that calling for *abolition* of the death penalty in the Middle East would be an exercise in futility. So in those countries, AI would simply aim to open up discussion of things like the ethics of executing pregnant women. Strategy for each target nation would be based on perceived soft spots, the very notion that the U.S. section was pushing in 1985 (Interview with Barbara Sproul, October 7, 1992).

42. Letter, Ian Martin to Curt Goering, January 30, 1990; "Policy on measures short

of total abolition," Amnesty International Program Against the Death Penalty, October 10, 1988.

43. Interview with Charles Fulwood, May 29, 1992. Fulwood's assessment of London's eventual acceptance of the necessity of incrementalism is shared by Larry Cox, who preceded him in the Death Penalty Program and was deputy secretary general at the International Secretariat when the trans-Atlantic debate was taking place.

Still, the London headquarters felt compelled to remind the Americans from time to time of the importance of constantly reiterating that its support for juvenile-exemption bills is in the context of its desire for total abolition.

44. The AIUSA Death Penalty Program monthly mailing, December 1990, included the following statement: "NOTE: On all MR bills, the lead must be taken by the ARC or related lobbies. The reasons for this are that the bills have the best chance of passage if they are not perceived as abolitionist and if the fight is headed up by an organization that represents MR interests. AI may play a large behind-the-scenes role, but the other organizations should be out front."

45. AIUSA Death Penalty Program monthly mailing, March–April 1992.

46. "National conference meets in D.C." *Lifelines* no. 37 (November/December 1987).

47. NCADP *Annual Report* (1987).

48. Interview with Diane Rust-Tierney, November 16, 1992.

49. U.S. Department of Justice, Bureau of Justice Statistics 1992a. Kansas's and New York's death penalty statutes specify a minimum age of 18, making them the 12th and 13th.

50. According to AIUSA death penalty mailings for that year, AI State Death Penalty Action Coordinators (SDPACs) were directly involved in drafting and/or promoting such bills in at least nine states—Arkansas, California, Colorado, Idaho, Missouri, Montana, New Jersey, New Mexico, and Oklahoma. Members of AIUSA and various state coalitions worked in less direct ways to support such bills in the rest of the 16 states where they were considered that year.

51. According to "Strategy against the death penalty approved by the board of directors, Amnesty International U.S.A.," November 18, 1984, mail identified as coming from AI members was routinely placed in a special file and ignored in Florida and other states. The governor of North Carolina made a public distinction among in-state, out-of-state, and international mail regarding clemency for Velma Barfield. Barfield was the only female to be executed in the United States since the reinstatement of the death penalty.

52. Interview, March 12, 1992.

53. Telephone interview with Rick Halperin, August 12, 1992.

54. Interview with William Bowers, April 27, 1992.

55. Letter, David J. Bradford to Michael Millman and Anthony Amsterdam, November 20, 1989.

56. Memorandum, Leigh Dingerson to NCADP executive committee et al., February 28, 1990.

57. Letter, Henry Schwarzschild to David J. Bradford, September 15, 1989; "Update on the status of the Death Penalty Information Center," January 1991; letter, Eugene G. Wanger to Hugo Bedau, November 14, 1990 (Papers of Hugo Adam Bedau); letter, Henry Schwarzschild to David J. Bradford, September 15, 1989.

58. "Update on the status of the Death Penalty Information Center, its future, and questions for the NCADP." Agenda Item VIII, NCADP board meeting, January 1992.

59. Ibid.

60. Ibid.

61. Comments by Earl Bender, 1991 NCADP conference, Seattle, Wash.; "Case Statement 1991," unpublished document, National Coalition to Abolish the Death Penalty.

62. Minutes of the NCADP Executive Committee, November 1, 1991; NCADP Director's Report, 1991, p. 6; "Case Statement 1991." Unpublished documents, National Coalition to Abolish the Death Penalty.

63. Interview with Leigh Dingerson, February 11, 1992.

64. Interview with Earl Bender, November 17, 1992.

65. Interview with Leigh Dingerson, November 20, 1992.

66. As this book was being written, a trial was being held in the case of O. J. Simpson. Simpson, a television sports commentator and former football hero, was accused of the brutal murder of his ex-wife and one of her acquaintances. Few homicide cases have had the notoriety of this one. It has received constant coverage in both the electronic and print media, including live television coverage of a chase of Simpson on the freeways in the Los Angeles area and of the preliminary hearing itself. The alleged facts surrounding the murders, the notoriety of the case, and the fact that Simpson is African American and both of his victims were Caucasian, might ordinarily make it a predictable death penalty case in California. But he is wealthy enough not only to hire his own lawyer—which most capital defendants are not—but to put together a "Dream Team" of highly skilled defense attorneys. They include Robert L. Shapiro, F. Lee Bailey, and Alan Dershowitz. This alone made it most unlikely that O. J. Simpson would ultimately be convicted on capital charges. The prosecution did not seek the death penalty.

67. At its 1991 annual general meeting in Washington, D.C., at least two resolutions on this topic were passed. Resolution C2 called on AIUSA to "[p]repare materials to enable local groups to meet with and educate local prosecutors about all aspects of the death penalty, and to serve as a resource to defense attorneys involved in capital cases." Resolution C4 established a task force "to explore the most effective way for local groups to take actions to prevent imposition and execution of an individual." The task force produced a set of proposed guidelines that were still under discussion a year later. They included suggestions for fact-finding in advance of meetings with prosecutors, and encouraged confronting them with research findings on the cost of capital cases, racism in the application of the death penalty, and other issues particularly well suited to pending cases. The guidelines also stressed how crucial it was to get the permission of defense counsel before meeting with prosecutors on specific cases. "Preventing the imposition of the death penalty: Amnesty International involvement with local prosecutors." Unpublished document, AIUSA, 1992.

What AIUSA had not yet determined is whether it was wise to visit prosecutors in connection with particular cases, or just to give them printed material and discuss AI's position on the death penalty in general. Interview with Claudia King, July 1, 1992.

68. Interview with Pat Clark (Death Penalty Focus), June 30, 1992; interview with Claudia King (Amnesty International USA, Humanitas, and Death Penalty Focus), July 1, 1992; interview with Ronald Hampton (National Black Police Association), November 25, 1992; interview with Nancy Otto (American Civil Liberties Union of Northern California), July 1, 1992.

69. AIUSA Death Penalty Mailing, July–August, 1992.

70. AIUSA Death Penalty Mailing, April–June, 1994.

71. There are occasional exceptions to this. Joe Giarratano became a skilled "jailhouse lawyer" while on death row in Virginia, wrote law review articles (Giarratano 1991), and originated a lawsuit concerning provision of counsel in federal habeas corpus proceedings that reached the U.S. Supreme Court (*Murray v. Giarratano,* 492 U.S. 1). Others, like Willie Darden and Gary Graham, have served as important symbols for

ADPM claims. And a handful of men who were convicted of murder but ultimately exonerated and released from prison have become active spokespersons for the movement *after their release.* Examples of such releasees-cum-activists are Robert Domer, Rubin "Hurricane" Carter, Clarence Brandley, and Randall Dale Adams.

72. Interview, April 27, 1992.

73. The bishops, by a 145–31 vote with 41 abstentions, went on record for the abolition of capital punishment in 1980. Earlier abolition resolutions came from the National Catholic Conference for Interracial Justice and the National Coalition of American Nuns in 1971, and the U.S. Catholic Conference in 1974 (Drinan 1994).

74. Interview with Leigh Dingerson, February 11, 1992.

75. Memorandum, Henry Schwarzschild to Ira Glasser, October 7, 1983.

76. Telephone interview with Kathy Lancaster, July 27, 1993.

77. "Statement on the occasion of lighting the torch of conscience, Atlanta, Georgia—April 14, 1989." Papers of Joseph Ingle, Northeastern University, Boston, Mass.

78. Memorandum, campaign committee to major participants, October 22, 1990.

79. Telephone interview with Kathy Lancaster, July 27, 1993.

80. Based on his contacts with a number of victims' groups, Kentucky attorney Kevin McNally estimates that the proportions of survivors favoring the death penalty are about the same as in the population at large (McNally 1988).

81. Prejean 1993; Rozzell 1986:2; interview with Leigh Dingerson, February 11, 1992; interview with Laura Magnani, June 30, 1992.

82. Telephone interview, January 27, 1993.

83. Interview with Marie Deans, November 18, 1992.

84. William J. Lucero, criminal justice task force coordinator, Unitarian Universalist Service Committee Unit of Kansas. Testimony of the Federal and State Affairs Committee in opposition to H.R. 2135, March 20, 1985.

85. Historically, many prison wardens have been outspoken critics of the death penalty. For example Lewis Lawes, the warden of New York's Sing Sing prison, was associated with the American League to Abolish Capital Punishment for many years. Two of his predecessors, George W. Kirchwey and Thomas Mott Osborne, were also abolitionists, as was warden Clinton Duffy of San Quentin. More recently Donald Cabana (former commissioner of corrections for the state of Mississippi and former warden at Mississippi's Parchman Prison) and Jennie Lancaster (female command manager at the North Carolina Division of Prisons and former superintendent at the North Carolina Correctional Institution for Women) were featured speakers at the 1992 NCADP Conference in Chicago. Both had been involved in supervising executions.

Participation in the ADPM by police has been less prominent than that of corrections officials. A national organization called Law Enforcement Against Death (LEAD) was formed in 1980 by Sheriff John Buckley of Middlesex County, Mass. Its members included chiefs and deputy chiefs of police, and at least one county prosecuting attorney. They testified before legislatures in Alabama, New York, Connecticut, and Massachusetts and at a number of murder trials. But after a promising start (see *New York Times* December 30, 1980), the group failed to achieve much prominence. And under the leadership of Ronald Hampton, the National Black Police Association has been critical of the death penalty. But many of the leaders of ADPM organizations agree that it would be very beneficial for the movement to attract more police officers and more prosecuting attorneys.

86. POMC was recently offered a $10,000 contribution by the president of the California Correctional Peace Officers Association if it would form a political action committee. The offer was interpreted by some as an effort to persuade POMC to endorse the death penalty (Ferriss 1993).

87. Memorandum, Marie Deans to participants in the Airlie conference, August 11, 1987; memorandum, Pat Bane to NCADP board of directors, May 2, 1992.

88. Interview with Pat Bane, July 8, 1993.

89. "Special report on the Journey of Hope," Murder Victim's Families for Reconciliation brochure, Fall 1993.

90. Interview with William Bowers, April 27, 1992.

91. Interview with Ali Miller, March 12, 1992.

92. Amnesty International USA, "November 1987 death penalty mailing," November 12, 1987, p. 2; "Report to the board on the international campaign against the death penalty in the U.S.," Unpublished document, n.d.
A similar approach was used in Illinois to increase the Latino community's awareness of death penalty issues. AIUSA's Midwest regional office, with the American Friends Service Committee and other groups, staged a press conference, rally, and march called "Dia de Solideridad con Latinos Sentenciados a Meurte"—Solidarity Day with Latinos on Death Row (AIUSA Death Penalty Mailing, September–October 1993).

93. "Campaign mailing #5," Amnesty International USA 1987 Campaign to Abolish the Death Penalty in the United States, May 6, 1987, p. 13.

94. Memorandum, Scharlette Holdman to Magdaleno Rose-Avila and Charles Fulwood, January 8, 1989; "Swainsboro, Georgia: A study of the imposition of the death penalty in the United States," Amnesty International USA, 1989.

95. National Coalition to Abolish the Death Penalty, "Affiliate relationships and affiliation process." Unpublished document, May 1, 1992.

96. Interview with Hugo Bedau, April 27, 1992; interview with Pat Clark, June 30, 1992.

97. Interview with Hugo Adam Bedau, April 27, 1992.

98. Interview, May 29, 1992.

99. Interview, May 29, 1992.

100. Interviews with Ron Hampton, November 25 and December 2, 1992; interview with Magdaleno Rose-Avila, June 26, 1992.

101. Interview with Charles Fulwood, May 29, 1992.

102. Interview with Ron Hampton, November 25, 1992.

103. Interview with Diane Rust-Tierney, November 16, 1992; interview with Ronald Hampton, November 25, 1992; interview with Leigh Dingerson, November 20, 1992.

Chapter 4

1. The litigators have been more reluctant to throw out the welcome mat than have the activists. This is particularly true of the "Airlie Conference," an annual gathering of death penalty litigators. A few, but only a few, nonlawyers have been invited to these conferences: "I have welcomed the increasing awareness by the people who put the conferences together (LDF and others) that the death penalty is a public-policy issue as much as a legal one, that this battle will not be won in the courts until the society, the culture, begins to think about it differently. That awareness is still rudimentary and reluctant, but I am indulgent with super-lawyerly types who not only have their own very real and very complex problems to deal with but who have internalized the professional myopia of the profession which can see no reality beyond the four walls of the courthouse. Still, in the past few years and again this year, a slightly larger number of non-litigators have been invited to attend and even to make presentations" (Letter, Henry Schwarzschild to Ed Monahan, September 11, 1986).

Nonlitigators are now invited to the conference to conduct sessions on such topics as pending legislation, investigations of potentially mitigating evidence, and dealing with the media. Lawyers like Ronald Tabak, Bruce Ledewitz, David Bruck, and Anthony Amsterdam, on the other hand, have been attending NCADP conferences and serving on the board of abolition groups for many years.

2. California attorneys were, in fact, instrumental in launching Death Penalty Focus, which is primarily a public education and advocacy group. As the resumption of executions approached, they recognized the importance of stirring up resistance to the death penalty among sympathetic yet complacent groups in the state (Interview with Pat Clark, June 30, 1992).

3. Interview March 10, 1992. Several of the people interviewed for this book suggested that some lawyers are becoming more aware of their limitations and more likely to welcome the contribution of lay activists. Interview with Robert Bryan, June 29, 1992; interview with Marie Deans, November 18, 1992; interview with Leigh Dingerson, February 11, 1992.

4. Interview with Ali Miller, March 12, 1992.

5. Speech written by Marie Deans and given by Jonathan Gradess to the NCADP regional conference, Albany, N.Y., October 10, 1986.

6. Interview, April 27, 1992.

7. Interview with Margaret Vandiver, April 27, 1992.

8. Interview with Pat Clark, June 30, 1992.

9. Interview with Michael Radelet, November 6, 1992.

10. Interview, April 27, 1992.

11. Interview, March 10, 1992. Schwarzschild sees Joseph Ingle as particularly guilty of this, but nevertheless respects him for giving so much of himself to death row work: "[W]hen it comes right down to it, Joe Ingle devoted himself to the people on death row in a way which I never did for a single solitary minute. He invested himself in that, and then he probably did them more human good than I did for a single moment. Now Joe and I had very different styles and very different languages and rhetoric and attitudes. But when all is said and done, you can't deny that whatever the pretentiousness and sentimentality and other problems, that he was there when they needed him. I wasn't, though I had other fish to fry."

12. Many of us either prefer not to know what goes on during an execution, or to imagine that the process is free of suffering or gore. Death penalty opponents have done their best to shatter these comforting assumptions by publicizing botched executions, such as those in which initial attempts at electrocution failed to kill inmates. In the first of these, malfunctioning equipment caused bursts of smoke and flames during the 1983 execution of John Louis Evans in Alabama. Three successive attempts to kill the inmate were required. Technical problems also arose in the electrocutions of Alpha Otis Stephens (December 12, 1984), William Vandiver (October 16, 1985), Horace Dunkins (July 14, 1989), Jesse Tafero (May 4, 1990), and Wilbert L. Evans (October 17, 1990). Less dramatic problems have occurred in one gas chamber execution and several lethal injections (see Haines 1992). Some abolitionists endorse proposals to *televise* executions, on grounds that fewer Americans would favor capital punishment if they witnessed it in action.

13. Interview with Doug Magee, October 9, 1992.

14. Interview, November 17, 1992.

15. Executed on March 15, 1988.

16. Executed in Florida on November 30, 1983.

17. Interview, April 27, 1992.

18. Interview, November 18, 1992.

19. Stab wounds on one of the victims were determined to have been inflicted by a right-handed assailant. Giarratano is not only left-handed, but suffers from partial paralysis on his right side. In his confessions, Giarratano claimed to have strangled one of the victims with his hands while raping her in a face-to-face position, but the medical examiners's report suggested that she had been strangled from behind with a broad object such as a forearm. Neither blood nor physical evidence of having been in a struggle were found on him when he turned himself in, a fact that was grossly inconsistent with the condition of the bodies and the murder scene. Furthermore, it was determined that Joe Giarratano's boots could not have made the bloody shoeprints found at victims' apartment, and new evidence suggested that the blood he found on his own boot did not come from the crime scene. Fingerprints and body hairs collected by police did not match Joe Giarratano. All the remaining evidence against him was circumstantial and could be explained by his having resided with the victims.

20. Restrictions of the introduction of newly discovered evidence are not confined to Virginia. As of May, 1993, the following time limits were in effect in states with death penalties: *5 days,* Oregon (limit can be waived); *10 days,* Florida, South Dakota, Utah; *14 days,* Idaho (limit can be waived); *15 days,* Missouri; *21 days,* Virginia; *30 days,* Alabama, Arkansas, Georgia (limit can be waived), Illinois, Indiana, Montana, Tennessee, Texas; *60 days,* Arizona; *120 days,* Ohio (limit can be waived); *one year,* Kentucky (limit can be waived), Louisiana, Maryland, Oklahoma, Washington; *two years,* Delaware, Nevada, New Mexico, Rhode Island, Wyoming; *three years,* Connecticut, Nebraska, New Hampshire. *Source:* 1993 briefing paper, National Coalition to Abolish the Death Penalty.

21. Interview with Margaret Vandiver, April 27, 1992.

22. Interview with Laura Magnani, June 30, 1992; *Lifelines* 1993.

23. Interview with Joseph B. Ingle, March 28, 1992.

24. There was also a quiet debate among some participants in the movement about whether or not it is morally appropriate to lie in order to prevent executions by the state. In an article in the *Israel Law Review,* Henry Schwarzschild raised the possibility of death penalty opponents lying about their views in order to gain admission to juries in capital cases and thus saving the lives of defendants. Without granting his unambiguous approval to such an act, he suggests that it might arguably be equivalent to withholding the truth from the Gestapo when they come to the door and demand to know if there are any Jews on the premises (Schwarzschild 1991:511).

25. Interview with Claudia King, July 1, 1992.

26. Interview with Pat Clark, June 30, 1992.

27. Interview, October 9, 1992.

28. Interview with Laura Magnani (Northern California Coalition Against the Death Penalty), June 30, 1992.

29. Letter to NCADP officers and executive committee members, May 3, 1988.

30. "Remarks on civil disobedience," NCADP annual conference, Washington, D.C., November 10, 1990.

31. Interview with Pat Clark, June 30, 1992. DPF has experienced difficulty in securing liability insurance, in part because of the danger of demonstration-related lawsuits. Lacking insurance throughout the Harris crisis of 1990–1991, DPF and its director were vulnerable to being sued.

32. Letter, Doug Magee to the members of the executive committee, May 27, 1988.

33. Interview, February 11, 1992.

34. Interview, February 11, 1992.

35. Interview with Bruce Ledewitz, August 20, 1992; interview with Michael Radelet, November 6, 1992.

36. Interview, November 6, 1992.

37. Life without parole has also been applied to habitual offenders and drug kingpins. A number of states and the federal government have enacted so called "Three Strikes and You're Out" statutes that impose LWOP sentences on persons convicted of a serious felony for the third time.

38. Interview with Robert Johnson, November 17, 1992. However, defense lawyers are far from unanimous in this assessment of LWOP's potential for preventing death sentences. Many fear that a sort of "sentencing inflation" will ensue, in which prosecutors will seek LWOP in nearly every murder case. This would result in more prisoners under life sentences without reducing the size of the death-sentenced population. There are also concerns that the elimination of parole eligibility will create a category of prisoner with nothing to lose and which thus constitutes a major security risk. Both the California Attorneys for Criminal Justice and the New York State Defenders Association went on record during the late 1980s as opposed to LWOP. For an overview of the LWOP issue from the litigator's perspective, see *Capital Report* 1987:5; *Capital Report* 1988:9; *Capital Report* 1989b:1; *Capital Report* 1993:7.

39. David Bruck, "Changing public opinion" (notes for a panel discussion at the Airlie Death Penalty Litigation Conference, August 9, 1986. Papers of Henry Schwarzschild.

40. Interview, November 17, 1992.

41. Telephone interview with Bob Gross, January 27, 1993.

42. AIUSA Death Penalty Mailing, November–December, 1990.

43. Interview, March 28, 1992.

44. Unitarian Universalists Service Committee and Citizens United for Errants, "Alternatives to the death penalty." *ACLU Briefing Book* 1986.

45. Interview with Robert Johnson, November 17, 1992.

46. Telephone interview with Richard Dieter, February 18, 1994.

47. Interview with Jan Marinesson, western regional office of the American Friends Service Committee, June 30, 1992; Mackey 1993:25, 28–30.

The Fellowship of Reconciliation's Capital Punishment Program emphasizes the point that the majority of violent crimes are crimes of passion, not premeditated acts, and are so overpublicized that they create an unrealistic fear among Americans. Public safety requires the confinement of only a small number of truly dangerous persons, probably no more than 100 in any single state. Such offenders "are obviously ill, and should be committed to secure, small medical facilities for treatment." Instead of pouring billions of dollars into punitive institutions, FOR contends, policy should emphasize crime prevention and restitution (Fellowship of Reconciliation Capital Punishment Program, n.d.).

48. Telephone interview with Jonathan Gradess, November 23, 1992.

49. Letter, Schwarzschild to Robert Johnson, March 1, 1985. Papers of Henry Schwarzschild. He characterized LWOP as "mindless," "humanly and economically wasteful," and "morally repellant in its very assumptions," and was willing to withhold his opposition only as "a reluctant gesture of legislative realism."

50. Interview with Therese Bangert and Bill Lucero, April 3, 1992.

51. Interview, November 18, 1992.

52. Telephone interview with Rick Halperin, August 12, 1992.

53. Interview with Pat Clark, June 30, 1992; interview with Earl Bender, November 17, 1992; interview with Michael Radelet, November 6, 1992; Radelet 1988.

54. Interview with Pat Clark, June 30, 1992; interview with Mary Dunwell, June 27, 1992.

55. Interview with Bruce Ledewitz and Pam Tucker, August 20, 1992.

56. Telephone interview, November 27, 1992.

57. "Sentencing alternatives to the death penalty." Information packet distributed by New York State Defenders Association.

58. Interview with Leigh Dingerson, February 11, 1992.

59. Letter, Eugene G. Wanger to NCADP officers and executive committee members, May 3, 1988. Emphasis in the original.

60. Interview with Bill Lucero, April 3, 1992.

61. Interview, November 6, 1992.

62. Interview, August 20, 1992.

63. Minutes of the NCADP executive committee meetings, November 17 and 18, 1985.

64. Interview with Jonathan Gradess, November 23, 1992; interview with Bob Gross, January 27, 1993; interview with Leigh Dingerson, November 20, 1992; interview with Mary Dunwell, June 27, 1992.

65. Interviews with Ronald Hampton, November 25 and December 2, 1992.

66. Interview, March 28, 1992.

67. Sensitivity about the NCADP's exclusive focus on the death penalty can be seen in connection with its participation in an interorganizational coalition to oppose the 1987 nomination of Robert Bork to the U.S. Supreme Court. On one level, it makes perfect sense for the core abolitionist group in America to have taken a stand against the nomination. While serving as Solicitor General of the United States in 1975, Bork had gone out of his way to file an amicus brief in support of the death penalty in North Carolina when the *Fowler* case was being heard, and again the next year during the Supreme Court's consideration of the *Gregg* and *Woodson* cases. He had introduced and enthusiastically defended Isaac Ehrlich's questionable (and subsequently discredited) findings concerning the unique deterrent value of capital punishment. Although the NCADP's participation in the "Block Bork" coalition received "overwhelming support" from its executive committee, "some concern was raised about the propriety of the NCADP taking a stand on an issue broader than the death penalty and the precedent of opposition to a particular judicial nominee" (Minutes of the NCADP executive committee meeting of September 12, 1987).

68. Interview with Hugo Bedau, April 27, 1992; interview with Rick Halperin, August 12, 1992; interview with Kathy Lancaster, July 27, 1993.

69. Interview with Pat Clark, June 30, 1992.

Chapter 5

1. Telephone interview, November 23, 1992.

2. Telephone interview with Bob Gross, January 27, 1993.

3. Interview, April 27, 1992.

4. "National coalition wish list," *Lifelines* no. 62, p. 2 (January–March 1994).

5. Interview with Magdaleno Rose-Avila, June 26, 1992.

6. Interview with Joe Ingle, March 28, 1992.

7. Interview with Earl Bender, November 17, 1992; interview with Pat Clark, June 30, 1992; interview with Marie Deans, November 18, 1992; interview with Leigh Dingerson, February 11, 1992; Rankin 1988a.

8. Interview with Ali Miller, March 12, 1992; interview with Bill Lucero, April 3, 1992; telephone interview with Donna Schneweiss, August 17, 1992.

9. Telephone interview with Bob Gross, January 27, 1994. In some of the states that lack adequately funded ADPM organizations, much of the death penalty work is supported informally by other groups. In Kansas, for instance, two of the three leading activists are

nuns, and their religious orders both accommodate their work against the death penalty and underwrite their travel. Similar arrangements exist elsewhere, but this is no substitute for fully staffed offices devoted exclusively to capital punishment.

At the same time, paid staff is not necessarily an indication of organizational vigor. ADP groups in Illinois and Massachusetts, for example, are able to pay a coordinator and thus maintain a fairly steady presence in their states. But both are in a constantly precarious financial state and have disappointing levels of member involvement (Rankin 1988b; interview with William Bowers, April 27, 1992).

10. Letter, Ricardo Villalobos to NCADP members, July 1994. The estimate of the state's annual expenditure on capital cases appears to be quite low because the 25 capital cases expected to be heard in Harris County alone during 1994 were costing about $2 million dollars each (Taylor 1994).

11. Interviews with Leigh Dingerson, February 11 and November 20, 1992; interview with Marie Deans, November 18, 1992; telephone interview with Bob Gross, January 27, 1993; telephone interview with Jonathan Gradess, November 23, 1992.

12. Interview, November 20, 1992.

13. Interview with Ali Miller, March 12, 1992.

14. Interview with Ali Miller, March 12, 1992; interview with Marie Deans, November 18, 1992; interview with Mary Dunwell, June 27, 1992.

15. Interview with Marie Deans, November 18, 1992.

16. Interview, November 20, 1992.

17. Interview with Diane Rust-Tierney, November 16, 1992; telephone interview with Rick Halperin, August 12, 1992.

18. Interview with Pat Clark, June 30, 1992; interview with Robert Bryan, June 29, 1992; interview with Nancy Otto, July 1, 1992; interview with Hilary Naylor, July 1, 1992.

19. Interview with Bill Lucero and Therese Bangert, April 3, 1992; telephone interview with Donna Schneweiss, August 17, 1992.

20. Telephone interview with Jonathan Gradess, November 23, 1992.

21. Interview with Hugo Bedau, April 27, 1992.

22. Interview, March 12, 1992.

23. Interview, March 10, 1992.

24. Interview with Michael Radelet, November 6, 1992.

25. Interview with Leigh Dingerson, November 20, 1992.

26. Interview, May 29, 1992.

Chapter 6

1. This figure includes only the trial and the first round of appeals, and thus is lower than most other estimates. On the other hand, it assumes that defendants will actually receive highly skilled, and rather costly, trial counsel. Many states that have reinstated capital punishment have cut corners in connection with the appointment of defense attorneys. The same may well occur now that capital punishment has returned to New York.

Nevertheless, the Criminal Justice Section of the New York Bar Association resolved in 1989 to oppose the reintroduction of the death penalty on the grounds that it would "devastate the already financially strained criminal justice system and overwhelm its ability to deliver proper prosecution, defense and judicial services to current and future caseloads," thereby creating "a crisis of unprecedented dimension in the Criminal Justice System of this state and in every county thereof . . . " (New York State Bar Association 1989).

2. Also see Memorandum, "Kansas Legislative Research Department regarding costs of implementing the death penalty—House Bill 2062," February 11, 1987; "Indiana Legislature, a fiscal impact statement re Senate Bill 531," 1989.

3. Telephone interview with Paula Sites, Indiana Public Defender Council, August 24, 1994.

4. Interview, August 20, 1992.

5. As of 1994, 20 Capital Resource Centers were operating in 18 states: Alabama, Arizona, Arkansas, California, Florida, Georgia, Illinois, Kentucky, Louisiana, Mississippi, Missouri (Kansas City and St. Louis), Nevada, North Carolina, Ohio, Oklahoma, South Carolina, Tennessee, and Texas (Austin and Houston). Another resource center was scheduled to open in Indiana during 1995, but is unlikely to do so due to Congressional resistance. Also during 1995, these Capital Resource Centers were officially renamed "Postconviction Defender Organizations." While their charge was expanded from training and support to the actual handling of capital appeals, their federal funding was in jeopardy (Telephone interviews with Richard Dieter and Norman Lefsting, July 5, 1995).

6. According to NCADP director Leigh Dingerson, there has been considerable debate within the movement as to the effectiveness of raising cost as an issue. Some feel that most death penalty supporters simply do not care about the expense. And some fear that the argument could collapse in states that cut corners by appointing poorly trained and unqualified defense counsel to indigent defendants. Dingerson maintains, however, that the NCADP leadership has finally reached a consensus that attacking the death penalty on the basis of its expense is a solid strategy that will prove effective (Interview, November 20, 1992).

7. Telephone interview with Richard Dieter, February 18, 1994.

8. An excellent, accessible summary of rational crime-reduction policies can be found in Elliot Currie's *Confronting Crime* (1985). Among other things, Currie makes a strong case for intensive rehabilitation programs for young lawbreakers, family planning services, improved parental leave and child care, community dispute-resolution programs, early education programs for children in poverty, more generous income support for poor families, and job creation by government.

9. Both men acted out of personal moral objection to capital punishment. Anaya commuted the death sentences of all five residents of New Mexico's death row the day before Thanksgiving, calling capital punishment "inhumane, immoral, anti-God—and . . . incompatible with an enlightened society" ("Statement by Governor Toney Anaya on crime and capital punishment, Sante Fe, New Mexico, November 26, 1986").

Celeste's action took place on January 10, 1991—74 hours before leaving office—and involved seven death row inmates. The state's attorney general who replaced him as governor sued to overturn the commutations, and a judge ruled in February 1992 that Celeste had acted illegally. The Ohio Supreme Court upheld the former governor's commutations in late 1994 (Brown and Kawa 1994; *Cincinnati Post* 1994; Kimmins 1994).

10. Lawmakers in several states are considering or have already passed bills that would increase the harshness of life in their correctional institutions. California, Florida, Louisiana, Mississippi, New York, North Carolina, Ohio, South Carolina, and Wisconsin have taken steps to restrict prisoner access to recreational sports facilities, television, and stereo equipment. California has authorized the banning of erotic materials (Nossiter 1994).

11. Comments at the 1993 Conference of the National Coalition to Abolish the Death Penalty, Pittsburgh, Pa., November 5–7.

12. Interview, July 1, 1992.

13. Interview with Michael Radelet, November 6, 1992.

14. Actually, enthusiasm for shock incarceration—the "boot camps" that so many states have built in recent years—may be on the wane. There is little evidence so far that this alternative reduces recidivism, and while it is clearly cheaper than traditional incarceration, those who receive it may be people who would normally receive probation, not prison. To the extent that this is true, shock incarceration may "widen the net" and fail even to save precious funds (Fisher 1994a; Katel 1994; MacKenzie, Shaw, and Gowdy 1993; Morash and Rucker 1990; Sechrest 1989). Nevertheless, the potential waste from the use of boot camps as alternatives to incarceration is likely to be far less than the waste deriving from prison overuse.

15. See American Civil Liberties Union *Annual Report, 1990;* ACLU, "Capital Punishment Project: A report on its functions and activities, 1991/1992"; ACLU Briefing Paper #2: "Crime and civil Liberties," n.d.; ACLU Briefing Paper No. 8: "The death penalty," n.d.

16. Interview with Ali Miller, March 22, 1992.

17. Prior to 1990, local AIUSA groups were prohibited from participating in other organizations or coalitions in order to protect AI's reputation for impartiality and independence. That year a resolution was passed at the annual general meeting that allowed groups to take part in state affiliates of the NCADP.

18. Interview with Earl Bender, November 17, 1992.

19. Interview, May 29, 1992.

20. Interview, March 10, 1992.

Afterword

1. Steven Hawkins, NCADP Executive Director's Report, June 1996.

2. Larry W. Yackle, Memorandum on the New Habeas Corpus Statute, Prepared for the National Legal Aid and Defender Association, April 24, 1996; Steven Hawkins, NCADP Executive Director's Report, June 1996.

3. Telephone interview with Abraham Bonowitz, Citizens United for Alternatives to the Death Penalty, January 12, 1999; telephone interview with Rick Halperin, AIUSA, January 20, 1999. Pat Clark of the American Friends Service Committee, on the other hand, feels that the Mumia movement is more interested in the larger issue of the death penalty than many mainstream abolitionists realize. She reports that she has often been invited to participate at events organized by his supporters and to speak about issues that transcend his case. The problem, Clark believes, is that many mainstream ADPM activists have difficulty "dealing with a group of folks who are far more radical, and far more *black*, than the normal abolitionist groupings." Telephone interview, January 22, 1999.

4. Telephone interview with Richard Dieter, Death Penalty Information Center, January 13, 1999.

5. Telephone interview with Abraham Bonowitz, January 12, 1999; telephone interview with Pat Clark, American Friends Service Committee, January 22, 1999; telephone interview with Steven Hawkins, National Coalition to Abolish the Death Penalty, January 15, 1999; telephone interview with George White, Journey of Hope—From Violence to Healing, January 11, 1999.

6. Telephone interview with Rich Cizik, National Association of Evangelicals, January 22, 1999.

7. Telephone interview with Rich Cizik, January 22, 1999.

8. Telephone interview with Pat Clark, American Friends Service Committee, January 22, 1999.

9. Telephone interview with David Dow, University of Houston School of Law, January 14, 1999. Telephone interview with Rick Halperin, AIUSA, January 20, 1999.

10. Life-without-parole is available as a sentencing option in Hawaii, Iowa, Maine, Massachusetts, Michigan, Rhode Island, Vermont, West Virginia, and the District of Columbia. Sentencing judges in Alaska and Wisconsin are empowered to set dates of parole eligibility so distant as to provide for *de facto* life-without-parole. Minnesota and North Dakota had enacted neither death penalty statutes nor LWOP at the time of this writing.

11. Telephone interview with Richard Dieter, January 13, 1999; telephone interview with Steven Hawkins, National Coalition to Abolish the Death Penalty, January 15, 1999; telephone interview with George White, Journey of Hope—From Violence to Healing, January 11, 1999.

12. Citizens United for Alternatives to the Death Penalty (CUADP), <http://www.abolition.org/>.

13. Citizens United for Alternatives to the Death Penalty (CUADP), <http://www.abolition.org/>.

14. Interview with Abraham Bonowitz, Citizens United for Alternatives to the Death Penalty, January 12, 1999; "History of Virginians for Alternatives to the Death Penalty" (web site), <http://www.vadp.org/history.htm>.

References

Abu-Jamal, Mumia. 1995. *Live from Death Row*. Reading, Mass.: Addison-Wesley.
———. 1997. *Death Blossoms: Reflections from a Prisoner of Conscience*. Farmington, Penn.: Plough.
Acker, James R. 1990. "New York's proposed death penalty legislation: Constitutional and policy perspectives." *Albany Law Review* 54:515–615.
———. 1993. "A different agenda: The Supreme Court, empirical research evidence, and capital punishment decisions, 1986–1989." *Law and Society Review* 27 (1):65–87.
Ad Hoc Committee on Federal Habeas Corpus in Capital Cases. 1989. "Committee report and proposal" (August 23). Washington, D.C.: U.S. Government Printing Office.
ALACP. 1929. *Bulletin to the members of the board of directors and the advisory committee*, no. 3 (July 9). American League to Abolish Capital Punishment, Inc. Sara B. Ehrmann Collection, Northeastern University Law School.
———. 1934. "Innocent men." *League News* 3 (April 25):1. Sara B. Ehrmann Collection, Northeastern University Law School.
———. 1953. *ALACP Bulletin* (April). Sara B. Ehrmann Collection, Northeastern University Law School.
———. 1961. "Innocence in the news." *ALACP Bulletin* (July). Sara B. Ehrmann Collection, Northeastern University Law School.
ALACP/Massachusetts Council for the Abolition of the Death Penalty. 1954. "The Pfeffer-Roche case: 'The ever-present possibility of executing an innocent man.'" *ALACP/MCADP Bulletin* (November). Sara B. Ehrmann Collection, Northeastern University Law School.
Allen, Harry, and Edward Latessa. 1983. "The conservative coup in crime policy and corrections." Paper presented at the Academy of Criminal Justice Sciences, San Antonio, Tex.
American Civil Liberties Union of Northern California. 1972. "Campaign underway for 'no on prop 17.'" *ACLU News* 37:1, 3 (September).
Amnesty International USA. 1986. "Attitudes in the state of Florida on the death penalty. Executive summary of a public opinion survey." Unpublished document.
———. 1987. *The United States of America: The Death Penalty*. London: Amnesty International Publications.
———. 1989a. *When the State Kills. . . . The Death Penalty: A Human Rights Issue*. New York: Amnesty International USA.
———. 1989b. "New York public opinion poll—The death penalty: an executive summary." Unpublished document.

———. 1991. *Amnesty International Handbook,* 7th ed. New York: Amnesty International Publications.

Amsterdam, Anthony G. 1982. "Capital punishment." In Hugo Adam Bedau, *The Death Penalty in America,* 3rd ed., 346–358. New York: Oxford University Press.

Applebome, Peter. 1993. "Mayoral races across country focus on crime." *New York Times,* October 18, p. 1.

Bailey, William C. 1975. "Murder and capital punishment." *American Journal of Orthopsychiatry* 45:669–688.

———. 1976. "Rape and the death penalty: A neglected area of deterrence research." In Hugo Adam Bedau and Charles M. Pierce (eds.), *Capital Punishment in the United States,* pp. 226–58. New York: AMS Press.

Bailey, William C., and Ruth D. Peterson. 1987. "Police killings and capital punishment: The post-*Furman* period." *Criminology* 25:1–25.

Baldus, David C., and James W. L. Cole. 1975. "Statistical evidence on the deterrent effect of capital punishment: A comparison of the work of Thorsten Sellin and Isaac Ehrlich on the deterrent effect of capital punishment." *Yale Law Journal* 85: 170–186.

Baldus, David C., George Woodworth, and Charles A. Pulaski, Jr. 1990. *Equal Justice and the Death Penalty: A Legal and Empirical Analysis.* Boston: Northeastern University Press.

Barkan, Steven E. 1986. "Interorganizational conflict in the southern civil rights movement." *Sociological Inquiry* 56:190–209.

Barry, Rupert V. 1979. "*Furman* to *Gregg:* The judicial and legislative history." *Howard Law Journal* 22:53–117.

Beccaria, Cesare. 1963. *On Crimes and Punishments.* Originally published 1764. Translated, with an introduction, by Henry Paolucci. New York: Bobbs-Merrill.

Bedau, Hugo Adam. 1967. "The struggle over capital punishment in New Jersey." In Hugo Adam Bedau (ed.), *The Death Penalty in America,* rev. ed., 374–395. Garden City, N.Y.: Anchor Books.

———. 1976. "Felony murder rape and the mandatory death penalty: A study in discretionary justice." In Hugo Adam Bedau and Chester M. Pierce (eds.), *Capital Punishment in the United States,* 54–75. New York: AMS Press.

———. 1977. *The Courts, The Constitution, and Capital Punishment.* Lexington, Mass.: Lexington Books.

———. 1980. "The 1964 death penalty referendum in Oregon: Some notes from a participant-observer." *Crime and Delinquency* 26(4):528–36.

———. 1987. *Death is Different: Studies in the Morality, Law, and Politics of Capital Punishment.* Boston: Northeastern University Press.

———. 1988. "Death penalty in America: Yesterday, today, and tomorrow." *Iliff Review* 45:43–51.

———. 1990. "Imprisonment vs. death: Does avoiding Schwarzschild's paradox lead to Sheleff's dilemma?" *Albany Law Review* 54:481–95.

———. 1992. *The Case Against The Death Penalty.* New York: American Civil Liberties Union Capital Punishment Project.

———, ed. 1964. *The Death Penalty in America.* Garden City, N.Y.: Anchor Books.

———. 1982. *The Death Penalty in America,* 3rd ed. New York: Oxford University Press.

Bedau, Hugo Adam, and Michael L. Radelet. 1987. "Miscarriages of justice in potentially capital cases." *Stanford Law Review* 40:21–179.

Benford, Robert D. 1993. "Frame disputes within the nuclear disarmament movement." *Social Forces* 71(3):677–701.

Berger, Raoul. 1982. *Death Penalties: The Supreme Court's Obstacle Course.* Cambridge, Mass.: Harvard University Press.

Best, Joel (ed). 1989. *Images of Issues: Typifying Contemporary Social Problems.* New York: Aldine de Gruyter.

Black, Charles. 1981. *Capital Punishment; The Inevitability of Caprice and Mistake,* 2nd ed. New York: Norton.

Blankenship, Bill, and John Boyette, Jr. 1987. "Cost factor intensifies death penalty debate." *Topeka Capital-Journal,* February 2, p. 1.

Bluestone, Harvey, and Carl L. McGahee. 1962. "Reaction to extreme stress: Impending death by execution." *American Journal of Psychiatry* 119:393–396.

Boer, Arthur. 1992. "Living forgiveness: A conversation with Marietta Jaeger by Arthur Boer." *The Voice* 1:8–9.

Bowers, William J. 1984. *Legal Homicide: Death as Punishment in America, 1864–1982.* Boston: Northeastern University Press.

———. 1988. "The effect of executions is brutalization, not deterrence." In Kenneth C. Haas and James A. Inciardi, *Challenging Capital Punishment,* 49–89. Beverly Hills, Calif.: Sage Publications.

———. 1993. "Capital punishment and contemporary values: People's misgivings and the Court's misperceptions." *Law and Society Review* 27:157–175.

Bowers, William J., and Glenn L. Pierce. 1975. "The illusion of deterrence in Isaac Ehrlich's research on capital punishment." *Yale Law Journal* 85:187–208.

———. 1980a. "Deterrence or brutalization: What is the effect of executions?" *Crime and Delinquency* 26:453–484.

———. 1980b. "Arbitrariness and discrimination under post-*Furman* capital statutes." *Crime and Delinquency* 26:563–635.

Bowers, William J., and Margaret Vandiver. 1991a. "New Yorkers want an alternative to the death penalty: Executive summary of a New York State survey conducted March 1–4, 1991." Unpublished paper.

———. 1991b. "Nebraskans want an alternative to the death penalty: Executive summary of a Nebraska State survey conducted April 26–28, 1991." Unpublished paper.

Bowers, William J., Margaret Vandiver, and Patricia H. Dugan. 1994. "People want an alternative to the death penalty: A new look at public opinion." *American Journal of Criminal Law.* no. 22(1):77–150.

Brown, Edmund G. (Pat). 1989. *Public Justice, Private Mercy: A Governor's Education on Death Row.* New York: Weidenfeld and Nicolson.

Brown, T. C., and Barry Kawa. 1994. "Death-sentence commutations upheld by court." *Cleveland Plain Dealer,* December 31, p. 1-A.

Bruck, David. 1984. "Public presentation of the abolitionist position." *Lifelines,* no. 9:1–3.

———. 1986. "Changing public opinion." Notes for panel at the Airlie Institute Death Penalty Conference, August 6–9.

———. 1987. "On McCleskey and abolition: 'The question is not whether . . . but when'." *Lifelines,* no. 34:2, 8.

Buckley, William F., Jr. 1977. "Amnesty group pushes open the wrong door." *Los Angeles Times,* December 20, sec. II, p. 5.

Buechler, Steven M. 1993. "Beyond resource mobilization? Emerging trends in social movement theory." *Sociological Quarterly* 34(2):217–235.

Burstein, Paul. 1991a. "Legal mobilization as a social movement tactic: The struggle for equal employment opportunity." *American Journal of Sociology* 96:1201–1225.

———. 1991b. "'Reverse discrimination' cases in the federal courts: Legal mobilization by a countermovement." *Sociological Quarterly* 32(4):511–528.

Cable, Sherry. 1984. "Professionalization in social movement organizations: A case study of Pennsylvanians for Biblical morality." *Sociological Focus* 17:287–304.

Caldeira, Gregory A. 1991. "Courts and public opinion." In John B. Gates and Charles A. Johnson, *The American Courts: A Critical Assessment,* 303–334. Washington, D.C.: CQ Press.

Callahan, Bill. 1994. "Lawyers no longer get millions in capital cases." *The San Diego Union Tribune,* June 26, p. A1.

Capital Report. 1987. "Is LWOP the answer to jury parole fears?" (September) 5.

———. 1988. "Life without parole—the debate continues." (January) 9.

———. 1989a. "Cost could be the winning issue." (May–June) 5–9.

———. 1989b. "LWOP—the continuing debate." (July/August) 1.

———. 1993. "State legislatures active on DP issues." (May/June) 1, 7, 11.

———. 1994. "Gary Graham wins chance to establish innocence." (March/April) 1, 12.

Castle, Michael N. 1991. "Alternative sentencing: Selling it to the public." Washington, D.C.: National Institute of Justice.

Caswell, Steve. 1974. "TRIAL interview: Hugo Adam Bedau." *TRIAL Magazine,* (May/June) 49, 51–53.

Chaiken, Marcia R., and Jan M. Chaiken. 1990. "Offender types and public policy." In Neil Alan Weiner, Margaret A. Zahn, and Rita J. Sagi, *Violence: Patterns, Causes, Public Policy,* 351–367. New York: Harcourt Brace Jovanovich.

Cheatwood, Derral. 1988. "The life-without-parole sanction: Its current status and a research agenda." *Crime and Delinquency* 34:43–59.

Chen, Connie. 1992. "A review and analysis of the 1982 New Jersey legislative decision making process reenacting capital punishment in New Jersey." In *Policy Conference Final Report: A Decade of Capital Punishment in New Jersey,* 28–52. Woodrow Wilson School of Public and International Affairs.

Chiang, Harriet. 1992. "Californians back death penalty, poll says." *San Francisco Chronicle,* April 2 p. A13.

———. 1993. "ACLU asks ban on gas chamber." *San Francisco Chronicle,* July 14, p. A18.

Christianity Today. 1998. "Editorial: The lesson of Karla Faye Tucker." April 6. <http://www.christianity.net/ct/8T4/8T4015.html>.

Christoph, James B. 1962. *Capital Punishment and British Politics: The British Movement to Abolish the Death Penalty, 1945–57.* Chicago: University of Chicago Press.

Cincinnati Post. 1994. "Death-penalty cases on line." September 19.

Cobin, Herbert L. 1967. "Abolition and restoration of the death penalty in Delaware." In Hugo Adam Bedau (ed.), *The Death Penalty in America,* rev. ed., 359–373. Garden City, N.Y.: Anchor Books.

Cohen, Jean L. 1985. "Strategy of identity: New theoretical paradigms and contemporary social movements." *Social Research* 52:663–716.

Comack, Elizabeth. 1990. "Law-and-order issues in the Canadian context: The case of capital punishment." *Social Justice* 17(1):70–97.

Congressional Digest. 1992. "Omnibus Crime Control Act," (April).

Cook, Philip J., and Donna B. Slawson. 1993. "The costs of processing murder cases in North Carolina." Terry Sanford Institute of Public Policy, Duke University.

Cooper, Claire. 1977. "ACLU's fight ended at 8:07 a.m." *Civil Liberties* 316:1, 4.

Coyle, Marcia. 1994. "Powell recants death penalty view." *National Law Journal,* June 13, p. A12.

Culhane, Chuck. 1988. "A fast to protest the death penalty." In *Organizing Against the Death Penalty: A Handbook,* 3rd ed., D13–15. Washington, D.C.: National Coalition to Abolish the Death Penalty.

Currie, Elliot. 1985. *Confronting Crime: An American Challenge.* New York: Pantheon Books.

Daily Oklahoman. 1992. "Death verdicts slip as no-parole grows." November 10.

Dallas Morning News. 1989. "Former death row inmate tries to recapture life." April 24.

Davies, Nick. 1991. *White Lies: Rape, Murder, and Justice Texas Style.* New York: Pantheon Books.

Davis, David Brian. 1957. "The movement to abolish capital punishment in America, 1787–1861." *American Historical Review* 63 (October):23–46.

DeAgostino, Martin. 1993. "Campaign fights death penalty." *South Bend Tribune,* June 1, p. 1.

Denno, Deborah W. 1992. Review Essay: "'Death is different' and other twists of fate." *Journal of Criminal Law and Criminology* 83 (2):437–467.

Dershowitz, Alan M. 1982. *The Best Defense.* New York: Random House.

Diani, Mario. 1992. "The concept of social movement." *The Sociological Review* 40 (February):1–25.

Dieter, Richard C. 1992. *Millions Misspent: What Politicians Don't Say About the High Costs of the Death Penalty.* Washington, D.C.: Death Penalty Information Center.

———. 1993. *Sentencing for Life: Americans Embrace Alternatives to the Death Penalty.* Washington, D.C.: Death Penalty Information Center.

———. 1994. *The Future of the Death Penalty in the U.S.: A Texas-Sized Crisis.* Washington, D.C.: Death Penalty Information Center.

———. 1998. *The Death Penalty in 1998: Year-end Report.* Washington, D.C.: Death Penalty Information Center.

Dingerson, Leigh. 1988. "Vigils—pro and con." In *Organizing Against the Death Penalty: A Handbook,* 3rd ed., D23–25. Washington, D.C.: National Coalition to Abolish the Death Penalty.

Ditzen, Stuart. 1998. "PA. High court upholds Abu-Jamal conviction." *Philadelphia Inquirer,* October 31, p. A01.

Doege, David. 1994. "McCann sees death penalty as costly, immoral." *Milwaukee Sentinel,* September 29, p. 11A.

Dorsen, Norman. 1968. *Frontiers of Civil Liberties.* New York: Random House.

Drell, Adrienne, and Lorraine Forte. 1997. "Critics of death penalty seek ban." *Chicago Sun-Times,* July 15. <http://www.suntimes.com:80/output/news/deth15.htm>.

Drinan, Robert. 1994. "Catholics and the death penalty." *America,* June 18, p. 13–14.

Edwards, Don. 1994. "Congressional overkill." *Washington Post,* March 8, p. A19.

Ehrlich, Isaac. 1975. "The deterrent effect of capital punishment: A question of life and death." *American Economic Review* 65:397–417.

Eisinger, Peter K. 1973. "The conditions of protest behavior in American cities." *American Political Science Review* 67:11–28.

Elliot, David. 1993. "5 of 6 witnesses could not identify Graham." *Austin American-Statesman,* May 2.

Elliot, Janet, and Mark Ballard. 1993. "Novel tack cracks clemency door." *Texas Lawyer,* August 23, pp. 1, 2B.

Ellsworth, Phoebe C., and Lee Ross. 1976. "Public opinion and judicial decision making." In Hugo Adam Bedau and Chester M. Pierce (eds.), *Capital Punishment in the United States,* 152–171. New York: AMS Press.

Epstein, Lee, and Joseph F. Kobylka. 1992. *The Supreme Court and Legal Change: Abortion and the Death Penalty.* Chapel Hill: University of North Carolina Press.

Espy, Watt, and J. O. Smykla. 1987. *Executions in the United States, 1608–1987: The Espy File.* [Machine-readable data file]. Ann Arbor, Mich.: Inter-University Consortium for Political and Social Research.

Fair, Kathy. 1992. "Texans give thumbs up to executions." *Houston Chronicle,* February 22, p. 25.

Fattah, Ezzat A. 1983. "Canada's successful experience with the abolition of the death penalty." *Canadian Journal of Criminology* 25:421–431.

Feieraband, Ivo, Rosalind Feieraband, and Betty Nesvold. 1969. "Social change and political violence: Cross national patterns." In Hugh David Graham and Ted Robert Gurr (eds.), *Violence in America: Historical and Comparative Perspectives,* 497–595. Washington, D.C.: Government Printing Office.

Feinberg, Kenneth R. 1984. "How the death penalty is hurting law enforcement." *Washington Post* (National Weekly Edition), June 4, pp. 22–23.

Fellowship of Reconciliation Capital Punishment Program. n.d. "Instead of the Death Penalty" (pamphlet). Nyack, N.Y.: The Fellowship of Reconciliation.

Ferree, Myra Marx. 1992. "The political context of rationality: Rational choice theory and resource mobilization." In Aldon D. Morris and Carol McClurg Mueller (eds.), *Frontiers in Social Movement Theory,* 29–52. New Haven: Yale University Press.

Ferree, Myra Marx, and Frederick D. Miller. 1985. "Mobilization and meaning: Toward an integration of social psychological and resource perspectives on social movements." *Sociological Inquiry* 55:38–61.

Ferriss, Susan. 1993. "Children's murders are shared horrors." *Fresno Bee,* August 10, p. A1.

Feuer, Lewis. 1969. *The Conflict of Generations: The Character and Significance of Student Movements.* New York: Basic Books.

Filler, Louis. 1952. "Movements to abolish the death penalty in the United States." *Annals of the American Academy of Political and Social Science* 284 (November):124–136.

Fireman, Bruce, and William Gamson. 1979. "Utilitarian logic in the resource mobilization perspective." In Mayer N. Zald and John D. McCarthy (eds.), *The Dynamics of Social Movements,* 8–45. Cambridge, Mass.: Winthrop.

Fisher, Ian. 1994a. "Prison boot camps prove no sure cure." *New York Times,* April 10, p. 43.

———. 1994b. "Pataki urging longer terms in crime plan." *New York Times,* October 12, p. A1.

Fox, James Alan, and Michael L. Radelet. 1989. "Persistent flaws in econometric studies of the deterrent effect of the death penalty." *Loyola of Los Angeles Law Review* 23:28–44.

Freeman, Jo. 1973. "The origins of the women's liberation movement." *American Journal of Sociology* 78:792–811.

French, Ron. 1994. "Tangled web of appeals process delays death, runs up legal bills." *Fort Wayne Journal-Gazette,* June 12.

Friedman, Debra, and Doug McAdam. 1992. "Collective identity and activism: Networks, choices, and the life of a social movement." In Aldon D. Morris and Carol McClurg Mueller (eds.), *Frontiers in Social Movement Theory,* 156–173. New Haven: Yale University Press.

Friedman, Lawrence M. 1993. *Crime and Punishment in American History.* New York: Basic Books.

Gale, Richard P. 1986. "Social movements and the state: The environmental movement, countermovement, and governmental agencies." *Sociological Perspectives* 29:202–240.

Galliher, John F., Gregory Ray, and Brent Cook. 1993. "Abolition and reinstatement of capital punishment during the progressive era and early 20th century." *Journal of Criminal Law and Criminology* 83(3):538–576.

Gallup, Alec, and Frank Newport. 1991. "Death penalty support remains strong." *The Gallup Poll Monthly* 309:40–45.

Gamson, William A. 1975. *The Strategy of Social Protest.* Homewood, Ill.: Dorsey Press.

Gamson, William A., and Andre Modigliani. 1989. "Media discourse and public opinion on nuclear power: A constructionist approach." *American Journal of Sociology* 95: 1–37.

Gelles, Richard J., and Murray A. Straus. 1975. "Family experience and public support of the death penalty." *American Journal of Orthopsychiatry* 45:596–613.

Gerth, Joseph. 1994. "Counties balk at paying experts to testify for indigents." *Louisville Courier-Journal,* April 4, p. 1.

Giarratano, Joseph M. 1991. "'To the best of our knowledge, we have never been wrong': Fallibility vs. finality in capital punishment." *Yale Law Journal* 100:1005–1011.

Goffman, Erving. 1974. *Frame Analysis.* Cambridge, Mass.: Harvard University Press.

Golway, Terry. 1995. "Albany sings executioner's song; Unlikely allies try to unplug chair." *New York Observer,* December 26–January 2, p. 1.

Gottlieb, David J. 1989. "The death penalty in the legislature: Some thoughts about money, myth, and morality." *University of Kansas Law Review* 37:443–470.

Gottlieb, Gerald. 1961. "Testing the death penalty." *Southern California Law Review* 34: 268–281.

Gowdy, Voncile B. 1992. *Research in Brief: Intermediate Sanctions.* Washington, D.C.: National Institute of Justice.

Gray, Ian, and Moira Stanley. 1989. *A Punishment In Search Of A Crime: Americans Speak Out Against the Death Penalty.* New York: Avon Books.

Greenberg, Jack. 1994 *Crusaders in the Courts: How a Dedicated Band of Lawyers Fought for the Civil Rights Revolution.* New York: Basic Books.

Gross, Rachel. 1984. "Death row support project." *Lifelines,* no. 11:1–2.

Gurr, Ted Robert. 1970. *Why Men Rebel.* Princeton, N.J.: Princeton University Press.

Gusfield, Joseph R. 1962. "Mass society and extremist politics." *American Sociological Review* 27:19–30.

Haines, Herbert H. 1984. "Black radicalization and the funding of civil rights: 1957–1970." *Social Problems* 32:31–43.

———. 1988. *Black Radicals and the Civil Rights Mainstream, 1954–1972.* Knoxville, Tenn.: University of Tennessee Press.

———. 1992. "Flawed executions, the anti-death penalty movement, and the politics of capital punishment." *Social Problems* 39 (2):301–314.

———. 1993. "Abolitionism in abeyance: The American League to Abolish Capital Punishment." Unpublished paper presented at the Meetings of the Midwest Sociological Society, Chicago, Ill., March 1993.

Hanna, John. 1987. "Lower costs seen for death penalty." *Topeka Capital-Journal,* February 13, p. 1.

Hayes, Patty. 1992. "Sam Sheppard speaks out against the death penalty." *Hingham Mariner,* May 7, pp. 16–17.

Henderson, Ky. 1997. "How many innocent inmates are executed? An Illinois coalition moves to stop the death penalty in the wake of startling statistics." *Human Rights* (Fall):10–11.

Hensel, Deborah Q. 1993. "Court stays Graham's execution." *Houston Post,* June 3, p. A1.

Hentoff, Nat. 1988. "A liberal—and an anti-abortionist, too," *Philadelphia Inquirer,* February 28.

Hewitt, Bill, Anne Maier, and Bob Stewart. 1998. "Reborn too late." *People*, February 2, p. 109.

Hoffer, Eric. 1951. *The True Believer: Thoughts on the Nature of Mass Movements.* New York: Mentor Books.

Hoffmann, Joseph L. 1989. "The Supreme Court's new vision of federal habeas corpus for state prisoners." *Supreme Court Review* 4:165–93.

Holding, Reynolds. 1994. "Gas chamber ruling strikes a nerve." *San Francisco Chronicle,* October 8, p. A23.

Holley, Joe. 1982. "Death race." *Texas Observer,* December 24.

Hood, Roger. 1989. *The Death Penalty, A World-Wide Perspective: A Report to the United Nations Committee on Crime Prevention and Control.* Oxford: Clarendon Press.

Hoppe, Christy. 1994. "Court uses Graham case to set up hearing procedure," *Dallas Morning News,* April 21, p. 1A.

Houston Post. 1986. "Death, dollars, and the scales of justice." December 7.

Immarigeon, Russ. 1990. "Instead of death: Alternatives to capital punishment." *National Prison Project Journal,* Summer:6–9.

Ingle, Joseph B. 1987. "From where I stand." *Southern Coalition Report* 15 (1):5.

———. 1990. *Last Rights: Thirteen Fatal Encounters with the State's Justice.* Nashville, Tenn.: Abingdon Press.

Jayewardene, C. H. S. 1972. "The Canadian movement against the death penalty." *Canadian Journal of Criminology and Correction* 14:366–389.

Jenkins, J. Craig, and Craig M. Eckert. 1986. "Channeling black insurgency: Elite patronage and professional social movement organizations in the development of the black movement." *American Sociological Review* 51:812–829.

Jenkins, J. Craig, and Charles Perrow. 1977. "Insurgency of the powerless: Farm workers' movements (1946–1972)." *American Sociological Review* 42:249–268.

Jenkins, Philip. 1994. *Using Murder: The Social Construction of Serial Homicide.* New York: Aldine de Gruyter.

Johnson, Robert. 1990a. *Death Work: A Study of the Modern Execution Process.* Pacific Grove: Calif.: Brooks/Cole.

———. 1990b. "Op-ed: An open letter to the governors of states with the death penalty." *Lifelines* no. 48:5.

Jones, Jim. 1998. "Churches to work to end death penalty." *Fort Worth Star-Telegram,* February 20.

Jones, Ramona. 1987. "Senate votes against executions." *Wichita Eagle-Beacon,* April 4, p. 1.

Kaplan, David A. 1991. "Pardon me, Governor Wilder." *Newsweek,* March 4, p. 56.

Katel, Peter, with Melinda Liu and Bob Cohn. 1994. "The bust in boot camps." *Newsweek,* February 21, p. 26.

Kaufman, Julia Cass, and Carol Morello. 1995. "Abu-Jamal's long climb to a world stage." *Philadelphia Inquirer,* August 13, p. A01.

Kaufman, Michael T. 1995. "Applause for death penalty brings opponents alive again." *New York Times,* January 4, p. B4.

Kazis, Israel J. 1967. "Judaism and the death penalty." In Hugo Adam Bedau (ed.), *The Death Penalty in America,* rev. ed., 171–175. Garden City, N.Y.: Anchor Books.

Killian, Lewis M. 1981. "Organization, rationality, and spontaneity in the civil rights movement." *American Sociological Review* 49:770–783.

Kimmins, Dick. 1994. "Celeste pardons being argued in Ohio's top court." *Cincinnati Inquirer,* September 20, p. B3.

Klandermans, Bert. 1984. "Social psychological expansions of resource mobilization theory." *American Sociological Review* 49:583–600.

———. 1986. "New social movements and resource mobilization: The European and American approach." *Journal of Mass Emergencies and Disasters* 4:13–37.

———. 1988. "The formation and mobilization of consensus." In Bert Klandermans, Hanspeter Kriesi, and Sidney Tarrow (eds.), *From Structure to Action: Comparing Social Movement Research Across Cultures. International Social Movement Research,* vol. 1, 173–196. Greenwich, Conn.: JAI Press.

———. 1992. "The social construction of protest and multiorganizational fields." In Aldon D. Morris and Carol McClurg Mueller (eds.), *Frontiers in Social Movement Theory,* 77–103. New Haven: Yale University Press.

Klandermans, Bert, and Sidney Tarrow. 1988. "Mobilization into social movements: Synthesizing European and American approaches." In Bert Klandermans, Hanspeter Kriesi, and Sidney Tarrow (eds.), *From Structure to Action: Comparing Social Movement Research Across Cultures. International Social Movement Research,* vol. 1, 1–38. Greenwich, Conn.: JAI Press.

Kleck, Gary. 1979. "Capital punishment, gun ownership and homicide," *American Journal of Sociology* 84:882–910.

Kornhauser, William. 1959. *The Politics of Mass Society.* Glencoe, Ill.: Free Press.

Kotok, C. David, and Jason Gertzen. 1995. "Opposition to death penalty killed many candidates' chances." *Omaha World-Herald,* November 17, p. 1.

Krauss, Clifford. 1994. "Crime levels fell in 1993, report says." *New York Times,* April 2, p. 21.

Kroll, Michael. 1988. "Florida Day." In *Organizing Against the Death Penalty: A Handbook,* 3rd ed., D4–D9. Washington, D.C.: National Coalition to Abolish the Death Penalty.

Layson, Stephen. 1985. "Homicide and deterrence: A reexamination of the United States time-series evidence." *Southern Economic Journal* 52:68–88.

Leahy, Bill. 1993. "The high cost of the death penalty." *Nuvo Newsweekly,* November 3–10, p. 8.

Leavy, Deborah. 1976. "The death penalty." Unpublished paper prepared for Biennial Conference of the American Civil Liberties Union, June 10–13.

———. 1977. "Utah deathwatch: renewed hope, then grief." *Civil Liberties* 316:4.

Leech, Elizabeth. 1987. "Death penalty foes say cost estimates were not inflated." *Kansas City Times,* March 4.

Lehr, Dick. 1993. "Death penalty foes seek a new debate, see stronger case." *Boston Globe,* January 10, p. 1.

Lewis, Neil A. 1993. "Crime: Falling rates but rising fear." *New York Times,* December 8, p. B6.

Lifelines. 1985a. "Civil disobedience in Georgia," no. 21 (April):4.

———. 1985b. "Peace pentecosters arrested at Supreme Court building," no. 22 (June):2.

———. 1986. "PAX defense fund," no. 27 (January–February):2.

———. 1993. "Abolitionists commit civil disobedience in Washington state," no. 59 (January–March):8.

Lindner, Charles L. 1993. "Capital cases are crippling state courts." *Sacramento Bee,* September 5, p. 1.

Los Angeles Times. 1979. "Mock executions staged at high court." November 24, p. I13.

Lowry, Beverly. 1992. *Crossed Over: A Murder, a Memoir.* New York: Alfred A. Knopf.

Lozier, John. 1976. "Tennessee death row visitation." *Southern Coalition Report* 3 (5):2.

MacCormack, John. 1990. "Brandley regains his freedom." *Dallas Times Herald,* January 24, p. A1.

MacKenzie, Doris Layton, James W. Shaw, and Voncile B. Gowdy. 1993. *Research in Brief: An Evaluation of Shock Incarceration.* Washington, D.C.: National Institute of Justice.

Mackey, Philip English. 1976. *Voices Against Death: American Opposition to Capital Punishment, 1787–1975.* New York: Burt Franklin.

———. 1982. *Hanging in the Balance: The Anti-Capital Punishment Movement in New York State, 1776–1861.* New York: Garland.

Mackey, Virginia. 1993. *Reflections on Twenty-Five Years: The History of the National Interreligious Task Force on Criminal Justice, 1968–1993.* Louisville, Ky.: Presbyterian Criminal Justice Program, Presbyterian Church (USA).

Mader, Ian. 1994. "It's taps for death penalty." *Juneau Empire,* February 1, p. 1.

Magagnini, Stephen. 1988. "Closing death row would save state $90 million a year." *Sacramento Bee,* March 28, p. 1.

Magee, Doug. 1980. *Slow Coming Dark: Interviews on Death Row.* New York: Pilgrim Press.

Mailer, Norman. 1979. *The Executioner's Song.* Boston: Little, Brown.

Malcolm, Andrew H. 1989. "Tainted verdicts resurrect specter of executing the innocent." *New York Times,* May 3, p. A18.

Marquart, James W., and Jonathan R. Sorensen. 1989. "A national study of the *Furman*-commuted inmates: Assessing the threat to society from capital offenders." *Loyola of Los Angeles Law Review* 23:5–28.

Marshall, Thomas R. 1989. *Public Opinion and the Supreme Court.* Boston: Unwin Hyman.

Mastrofski, Stephen D. 1992. "What does community policing mean for daily police work?" *National Institute of Justice Journal,* August 23, p. 27.

Masur, Louis P. 1989. *Rites of Execution: Capital Punishment and the Transformation of American Culture, 1776–1865.* New York: Oxford University Press.

Mattox, Jim. 1993. "Texas' death penalty dilemma." *Dallas Morning News,* August 25, p. 23A.

McAdam, Doug. 1982. *Political Process and the Development of Black Insurgency, 1930–1970.* Chicago: University of Chicago Press.

McAdam, Doug, John D. McCarthy, and Mayer N. Zald. 1988. "Social movements." In Neil J. Smelser (ed.), *Handbook of Sociology,* 695–737. Newbury Park, Calif.: Sage Publications.

McCarthy, John D., and Mayer N. Zald. 1973. *The Trend in Social Movements in America: Professionalization and Resource Mobilization.* Morristown, N.J.: General Learning Press.

———. 1977. "Resource mobilization and social movements: A partial theory." *American Journal of Sociology* 82:1212–1241.

McCraw, Vincent. 1992. "District voters reject death penalty." *Washington Times,* November 4, p. B1.

McNally, Kevin. 1988. "Working with survivors: What can a defense lawyer, an activist against capital punishment, say to Parents of Murdered Children?" *Fellowship,* March:14–15.

McNulty, Timothy. 1977a. "1,000 march in Atlanta for end of death penalty." *Chicago Tribune,* April 10, p. 1.

———. 1977b. "For some, life in jail is a victory." *Chicago Tribune,* May 27, p. 1.

Megivern, James. 1981. "Biblical argument in the capital punishment debate." *Perspectives in Religious Studies* 8:143–153.

Meier, Barry. 1993. "Reality and anxiety: Crime and the fear of it." *New York Times,* February 18, p. A14.

Meltsner, Michael. 1973. *Cruel and Unusual: The Supreme Court and Capital Punishment.* New York: Random House.

Melucci, Alberto. 1980. "The new social movements: A theoretical approach." *Social Science Information* 19:199–226.

———. 1981. "Ten hypotheses for the analysis of new movements." In D. Pinto, (ed.), *Contemporary Italian Sociology,* 173–194. Cambridge, Mass.: Cambridge University Press.

———. 1989. *Nomads of the Present: Social Movements and Individual Needs in Contemporary Society.* Philadelphia: Temple University Press.

Memphis Commercial Appeal. 1994. "Death sentences fall in Tenn.; costs cited." September 6.

Miami Herald. 1980. "Death penalty protesters unable to disrupt Graham." August 15.

———. 1988. "Bottom line: Life in prison one-sixth as expensive." July 10.

Milligan, Charles S. 1967. "A protestant's view of the death penalty." In Hugo Adam Bedau (ed.), *The Death Penalty in America,* rev. ed., 175–182. Garden City, N.Y.: Anchor Books.

Minor, Elliott. 1989. "Spotlight turned on Swainsboro in anti-death penalty campaign." *Savannah Evening Press,* June 28, p. 1.

Minor, Emily J. 1990. "Imprisoned by freedom. New ordeals face man wrongly convicted of killing his children." *San Francisco Examiner,* May 13, p. 1.

Moran, Richard. 1989. "High cost of execution." *Boston Globe,* December 4, p. 19.

Morash, Merry, and Lila Rucker. 1990. "A critical look at the idea of boot camp as a correctional reform." *Crime and Delinquency* 36:204–222.

Morris, Aldon. 1984. *The Origins of the Civil Rights Movement.* New York: Free Press.

Morris, Norval, and Michael Tonry. 1990. *Between Prison and Probation: Intermediate Punishments in a Rational Sentencing System.* New York: Oxford University Press.

Muller, Eric. 1985. "The Legal Defense Fund's capital punishment campaign: The distorting influence of death." *Yale Law and Policy Review* 4:158–187.

Murray, Alice. 1977. "Atlanta rally to protest death penalty." *Atlanta Journal and Constitution,* April 2, p. 7B.

Myers, Roger. 1987. "Death penalty foes testify." *Topeka Capital-Journal,* January 22, p. 1.

Nadelmann, Ethan A. 1992. "America's drug problem: A case for decriminalization." *Dissent.* Spring:205–212.

Nagel, Joane. 1990. "Cycles of protest and cycles of reform: From termination to self-determination in federal Indian policy, 1950–1980." Paper delivered at the annual meetings of the American Sociological Association (August) Washington, D.C.

Nagorka, Jennifer. 1993. "Fear of crime up, but murder rate in U.S. same as in '74." *Dallas Morning News,* March 29, p. 6A.

National Coalition to Abolish the Death Penalty. 1990. *The 1991 Abolitionist's Directory.* Washington, D.C.: National Coalition to Abolish the Death Penalty.

National Council on Crime and Delinquency. 1992. *Criminal Justice Sentencing Policy Statement.* National Council on Crime and Delinquency.

———. 1993. *Reducing Crime in America: A Pragmatic Approach.* San Francisco, Calif.: National Council on Crime and Delinquency.

National Institute of Justice Journal. 1992. "Community policing in the 1990's." August, pp. 1–8.

National Interreligious Task Force on Criminal Justice. 1979. *The Death Penalty: The Religious Community Calls for Abolition.* New York: NITFCJ Work Group on the Death Penalty.

National Law Journal. 1993. "Washington Brief: Death penalty centers come under pressure." October 11, p. 5.

Neier, Aryeh. 1982. *Only Judgement: The Limits of Litigation in Social Change.* Middletown, Conn.: Wesleyan University Press.

New York State Bar Association. 1989. Report of the Criminal Justice Section, Reinstitution of Death as Punishment.

New York State Defenders Association. 1982. "Capital losses: The price of the death penalty for New York State." A report from the Public Defense Backup Center to the Senate Finance Committee, the Assembly Ways and Means Committee and the Division of the Budget. April 1.

New York Times. 1971. "Supreme Court decision prompts meeting here of 100 lawyers battling execution of their clients." May 16, p. 36.

———. 1972a. "Parole in capital cases less likely, officials say." *New York Times,* June 30:1.

———. 1972b. "Florida becomes first to reinstate the death penalty." December 9, p. 32.

———. 1973. "Death penalty has been restored by 13 States." May 10, p. 18.

———. 1975. "Court to hear test today on death penalty return." April, 21, p. 1.

———. 1976a. "'Team Defense' uses new methods to avoid death penalty for clients." December 4, p. 60.

———. 1976b. "Vigils in 4 states in South protest death penalty." December 26, p. 22.

———. 1980. "Law enforcement officers unite to fight death penalty." December 30, p. A6.

———. 1994. "Justice Powell's new wisdom." June 11, p. 20.

Newbold, Greg. 1990. "Capital punishment in New Zealand: An experiment that failed." *Deviant Behavior* 11:155–174.

Niebuhr, Gustav. 1998. "Tucker case may split evangelical Christians." *New York Times,* February 4, p. A20.

Niller, Eric. 1990. "Death penalty support 'broad but not deep.'" *Charleston Gazette,* January 25, 1990.

Nordheimer, Jon. 1977. "Gilmore is executed after stay is upset; 'Let's do it!' he said." *New York Times,* January 18, pp. 1, 21.

Norman, Tony. 1998. "Mumia Must Have a Retrial." *Pittsburgh Post-Gazette,* November 13, p. D1.

Nossiter, Adam. 1994. "Making hard time harder, states cut jail TV and sports." *New York Times,* September 17, p. 1.

Oberer, Walter E. 1961. "Does disqualification of jurors for scruples against capital punishment constitute denial of fair trial on issue of guilt?" *Texas Law Review* 39: 545–567.

Oberschall, Anthony. 1973. *Social Conflict and Social Movements.* Englewood Cliffs, N.J.: Prentice-Hall.

Oney, Steve. 1979. "One man's war against the death penalty." *Atlanta Journal and Constitution Magazine,* March 25, p. 13.

O'Reilly, David. 1998. "Gathering of the young rallies for Abu-Jamal." *Philadelphia Inquirer,* July 20, p. B01.

Oreskes, Michael. 1990. "The political stampede on execution." *New York Times,* April 4, p. A16.

Paduano, Anthony, and Clive A. Stafford Smith. 1989. "Deathly errors: Juror misperceptions concerning parole in the imposition of the death penalty." *Columbia Human Rights Law Review* 18:211–257.

Passell, Peter. 1975. "The deterrent effect of the death penalty." *Stanford Law Review* 61: 61–80.

Paternoster, Raymond. 1991. *Capital Punishment in America.* New York: Lexington Books.

Peterson, Ruth D., and William C. Bailey. 1988. "Murder and capital punishment in the evolving context of the post-*Furman* era." *Social Forces* 66:774–807.

Phillips, David P. 1980. "The deterrent effect of capital punishment: New evidence on an old controversy." *American Journal of Sociology* 86:139–148.

Piven, Francis Fox, and Richard Cloward. 1977. *Poor People's Movements: Why They Succeed, How They Fail.* New York: Vintage.

Pizzorno, Alessandro. 1978. "Political science and collective identity in industrial conflict." In Colin Crouch and Alessandro Pizzorno (eds.), *The Resurgence of Class Conflict in Western Europe since 1968,* 277–298. New York: Holmes and Meier.

Post, Albert. 1944. "Early efforts to abolish capital punishment in Pennsylvania." *Pennsylvania Magazine of History and Biography* 68 (January):38–53.

Prejean, C. S. J. Helen. 1993. *Dead Man Walking: An Eyewitness Account of the Death Penalty in the United States.* New York: Random House.

Radelet, Michael L. 1988. "The successes of the abolition movement: An optimistic view." Paper presented to the Florida Chapter of the American Civil Liberties Union, Tampa, Florida, October 1.

Radelet, Michael L., Hugo Adam Bedau, and Constance E. Putnam. 1992. *In Spite of Innocence.* Boston: Northeastern University Press.

Rankin, Mary Alice. 1988a."The Illinois Coalition Against the Death Penalty: A history." In *Organizing Against the Death Penalty: A Handbook,* 3rd ed., A10–A15. Washington, D.C.: National Coalition to Abolish the Death Penalty.

——. 1988b. "Four years later: Continued chronicle of the Illinois Coalition Against the Death Penalty." In *Organizing Against the Death Penalty: A Handbook,* 3rd ed., A16. Washington, D.C.: National Coalition to Abolish the Death Penalty.

Reidel, Marc. 1976. "Discrimination in the imposition of the death penalty: A comparison of the characteristics of offenders sentenced pre-*Furman* and post-*Furman.*" *Temple University Law Review* 49:261–286.

Robbins, William. 1972. "Nixon backs death penalty for kidnapping, hijacking." *New York Times,* June 30, p. 1.

Roderick, Kevin. 1990. "67% favor life term over gas chamber." *Los Angeles Times,* March 1, p. A3.

Rosenthal, Naomi, and Michael Schwartz. 1989. "Spontaneity and democracy in social movements." In Bert Klandermans, (ed.), *Organizing for Change: Social Movement Organizations in Europe and the United States. International Social Movement Research,* vol. 2, 33–59. Greenwich, Conn.: JAI Press.

Rothman, David. 1971. *The Discovery of the Asylum: Social Order and Disorder in the New Republic.* Boston: Little, Brown.

Royal Commission on Capital Punishment. 1953. Report. London: Her Majesty's Stationery Office.

Rozzell, Liane. 1986. "Abolitionists share strategies, information, at annual meeting." *Lifelines,* no. 27:1–3.

San Francisco Examiner. 1983. "Protest against death penalty." May 26.

Sanchez, Rene. 1992. "District rejects death penalty measure." *Washington Post,* November 4, p. A33.

Sarat, Austin D., and Neil Vidmar. 1976. "The public and the death penalty: Testing the Marshall hypothesis." In Hugo Adam Bedau and Chester M. Pierce (eds.), *Capital Punishment in the United States,* pp. 190–223. New York: AMS Press.

Savage, David G. 1992. *Turning Right: The Making of the Rehnquist Supreme Court.* New York: John Wiley and Sons.

Schmetzer, Uli, and Blair Kamin. 1987. "The plea from Italy: Spare Gary murderer." *Chicago Tribune,* August 26, sec. 2, p. 1.

Schwarzschild, Henry. 1979. "The Capital Punishment Project: Mandate, operations, and needs. A report for the capital punishment project review committee." Unpublished report. American Civil Liberties Union Archives, Volume V, Princeton University.

———. 1990. "Remarks—The death penalty as a controversy over social values." *Albany Law Review* 54:497–500.

———. 1991. "Reflections on capital punishment." *Israel Law Review* 25:505–511.

Schwarzschild, Henry, and George H. Kendall. 1985. "The death penalty and the ACLU." Paper prepared for the Biennial Conference of the American Civil Liberties Union, Boulder, Colorado, June 13–16.

Schwed, Roger. 1983. *Abolition and Capital Punishment: The United States' Judicial, Political, and Moral Barometer.* New York: AMS Press.

Scott, Steve. 1993. "Prosecutors find juries balking at death penalty." *Dallas Morning News,* December 26, p. 41A.

Sechrest, Dale K. 1989. "Prison 'boot camps' do not measure up." *Federal Probation* 53: 15–20.

Sellin, Thorsten. 1959. *The Death Penalty.* Philadelphia: American Law Institute.

———. 1967. "Does the death penalty protect municipal police?" In Hugo Adam Bedau (ed.), *The Death Penalty in America,* rev. ed., 284–301. Garden City, N.Y.: Anchor Books.

Shorter, Edward, and Charles Tilly. 1974. *Strikes in France, 1830–1968.* London: Cambridge University Press.

Simon, Ellen. 1993. "Death be not cheap." *Connecticut Law Tribune* 19:12–15.

Skelton, George. 1992. "Death penalty support still strong in state." *Los Angeles Times,* April 29, p. 1.

Smelser, Neil. 1962. *Theory of Collective Behavior.* New York: Free Press.

Smith, Doug. 1993. "For death penalty, but. . . . " *Arkansas Times,* February 4.

Smith, M. Dwayne, and James Wright. 1992. "Capital punishment and public opinion in the post-*Furman* era: Trends and analyses." *Sociological Spectrum* 12:127–144.

Smith, Pamela. 1977. "Death penalty blasted at Liberty Bell vigil." *Philadelphia Tribune,* April 12, p. 1.

Snell, Tracy. 1998. *Bureau of Justice Statistics Bulletin: Capital Punishment, 1997.* Washington, D.C.: U.S. Department of Justice, Bureau of Justice Statistics.

Snow, David A., and Robert D. Benford. 1988. "Ideology, frame resonance, and participant mobilization." In Bert Klandermans, Hanspeter Kriesi, and Sidney Tarrow (eds.), *From Structure to Action: Comparing Social Movement Research Across Cultures. International Social Movement Research,* vol. 1, 197–218. Greenwich, Conn.: JAI Press.

———. 1992. "Master frames and cycles of protest." In Aldon D. Morris and Carol McClurg Mueller (eds.), *Frontiers in Social Movement Theory,* 133–155. New Haven: Yale University Press.

Snow, David A., and Susan Marshall. 1984. "Cultural imperialism, social movements, and the Islamic revival." In Louis Kriesberg (ed.), *Social Movements, Conflicts and Change,* vol. 7, 131–152. Greenwich, Conn.: JAI Press.

Snow, David A., E. Burke Rochford, Jr., Steven K. Worden, and Robert D. Benford. 1986. "Frame alignment process, micromobilization, and movement participation." *American Sociological Review* 51:464–481.

Spangenberg, Robert L., and Elizabeth R. Walsh. 1989. "Capital punishment or life imprisonment? Some cost considerations." *Loyola of Los Angeles Law Review* 23: 45–58.

Stack, Steven. 1987. "Publicized executions and homicide, 1950–1980." *American Sociological Review* 52:532–540.

Staggenborg, Suzanne. 1988. "The consequences of professionalization and formalization in the pro-choice movement." *American Sociological Review* 53:585–606.

———. 1989. "Stability and innovation in the women's movement: A comparison of two movement organizations." *Social Problems* 36:75–92.

———. 1991. *The Pro-Choice Movement: Organization and Activism in the Abortion Conflict.* New York: Oxford University Press.

Stark, Shelley. 1994. "Life sentencing in Pennsylvania: To parole or not to parole." *Pittsburgh Legal Journal,* December 28, pp. 1, 4.

Stoecker, Randy. 1995. "Community, movement, organization: The problem of identity convergence in collective action." *Sociological Quarterly* 36(1):111– 130.

Streib, Victor L. 1987. *Death Penalty for Juveniles.* Bloomington, Ind.: Indiana University Press.

Tabak, Ronald J., and J. Mark Lane. 1989. "The execution of injustice: A cost and lack-of-benefit analysis of the death penalty." *Loyola of Los Angeles Law Review* 23: 59–146.

Tarrow, Sidney. 1988a. "Old movements in new cycles of protest: The career of an Italian religious community." In Bert Klandermans, B. Kriesi, and Sidney Tarrow (eds.), *International Social Movement Research,* vol. 1, 281–304. Greenwich, Conn.: JAI Press Inc.

———. 1988b. "National politics and collective action: Recent theory and research in Western Europe and the United States." *Annual Review of Sociology* 14:421–440.

———. 1989. "Struggle, politics, and reform: Collective action, social movements, and cycles of protest." Ithaca: Cornell University Western Societies Program, Occasional Paper No. 21.

———. 1992. "Mentalities, political cultures, and collective action frames: Constructing meanings through action." In Aldon D. Morris and Carol McClurg Mueller (eds.), *Frontiers in Social Movement Theory,* 174–202. New Haven: Yale University Press.

Taylor, Gary. 1994. "Death works double-time in the Lone Star State." *National Law Journal,* October 3, p. A7.

Taylor, Verta. 1989. "Social movement continuity: The women's movement in abeyance." *American Sociological Review* 54(5):761–775.

Taylor, Verta, and Nancy E. Whittier. 1992. "Collective identity in social movement communities." In Aldon D. Morris and Carol McClurg Mueller (eds.), *Frontiers in Social Movement Theory,* 104–129. New Haven: Yale University Press.

Thomas, Robert H., and John D. Hutcheson, Jr. 1986. "Georgia residents' attitudes toward the death penalty, the disposition of juvenile offenders, and related issues." Unpublished paper, Center for Public and Urban Research, College of Public and Urban Affairs, Georgia State University.

Tilly, Charles. 1978. *From Mobilization to Revolution.* Reading, Mass.: Addison-Wesley.

Topeka Capital-Journal. 1986. "Panel urged to reinstate death penalty." May 7.

Touraine, Alain. 1985. "An introduction to the study of social movements." *Social Research* 52:749–787.

Tugend, Alina. 1993. "Death penalty's high cost." *Orange County Register,* August 9, p. 1.

Turner, Ralph H., and Lewis M. Killian. 1957. *Collective Behavior.* Englewood Cliffs, N.J.: Prentice Hall.

———. 1987. *Collective Behavior,* 3rd ed. Englewood Cliffs, N.J.: Prentice-Hall.

Turner, Wallace. 1979. "Murderer in casino executed in Nevada." *New York Times,* October 23, p. 1.

Uelmen, Gerald F. 1992. "At what cost the death penalty?" *San Jose Mercury News,* September 20.

Urofsky, Melvin L. (ed.). 1987. *The Douglas Letters.* Bethesda, Md.: Adler and Adler.

U.S. Department of Justice, Bureau of Justice Statistics. 1988. *Report to the Nation on Crime and Justice,* 2nd ed. Washington, D.C.: U.S. Government Printing Office.

———. 1991. *Bureau of Justice Statistics National Update.* October. Washington, D.C.: U.S. Government Printing Office.

———. 1992a. *Sourcebook of Criminal Justice Statistics, 1991.* Washington, D.C.: U.S. Government Printing Office.

———. 1992b. *Census of Adult Correctional Facilities, 1990.* Washington, D.C.: U.S. Government Printing Office.

———. 1992c. *Justice Expenditure and Employment, 1990.* Washington, D.C.: U.S. Government Printing Office.

———. 1994. *Sourcebook of Criminal Justice Statistics, 1993.* Washington, D.C.: U.S. Government Printing Office.

U.S. General Accounting Office. 1989. *Criminal Justice. Limited Data Available on Costs of Death Sentences.* Report to the Chairman, Subcommittee on Civil and Constitutional Rights, Committee on the Judiciary, House of Representatives. Washington, D.C.: U.S. Government Printing Office.

U.S. House of Representatives Subcommittee on Civil and Constitutional Rights. 1993. *Innocence and the Death Penalty: Assessing the Danger of Mistaken Executions.* Reprinted by the Death Penalty Information Center, Washington, D.C.

van den Haag, Ernest. 1990. "Why capital punishment?" *Albany Law Review* 54:501–514.

Verhovek, Sam Howe. 1998a. "As Woman's Execution Nears, Texas Squirms." *New York Times,* January 1, p. A1.

———. 1998b. "Divisive Case of a Killer of Two Ends as Texas Executes Tucker." *New York Times,* February 4, p. A1.

———. 1998c. "Karla Tucker Is Now Gone, But Several Debates Linger." *New York Times,* February 5, p. A12.

Vidmar, Neil, and Phoebe Ellsworth. 1974. "Public opinion on the death penalty." *Stanford Law Review* 26:1245–1270.

Visher, C. A. 1987. "Incapacitation and crime control: Does a 'lock 'em up' strategy reduce crime?" *Justice Quarterly* 4:513–544.

Vito, Gennaro F., and Thomas J. Keil. 1989. "Attitudes in the State of Kentucky on the death penalty." Unpublished paper.

Vulliamy, Ed. 1997. "Former Panther Fights for Voice from Death Row." *The Guardian,* September 1, p.15.

Waldron, Martin. 1972. "Ruling cheered on Florida death row." *New York Times,* June 30, p. 14.

Walker, Samuel. 1990. *In Defense of American Liberties: A History of the ACLU.* New York: Oxford University Press.

Walsh, Edward J. 1981. "Resource mobilization and citizen protest in communities around Three Mile Island." *Social Problems* 29:1–21.

———. 1988. *Democracy in the Shadows: Citizen Mobilization in the Wake of the Accident at Three Mile Island.* New York: Greenwood Press.

Warren, Susan. 1993. "Taking offense at death-row defense." *Houston Chronicle,* November 7, p. 20A.

Weir, Ed. 1993. "Expense halts death penalty." *Rural Southern Voice for Peace,* September/October, p. 15.

Weisberg, Robert. 1983. "Deregulating death." In Philip B. Kurland, Gerhard Casper, and Dennis J. Hutchinson (eds.), *The Supreme Court Review, 1983,* 305–395. Chicago: University of Chicago Press.

West, Louis Jolyon. 1975. "Psychiatric reflections on the death penalty." *American Journal of Orthopsychiatry* 45:689–700.

White, Welsh S. 1987. *The Death Penalty in the Eighties: An Examination of the Modern System of Capital Punishment.* Ann Arbor: University of Michigan Press.

———. 1991. *The Death Penalty in the Nineties: An Examination of the Modern System of Capital Punishment.* Ann Arbor: University of Michigan Press.

Wicker, Tom 1976. "A Christmas vigil." *New York Times,* December 26, sec. IV, p. 9.

———. 1977. "Rally against death." *New York Times,* April 12, p. 33.

Williams, Janet E. 1993. "Accused won't face the death penalty." *Indianapolis Star,* August 18, p. 1.

Williams, Randall. 1978. "The legacy of legalized murder." *Southern Exposure* 6(4): 70–73.

Wolfe, Burton H. 1973. *Pileup on Death Row.* Garden City, N.Y.: Doubleday.

Wolfgang, Marvin E., and Marc Reidel. 1976. "Rape, racial discrimination, and the death penalty." In Hugo Adam Bedau and Chester M. Pierce (eds.), *Capital Punishment in the United States,* 99–121. New York: AMS Press.

Wood, Toni, and Miriam Pepper. 1987. "The walk to death row long and costly." *Kansas City Star,* January 24, pp. 1A, 6A.

Woodward, Bob, and Scott Armstrong. 1979. *The Brethren: Inside the Supreme Court.* New York: Simon and Schuster.

Woolf, Michael. 1987. "Winning in Kansas!" *Death Penalty Exchange,* July, p. 1.

Wright, Julian H., Jr. 1990. "Life-without-parole: An alternative to death or not much of a life at all?" *Vanderbilt Law Review* 43:529–568.

Zald, Mayer N. 1992. "Looking backward to look forward: Reflections on the past and future of the resource mobilization research paradigm." In Aldon D. Morris and Carol McClurg Mueller (eds.), *Frontiers in Social Movement Theory,* 326–348. New Haven: Yale University Press.

Zald, Mayer N., and John D. McCarthy. 1987. "Religious groups as crucibles of social movements." In Mayer N. Zald and John D. McCarthy (eds.), *Social Movements in an Organizational Society,* 67–96. New Brunswick, N.J.: Transaction Books.

Zald, Mayer, N., and Bert Useem. 1987. "Movement and countermovement interaction: Mobilization, tactics and state involvement." In Mayer N. Zald and John D. McCarthy (eds.), *Social Movements in an Organizational Society,* 247–272. New Brunswick, N.J.: Transaction Books.

Zawitz, Marianne W., Patsy A. Klaus, Ronet Bachman, Lisa D. Bastian, Marshall M. DeBerry, Jr., Michael R. Rand, and Bruce M. Taylor. 1993. *Highlights from 20 Years of Surveying Crime Victims: The National Crime Victimization Survey, 1973–92.* Washington, D.C.: U.S. Government Printing Office.

Zimring, Franklin E. 1983. "Idealizing the 'angels' on death row." *Los Angeles Times,* February 24, section II, p. 7.

————. 1993. "On the liberating virtues of irrelevance." *Law and Society Review* 27 (1): 9–17.

Zimring, Franklin E., Joel Eigen, and Sheila O'Malley. 1976. "Punishing homicide in Philadelphia." *University of Chicago Law Review* 43:227–252.

Zimring, Franklin E., and Gordon Hawkins. 1986. *Capital Punishment and the American Agenda.* New York: Cambridge University Press.

Index

Abernathy, Rev. Ralph, 59
Abeyance, 21
Abolition dividend, 177
 and crime prevention, 186–93
 and enhanced local law enforcement,
  183–86
 and mandatory sentences, 178–83
Abortion. *See* right-to-life movement
Abu-Jamal, Mumia, 200–202, 231n.3
Accomplices to murder, death sentences
 for, 75
ACLU. *See* American Civil Liberties
 Union
ACT UP!, 131–32, 161
Ad Hoc Committee on Federal Habeas
 Corpus in Capital Cases, 217–18n.2
Adams, James, 124, 220n.33
Adams, John P., 215n.10
Adams, Randall Dale, 88–89, 223n.71
Adams v. Texas, 56
Aggravating circumstances, 46, 51, 56, 75
AI. *See* Amnesty International
AIDS activists, 131–32
Airlie Conference, 224–25n.1
Aikens v. California, 37, 211n.12
AIUSA. *See* Amnesty International USA
ALACP. *See* American League to Abolish
 Capital Punishment
*Albertson v. Subversive Activities Control
 Board*, 40
ALI. *See* American Law Institute
Alienation, 16
Alternatives to capital punishment, 94, 99,
 135–43, 163, 165, 168, 177, 179
Alternatives to incarceration, 186–87
American Baptist Church in the USA, 104

American Baptist Churches, 105, 215n.12
American Civil Liberties Union: 15, 20,
 48, 61, 102, 119, 121, 215n.12
 and alternatives to capital punishment,
  191
 Capital Punishment Project, 49–50, 52,
  61–62, 69, 72, 81–82, 116, 125,
  219n.15
 emphasis on lobbying and public education, 30, 49–50, 82, 153
 and federal death penalty, 82
 and Gilmore execution, 57–59, 125
 Litigation Centers, 219n.18
 and moral arguments, 191
 multi-issue focus, 146, 209–210n.7
 of Northern California, 49, 82, 185
 position against capital punishment, 25
 priority of ADP work, 81–82, 219n.18
 reaction to *McCleskey v. Kemp*, 79
 role in 1960s litigation, 14, 25, 30, 32,
  35, 41, 211n.14
 state affiliates, 49–50, 57, 200n.19
 volunteer lawyers, 60
American Ethical Union, 215n.12
American Friends Service Committee, 62,
 80, 105, 138, 215n.12, 224n.92
American Law Institute, 13, 172
American League to Abolish Capital Punishment (ALACP), 10–11, 36
 decline of, 41–42, 48
 on juvenile and mentally retarded defendants, 94
 on miscarriages of justice, 87, 220n.31
 papers of, viii
 prison wardens in, 223n.85
 role of, 62

251